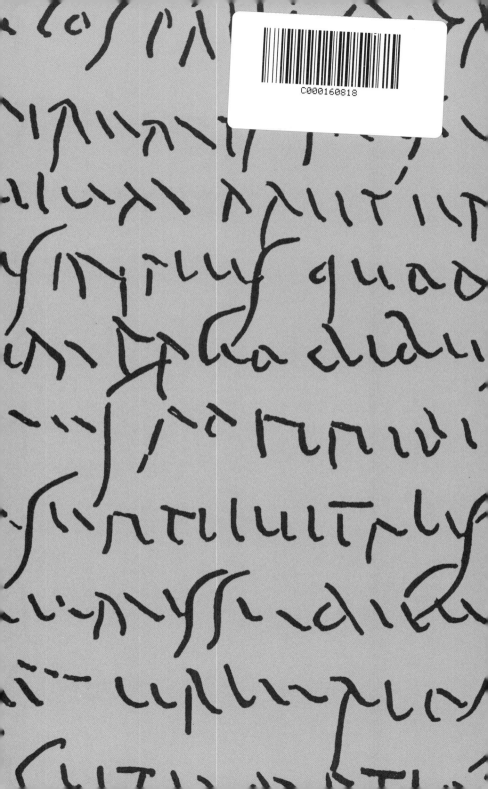

EARLY ENGLISH ARBITRATION

Also by Derek Roebuck
published by HOLO Books: The Arbitration Press

The Charitable Arbitrator 2002
Ancient Greek Arbitration 2001
A Miscellany of Disputes 2000

with Bruno de Luynes de Fumichon
Roman Arbitration 2004

EARLY ENGLISH ARBITRATION

DEREK ROEBUCK

Sponsored by Dewey & LeBoeuf

HOLO BOOKS
THE ARBITRATION PRESS
OXFORD
2008

First published 2008 by
HOLO Books: The Arbitration Press
Clarendon House
52 Cornmarket
Oxford OX1 3HJ

email: holobooks@yahoo.co.uk
www.holobooks.co.uk
and www.centralbooks.com

ISBN 978-0-9544056-1-8

The author thanks Arthur Marriott and his firm, Dewey & LeBoeuf,
for their generous support, not only financial, without which
this publication would not have been possible.

10   9   8   7   6   5   4   3   2   1

Maps drawn by two dot media
Designed and produced for HOLO Books: The Arbitration Press by
Chase Publishing Services Ltd, Fortescue, Sidmouth EX10 9QG
Printed in the European Union

For my children
Derek, Lucy and Paul
who make me so proud

Author's Note
I have tried to make the footnotes and the bibliography as
comprehensive as I can but there must be gaps that readers can fill.
New research is published all the time. With your help I shall try to
keep this book up-to-date, as I will *Ancient Greek Arbitration* and
Roman Arbitration at www.holobooks.co.uk. I welcome any
contribution to derek@holobooks.co.uk

CONTENTS

PREFACE

I ask that every reader who shall read this book may excuse me for daring to write so much of this after so many others, like a chattering bird or like a certain useless arbitrator, *quasi garrulus avis vel quasi quidam invalidus arbiter*. I give way to anyone who shall be sufficiently more knowledgeable in that skill than I.

Nennius *History of the Britons* preface cAD800

Lord Eberhard had this book of laws written. Wise to the wise he gave it. Anyone who wants to know about all the legal cases and wants to seem a famous arbitrator himself, will eagerly and longingly explore it with eyes and brain.

Lupus of Ferrières cAD836[1]

This is an attempt to tell the story of how disputes were managed in England from the earliest times to about AD1154. Then Henry II began to create a new legal system, which became the Common Law of England first, then of most of the British Empire, and now prevails in the United States and the Commonwealth and in other jurisdictions as different as Ireland and China's Special Administrative Region of Hong Kong. Before the Common Law, the different communities in England handled their disputes in traditional assemblies according to their various customary laws.

The writing of history should never be driven by the urge to prove a case, still less to vindicate an ideology. The way to reduce the ever-present risks is to be aware that the temptation does not decrease as research progresses but grows from the confidence that greater knowledge appears to justify. I started with no conscious agenda other than to describe the development of dispute resolution as accurately and fully as the sources would allow. But now I know that, at the back of my mind, I may have been trying to show, in this as in earlier work, how natural and pervasive mediation and arbitration are and always have been, partly because I believe that it would be wise to increase their use now, not only in private but in international disputes.

The history of arbitration is in its infancy. As a fine scholar working on a later period said, faced with having to do the linguistic spade-work:[2]

At no point is it unlikely that a further week's reading would not modify the details of the discussion. Many readers, no doubt, will be in a position to supply information which so often I have lacked. A beginning, it may be agreed, had to be made.

1. Patrick Wormald *The Making of English Law* p32.
2. JP Collas (1964) 81 *Selden Society* xii.

If you will not even allow me that, I am just happy to say with Maitland, slyly: 'Perhaps I was not the man for the work; but I have liked it well.'[3] A reviewer said of an earlier book of mine on arbitration history that it was clear I had written it for my own enjoyment. I take that as a compliment. Why else would any sensible writer produce such a book? Money? Fame? Well, perhaps to give others a share in the pleasures of understanding more, and that is enjoyable too.

I am aware that it may be some time before anyone else attempts the same task and that fills me with a sense of responsibility for accuracy above all but also care in making large claims. When I have let my imagination run, I hope I have remembered to say so.

I have quoted the primary sources in translation throughout the text. For ease of reference each translated passage has been given a number, printed in bold figures, so that **3.5** refers to the fifth quotation in Chapter 3. I am solely responsible for nearly all the translations. I have been greatly helped by the distance teaching of Steve Pollington. It would be woeful ingratitude if I were to allow the impression that he is in any way responsible for the shortcomings of my Anglo-Saxon.

I hope that readers will find useful the glossary index, where unfamiliar or technical words are explained, and will make easy reference to the chronology.

My greatest debt is to Patrick Wormald. The fact that I respond to his challenges and sometimes find a different solution takes nothing away from the tribute I want to pay to his memory. The words he used of Maitland are as true of him:[4] 'he had in full measure the great scholar's maddening tendency to have noticed what one thought one had been first to notice oneself'. I wish he had stayed to argue with me and put me right.

Francis Pryor's three books, *Britain BC, Britain AD* and *Britain in the Middle Ages* stimulated me to think again as I began to write but it was a clutch of new books, based on the latest research in genetics, published after I had finished the first drafts of most chapters, which required an enjoyable self-re-education and comprehensive rewriting.[5] How much poorer this book would have been if I had not had to take account of their radically new ideas, which forced me to make many changes but made me more secure in what I had thought were my own fancies. Then younger scholars like Robin Fleming have reassured me that perhaps it will not be too long before someone else takes on at least some parts of my period and does it better. I have tried to avoid being side-tracked into arguments with other scholars

---

3. FW Maitland *Bracton's Note Book* I ix.
4. Patrick Wormald 'Anglo-Saxon Law' p15.
5. For example: Robin McKie *Face of Britain*; David Mattingly *An Imperial Possession*; David Miles *The Tribes of Britain*; Stephen Oppenheimer *The Origins of the British*; Chris Stringer *Homo Britannicus*.

and, where I have failed, to keep them to the footnotes, giving references full enough for those interested to follow.

My interest in problems of language, and conviction that dispute resolution cannot be understood without its linguistic background, caused me first to overload the text and then to put my thoughts into appendices. The first attempts to describe the use of languages in dispute management from the Stone Age to the end of the Anglo-Norman kings. The second suggests an emendation to the text of the laws of Hlothhere and Eadric.

Many friends in the arbitration community have given me encouragement. I have relied on Neil Kaplan's since, fourteen years ago, he first put the words 'arbitration' and 'history' together for me and challenged me to do something about it. Arthur Marriott's support is of the same vintage and now he has arranged for the international law firm of which he is a partner, Dewey & LeBoeuf, to provide the sponsorship without which this publication would not have been possible. It is heart-warming to know that there are still scholar-patrons for scholar-clients to rely on.

Another friend, Ray Addicott of Chase Publishing Services Ltd, has now, for the fifth time, transformed my text files into a book, without once referring to sow's ears. I am ever fuller of wonder at his skills and grateful for them.

A book like this, which draws on so many different disciplines and covers such a long period needs many a critical eye. I have been fortunate to have criticism of parts of the text from, in chronological order, Barry Cunliffe, Tony Honoré, Roger Tomlin, Nick Higham, Bruce O'Brien, and David Bates. I hope I have been able to express to them the depth of my thanks, more than anything for confirming my conviction that generosity is a part of true scholarship.

I have had friendly and professional help again from the Bodleian, Sackler and Taylorian libraries in Oxford, the British Library, and especially Jules Winterton and his library at the Institute of Advanced Legal Studies.

I thank Roger Tomlin and the Bibliothèque Nationale for permission to use their illustrations for the endpapers and dustjacket respectively.

The knowledge that all my drafts have to pass under the eye of my wife, Susanna Hoe, makes me try harder. Her historian's judgment, careful editing and daily encouragement have kept me from many errors. She also demands, in mine as in her own work, that it is the author's duty to make the reader's task as pleasant as possible. She makes my working hours a delight and the credit is hers.

Derek Roebuck
Oxford
December 2007

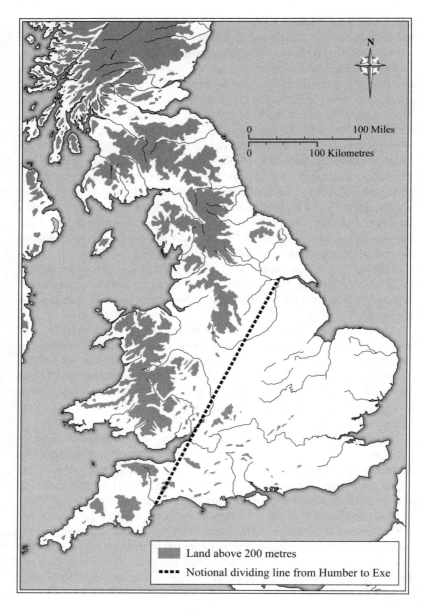

Map 1   Highland and Lowland Zones

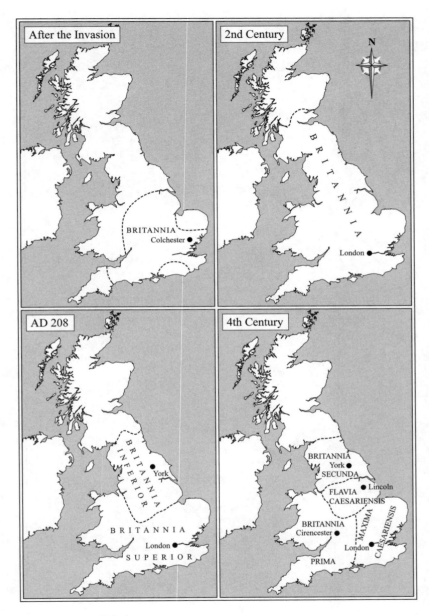

Map 2   Roman Britain

Map 3   Anglo-Saxon Kingdoms

Map 4   England and Normandy 1066

ENGLAND'S EARLIEST SURVIVING ARBITRAL AWARD

Stilus writing tablet of 14 March AD114 from the Walbrook, London **3.25**
Drawn by Dr Roger Tomlin and reproduced here and on the endpapers with his kind permission.

1 INTRODUCTION

We try to find the truth about this or that, not about things in general. Our work is not to see life steadily and see it whole, but to see one particular portion of life right side up and in true perspective.

GN Clark *Historical Scholarship and Historical Thought* p11

As in the natural sciences, fundamental propositions in legal history may stand or fall not with single facts but with their power to explain all the facts.

SFC Milsom *A Natural History of the Common Law* p76

INTRODUCTION

This work studies that portion of life in which disputes are managed. Its purpose is to increase understanding of the ways in which people recognised, classified and provided systematic methods of dealing with conflicts in the hope of ending strife. If that increased understanding proves helpful for those who concern themselves with present-day problems and future reform, so much the better, but I have tried hard not to let such concerns affect the inquiry or the results.

To the historian ordinary people are often invisible. It is all too easy to work on the assumption that one can extrapolate from the few distinguished individuals mentioned in the sources to the people and the nation as a whole. Even archaeologists are not always above this temptation: the invisible majority may have left middens but were usually too poor to be commemorated in death either by inscriptions or fancy graves. Until modern times, most ordinary people in England could not write and the few who could had to do so in a language not their own. So we do not hear their voices, even in the partial sources which survive. But we can be sure they had disputes and regular ways of dealing with them.

Because there are so few direct references to mediation and arbitration in any part of our period, though they become more plentiful near the end, every piece of evidence is precious, however small or faint. Plankton sustain the basking shark: single facts when ordered and explained may have the power to illuminate processes.

SCOPE

Area This study deals only with that part of the British Isles which is now called England and here it is by convention given that name from the

1

beginning, even though it did not correspond to the present country during the period covered by this study. That is not just for convenience but to ensure consistency, so that everyone knows where I am referring to. Ireland, Scotland and Wales have different legal histories, and some of their sources are in languages I cannot read. Modern England was never the same size as what the Romans called Britannia, so that the Roman terms for their provinces are sometimes necessary for precision. After the Romans left, it was some centuries before England became a nation and it did not acquire its present boundaries nor a uniform legal system until after our period.

The imbalances of the surviving sources ensure an overemphasis on England's South and East, perhaps because agricultural societies there allowed more civilisation earlier; but it does not follow that the processes for managing disputes were any better developed there.[1]

This restricted scope makes all the more important constant reference to the rest of Britain, to Europe and even beyond, to wherever there may be a helpful analogy. Travel was never as difficult as we may suppose. There is plenty of evidence of trips to Rome and it was usually quite easy to get on a boat across the Channel. There is plenty of evidence of communication. Analogies must be carefully handled, though, and the essence of parallels is that they do not meet.

Time   This is a study of disputes in England from the earliest times through the Norman Conquest to about 1154, when the first signs of what was to become the English Common Law can be demonstrated. It was necessary to start in prehistoric times because it was then that the first signs were left of people assembling to deal with disputes, no doubt according to the customary law of their groups. Continuing to the mid-12th century allows the sources from that time to declare what writers then wished to present as Anglo-Saxon laws, the *laga* of good king Edward, the old customary laws as they insisted they still applied. For political purposes they pretended they remained unchanged, though they were reconstructing them to fit the needs of their own time, as their forebears had always done. Throughout this period of many thousands of years, this is the story of dispute management by customary law, including spoken and written dooms when they arrive. It ends as customary law is becoming ancillary to a new centrally administered legal system, which we now recognise as the Common Law. By 1154, too, there are signs of a legal profession, of full-time judges, of central courts and even of indigenous legal scholarship within the wider realm of Catholic Europe.[2]

---

1. State-run systems of dispute resolution are not self-evidently superior to informal ones, even today, for example in Turkey, Sarah Rainsford 'The Turkish Peacemaker', or the failure of state control of teenage gang feuds in London or Manchester.
2. With papal domination of ideology, from Gregory VII's 1074 failure, through Urban 1095 onwards.

DEFINITIONS AND CATEGORIES

Function   Definitions are important; they may be allowed to fix the limits of a study. Once the categories are decided, material which does not fit into them may be automatically rejected as irrelevant. But that is not my approach:[3]

> The technique employed here has not been to define arbitration and then to sift the sources for phenomena which satisfy the elements of the definition... it has been to collect and examine every source within the period, which might increase understanding of the ways in which disputes have been resolved....

The concepts of dispute resolution must be carefully defined but it must always be remembered that the categories are either those of our sources or our own. Rarely will they coincide. If we choose ours, we artificially force in or out of them the material from which we want to extract knowledge. The sources will then reveal what is not there, usually what we would like to find. Here I have tried to create definitions to fit my purpose, empirical not a priori, functional tools fashioned unashamedly to fit the study, which is a history of practice not of thought about it, except as evidence of that thought shows what was being done.[4]

Private and Public Arbitration   If the parties are able to dispose of their dispute themselves, by negotiating a settlement unaided, or by enlisting the help of a mediator, or by agreement to allow a third party to decide between them, the community is usually happy to leave it to them to sort out their dispute. That is private arbitration.

If those with power in the community discover that one party to a dispute refuses to submit to private processes of settlement, despite the request of the other – and request and refusal may be express or implied – the community may impose a process of dispute resolution upon the parties. When a society has formal tribunals of sufficient regularity, the choice of processes includes one which we call 'litigation'. Without them it does not. There was litigation before there were courts. While the definition of 'litigation' is satisfied by the formality and regularity of procedure before a public tribunal, a court requires more: at least the regular performance of adjudication by the same experienced personnel. But even in a society without courts or litigation, the community may impose arbitration on parties even against their will. The choice of arbitrator is not usually left to the parties, because they are unlikely to agree. That is public arbitration.

3. Derek Roebuck *Ancient Greek Arbitration* p11.
4. I dealt with these problems in *Ancient Greek Arbitration* pp17–23 and reproduce the arguments here, somewhat edited, for convenience and to show consistency of treatment; also Derek Roebuck and Bruno de Loynes de Fumichon *Roman Arbitration* pp11–14. Susan Reynolds *Fiefs and Vassals* pp13–14 is typically trenchant and valuable: 'Starting our investigation of phenomena by focusing on particular words is a sixteenth-century habit that needs to be dropped.'

***Categories of Dispute Management*[5]**   In thinking about processes
whose purpose is to resolve disputes,[6] it is helpful to have some kind of
classification. For comparative purposes such a system of categories is
essential. The familiar metaphor is a spectrum, depending on the response
of the complainant, which may be represented something like this:

Litigation
Arbitration/
Mediation (Conciliation)/
Negotiated Settlement/

Self-Help/
Seeking a Concession/
Doing Nothing/

That two or more of these categories may be mixed or even compounded
– and usually were – does not reduce the usefulness of the typology or the
appropriateness of the formality factor. The modern 'med-arb', where the
tribunal plays a mediating as well as and sometimes alternately with its
adjudicatory role, is a contemporary example (with a respectable history)
of a composite category or confusion of categories, because in it two
categories may operate simultaneously.

Yet it should be possible to take each process and describe it in such a
way as to distinguish it clearly from all others. Not only does this help any
kind of thinking about dispute settlement in any language, it has obvious
advantages for those who have to think about dispute resolution in more
than one language, particularly in translating from one to another.[7]

Doing Nothing   Most people who feel aggrieved do nothing, many
even though the grievance is not trivial. That will, of course, please many
a wrongdoer and it may even appear best for the community, which has
other priorities. The victim puts up with it willy-nilly, out of fear, lethargy,
or impotence. That is our common experience and it is supported by
scholarly studies.[8]

Seeking a Concession   If we do decide to do something about our
grievance, we may start by seeking a concession from the person we consider
has injured us. Depending on our personality, we may take back to the shop

---

5.   Legal theory has its own scheme, well expressed and analysed in Charles Jarrosson *La
     Notion d'Arbitrage* and Bruno Oppetit *Théorie de l'Arbitrage*.
6.   Simon Roberts and Michael Palmer *Dispute Processes*; Peter Stein *Legal Institutions: the
     Development of Dispute Settlement*.
7.   There is extensive anthropological literature which deals with all aspects of dispute
     resolution, too large to be listed here, but see Roberts and Palmer *Dispute Processes*;
     Simon Roberts *Order and Dispute: An Introduction to Legal Anthropology* pp53–79
     and 'The Handling of Disputes'; Thorstein Eckhoff 'The Mediator, the Judge and the
     Administrator in Conflict-Resolution' pp148–7; Vilhelm Aubert *Sociology of Law*; Stein
     Legal Institutions; OG Chase *Law, Culture, and Ritual*.
8.   Hazel Genn *Paths to Justice*; Michael Zander *The State of Justice*.

something we have bought, even if the shortcoming is trivial: one bad peach out of an otherwise acceptable punnet. But, unless we consider the damage to be substantial, or the refusal to concede is insultingly dismissive, we are not likely to go further, unless we have access to some means of self-help.

Self-Help   Even if the damage we have suffered is quite small, we will help ourselves to a remedy if we can. Perhaps the most widespread example is that of buyers, disappointed by the quality or non-delivery of goods, just refusing to pay the price or not shopping there again. In some societies the appropriate, sometimes the required, response is violence. Fighting among individuals and groups – war if the groups are big enough – is still a widespread phenomenon.

Negotiated Settlement   Much more pervasive – so obvious that its relevance and importance may not be seen – is negotiating towards a settlement at all stages of a dispute, including arbitration and litigation. An agreement to submit to arbitration is a step towards settlement. Even an arbitration clause in a contract is a settlement in part, at least of the chosen procedure. And experience shows that it is not at all unknown for the parties to substitute a negotiated settlement after (and substantially different from) a formal judgment or award, perhaps to ensure that commercial relations continue between the parties. The judgment or award may decide the parties' respective rights. It may even do so to their mutual satisfaction. It says nothing of their respective power.

In most societies there is folk wisdom, some proverb on the lines of 'better a bad compromise than a good case' or 'it is better to give a little early than to gain a little late'. As old farmer Hesiod wrote 27 centuries ago: 'Fools, who do not know that the half is better than the whole.'[9]

Mediation (Conciliation)   When parties find that they are unable to produce a settlement by their own negotiations, they may seek a third party's help, provided that both sides still see advantages in compromise. The chosen mediator may be just a conduit, doing no more than easing the tension by carrying messages from one side to the other. Or the go-between may also make suggestions independent of any offer of either party. The parties may go further and empower the mediator to present them with suggested solutions which, if they do not lead to agreement, will be followed by adjudication, the mediator then assuming the role of arbitrator and making an award, enforceable whether the parties like it or not.

'Mediation' and 'conciliation' are synonyms unless the user gives them a particular meaning. Sometimes, for scientific use in legislation or scholarly analysis, attempts have been made to give them distinguishing characteristics by placing in one an ingredient missing from the other, for example the

9. Hesiod *Works and Days* 40.

intrusion of the third party in suggesting compromises to the parties may be termed conciliation, while the passive process of exchanging information may be called mediation. But the exact opposite is sometimes preferred. There is still no consistent or accepted usage even among English-speaking professionals and the terms are most often used interchangeably. Mediation is the term used in this book.

Arbitration   English attempts to define arbitration have usually been unsatisfactory. They have tended to concentrate on only a part of what is a multifaceted process, for example 'the *submission* of a dispute to arbitrators'.[10] Any satisfactory definition must include the whole process by which the dispute is resolved. Legal definitions must be specific to and confined to a jurisdiction. They are not usually intended to be scientific but prescriptive. Those of arbitration provided by the English case law are sketchy, for example:[11] 'An arbitration is a reference to the decision of one or more persons, either with or without an umpire, of a particular matter in difference between the parties.' There do not seem to be any statutory definitions, which must mean that none have ever been considered necessary, or even useful.[12]

Moreover, it must be stressed that this work is a history of arbitration as a social phenomenon, as an institution or process, rather than of the law which controls it.[13] It would therefore be helpful to have the input of scholars in other disciplines, for example economists and sociologists,[14] if an exhaustive or clinically accurate definition were required. But for our purposes, a definition needs to be useful, rather than scientifically adequate, provided it can be used consistently. This may suffice:[15]

> 'Arbitration is the processes (other than litigation) by which parties to a dispute submit it to a third party to resolve and by which that resolution is reached and enforced.'

10. Ivan Horniman *Wharton's Law Lexicon* 'the submitting of a matter in dispute to the judgment of one, two, or more persons, called arbitrators'; Clifford Walsh *Jowitt's Dictionary of English Law* 'the determination of a dispute by an arbitrator or arbitrators, who in case of difference usually call in an umpire to decide between them'.
11. Romilly MR in *Collins v Collins* 28 LJ Ch 186.
12. There are none in the English Arbitration Act 1996 (though s6 defines arbitration agreement), the United States Arbitration Act, or the UNCITRAL Model Law; nor do other jurisdictions have legislation which defines arbitration, Emmanuel Gaillard and John Savage eds *Fouchard Gaillard Goldman on International Commercial Arbitration* Chapter 1; Bruno Oppetit *Théorie de l'Arbitrage*.
13. Susan Reynolds *Kingdoms and Communities* p26 n51: 'The distinction between compromise and judgement... does not seem to coincide with that between an arbitration and a law-suit in modern terms.' The text provides comparative insights and the footnote helpful references.
14. Useful contributions are, from an economist Lord Peston 'The 1997 Bernstein Colloquium: Arbitration – An Economist's View' pp19–27 and from lawyer-anthropologists Roberts and Palmer *Dispute Processes*.
15. This is another refinement to my previous attempts. I doubt whether the process is over.

The first criterion is that arbitration is not litigation. It is easier to discern in a society where there are courts from whose procedures and jurisdiction it can be distinguished. But arbitration may just as well exist in a society where there are no courts. There it is an alternative to some form of non-adjudicative mediation or to self-help. Allowing one's dispute to be resolved by the representatives of the community, rather than taking the law into one's own hands, has been seen as a sign of civilised behaviour since the time of Homer.[16]

The second criterion is that the process must be, at least potentially, adjudicative and intended to lead to a third party's award (rather than agreement between the parties) disposing of the dispute. This element distinguishes arbitration from mediation, though, as we have seen, it is natural to have adjudication and mediation mingled in one process, for which arbitration is still, in English, the most common name.

A third criterion is often prescribed, that the parties must have submitted their dispute voluntarily, or at least as part of a process which one or both initiated. But this is a criterion not of arbitration as a whole but of one kind only, called in this book '*private* arbitration'. For scholarly purposes, there is little interest in a method which occurs only accidentally or in isolated and unrelated instances. The procedure must have enough formality and regularity for likelihood of replication to be inferred. But accounts of private *ad hoc* arbitrations may show that a community recognises them as normal procedures, regularly available to those whose unaided negotiations fail and who, for whatever reason, prefer to avoid litigation, self-help, or leaving things as they are.

In a historical and comparative study, the criterion of voluntariness may be relaxed to include *public* arbitration. This book will show how public arbitration may lie at the heart of a community's system of dispute resolution. Even in modern times, there is a form of arbitration which is ordered or suggested by a court, or other authority representing the community, in which a dispute, in whole or in part, is referred to arbitrators who examine the evidence and either make a decision or report their findings back to a court which decides.[17]

Litigation   For our purposes there is no need for a definition of litigation more technical than 'the action and process of a law suit'. There need be no professional lawyers, or even regular judges. But, at least for the purposes of this book, a court is an institution established by the state.[18]

16. Homer *Odyssey* 9.112 on the Cyclopes: 'They have no assemblies where counsel is taken nor customary laws', each head of the family deciding disputes.
17. For example, the use of arbitrators by the Council in England in the time of Elizabeth I. From Homer's time it has been common to have one body work out the solution and another proclaim it.
18. Susan Reynolds *Kingdoms and Communities* p24: 'Assembly is a better word here than court' with helpful references in n42.

Importance of Definitions   Definitions may determine more than scope. They fix the observer's focus. For example, in *The Blackwell Encyclopedia of Anglo-Saxon England*, Patrick Wormald wrote of: 'Laws, defined as written statements of observed and enforceable social norms...'[19] Such a definition needs to be explained, indeed to be justified. It will work only if it is made clear that no special status is given to written as distinguished from oral laws. If you say 'laws' are written legislation, some other name needs to assigned to those laws which are not written (which include oral legislation in part of our period). That unwritten law is often called 'custom' but that is easily taken to mean that customary unwritten law is not law at all but something less than law. Names have great power when used as tokens in thinking. Imprecision has led to misunderstanding of the law, for example at the end of our period when unwritten customary law still prevailed in much of the legal system of the Norman kings, despite the existence of 'laws'.

It is well to heed the warning that Susan Reynolds gives in another context, that of the concept of 'corporation', but which works just as well for 'arbitration':[20]

> When Innocent IV, for instance, is found making a remark which sounds more or less compatible with modern ideas, he is applauded as if he were 'getting warm' in some game of Hunt the Concept. But the idea of Hunt the Thimble only makes sense if a single thimble is there all the time, if one is trying to find it, and if there is someone who has hidden it and knows where it is. Legal concepts are not like thimbles.

We may congratulate ourselves on 'getting warmer' only when we occasionally see through the eyes of those who used the thimble.

LANGUAGE AND TRANSLATION

A history of dispute management is a story of how words have been used. It is true that communities have often resorted to violence and sometimes made it formal, as with trial by battle. But, except for the underlying threat of the feud, which enabled the enforcement of awards and agreements, such methods are aberrant; as are calls for divine intervention, like the ordeal.

Language is the tool which enables the primary parties and third parties, including the representatives of the community, to work towards a solution. When the first draft of this book was completed, it became clear that the story it was trying to tell was weighed down by the amount of detail I had felt it necessary to include on language problems. I have therefore put that into Appendix A, which explains its importance. Appendix B is an attempt to show how a small textual emendation can make all the difference to our understanding of an important source.

Functions Translations, like definitions, are functional.[21] One which is appropriate for a lawyer may not be for a linguist. Moreover, those who wrote our primary sources wrote for their contemporary readers. They had much in common which they could assume. They might not have written as they did, if they had known we were going to rely on their work many centuries later. They might have taken the trouble to explain matters more carefully to ensure we did not go wrong by manipulating their ideas into forms we find more familiar, more comfortable, and which fit our preconceptions better.

My purpose is straightforward: to enable the reader to understand as accurately as possible the processes by which disputes were then managed. I have therefore made my own translations because I want to be sure that I have looked at every original source with fresh eyes and because, as far as I can possibly ensure it, I want the reader to be able to judge whether I have introduced any slant. You can see what I am up to and that I am not pretending that a 'literal' translation is inert. Yet sometimes technical terms are best left in Anglo-Saxon words; I could not improve on 'deem right dooms' in the Laws of Edgar.[22]

The risk of mistranslation is real, as the errors of even the best of scholars prove.[23] For example, both Robertson and Attenborough translate *folcriht*, the word used regularly for customary law, as 'public law', an English phrase without a concept to fit it for many centuries to come.[24] Their mistranslations may well be largely responsible for the general misunderstanding of the comprehensiveness of customary law in England until well after the Norman Conquest.

The lesson is most striking when a more careful translation makes an apparent reference to arbitration disappear. Appendix B suggests an emendation to the generally accepted text which sadly reduces by one the

21. I have set out my theoretical foundations in *Ancient Greek Arbitration* Chapter 3 pp26–35 and the other work cited there.
22. III Edgar 1, **8.30**.
23. Bruce Dickins, in his Prefatory Note to GN Garmondsway's translation of *The Anglo-Saxon Chronicle*, gives examples only from historians who became Fellows of the British Academy. The dangers of attempting to write history with no knowledge of the languages of the sources are amply shown by JM Stearns *The Germs and Developments of the Laws of England*.
24. AJ Robertson ed and tr *The Laws of the Kings of England from Edmund to Henry I*; FL Attenborough *The Laws of the Earliest English Kings*. They may have been misled by their misunderstanding of Liebermann's translation of *folcriht* as *Volksrechte* – literally 'laws of the people', confusing it with *Völkerrechts* – 'international law', or perhaps by the Latin equivalent *ius publicum*. RL Venezky and A di P Healey *Microfiche Concordance to Old English* 'suggest that folkright (*folcriht, folcryht, folcryhte*) also had a fairly wide range of meanings: cf *folclaga, folclage*', Susan Reynolds *Fiefs and Vassals* p325 fn5.

tiny handful of references to arbitration in the surviving corpus of Anglo-Saxon literature.

Terminology   There are some oddities of nomenclature that need to be remembered. The Scots, or at least those called *Scotii* in Latin, may have come from Ireland. The language which became Welsh was not confined to what became Wales. Those who are now called Celts in modern English are not the same people as those the Greeks called *Keltoi*, who are different again from Caesar's and Tacitus's *Celtae*. The Franks were Germans, like many invaders since. Anglo-Saxon is not the English version of people or language from Saxony. I have stuck with the name 'Anglo-Saxon' because that is how the language is known among ordinary readers, though scholars now justifiably prefer 'Old English'. The Anglo-Saxon *æ* is shown in English as ae, *đ* and *þ* as th. I have preferred the names most likely to be readily recognised today: Cnut rather than Canute and Boudicca rather than Boadicea but Swein, not Swegn and Aethelberht, not Ethelbert.

Anachronism   The dangers of anachronism are ever present. As Susan Reynolds insists:[25]

> We may often legitimately want to investigate the history of concepts or phenomena of which people in the past were not aware, like Vitamin C deficiency... But when the subject under investigation involves notions or attitudes held by people in the society concerned it is vital to distinguish whether a concept is ours or theirs.

Sometimes anachronism can be avoided by a simple explanation. We can use 'England' appropriately to describe that area of land now called by that name, long before there was any such entity. Similarly with Somerset and even Lancashire, which did not exist as an entity until after our period. But it is better not to use 'Wales' for what it was to become, when still there was nothing but independent British kingdoms, which they were throughout this period.

I hope to show, too, that there was no such thing as a code, as *codex* is often mistranslated or as piecemeal legislation is called. The word 'code' is best kept for attempts to make law systematically, and that is its modern use, which must colour any discussion of the early law. No one in this period used it in that sense.[26] Until Cnut there were only collections with no pretensions to a scheme.

Moreover, it is misleading to talk of compensation in the tariffs of the early laws. Aesthetics must give way to clarity, even if that requires, for example, the Old English word *bot*, usually translated 'compensation', to be clumsily

---

25. Susan Reynolds *Fiefs and Vassals* p13.
26. TFT Plucknett *Edward I* pp3 and 7: 'There is no sign in the Anglo-Saxon laws that the greatest and most general lesson of Roman law had been learned: the texts present no trace whatever of any attempt to arrange their material.'

paraphrased as 'reconciliation-payment'. The amount stated in the lists of tariffs was not an attempt to quantify in money terms the damage the victim had suffered. Nobody thought a king was worth three bishops or a lord's wound needed five times as much reparation as a slave's. But they did know that it would be shameful for a nobleman to accept the same money for a wrong as a commoner would, instead of fighting for his honour.[27]

This insistence on the careful use of technical terms comes not from aesthetic nicety but determination to use powerful words with precision, and to avoid as much as possible the misunderstanding that comes from confusing old things and concepts with their nearest modern equivalents.

The same may be said of the use of 'witness' for the person whose name appears at the end of a document. A witness now is one who authenticates a signature but then witnesses were used to ensure that, if the document were challenged, those who had attested could confirm together the donor's intent. They were likely to be the very same thegns, those of the rank of landholding fighting men, as would have to manage the dispute. The witnesses who now appear in court or arbitration just give evidence to the decision-makers. In our period their functions included to recollect both the facts and the law, to hear argument and then to decide.

As in Rome, an *arbiter* is not quite the same as an arbitrator.[28] It should not be translated 'judge' either, as it often is. Nor should *iudex*, for the same reason: there were no judges until well after the Conquest, with the attributes inherent in the term: those who made judging a profession and were regularly employed as such.[29] That is not to say that the Anglo-Saxons did not know what judges were. Not only had they the Biblical examples and those of other literature, there is evidence from Alfred of a concern that those who exercised decision-making authority should have the highest moral standards. There is even a short treatise, called *Judex*, from the time of Edgar on the subject.[30]

For most of the period, till well after the Norman Conquest, meetings to resolve disputes did not derive their authority from the state or the king. They are best not called courts until they do. From beginning to end there were no courts, judges or lawyers as we know them. All litigation lay before customary assemblies, except perhaps in part of Britannia under the Romans and some courts of the Norman kings. Even the totalitarian administration of a Roman colony left private disputes to the parties and to customary groups

---

27. Though Patrick Wormald says, 'Anglo-Saxon Law' p14: 'it means compensation to God, Church, king or community at large', he understands its force better than most: 'It was the price of mercy.'
28. The Roman law of dispute resolution was discussed in *Roman Arbitration*. The legislation of Justinian was described there sufficiently for the purposes of this book, especially because it came more than a century after England ceased to be part of the Roman Empire.
29. EG Stanley 'The Administration of Law in Anglo-Saxon England' pp60–4.
30. Patrick Wormald *Making* pp382–3.

and their law, so long as they did not threaten the power of the state and the order it required, as many totalitarian governments have done since.

It is easy when writing of the past, and a particular danger for non-lawyers, to display an uncertain command of technical legal terms, infusing a modern criminal flavour into all law, before such distinctions existed in the minds of the creators of the sources. The technical term of criminal law, 'charge', is wrongly used as the name of any claim, as is 'penalty' for any payment, where the word in the original source is plain and general.[31]

METHOD

Even if there had been ample literary sources, an interdisciplinary study would have been advisable: their absence makes essential the greatest possible exploitation of the work of scholars in history, archaeology, anthropology, linguistics, the physical sciences and most recently genetics.

Though hard to interpret for our purposes, the archaeological evidence has one great advantage over the literary: the material is affected only by the touch of the examiner, not by its creator, who could rarely have had any thought of its significance for the future, let alone for historians. Literary remains are twice tainted, by what both writer and reader want.

Together the literary and archaeological evidence tells a story which reveals much about later developments in historical times and which can be used to correct entrenched misunderstandings:[32] 'If the historical models that we construct are not to be mere toys, then the models require detailed testing based on the use of the archaeological sources.' Until recently, archaeology's contributions to knowledge have depended on painstaking collection and sorting, usually followed by slow publication. Now the more dramatic results are often published quickly in popular television programmes.

Other scientific disciplines now challenge old assumptions. Objects can be dated with much greater accuracy. The most radical attacks on old assumptions come from the new research which illuminates genetic origins, not only in prehistoric times but up to the end of our period.[33] Interpretations are changing faster in ancient than in modern history. But we must heed Catherine Hills' warning and:[34]

> note the alacrity with which proponents of differing views have seized on new scientific research which appears to support their own case, ignoring or playing down contradictory findings... we have been following our prejudices and choosing the science which fits those best.

---

31. Even the best scholars are guilty, e.g. Liebermann, Attenborough, Robertson and Oliver.
32. Dominic Powlesland 'Early English Settlements' p101.
33. E.g. Stephen Oppenheimer *The Origins of the British* and 'Myths of British Ancestry' and the work being done by Sir Walter Bodmer's team in Oxford.
34. 'Anglo-Saxon Attitudes' in Higham *Britons in Anglo-Saxon England* p25.

I have avoided giving religious explanations in default of better. We all tend to see what we are looking for. Those who make a study of other people's religious beliefs are usually more careful than the general scholars, historians or archaeologists, who see religious significance whenever they are lost for another explanation, so that formal procedures must be ritual, technical skill is magic, a carefully placed stone or heaped up earth has a sacred rather than a practical significance. Few historians are fundamentalists. They do not treat sacred texts as history. They recognise that they were not written to record facts, nor were the other religious writings which appeared throughout our period.

I have tried to give credit to all the scholars whose work I have read, by footnotes and bibliography. Some have been so rich in their gifts that they must sometimes seem to have been overlooked and my debt is often implicit, for example to Patrick Wormald, Francis Pryor, Susan Reynolds and Stephen Oppenheimer, just because they and others have so often challenged me to think again about my assumptions. It will be clear when I have dared to disagree. The scale is so vast that I can often present only the conclusions of others' specialist work, with references in the footnotes to where their arguments are to be found. I know there will be those who will be satiated by too many footnotes. Others will be disappointed. The former may happily skip; the latter will find much more if, like me, they delight in chasing serendipity down the rabbit holes of an unsparing bibliography.

There are so many controversies, none of them about dispute resolution itself but whose solutions govern this study, that I must do my best, seeking the advice of experts, and making choices to find the most internally coherent and consistent sense.

SOURCES

The evidence found by metal detectors may be better than Bede if you can interpret it. Archaeology is a powerful antidote to myth. It may not establish a full picture but it can often prove conclusively that a part of the tradition cannot be true. Moreover, charters have been shown to be subject to regular and systematic forgery. Those who made them often did so to strengthen their title to land, or, as they saw it, God's ownership. As so often then as now, truth for them was what should be true.

Writers write for a present audience. We do not bother to explain what the readers already know. Nor do we commonly seek readers far into the future. Neither did our sources. It is unfortunate for us that, perhaps for fear of boring their readers, they left out all the commonplace things that we would find so useful in creating a truer picture of how they lived.

Moreover, in every place and generation we have wasted the evidence, archaeological and literary, so that we must make do with random bits and pieces, not only partial but ambiguous. The gaps allow, indeed require, imaginative filling. And what a wonderful thing is ambiguous evidence: it allows historians to exploit it to construct an ideologically motivated message to satisfy themselves. The genetic evidence is still all there, awaiting new exploitation and explanation; archaeologists make new finds and reinterpret old ones; even the literary evidence, though rarely expanded, is still full of opportunities for new interpretations.

There are few references to arbitration in the surviving manuscripts. To discover how mediation and arbitration worked requires interpretation of sources of a more general kind and inferences from what was happening elsewhere. Even of that general information little is certain and what facts have been established are controversial and differently interpreted. Perhaps because the literature is so scant, whatever facts it provides have been accepted as reliable until recently, when new techniques have made it easy and necessary to cast doubt.

There are few relevant inscriptions; no papyri like those from Roman Egypt. The only important physical writing from Roman Britannia is on a handful of writing tablets and just one refers to the resolution of a dispute.

CONCLUSIONS

There has never been in any language anything like a comprehensive general treatment of Anglo-Saxon law which can be relied on, and none at all of Romano-British law, so that the relevant parts of those legal systems need to be discussed here. To understand how disputes were handled, more of the background needs to be established, firmly and afresh, not only of the legal system but generally, than was necessary in describing arbitration in Ancient Greece or Rome. There are matters wider than dispute resolution which need to be settled. Because we so often have few relevant particulars, we need all the more to be as sure as we can of the soundness of the general base on which we try to build hypotheses by analogy and imagination.

2 PREHISTORY

First, the British Isles were cleared of people after the last Ice Age, thus avoiding the complication of a Palaeolithic gene pool. Second, and uniquely for such a small region in Europe, there is a deep genetic line dividing the English from the rest of the British. Third, the separate genetic source regions for the English and the Atlantic Celts are clear and distinct, and correspond to scientific interpretations of the cultural evidence.

Stephen Oppenheimer *The Origins of the British* p15

It is this long time scale that allows us to discover social change. The past is camouflaged and we recognise it when something moves.

Richard Bradley *The Social Foundations of Prehistoric Britain* p167

My understanding and experience of British prehistory lead me to the view that the Ancient Britons were a resourceful bunch. Their insular society worked well: they seem to have kept their feuding to manageable proportions.

Frances Pryor *Britain BC* p438

INTRODUCTION

For more than 700,000 years there have been people in what is now England, living in communities, cooperating in hunting, making and possibly trading in tools, and for half a million years carefully burying their dead.[1] They have been talking to one another since at least 300,000BC.[2] Perhaps some of them were like us in many basic ways, social as well as genetic. The recent discovery of a jawbone suggests that *homo sapiens*, our own kind, lived here more than 37,000 years ago. New finds keep pushing these dates back but they tell us nothing of how those who lived then managed the disputes they must have had.

The last great Ice Age, about 16,000 years ago, brought ice a mile high in places and froze out all those humans who could escape from England, south to Iberian refuges. When the ice began to melt, about 12,000 years ago, humans started to repopulate England from scratch. Until about 8,000 years ago, England was part of the land mass of north-western Europe.

---

1. SA Parfitt and 17 others 'The Earliest Record of Human Activity in Northern Europe'.
2. From studies of earbones, tongue, brain and neural connections, e.g. I Martinez and 9 others 'Auditory Capacities in Middle Pleistocene Humans from the Sierra de Atapuerca in Spain'; Sverker Johansson *Origins of Language – Constraints on Hypotheses*.

Then the strip by which travellers could walk to and from the peninsula was finally inundated and the British Isles took their separate form.

Recent advances in the application of genetics to prehistory have revealed the stories of our present genes and the DNA of old bones. Most of the facts are agreed but the interpretations differ. If only because they require radical rethinking of many assumptions accepted by mainstream historians until recently, any new history must accommodate these findings. Whatever else, the uncertainties of the present state of knowledge are a better foundation for specialised studies than outdated assumptions that can be shown to be false.

Some points at issue are relevant to this work. It will become important to know where the people of England came from, where they got traditions and what languages they used for managing their disputes. Most of the new knowledge has been made accessible to the non-specialist and can be quoted to advantage here.[3] The analysis of mitochondrial DNA shows who our maternal ancestors were. All agree they came soon after the last Ice Age allowed them back from their refuges in Europe. Most came from what is now Southern France and Northern Spain:[4] 'over half our maternal ancestors arose from southern refuges and arrived in north-west Europe just as soon as the melting ice allowed'. Sykes confirms this:[5]

> After that the genetic bedrock on the maternal side was in place. By about 6,000 years ago, the pattern was set... Once here, the matrilineal DNA mutated and diversified, each region developing slightly different local versions, but without losing its ancient structure.

Analysis of the specifically male Y chromosome shows where our male ancestors came from:[6]

> While the older Iberian post-LGM [last Ice Age] influence reaches its highest rates in Ireland and the west coast of Britain, it is still present in 60–75% of males, even in England. This English genetic conservatism tends to undermine the idea of complete recent replacement by Anglo-Saxons, since the effect is seen whether one looks at broader gene groups or exact matching gene types between the two potential sources of gene flow – Iberia or the 'Germanic–speaking' regions. In the Neolithic or before, an east/west division, or differentiation, began and progressed. The dividing line stretched from the Scottish Grampians in the north to Wessex in the south, between the west and east coasts of Britain.

3. Stephen Oppenheimer *The Origins of the British*; Chris Stringer *Homo Britannicus* presenting the work of the 'Ancient Human Occupation of Britain' project; Brian Sykes *Blood of the Isles* (in USA *Saxons, Vikings and Celts*); and the work of Sir Walter Bodmer's 'The People of the British Isles' project, to be concluded in 2009, on which Robin McKie's *Face of Britain* is an accessible interim report; and from an archaeologist Barry Cunliffe *Facing the Ocean: The Atlantic and its Peoples*.
4. Oppenheimer *Origins* p107.
5. Sykes *Saxons, Vikings and Celts* p281.
6. Oppenheimer *Origins* p265.

The differences are apparent in male genetic lines and cultural influence coming in from two distinct sources... On the east coast of Britain, the Neolithic cultural influence was more clearly derived from north-west Europe, which is consistent with the introduction of new male gene lines to England from that part of the Continent.

Now we think of England, Ireland, Scotland and Wales but we recognise that those nation-states are comparatively very recent. Yet these advances in genetics appear to show a primordial split in our ancestral make-up.

There is every reason, therefore, to take the return from the last Ice Age refuges as a realistic starting point for a study of dispute resolution in England and to restrict this study to those parts of the British Isles whose cultural, linguistic and legal foundations have more recently become Anglo-Saxon. To have tried to include the parts now known as Celtic would have been to expand unwisely an already ambitious scope. The histories of Ireland, Scotland and Wales have their own literary sources, in languages I cannot read, and their own legal traditions beyond my knowledge.

SOURCES AND ARCHAEOLOGY

The written record starts only 2,300 years ago and most of it is unreliable. The first glimpses are from surviving fragments of the lost work of Pytheas, from the Greek colony Marseilles, who described his visit to Britain in the Iron Age, about 320BC. Barry Cunliffe has shown him to be a more dependable source than he has often been given credit for:[7]

> The totality of the data now available allows us to glimpse the dynamics of the world that Pytheas inhabited. It was a world of change, of developing horizons, of contacts over huge distances, of commodities and ideas flowing and knowledge expanding.

Long before this, however, there is the better evidence of archaeology, which, though it says nothing directly about how disputes were resolved, tells us much about what was going on in the evolving communities.[8] It may take imagination to produce pictures from the faint hints which lie scattered in the astonishing scholarship of the archaeological reports, but they should not be ignored.

Archaeological evidence does not usually provide what we are looking for directly; as Jacquetta Hawkes wrote:[9] 'The evidence for historical events during those centuries is tenuous and as easily broken as a cobweb. Archaeology catches so much of general life, so little of particular events.' For example, though there is no direct evidence for how they resolved disputes, it is inconceivable that the people, who 4,000 years ago devised

7. Barry Cunliffe *The Extraordinary Voyage of Pytheas the Greek* p4.
8. Neil Faulkner *Decline and Fall of Roman Britain* pp259–62.
9. Jacquetta Hawkes *Dawn of the Gods* p66.

Stonehenge or over 3,000 years ago used the exquisite gold cups found at Rillaton in Cornwall or recently in Woodnesborough in Kent (both now in the British Museum), had not worked out a system for coping with at least some of their differences in a peaceful way, with replicable routines and the expectations of fairness they arouse. Even if their technology had been rudimentary, that would have been no evidence of a lack of social skills.

SOCIETY

Earlier volumes[10] have been about dispute resolution in societies dominated by cities, civilised at least in that sense. Athens was a city and Greece a land of city-states. Rome, too, was a city and the centre of a great empire with many cities. England was not a land of cities.

Though England was repopulated from soon after the ice receded, there appears to have been enough room for all. Many communities were little larger than an extended family. Larger groupings were based on extended kin. But there is plenty of evidence that they gathered together for social purposes. The larger social group, whether called kin or clan or tribe, provided insurance against some of the risks of life, including the ill-effects of disputes, which arise naturally in every society. If families do not attend such gatherings, they live in backwardness, says Homer of the Cyclopes in a precocious flash of anthropological insight: 'they have no assemblies where counsel is taken nor customary laws'.[11] Even in the Mesolithic, from say 8000 to 5000BC, when the population grew more rapidly: 'people didn't live in such close proximity that disputes and rivalry for scarce resources could give rise to social competition'.[12] That means competition between groups, of course; there must have been some normal competition within the group.

Up to this time, Stone Age people had fed themselves by gathering food in the wild or by hunting. About 4000BC they gradually added farming, which allowed them to cluster more densely but required the exchange of stock for breeding, if not the trading of surplus:[13] 'It allows many more people to live in the landscape, and that in turn means that communities have to live alongside each other. So they must find ways of settling disputes....'

The first hunter–gatherer–farmers were still nomadic too, to some degree, but eventually, probably after c3000BC, they foraged abroad

10. *Ancient Greek Arbitration* and *Roman Arbitration*.
11. Homer *Odyssey* 9.112; *Ancient Greek Arbitration* p70.
12. Francis Pryor *Britain BC* p104.
13. Pryor *Britain BC* p111. It used to be accepted that farming was introduced by an 'invading wave' from abroad but archaeological scholarship and the results of mitochondrial DNA tests do not now support that. Indeed, modern scholarship finds little evidence of 'invading waves' at any time.

less often and came to settle on a piece of land they called their own. Not in individual ownership, of course, but part of the clan, inalienable, belonging to all its members, dead and living and still to be born, in the temporary stewardship of those alive who represented the clan. That is hard enough for us to comprehend but even harder is to realise that there were land rights determined in more complex ways than our simple linear boundaries. Most of us now cannot think of boundaries except as lines drawn round plots. That is the only way in which we now fix an area to be owned. It was possible for earlier communities to grade the authority they had over land according to its nearness to their ancestral sites, often the burial places of ancestors. Boundaries are then circumferences from central ancestral burial places, so that the community (clan members alive or dead) might have exclusive rights to occupy land near the nodal points, but diminishing rights of use the further away they went, perhaps to grow things in their 'slash and burn' horticulture, to keep animals nearby, and to hunt and gather further away, where they might share those rights with other groups. That is still the way land ownership is thought of in some communal societies today:[14]

> The forest ground is not delimited by boundaries which determine areas but by a complex network of points, each of which is the centre of a land area, defined in relation to a periphery. These fixed points are the tombs of ancestors... The law is written down in this vast number of funeral points... This area knows no *insides* or *outsides*, it is said to be *near* a funeral site.

There is no direct evidence that it was ever so in England but:[15]

> One clue may be provided by a series of large Bronze Age burial mounds, often with multiple circular ditches surrounding them, which appear to be evenly spaced at roughly half-kilometre intervals along the southern part of this landscape. It's as if some time around 2500BC people decided that the fertile pastures of the southern Welland Valley had to be parcelled up in an equitable fashion, and enlisted the help of their dead ancestors to ensure that the arrangement was not abused.

My suggestion that prehistoric societies in England may have had more complex concepts of space and boundaries and ownership and land rights is based not only on the evidence from a contemporary community in the Solomon Islands, whose 'industrial technology' was in some ways similar to England's in the New Stone Age, but also on hints, nothing more, from the Neolithic sites in the Valley of the Boyne in Ireland.[16]

---

14. Daniel de Coppet 'Gardens of Life, Gardens of Death in Melanesia' p22.
15. Francis Pryor *Britain AD* pp79–82 and 226: 'barrow burial is about territoriality'.
16. Where the Knowth 'macehead' was found, described below under 'Assemblies and Dispute Resolution'. The evidence of different disciplines from the valley of the Boyne is attractively presented in Gabriel Cooney ed *Brú na Bóinne*.

TRADE

There is some evidence of trade in Palaeolithic times, including half-finished flint tools and Baltic amber in the form of beads. There is ample evidence of trade along the south coast of England in Mesolithic times.[17] There cannot be trade without disputes. Regular patterns of reiterated trade would be unlikely if commercial disputes could only be resolved by violence when the parties could not settle them for themselves. Traders would not come back and their hosts knew that. The definition of 'trade' at that time is debatable but not during the period of our study, the following eight millennia. For our purposes it does not matter whether goods have become commodities, exchanged within a market economy. There was widespread distribution all over England of stone axes in the New Stone Age.[18] Some could be used to chop down trees. Others would have shattered and must have been prized by their recipients for their appearance. They were exchanged for something, goods or services or privileges, of value to those who received them, though those who parted with them need not themselves have seen much value in what they gave. The anthropologists who have studied the Kula ring and other forms of reciprocity have shown how such systems may work.[19] They have a meaning beyond trade:[20] 'These axes are the physical manifestation of a long-gone network of social relations, of marriages, gifts and exchange across the entire British Isles.'

There was cross-Channel trade for 3,000 years before the Romans interfered with it. The main exports were slaves, corn and raw materials. The discovery on the seabed off Dover of a cargo of 352 bronze implements, exported from France, is only one bit of evidence for cross-Channel trade about 1500BC, perhaps two centuries before the first wheel discovered in England was made.[21] The Veneti of Brittany had their own trading-posts in England.[22] Recent finds from wrecks off Salcombe and Dover, dating from c1200–1000BC, show cross-Channel trade flourished then between south-west England and Brittany in wines, figs, glass and other luxuries to supply the requirements of the sophisticated inhabitants of Britain. It continued until Caesar's attacks on Brittany in 57BC, after which most trade switched to Kent and the Thames estuary.

There is archaeological support for the stories preserved by Pliny and Herodotus of exports of tin from Cornwall c600BC. Strabo, writing cAD20, said the Phoenicians took care to monopolise the trade and kept the route

---

17. Oppenheimer *Origins* p141.
18. Pryor *Britain BC* pp150–1.
19. Bronislaw Malinowski *Argonauts of the Western Pacific*, essential reading for an understanding of England in the Stone Age.
20. David Miles *Tribes of Britain* p73.
21. Pryor *Britain BC* pp297, 300.
22. Barry Cunliffe 'Britain, the Veneti and Beyond'.

a secret, until Publius Crassus, governor of Hispania Ulterior, managed the voyage to Cornwall (c95BC) and saw how tin was mined and found the people peaceable.[23] The Phoenician merchants not only knew the sea-routes; they used their knowledge of the markets to sell tin throughout the Mediterranean. Nothing is known of how they settled their disputes with their suppliers in England, though there is no reason to suppose they forwent the techniques and procedures they were used to elsewhere.[24] 'Scrap metal was being traded across the Channel by the Middle Bronze Age (c1200–1100BC)' as the wrecks off Salcombe in Devon and Langdon Bay in Kent show.[25] If there is trade in scrap metal, can you imagine there being no disputes which required some systematic process for their resolution?

LANGUAGE

What languages were used in dispute resolution, or indeed at all, is quite unknown. It is possible to speculate about what they were like, what families they belonged to and where they came from. I have done so in Appendix A. It is likely that they fell into two large families on either side of the 'Neolithic geographical divide', roughly – very roughly – more or less north and west against south and east, and that there were others which did not fit. Though there is no direct evidence, I cannot believe that the prehistoric inhabitants of England managed without inventing pidgins and, possibly, one or more *linguae francae*.

CUSTOM AND LAW[26]

Wherever humans are found, at whatever time in history, they are social animals. If circumstances force them to be alone, they seek to rejoin the group when they can. It may well be that a permanent grouping is necessary for the survival of human young. The smallest group, the family, is in communal or pre-state societies not just a mother, father and their children. These extended families have relations with other neighbouring groups and wider kin with whom they congregate at certain times for agreed purposes. This seems to be a universal phenomenon: even the aboriginal Tasmanians, who were scattered at the ratio of one person to every seven square miles, came together in large congregations for consultation, resolution of differences and other social reasons.

23. Strabo *Geographica* 3,5,10–11; TW Potter and Catherine Johns *Roman Britain* pp14–15.
24. It is possible to speculate that the root of 'arbit-' words is to be found in Phoenician traders' pidgin, *Roman Arbitration* p19.
25. Potter and Johns *Roman Britain* p13.
26. Much of what follows is taken from my *Background of the Common Law*, Chapter 2, 'Communal Societies and Customary Law' and some has been published in my 'Customary Law Before the Conquest'. See now Adam Kuper *The Reinvention of Primitive Society*.

Any group of humans living together as a community needs some common rules to govern the behaviour of the individuals within it. Even within a group seeking to function as a family there must be some system, however rudimentary and implicit. The rules of a kin group have more effective sanctions than those of a state. Life in such communal societies has been observed in recent times by anthropologists.[27] It is fair to accept, if great care is taken, that some fundamental characteristics of modern communal societies are the same as those in earlier societies which archaeology shows had similar ways of life.

Communal life is public. There is little privacy and opportunities for eccentricity are limited. There is little chance of antisocial conduct passing unnoticed or being attributed to the wrong person. Moreover, the sanctions are often immediate and applied until they work, that is until the culprits give up their antisocial behaviour and admit their faults, or have their capacity to misbehave removed.

The rules are, of course, unwritten, but they are better known in their entirety than modern laws are to citizens of states. The greatest technological advance in the law is the use of writing, which reduces individual and communal memory as it provides the techniques of recording and reminding. But an even more basic difference is economic. Economic relations are far more complex in more modern societies and much of the complexity of their laws is the result. On the other hand, a great deal of the complexity of communal law stems from the group's concern to control much more of what would now be considered the private lives of its members. For example, communal groups have comparatively few members so that selection of spouses from within them is limited. The health of the group requires a wider definition of incest. In our society, anonymous adoption has made possible the unwitting marriage of siblings. All the members of any communal group know the rules in detail and expect hard punishment for their breach and the facts are not likely to be in dispute. Everywhere in modern communal societies there are legal rules of a complexity, sophistication and abundance that modern legal scholars find hard to comprehend.[28] There is no reason to doubt that the rules of customary law were like that in prehistoric England.

It is also fair to assume that the customary laws of the various groups shared certain characteristics. Modern law has categories, used for the purposes of exposition and application: public and private; civil and criminal; property and obligations. Customary law does not, all law being one, consecrated by long use, general acceptance and the group's religion,

---

27. I prefer 'communal' to 'traditional' or 'primitive' for those societies, found everywhere in the past and still existing in some places, where social and economic relations are common not to a nation but to a small ethnic group.
28. My favourite example is in Peter Lawrence *The Garia* pp178–85.

superstitions, magic, whatever we choose to call what they believed. Customary law cannot be openly questioned by anyone on the grounds of utility or fairness. It is an essential attribute of the group. Yet it is always assumed, for that very reason, that to find it you must look for whatever rules produce a result in the best interests of the group (or those with power within it). Expediency is all, whatever formula is needed to produce it. That does not mean that there are no legal principles; just that, after they have been clarified and applied to the problem, there is no danger of the heavens falling.

The ideology of the group insists that customary law is unchanging and unchangeable but it constantly responds to new challenges, particularly technological, without any intention to reform, perhaps with no idea of progress.

Francis Pryor expresses his insights into customary procedures with convincing simplicity. In describing the landscape architecture of Avebury and Stonehenge and the effects its creators over millennia may have intended, he explains how those who walked through it may have felt that they were moving from one 'realm' to another:[29]

> The emotions of awe, tension and foreboding would build up as parties approached the great circles along the Avenues. But it isn't an easy matter to enter into the thoughts and emotions of ancient people. Even on the off-chance that we believe in anything supernatural at all, our ancestors and gods are safely tucked away 'up there' somewhere. We have also grown used to living in a society where, for practical day-to-day purposes, laws are imposed on us... As a consequence, it's easy to assume that in prehistory similar hard-and-fast laws applied, and that they were obeyed by everybody. But it wasn't like that. People of different communities had the freedom to make laws for themselves.

Freedom to make laws for themselves? That is a strange claim but a bright insight. It depends on who you mean by 'people'. They must be those with power. They are those who in the assemblies declared what the customary law was, and those who in applying it fixed the details of its rules not just for that dispute but in the memories of all the kin for the future. We do not know whether women were consulted but we can be sure that slaves were not.

ASSEMBLIES AND DISPUTE RESOLUTION

If it can be assumed that there must have been a substantial and fairly regular number of disputes, can it be shown that prehistoric communities are likely to have worked out systems by which to manage them?

---

29. Pryor *Britain BC* p244.

From about 4000BC the Stone Age inhabitants of England started to build a variety of spectacular communal edifices which we now call monuments. All of them may have relevance to dispute resolution. To take causewayed enclosures first, found all over southern England.[30] Most of them were probably not dwellings, as first thought, nor tombs, but many were provided with a front courtyard admirably suited for assemblies 'for the transaction of the necessary business of tribal life'.[31]

The fact that a site was used for burials does not mean that was its sole or major purpose. Nor were the various functions of assemblies necessarily separated, to be discharged on different occasions. As the archaeologist Howard Williams has written:[32]

> These were not only assemblies for the living, but also places for assembling and burying the dead in order to create the impression of communality and ancestors in a landscape... Funerals are often occasions for a range of social activities including feasting, settling disputes and forming alliances through gift giving.

Archaeologists usually portray the evidence as showing that a site's primary function was for burials and that other activities were carried on there, but is it not more likely that the emphasis should be the other way, that burial grounds are often at or adjacent to traditional assembly sites? Perhaps it is of no great significance that funerals were part of what happened at the assembly ground – they probably would not wait for the next regular meeting anyway – rather than that those assembled for a funeral took advantage of the opportunity to settle disputes.[33]

A common feature of such enclosures is a line of posts, often of impressive size.[34] Beasts could have been tied to them, though they are usually bigger than necessary for that purpose. It is common to find animal bones there, with evidence of some eaten there and others slaughtered to be eaten elsewhere.[35] Some may have been akin to totem poles. They could

---

30. Pryor *Britain BC* pp162–73.
31. Isobel Smith *Windmill Hill and Avebury* p19. This is not the place to speculate about their religious uses.
32. Howard Williams 'Assembling the Dead' pp127, 115.
33. Still a widespread practice, e.g. among the Sukuma of Tanzania, where on a death the traditional horn whistle calls people together and the resulting *nzengo*, the feeling of community, makes possible 'discussions and reconciliations – resolving misunderstandings between family members, distributing any wealth left by the deceased', Plan UK 'A Slice of Life in Tanzania 2007: Togetherness'.
34. There is a splendid drawing in *Britain BC* p203, figure 36. There were massive wooden poles at Stonehenge thousands of years before the stones, Cunliffe *Facing the Ocean* pp138–9; and in Ireland, Cooney *Brú na Bóinne*.
35. Once an animal was killed, it had to be eaten within a few days. Surplus fresh meat could not be stored. When herds outgrew the food to feed them or the labour to tend them, there had to be a feast. When labour greatly exceeded the need for it, did communities join in building monuments? Richard Bradley *Social Foundations* is a scholarly treatment of these and allied problems, especially at pp64 and 166.

also mark the places where the elders stood or sat in the assembly, like the polished stones in the *Iliad*, below **2.1**.[36]

Small pits have often been found, too, with objects symbolic of something, though no one can be sure of what. Pryor takes care to separate what he can prove from his speculation:[37]

> The tradition of digging and filling pits was intended to transform a temporary event or occasion into something enshrined within tribal lore and ideology. It's a process of creating and fixing history, and with it come new, or renewed, social relationships. With this process of transformation come added dimensions of meaning and significance. So a marriage, for instance, becomes more than a union of two people.

There may have been religious elements in this process of digging and filling, whatever that means at that time. 'Religious' is a category which comes easily to the pen. A historian of religion may well find a different significance from a historian of dispute resolution. There is plenty of evidence that many barrows had nothing to do with burials. Why then assume that religion was involved? No doubt there was 'ritual', as there is in most things we do publicly now, from umpires walking out together to start a cricket match to many aspects of the most modern arbitral hearing, with electronic timers unconsciously but exactly replicating the water-clocks of their forebears in Ancient Greece. In prehistoric times we can call it ritual or magic if we like. We could as easily think of it as early science, particularly when it is a part of technologies we are not used to giving credit for, such as the mines at Great Orme in north Wales, 'thought to have yielded a rather extraordinary 175 to 238 tons' of copper in the Bronze Age.[38] Recent research shows quite large-scale agriculture in southern England then: carefully designed field systems with stockproof fences and gates, cowpens and sheep races, with some of the produce for export.[39] Rather than put labels on phenomena like 'science' and 'religion' – or, indeed 'art', whether 'performance art' or otherwise – it is better to stick with what we can be confident about: the processes in the assemblies were clearly accompanied by acts which were customary and replicated and intended to have some consequence.

36. There are also striking similarities in overall shape and interior disposition of space between the reconstructions of the long barrow at West Kennet, Pryor *Britain BC* p201 figure 35, and of the tomb at Apesokari in Crete, Nano Marinatos *Minoan Religion* p12 figure 14 and p19 figure 19. Both have a space in front of the entrance suitable for public gatherings. Marinatos writes (p14, her italics): 'Cult implements and offerings were found *outside* the tombs, thus suggesting periodic visitation... by *sizable groups of people*... The area outside the tombs is spacious, capable of serving communal gatherings.'

37. Pryor *Britain BC* p178.

38. Pryor *Britain BC* pp264–75. It is scarcely possible that, in 5km of passages, some 70m deep, and some so tiny that only children could have worked them, mining could have been carried out without disputes arising.

39. DT Yates *Land, Power and Prestige*.

The assemblies could well have been seasonal, which would have avoided the need to give notice, but they could also have been called whenever necessary, perhaps for funerals. The location of causewayed enclosures beside rivers may be significant if they were used for dispute resolution. The river was often not just a border between the territories of different kin groups; it was a safer way of getting there than crossing alien land.

Other kinds of Stone Age edifice are the chambered tomb and the barrow. It may, like the chambered tomb at West Kennet near Avebury, greet you with impressive stones standing at the entrance. When chambered tombs were filled with earth, that seems to have signified some kind of completion, 'to seal or endorse a range of new family ties and obligations',[40] including perhaps the settlement of a dispute. The artefacts buried in a round barrow at Lockington, south of Derby, may have been intended to recognise such a settlement, around 2100–1900BC.[41] They include two decorated gold armlets, significantly not a pair, and a long copper dagger, probably imported from Brittany and found in the remains of its scabbard. Rather than assume these were intended to accompany some dead man to another world, would it not be simpler – though of course still the merest speculation – to suggest that the parties each gave an armlet to the other and with them buried the hatchet, or rather the dagger, significantly sheathed?[42] Will archaeologists in 4,000 years' time still be giving religious significance to what is buried today:[43]

A spear buried on the common border of two nomadic-pastoralist communities in the North Rift region of Kenya marked the end of bloody clashes a couple of decades ago… Elders of the Pokot and the Samburu… buried a spear… The ceremony was a symbol that all weapons of violence had been buried.

The great advantage which the state has over non-state communities is the organised physical power to enforce its orders, including decisions which resolve disputes. If there are no police or bailiffs, what about magic? After 'ritual' preparation (nearly as awe-inspiring as a visit to a solicitor's office, followed by a conference with a QC in an inn of court and then the full majesty of a civil trial) the parties would have their dispute determined by some kind of tribunal in a public traditional assembly. The award would be

---

40. Pryor *Britain BC* p198.
41. Gwilym Hughes ed *The Lockington Gold Hoard*, particularly Stuart Needham 'The Gold and Copper Metalwork' pp23–47, 45–7: 'The Lockington hoard, with its Armorico-British dagger and fine goldwork, will readily evoke comparisons with Wessex grave groups. This however proves to be a false analogy on virtually every front. Firstly, the Lockington group was not placed in a grave.'
42. Miles *Tribes* pp100–1; Colin Pendleton 'Firstly, Let's Get Rid of Ritual' pp170–8, 174: 'if the metal items were deliberate offerings, then it appears that domestic rubbish was as well'.
43. Fredrick Nzwili 'Stories of Transformation'; I have my wife Susanna Hoe to thank for this reference.

'sealed' and its terms remembered by solemn repetition accompanied by 'ritual' depositing of the tokens of settlement – why not exchanged armlets? – and the customary sheathing and burying of an expensive imported dagger. Where there is no writing, it is common to use objects as mnemonics.[44]

Assemblies in the Bronze Age were clearly more than religious ceremonies. Farmers need to meet to exchange livestock to renew the bloodline, even if they do not have to sell their surplus stock. There is evidence of conspicuous consumption at feasts. Is there any evidence that disputes were settled there? Pryor asks the question:[45] 'Why had many of the Bronze Age implements dredged from the River Thames... been partially melted down?' His answer is that they were 'votive offerings':

> Now I think I'm beginning to understand what might have been in people's minds as they partially melted down their spearheads, then dropped them into the river – doubtless with a spectacular hissing explosion of steam. It would be hard to imagine a stronger symbolic statement.

Symbolic of what if not of the ending of hostilities, of settlement of a dispute? Is any other explanation more likely? In his later work, *Britain AD*, Pryor writes:[46] 'In most cases, those offerings reflect rank, status or the avoidance of conflict... conflict that has been avoided through some symbolic act.'

The most compelling object of all, however, is also perhaps the most beautiful. It was made of polished flint about 3200BC. Though found not in England but in Ireland, at Knowth in the valley of the Boyne, it may be of direct relevance.[47] It is usually called a 'macehead'. That term is used by archaeologists for clubs made more effective by the addition of a heavy head, originally stone but later metal. This is too small, too light and too fragile for that. Nor is it likely to have worked as a mace, in its

---

44. MT Clanchy *From Memory to Written Record* 2nd edn particularly pp38–40 and 258–9 and 'Medieval Mentalities' p90, where he quotes PJ Geary *Phantoms of Remembrance* p180: 'Texts, names, traditions, inscriptions and objects continued to haunt the landscape of the eleventh and twelfth centuries, wraiths of earlier ages that fit uneasily into the constructed pasts of our memory specialists.'

45. Pryor *Britain BC* pp275–6.

46. Pryor *Britain AD* p217. Weapons from the Viking Age, well over a millennium later, have been dredged from the Thames and 'a Viking sword in a wooden scabbard of willow poplar with fleece lining from Skerne in East Yorkshire... These deposits were probably ritual sacrifices....' JD Richards *Viking Age England* p41.

47. It is on display with other maceheads in the National Museum in Dublin and published in (1982) 112 *Journal of the Royal Society of Antiquaries of Ireland* 123–38. I know Knowth is in Ireland and this study is restricted to England but this specimen is irresistible. Maceheads both of antler and stone have been found in England, Bradley *Social Foundations* pp46, 48–9, 55. A few of sandstone and of quartzite are described and illustrated in WF Rankine 'Stone Maceheads with Mesolithic Associations'. I dare not suggest a ceremonial use for the 'batons', perhaps 6,000 years old, found in Gough's Cave, discussed and beautifully illustrated in Stringer *Homo Britannicus* pp206–8.

modern meaning of a symbol of power. But just looking at it is enough to proclaim (to me) its association with public speaking. It is a stylised human head, only about 80mm tall and 60mm wide, not much bigger than a knob on a walking stick, of polished brown and white flint, with stylised eyes and a great gaping mouth. It would fit easily into the palm of your hand. It does have a cylindrical hole which would have allowed it to be fitted to the top of a staff.[48] Do we know anything about such 'speaking-staffs' in other times and places? We do indeed! Homer's *Iliad* and *Odyssey* are full of descriptions of assemblies. The fullest account of an arbitration is in the description of the assembly portrayed on the shield of Achilles.[49]

> **2.1** Men were crowded together in an assembly. A dispute had been stirred up there, and two men were arguing about the reconciliation-payment for a man who had been killed. One was pleading 'all to be yielded', pointing it out to the citizens, but the other refused to accept anything. Both men had put it to a knowing-one to reach an end. And men, supporters of each side, were cheering on both of them, so marshals were restraining the crowd. The elders sat on polished stones in a sacred circle and one after another took the speaking-staff (*skeptron*) of the shouting marshals in their hand and adjudicated.

The elders are given seats on polished stones in the sacred circle.[50] Each elder takes the speaking-staff from one of the marshals, whose function is to keep the crowd in order, and speaks out in turn. No speaking-staff has so far been found by archaeologists in Greece, to my knowledge, but it would not be surprising if the imagery were similar.[51] The wide-open mouth has double significance. It proclaims the authority of the president of the assembly to conduct proceedings. He or his marshal calls for order and he decides who shall speak. Similar formality survives even now in the body language of a French meeting, when the *président* decides to *donner la parole*, rather like a modern conductor without a baton. But the primary purpose is to show clearly that only one person may speak at a time and that is the one holding the staff. That is a convention which all must honour at the risk of being shunned as a lout. That is the dramatic point of the earlier passage in the *Iliad*, when Achilles, the demi-god celebrity

---

48. But then it would have faced upwards, not forward. My best guess is that it was meant to be held in the hand, like a modern microphone, but as a symbol of the right to speak.
49. Homer *Iliad* 18.497–508. The references to other passages in the *Iliad* and *Odyssey* and in later literature are in *Ancient Greek Arbitration*, where the speaking-staff is more fully discussed.
50. Until recently they still did sit on polished stones in a half circle in Rarotonga, in the Cook Islands, to deliberate in the assembly. I have seen and photographed the stones.
51. Many maceheads, i.e. clubs with fitted heads, have survived from Ancient Egypt, the earliest from the fourth millennium BC; they were used there as 'ceremonial symbols' – maces in the modern sense – from the early Neolithic; in China, too, but not, apparently, in Greece, SM Caza *Maces*.

superstar athlete, behaves so petulantly, turning on his commander-in-chief Agamemnon, who has taken his slave girl:[52]

> **2.2** You drunk with the face of a dog and the heart of a doe, you never have the guts to fight... you just take the booty of anyone who stands up to you.... You listen to me – I swear a great oath by this staff which the Greeks hold in their hands when they turn over their judgments in their minds – they who (for Zeus) guard customary law – I swear you this great oath – you'll be sorry!

And he does the unthinkable – he throws the staff down.

That was in the Bronze Age in Greece.[53] Some Australian aboriginal communities still use the 'talking-stick'. Could some of the many so-called 'maceheads', and perhaps other ceremonial objects of stone or horn found in England, have served the same purpose?

CONCLUSIONS

In Iron Age England and the surrounding parts of the British Isles, there were large tribes, some led by chiefs, warlords who would be kings, both peoples and rulers known by name from later sources. Pryor suggests that there were places on their borders where they met in assemblies, before Roman occupation curtailed a trend towards conglomeration in larger kingdoms.[54] He finds 'little trace of feuds', by which he means violent vendettas rather than the kin-enforced resolution of disputes discussed in Chapter 4 below. This was a land of socially highly developed and economically prosperous communities.[55]

> From a technological point of view, the native inhabitants of Britain had been fashioning iron tools and weapons for some seven hundred years. They grew most of the common crops that we see in the modern countryside, and they had possessed sophisticated wheeled vehicles for well over a thousand years. Their clothes were made from brightly dyed woven cloth, and their artists and craftsmen were capable of producing works of art that could hold their own alongside the finest creations offered by the ancient world.

Pryor insists that prehistory teaches us that we must all learn to think in the long term. That is the justification for this first chapter. In trying to understand how dispute resolution has developed in England, there

---

52. Homer *Iliad* 1.224–45.
53. The *festuca* of the Roman *lictor*, which Gaius (*Institutes* 4.16) said was used like a spear as a sign of rightful authority, *iusti dominii*, reappears in the *Lex Salica*: *Pactus Legis Salicae* 46.1, Paul Fouracre 'Disputes in Later Merovingian Francia'.
54. Bradley *Social Foundations* p167. Catherine Hills 'Anglo-Saxon Attitudes' in Higham *Britons in Anglo-Saxon England* p23: 'Most of lowland England has been more or less continuously exploited since at least the Iron Age.'
55. Pryor *Britain BC* pp405–6, 409, 431. This chapter has been stimulated and informed by his two recent, comprehensive, accessible and lively books: *Britain BC* and *Britain AD*. No one who has not read them can rely on their old general knowledge of England's early history, however much they may want to argue with his conclusions.

are obvious advantages to starting from the beginning, even if there is little direct evidence. It is helpful, for example, to know that the people of England were so technically advanced when the Romans came. But, even had they not been, we would have had no right to assume that their dispute management was primitive. As far as we can tell, they had the processes they thought they needed. What little evidence there is tends to show they settled their private disputes in assemblies. There is no evidence that the parties regularly resorted to violence when they could not settle private disputes amicably themselves, though there is evidence that they did fight battles, for example the large numbers of arrowheads found at Crickley Hill.[56]

Our first written sources are Roman. They portray the people of England as inferior outsiders on the edge of the world. The new colonials were primarily interested in opportunities for military conquest and exploitation of natural resources but they have left evidence which reveals something about the people in what became their colony of Britannia, even traces of how they managed their disputes.

---

56. Philip Dixon 'Crickley Hill'.

3 BRITANNIA[1]

The Roman policy towards subject or subjugated races, though at first exclusive, had become, during the Roman dominion in this country, extremely liberal and enlarged. The ideas of the Romans on this subject, as on all others, advanced and expanded with the growth of their mighty empire, and at the very time when their dominion here had become firmly settled, their law had attained its highest development of excellence, and their policy towards their provincial subjects had reached the highest point of enlightenment.

WF Finlayson, *Reeves' History of English Law* pv

INTRODUCTION

The history of dispute resolution in Britannia, as Roman Britain will be called here, cannot be based on such wishful nineteenth-century conjectures. It is to be found in a few scattered references in the literature with substantial help from archaeology and not a little from analogy. The literature left by Roman writers allows a few, unconnected glimpses of how Roman law and administration affected the people who lived here then. No one wrote in the indigenous languages. Archaeological evidence provides a quite detailed background and just a little about the legal system.[2] Yet, provided it is recognised that any picture will be fragmentary and uncertain, all is not dark.

It is permissible to argue, though not to assume, that the Roman colonial legal system applied *mutatis mutandis* in Britannia much as it did in other provinces,[3] but that the administration required only those who were citizens to transact their private business according to Roman law. Law, custom and practice might differ in detail from province to province and between an Italian town and a British province but the system which the Roman colonial administration applied was likely to have been similar.[4]

1. A previous version of this chapter appeared as 'Bricks Without Straw: Arbitration in Roman Britain' but it has been rethought and revised in the light of recent scholarship, particularly in genetics, and of David Mattingly *Imperial Possession*, which has a full and up-to-date bibliography.
2. The evidence of how people lived is substantial, Martin Millett *The Romanization of Britain: An Essay in Archaeological Interpretation* and TW Potter and Catherine Johns *Roman Britain*. The fullest description of the sources, particularly of the individuals in the Roman administration, is now AR Birley *The Roman Government of Britain*.
3. The argument is made more fully by Andrew Lintott *Imperium Romanum: Politics and Administration* and in Derek Roebuck and Bruno de Loynes de Fumichon *Roman Arbitration* pp8–10.
4. Joan Liversidge *Britain in the Roman Empire*, particularly Chapter 11.

The result would still depend on the product of Roman law on local conditions. The archaeological evidence supports this, particularly the remains of wax tablets recording legal transactions, **3.25**.[5]

For most of the inhabitants of the new Roman colony, and throughout its four centuries, disputes were no doubt managed as they had been from time immemorial, in local assemblies according to customary laws, which developed over that time in their own ways. And that is how they were determined after the Romans left.

Except for Caesar and Tacitus, who wrote about their own times and what they knew, the literary descriptions in Latin or Greek of life in Britannia are for the most part untrustworthy, written from afar and long afterwards, unless we can catch them unawares, when they tell us something dependable by chance, in texts prepared always for a purpose other than to preserve the facts. And there are just a few reliable primary legal sources which are direct evidence of practice in Britannia. Perhaps paradoxically, that least reliable of tools, analogy, may here be of most use. Inferences from what we know of law and practice elsewhere, though they can tell us nothing directly about Britannia, may provide the most reliable general knowledge where there is evidence that the administration functioned similarly.[6]

Archaeological evidence can provide reliable information, if it is interpreted with care:[7]

> Can we really use the archaeological evidence to fill out the gaps? Yes but only if we turn a blind eye to the fact that all life turns on chance events, random experiences and the dynamic of personalities that can't possibly survive in the archaeological record. If you want a cautionary tale, take Julius Caesar. He invaded Britain twice, in 55BC and 54BC. There isn't the slightest piece of archaeological evidence for those events. We only have his word for it.

By great good luck, one of the scraps of wood and blocks of stone on which contemporary writing has survived makes reference to a dispute, **3.25**. It will be made to carry a heavy and lonely burden but we have no means of knowing whether it is representative.[8]

5. RSO Tomlin 'The Girl in Question', 'A Five-Acre Wood' and 'A Roman Will'.
6. But Mattingly *Imperial Possession* p43: 'One must also admit the caveat that the Roman empire was not run according to an unvaried rule book and there are numerous examples of local variations in procedures and of the adoption of short term, *ad hoc* solutions. When we employ analogy, therefore, we are constructing theories for further testing, not establishing fact.' We cannot follow too closely what we know to have happened among the Germans of these times, whose customary laws were quite different: EA Thompson *The Early Germans* p10.
7. Guy de la Bédoyère in *BBC History* June 2006 42 and his *Roman Britain: A New History*.
8. RSO Tomlin 'A Five-Acre Wood'; Edward James *Britain in the First Millennium* p47: 'In the first three centuries of the Empire 225 million pay-records would have been produced for the army – of which precisely *three* survive' from RO Fink *Roman Military Records* p242. Roger Tomlin tells me that another has since been found at Masada, making four.

SOCIETY

The primary source of information about what England was like when the Romans first invaded and before they conquered it is Julius Caesar's own account, *On the Gallic War*, written after his triumphal return to Rome in 50BC. The well-known words with which he begins, describing the people of Gaul, deserve to be read with as much care as he used in crafting them:[9]

> **3.1** The whole of Gaul, *Gallia*, is divided into three parts, of which the *Belgae* inhabit one, the *Aquitani* another, and the third those who are called the *Celtae* in their own language, in ours the *Galli*. They all differ from one another in language, institutions and laws. The Garonne separates the *Galli* from the *Aquitani* and the Marne and the Seine separate the *Galli* from the *Belgae*.

From this passage it is clear that Caesar recognised that there was a possibility for confusion arising from the ambiguity of the name Galli which he took pains to resolve. There was a place called Gallia and a people called Galli. They did not fit. Those people the Romans called Galli inhabited only the middle bit of Gallia. They did not call themselves Galli. Their own name for themselves was Celtae.

How did the people of Gaul relate to those in what Caesar already called Britannia? Caesar first describes the Britons, saying that some of them were immigrants from Gaul:[10]

> **3.2** By general agreement they entrusted the high command to Cassivellaunus. A river called the Thames divides his boundaries from the maritime communities, *civitates*, about 80 miles from the sea. In earlier times there had been never-ending wars with the other communities but when we arrived the Britons were forced to appoint him commander-in-chief for the whole war.
>
> The interior part of Britannia is inhabited by those who say that they are the ones who are native to the island; the maritime part by those who crossed from *Belgium* to get booty from war. They are nearly all called by the names of communities from which they emigrated. When the war was over they settled there and began to cultivate the fields. The multitude of people is infinite and their buildings are packed very tight, with a great number of cattle.

As Caesar says, there were people with the same names on both sides of the Channel, Parisii and Belgae for example. Then he places them geographically:[11]

> **3.3** The island is shaped like a triangle, with one side opposite Gaul. One angle of this side faces east. That is Kent, *Cantium*, where nearly all the ships from Gaul put in. The lower angle faces south. This side is about 500 miles long.

9. Caesar *Gallic War* 1.1.
10. Caesar *Gallic War* 5.11–12.
11. Caesar *Gallic War* 5.13.

The second side turns toward Spain, *Hispania*, and the west. On this side is Ireland, *Hibernia*, smaller by half than Britannia, it is estimated, and the same distance [from Spain] as Gaul is from Britannia...

The third side faces north, with no land opposite it, but the angle on that side mostly faces towards *Germania*.

Caesar had already picked out the people of Kent as having a 'Gallic' lifestyle, unlike those who lived inland:[12]

> **3.4** Of all these by far the most civilised, *humanissimi*, are those who live in Kent, which is an entirely maritime district, and they do not differ much from the Gallic in custom, *Gallica consuetudine*.
>
> Most of those who live inland do not sow corn. They live on meat and milk and are dressed in leather.

If we can trust Caesar, and there is no obvious reason here why we should not,[13] the Gauls who called themselves Celtae had different 'language, institutions and customs' from the Belgae and Aquitani. Those who lived in the maritime regions, which included Kent, were the most civilised and differed little from the Gallic way of life. Were they like the Celtae or the Belgae? From their proximity across the Channel, they must have been like the Belgae. In language, too, as well as institutions and custom?[14]

Julius Caesar did not stay. Before he came there had been ready and regular travel and trade between Britain and the Roman provinces across the Channel for many years. Roman merchants settled in Britain. After Caesar's invasions, Cunobelinus (Cymbeline) became king of most of the south and had coins minted, perhaps a million or more gold staters and many more bronze coins, naming himself on some '*Rex Brittonum*'.[15] Trade flourished between his capital Camulodunum (Colchester) and the Roman-occupied Rhineland. His kingdom fell apart when he died in AD40. When Verica's rule ended in the other great kingdom of lowland Britain in AD43, the emperor Claudius grasped the opportunity to invade with 40,000 troops.[16] A new Roman province was quickly settled, encompassing most of the southern half of the present England, though not Wales or Cornwall.

The Romans, like later imperialists, were not always alert to the niceties of other people's cultures. They were, like the Greeks, quick to disparage the different ways of the barbarians. But Tacitus was not a typical historian. He knew from personal experience a lot about colonial life, particularly in

---

12. Caesar *Gallic War* 5.11 and 5.12.
13. Though archaeological research has shown that he was wrong about the lack of agriculture among 'those who live inland', Mattingly *Imperial Possession* p50.
14. And these relations were nothing new: 'The earliest coins in south-east Britain were second-century BC imports from northern Gaul, the so-called Gallo-Belgic series', Mattingly *Imperial Possession* p69, who explains the importance of early coinage evidence, pp73–4.
15. Potter and Johns *Roman Britain* p34.
16. John Creighton *Britannia: The Creation of a Roman Province*.

Gaul. His father and grandfather had been in the colonial civil service and probably served in Gaul where the family had its origins.[17] He studied rhetoric and may have studied law. He became a successful imperial officer and consul in AD97, publishing the *Agricola* the following year. In this biography of his father-in-law, Agricola, who was governor here AD78–85, he compared the people in Britannia and Gaul:[18]

> **3.5** Anyway, who the first mortals were who lived in Britannia, whether indigenous or immigrants, is not sufficiently proved, as usual among foreigners. The physical types vary and the inferences drawn from that. The red hair and big limbs of those who live in *Caledonia* declare their Germanic origin. The swarthy faces and curly hair of the *Silures* and their position opposite Spain are evidence that ancient Iberians, *Hiberos*, crossed over and occupied those sites.
>
> Those nearest to the *Galli* are like them, either because of the continuing strength of origin or because the two countries run close together from opposite directions, so that the weather gives them their physical appearance. But taking everything into account it is likely that the *Galli* invaded the neighbouring island. You can detect their religion there, and their superstitious persuasions. Their speech is not much different at all....

The Caledonians are outside our study to the north. The Silures lived in what are now Glamorgan, Monmouth and south Brecknock and had not been conquered when Tacitus wrote. But who were the Galli and who were the people closest to them? Did Tacitus give the same meaning to the word Galli as Caesar did? All the Gauls? Just the Celtae? Neither meaning seems likely. I hesitantly suggest that Tacitus did not keep to Caesar's careful distinction. The Galli whom he compares with Britons and distinguishes from the redheaded Caledonians and the swarthy Silures live across the Channel from Gaul. They are not the Celtae who live in central Gaul but the Belgae to their north. They are the Galli who invaded and settled. It is their customs and religion and language which are similar to those in Britannia.

The population was probably over two million; agriculture flourished in the south-east and, with the help of new Roman technology, was able to provide a surplus of corn to feed the army[19] and wealth for the high-ranking colonials and those at the top of the tribal hierarchies to spend on imported luxuries. There was soon a flourishing export trade all the way to Rome. Oysters were caught in vast numbers. In London they were cheap but in Rome a dozen cost half a day's wage for a labourer.[20]

Few of the new colonials had any roots in Rome itself. Only a few of even the highest rank had been born or educated there. The others came

17. Tacitus *Agricola* RM Ogilvie and IA Richmond eds p7; the best new translation is by AR Birley.
18. Ogilvie and Richmond *Agricola* 11 p99.
19. Stuart Piggott 'Native Economies'.
20. John Morris *Londinium* pp270–1.

from all parts of the empire. Most of the soldiers and settlers, men and women, could well have been from the nearest provinces in Gaul, of much the same stock and speaking similar languages to some of the British, whether they came from Celtica or Belgica, or even Aquitania, perhaps even beyond Gaul in Germania.[21]

Though there may have been a general policy against serving in a legion in your own country, there is plenty of evidence that legions did recruit locally,[22] and you could join a cohort of foreign auxiliaries. A tombstone found at Mumrills on Hadrian's Wall reads:[23]

> **3.6** To the spirits of the dead and to Nectovelius, son of Vindex, aged 29, nine years' service, Brigans by nationality, served in the Second Thracian Cohort.

There were people called Brigantes elsewhere in the Empire,[24] but this soldier with a British name was a local, though his father's name was Roman.

A *colonia* of retired legionaries was set up in Camulodunum as early as AD49. A *colonia* was a distinctly Roman settlement, its citizens governed by and privileged to enjoy Roman law. There and in the *coloniae* founded later, Lincoln, Gloucester and York, there was no room for any British customary law. In the new town of London, one of very few to be set up anywhere in the Empire where there was no existing settlement, Roman law applied from the start.[25]

In AD61 the army crushed the uprising against Roman tyranny led by Boudicca. Thereafter the borders of Rome's British provinces stretched to what are now Scotland, Wales and Cornwall, with castles to keep other British at bay, and later Hadrian's Wall to keep out the Picts and also the Scoti, who were probably colonisers from Ireland.[26]

The Romans never imposed a civil administration even over all within their borders. Unlike most other provinces, Britannia had many unsettled areas, and only some of them were subject to Roman military occupation. Approximately, there was civil government in the south and east, military

---

21. At Vindolanda 'Most of the troops were Batavians or Tungrians from the Low Countries (modern Netherlands and Belgium) around the mouth of the Rhine, part of what Julius Caesar called Gallia Belgica', Miles *Tribes* p122.
22. RG Collingwood and RP Wright *The Roman Inscriptions of Britain* 369 from Caerleon.
23. Collingwood and Wright *Roman Inscriptions of Britain* 2142; *Corpus Inscriptionum Latinarum* vii 1091; E Birley *Roman Britain and the Roman Army*. Nicholas Higham *Rome, Britain and the Anglo-Saxons* p50 has doubts about Britons serving in the Roman army in Britannia but 'analogy from other provinces and the growth of "civil settlements" outside Roman forts makes it very likely' (personal communication from RSO Tomlin).
24. ALF Rivet and Colin Smith *Place Names of Roman Britain* p279.
25. Morris *Londinium*.
26. This book is concerned only with what is now England; it does not attempt to include Wales; or Ireland, never colonised by Rome; or Scotland, of which large parts came under some Roman control from time to time, IA Richmond *Roman and Native* and Peter Salway *The Frontier People of Roman Britain*.

occupation further north and west. The British client-queen Cartimandua and her Brigantes provided a buffer.[27] The division is sometimes even more roughly made into lowland and highland, though many of the most fertile parts were under military control, not civil administration, for example the Cheshire plain from Chester and the Vale of York from York.[28] About AD150 Appian, an Egyptian who became an advocate in Rome and later attained the high judicial-administrative office of procurator, wrote in Greek of the extent of Roman dominion:[29]

> **3.7** Crossing the northern ocean to Britannia, itself a continent, they have taken the more important part, over half, and are not concerned with the rest. Indeed, what they have is not much use to them.

Within those parts subject to civil Roman colonial government, however, the upper class adopted Roman ways and prospered and at least the slaves and other workers were not subject to wholesale and indiscriminate slaughter. The Roman god to which the British and Romans assimilated the existing British god or gods seems more often to have been Mercury, the god of commerce among other things, than Mars. As most British were not allowed to be fighters or even to carry weapons, they could not aspire to military glory. By AD49 lead mined in the Mendips was being used for building in Pompeii.[30] Roman senators were forbidden by law from engaging in commerce, though they regularly evaded it by charging rents or using slaves as managers, and it is unlikely that that law, which did not apply to others of the nobility, was enforced in Britannia.[31]

British society remained tribal and the imperial administration, where it could, co-opted existing tribal leaders, those with power over land and people, and strengthened their control so long as they performed the functions the Romans allotted them. From the Romans' point of view, the most important was to keep order, including the settlement of disputes. The provincial government with the governor at its head, assisted by his finance minister, the *procurator*, controlled the settled areas, with a small staff of civil servants, technically in military service. They eventually established *civitates*, administrative regions, with *capita*, centres where they relied on the local leaders to ensure law and order, facilitate the extractive industries and collect taxes.[32]

27. John Clarke 'Roman and Native, AD80–122' in Richmond *Roman and Native* pp28–59, at pp32–7.
28. Andrew Sargent 'The North–South Divide Revisited: Thoughts on the Character of Roman Britain'.
29. Appian *Roman History* preface 5.
30. Potter and Johns *Roman Britain* p45.
31. Tacitus *Annals* 14.32. We know that the law against slaves owning slaves was not observed, RSO Tomlin 'The Girl in Question'.
32. Tacitus *Agricola* 12, 13.

3.8 The Britons show more ferocity, those who have not yet been softened by longlasting peace... which happened to the Britons who were conquered a while ago. The others have remained like the Gauls once were... Rarely do two or three tribes come together to repel a common danger. They fight on their own and are conquered all together...

The British people readily put up with duties and taxes and colonial impositions, unless they are wronged. They will not tolerate that. They can bear being mastered but will not be slaves.

In the second century, Britannia stretched as far as Hadrian's Wall. In the third it was divided into Britannia Inferior in the north and Britannia Superior in the south. Early in the fourth century Britannia became the Diocese of the Britannias, under the rule of the *vicarius* and divided into four provinces: Britannia Prima in the south-west; Britannia Secunda in the north; Flavia Caesariensis in the midlands and Maxima Caesariensis in the south-east.

Many people lived in the towns, of which there were more in Roman times than for centuries to come after the Romans left. Indeed, the population may have reached a peak of three or even four million or more, higher than it was at the time of the Domesday Book census.[33] More than two million lived in the countryside and half a million in urban settlements and military camps. Moreover, there was a flourishing trade with the Belgae in Normandy and with Armorica, now Brittany. Disputes arising out of that trade, if they came to the notice of the colonial authorities, must have been dealt with according to rules and practices which were influenced, when they were not completely governed, by Roman law. It would not be surprising, however, if most were dealt with by older customary methods. There is no evidence.

TRADE

Strabo wrote in Greek. His compendious geography of cAD20 describes, or rather assumes, regular trading links between Britannia and the Continent from the Rhine, Seine, Loire and Garonne. He says that a ship could leave Gaul one evening and be in Britannia the next day:[34]

3.9 It is less than a day's run from these people to Britannia...
The passage to Britain from the rivers of Celtica is 320 *stadia* [c60km]. If they sail in the evening on the ebb tide, they land on the island the next day, about the eighth hour.

Even when the economy of Gaul across the Channel was ruined later in the third century, that of Britannia still flourished. It became the most important northern supplier of corn for Rome itself, as well as exporting iron, tin,

33. The estimates vary: KO Morgan *The Oxford History of Britain* p4; Potter and Johns *Roman Britain* p68; Millett *Romanization* p181 are much higher, as many as 3,665,000.
34. *Strabo* 4.1.14, 4.3.4.

copper and some gold. Rome looked to its British colony for money and men. Taxes were increased and forced labour was drafted for work on fortifications and even, perhaps, for work in Gaul.[35] Agricultural workers were more closely bound to the land. With no more conquests to provide wealth and slaves, the Roman administration of its colonies became not only more repressive but totalitarian: every walk of life, including much of commerce, fell under state control.

LANGUAGE

The Romans brought Latin with them. It was the language of the administration and the army, at least of the legions, and the auxiliary troops must have had a smattering. It was not the language of the Roman senate, let alone of the classical writers, like Caesar and Tacitus who wrote about Britannia. Some forms of it, including pidgins, must have been spoken by those who traded with or served their colonial masters, including some of the women with whom they lived and the children they had by them. Tacitus says Agricola fostered the learning of Latin by the upper classes. I have tried to discover and describe its use in Appendix A.

A letter from Vindolanda, **A.3**, shows that ordinary documents of trade, in that case a letter asking for payment of a debt, might be in reasonable Latin. The Latin of **3.25** can hardly be faulted.[36] In the management of disputes, those who were comfortable in their command of Latin were no doubt more likely to make use of the Roman legal system and arbitration in the Roman style; there would be other factors, including cost and accessibility, to inhibit their use by others.

Whatever languages were used by the British people when the Romans came no doubt continued as their mother tongues. In Appendix A I have tried to determine what they may have been. Language use must have determined the choice of system of dispute resolution in most cases, though for some disputes it might well have depended on whether one or more of the parties was a Roman citizen.

No evidence from Roman Britain discloses old Celtic, Germanic, or indeed Roman practices, linguistic or otherwise, which survived to influence the way disputes were managed later in Anglo-Saxon England.

CUSTOMARY LAW

Caesar tells how disputes were settled in Gaul:[37]

> **3.10** In all Gaul... [are] two categories of men of substance and dignity... one is of druids, the other of knights. [The druids] are the ones who lay down the law for almost all disputes, public and private, and whether something is considered

---

35. Neil Faulkner *The Decline and Fall of Roman Britain* pp157–61.
36. RSO Tomlin 'Five-Acre Wood' p212.
37. Caesar *Gallic War* 6.13–14.

a crime, and whether there has been a killing, and if there is a dispute about inheritance or boundaries they settle it. They lay down remedies and penalties. If any individual or group does not abide by their decision, they ban them from sacrifices; for them this is the gravest punishment. Those that they ban are held to be impious and accursed and everyone keeps clear of them, cutting them and refusing to talk to them, lest they suffer some harm from contact with them. If they try to exert their rights they will not be given them and they are granted no honour.

Note how careful Caesar was to say that this system applied in all Gaul, *in omni Gallia*. Not just among the *Celtae*. He says that the community relied on the druids to lay down the law, which of course was customary law then. He also stresses that they had no written laws but the druids kept them in their memory. Though there is no reason to accept this without question as evidence even of how the Gauls resolved their disputes, their British kin had similar druids, and it is likely that they too had a hand in resolving disputes. Though the Romans had no objection to communities resolving their own disputes by customary law, they did not find druids an acceptable alternative authority. Tacitus says that the Romans massacred the last of them on Anglesey, on the pretext that their human sacrifices were abhorrent.[38]

Druids or no, those well developed British communities had systems for resolving disputes which continued after the Romans set up their colonial government. That administration never attempted to do more than provide a legal system for some people in some parts of England. There is evidence that those indigenous systems continued to function in much the same way long after the Romans had gone, enforcing decisions by the effective sanction of outlawry. Perhaps, at least in the west, in similar languages as before the Romans came.

ROMAN LAW

The history of Britannia starts not long after the beginning of the Roman Empire, runs for four centuries and ends as the empire declines. The Roman law in Britannia is the law of the Empire as it developed over that period. The Roman imperial system of law and administration assumed – usually without stopping to think about it – that practice in the provinces would follow the customary ways of the various groups, of tribe, clan, trade,[39] or religion where like the Jews they had their own laws. Nor did the Romans make laws for the people of their provinces except where they had an interest in imposing a different solution. In those parts of Britain where this delegated administration was not possible, disputes which did

---

38. Tacitus *Annals* 14.30.
39. There was a craft guild in Colchester by the end of the first century AD: JE Bogaers 'King Cogidubnus' in RG Collingwood and RP Wright *The Roman Inscriptions of Britain* p91.

not attract the attention of the military command were no doubt settled as they had been before the Romans came and, indeed, after they left. There is nothing to tell us how that worked or anything of the content of the customary law. And there were large tracts of land which the Romans never tried to rule. There they usually let sleeping dogs lie, for they found, when they provoked them, they could bite.

The Latin of the Vindolanda tablets and the script used in Britannia to write it are close to those in Egypt at the same time,[40] which is some evidence to support the argument that other practices, including the legal system, were similar in quite different provinces. While it lasted, law and practice that began at the centre of imperial power or was deliberately intended for the provinces must have affected Britannia.

A few documents recording legal transactions survive and no doubt more will be found, particularly in the programmes of excavations in London. One is a transfer of land according to Roman law.[41] A part of a will found in a Welsh bog follows the Roman form.[42] Another tablet records the sale of the slave girl Fortunata to Vegetus, himself the slave of a slave, some time about AD75–125, in what is now Poultry in the City of London. It follows a standard Roman law precedent, though strictly Roman law did not allow a slave to own a slave.[43] Most interesting in the history of dispute resolution, though, is the stilus tablet discussed below, **3.25**, which shows how Roman citizens in London in AD118 dealt with a dispute over land in Kent. Together these documents make it clear that Roman citizens here used Roman forms familiar from survivals in other provinces. What else would they use?

So long as a place was under military rule, the commander was responsible for law and order and expected to hear petitions and resolve such disputes as the people were brave enough to present to him or which threatened his control. In times of peace it is unlikely that he intervened much in local and private matters. There is little direct evidence from Britannia[44] but in other Roman provinces villages were allowed to elect their own magistrates who dealt with all but the most serious disputes and those which involved a party from another village. We know that the political administration of some municipalities, not only the *coloniae* but also the *municipia*, was in the hands of *decuriones*, at first elected then co-opted, notionally a hundred

---

40. Potter and Johns *Roman Britain* p54.
41. EG Turner 'A Writing Tablet from Somerset'.
42. At the edge of Roman control, perhaps on land granted to a veteran, RSO Tomlin 'A Roman Will from North Wales' with a photograph, drawing, translation and commentary.
43. RSO Tomlin 'The Girl in Question'. Slaves were allowed to have their *peculium*, which in strict law was part of their master's property but separate from it. By custom and in practice slaves treated it as their own.
44. An inscription which survives from Caerwent is evidence of the grant of a constitution to the Silures, creating them a self-governing city-state, Faulkner *Decline* p34.

in number.[45] They elected two or more sets of *duumviri* or *duoviri*, the 'two-men'. The most senior pair, *duumviri iuri dicundo*, the 'two-men with jurisdiction' were magistrates in charge of legal matters. They dealt with all but the most serious criminal prosecutions and had a civil jurisdiction limited by the value of the claim.[46] Other parallel jurisdictions grew up, of military courts and of the *defensor civitatis*, at first appointed by the emperor, later elected by the *decuriones*. Some governors delegated their judicial powers to *iudices pedanei*.[47] Appeals went from all of them to the governor, to whom higher jurisdiction was reserved. If it was made up mainly of Roman citizens, a municipality's constitution might, like that of a *colonia*, bestow the boon of Roman law on all of them. If not, it could be granted lesser 'Latin rights', as they were called.

A town of any size had a main square, the forum, one side of which was the *basilica*, typically a large, long, rectangular room with an internal aisle and outside colonnade. The inside might be plastered with frescoes and the outside graced with statues. London's first was all of 150 metres long. Merchants traded outside in the porticoes. Inside the magistrates adjudicated. It is not too much, perhaps, to imagine that that was where the arbitrators, public and private, did their work.

An edict of Caracalla in AD212, the *Constitutio Antoniniana*, gave full citizenship to all free inhabitants of the empire. As Tony Honoré puts it:[48]

> To extend citizenship to all free people, whatever their sex, economic status, or ethnic origin, could not be popular with those whose privileges were diluted as a result; but it fitted the Zeitgeist. It gave many millions, perhaps a majority of the empire's inhabitants, new names, new capacities (for example to hold public office), and a new consciousness of being Roman. It put them under a new system of law.

But what happened in practice?

> The extension of citizenship did not at first dramatically affect the administration of law in the provinces. Provincial governors showed patience and tact in applying Roman law to the new citizens. Those who find this surprising underestimate the Roman administration. Why provoke discontent by rigidly insisting on unfamiliar norms of Roman law? Indeed until governors had regular legal assistance in the form of assessors, which became standard practice in the fourth century, they were not well placed to do so. They and other judges imposed the Roman legal system on the new citizenry incrementally... The legal technique available for this policy of gradualism was custom... The provincial governor will reach a decision after ascertaining what has been decided in the town in question in disputes of the kind with which he is now faced, since *preceding custom and the reason that led to the adoption of the custom* must be respected.

---

45. *Codex Theodosianus* 11.7.2, see fn55 below.
46. *Roman Arbitration* pp78–9 on the *Lex Irnitana*.
47. Paul Schaffner 'Britain's *Iudices*' p152; there is no evidence of them from Britain.
48. Tony Honoré 'Roman Law AD200–400: From Cosmopolis to Rechstaat?' pp114–16.

Though the italics are Honoré's own, it will be seen that the emphasis is essential if future developments are to be understood. The magistrates were likely to be appointed from the local landowning class or local chiefs, depending on the district, and to know the customary law as well as anyone. The governor, even though a foreigner, would take care to take advice and apply the local law.

The process did not happen throughout Britannia all at once, and probably never, but Neil Faulkner paints a picture which serves as a useful and dependable background of the administrative system in which to try to fit any pieces of evidence about dispute resolution:[49]

> Roman policy was to win over the bulk of the British aristocracy and to convert the warrior-chieftains of yesteryear into Roman gentleman-landlords... by reconstituting the old tribes as local government districts (*civitates*), each with its own county town (*civitas*-capital), governed by an administrative council (*ordo* or *curia*) made up of the leading local landowners (*decuriones* or *curiales*)... Thus local government was in the hands of a property-owning oligarchy descended from the Iron Age nobility. All that was required by the provincial government – the governor, the *procurator* (or finance minister), and the army commanders, each with their small staff of officials, clerks and soldiers – was that the town oligarchs ensure law and order in country areas, collect and forward the taxes due, and maintain the local infrastructure in a usable condition. Otherwise they could do pretty much what they liked.

It cannot therefore be accepted without qualification that: 'Roman rule imposed a world based on recognised, written civil and criminal law for one in which tribal custom and the ever present threat of local warfare dominated relationships.'[50] The colonial government applied Roman law directly to Roman citizens but respected and imposed the customary law on all others. Nor can it be assumed without evidence that the law of Rome would have provided a more acceptable procedure for resolving the civil disputes of the indigenous people than 'tribal custom'. The prime concern of the parties to a dispute is rarely the refinement of the law and procedure applied to it. It is to win. But, if they lose, an acceptable process based on mutually accepted traditional law may persuade them to give at least a grudging if unacknowledged recognition that the result is fair according to the facts, the merits and the norms they know.

49. Faulkner *Decline* p31. The evidence, and the lack of it, are neatly handled by JM Reynolds 'Legal and Constitutional Problems' pp70–5. Morris *Londinium* argues for British *civitates* by analogy with those elsewhere in the Empire, pp62–72.
50. Peter Salway *Roman Britain* pp526–7. In *The Frontier People of Roman Britain* p202 he goes further: 'Though the material culture of many changed but little, the people were for the first time subjected to the greatest of the benefits which Rome conferred on her empire, the institution which in future ages was not only to regulate but make possible both personal liberty and the proper ordering of society – the rule of law.' I wonder how many of the 'frontier people', the Brigantes say, saw it like that.

Two things, however, are incontrovertible and important. First, Roman law forbade, and the Roman administration strictly prevented, civilians from carrying arms. So far as that law could be enforced, it inhibited private feuds and duels. Secondly, every soldier in a Roman legion and many of the auxiliaries had opportunities to learn to read and write in Latin and the widespread acquisition of the language by the better-off, those most likely to have substantial disputes and to be asked to mediate and arbitrate for others, must have meant that there were many who had at least some smattering of their rights and duties under Roman law and knew how to take advantage of it in resolving their disputes.

HOW ROMAN LAW WAS APPLIED

Britannia was a long way from Rome. Travel and communications, though regular and efficient for the authorities, were neither cheap nor convenient for subjects or private citizens. It is hardly surprising that there are few Roman records of cases from here. What few there are, though, show that they were dealt with uniformly with cases from elsewhere. When imperial authority made a decision, called a rescript, in a private dispute, it had the force of law not only for the parties but for everyone else. Not only the decision itself but the reason for it was authoritative. The modern distinction between case law and legislation was not so sharply drawn until AD398, when a law provided that 'past and future rescripts, given when a judge has consulted the emperor on a point in the case before him, have effect only for the case about which the emperor was consulted'.[51]

Britannia's subjection to Rome had been over for more than a hundred years when Justinian proclaimed his great compilation of Roman law, the *Corpus Juris*. The *Code* of AD529 (revised AD534) is a collection of all the imperial legislation current at that date. The *Digest*, stating the law as at AD533, gives the force of legislation to legal rules drawn from statements by jurists in treatises published centuries earlier. Many were based on opinions they had given in real or hypothetical disputes. The *Institutes* are a textbook for students.[52] Though they come after Roman Britannia, these sources are important because they provide evidence of what happened there. Justinian's *Code* and the *Theodosian Code* before it include imperial rescripts, just a few of which arose from litigation in Britannia.[53]

On 20 November 319 the emperor Constantine wrote to Pacatianus, *vicarius* (deputy governor) of the Britannias:[54]

51. Honoré 'Roman Law AD200–400' p129.
52. The story is told in *Roman Arbitration* pp39–42.
53. I have been greatly and generally helped by the work of ME Jones 'The Legacy of Roman Law in Post-Roman Britain' and particularly at pp52–6. He points out that there are other rescripts made by emperors while they were in Britannia but not specifically referring to Britannia.
54. *Codex Theodosianus* 11.7.2.

3.11 Every *decurio* is bound to pay the portion for which he himself is liable, or the amount which his tenant (*colonus*), or a taxpayer for whom he is liable (*tributarius*) must pay (and he collects); but he is in no way liable for any other *decurio* or other magistrate's jurisdiction (*territorium*).

This shows that *decuriones* in Britannia were subject to the same obligations as their counterparts elsewhere in the collection of imperial taxes and is some evidence for the more general conclusion that the local government of municipalities was organised in much the same way throughout the empire.

Technical questions of the inheritance law which applied to Roman citizens in Britannia would, if abstruse enough, require the authoritative opinion of a leading lawyer. A passage in the *Digest* quotes the famous jurist Javolenus Priscus, who served as *iuridicus* in Britannia. He gave an opinion on a matter of inheritance which arose here as early as the second half of the first century:[55]

3.12 Seius Saturninus, a chief pilot from the Britannic fleet, by will appointed Captain Valerius Maximus his heir on trust, requiring him to restore the inheritance to his son Seius Oceanus when he reached sixteen years. Seius Oceanus died before he reached that age. Now Malleus Seneca, who says he is Seius Oceanus's uncle, claims these goods by right of family relationship. But Captain Maximus claims them for his own, because he to whom he was instructed to restore them is dead... My opinion was that... the goods belong to whomever the other goods of Oceanus belonged.

Early in the second century, Neratius Priscus, a leading jurist in Rome, sent an opinion to his brother Marcellus, almost certainly at that time in authority in Britannia. He advised that, according to Roman law, a general bequest of the contents of a house would include clothes:[56]

3.13 Especially as in this case, where the testator had excluded the silver and the books of account. Because, he says, anyone who excluded these things must have intended to include everything else that was in the house.

An inheritance might need the intervention of the emperor himself. A rescript of Septimius Severus and Caracalla, addressed around the end of the second century to the governor, *Brittanniae praeses*, instructed him how to deal with a problem which arose from the distinctive Roman practice of a father making a will for his under-age child. This is reported in the *Digest*, citing the jurist Julian:[57]

3.14 It is Julian's opinion that he ought first to appoint an heir for himself and then for his son. If, however, he should make a will first for his son and then for himself, it will be invalid. This opinion was approved in a rescript of our emperor

55. *Digest* 36.1.48.
56. *Digest* 37.7.12.43; Morris *Londinium* p185.
57. *Digest* 28.6.2.4.

to Virius Lupus, governor of Britain, and rightly so, because it is accepted that there is one will, even though there are two inheritances.

Conviction of a serious crime could deprive the criminal of testamentary capacity. The criminal might try to preserve the efficacy of a will by committing suicide before the formal deprivation. That would not work. But suicide was not a crime and did not itself affect testamentary incapacity. The *Digest* quotes a letter from the emperor Hadrian to someone called there Pomponius Falco, who was probably the Pompeius Falco who was governor of Britain under Hadrian:[58]

> **3.15** But anyone who commits suicide because they are tired of life or cannot bear ill health or to make a point, like some philosophers do, their wills are valid. In a letter to Pomponius Falco, the divine Hadrian said that the same distinction applied to a soldier's will, so that if he preferred to die because he realised he had committed some military offence, his will was invalid. But if he was tired of life or in pain or grief, his will was valid.

How much could be read into those dry words about the life of a Roman soldier in Britain! Though the *Digest* has no room for overt sentiment, the legal problems it reports often arise from personal tragedy. Sometimes the victims have names, even the women, but not in this bleak story, apparently from Britannia, in the chapter on the redemption of prisoners of war:[59]

> **3.16** A woman was sent to the salt works for her crime. She was taken from there by foreign bandits and sold according to commercial law. She was redeemed and restored to her proper situation. Her price must be repaid to Cocceius Firmus out of public funds.

If records had survived, they would no doubt tell many more stories of life in Britannia and how the Roman legal system worked. For our purposes, though, it remains to be shown that this evidence of the application of Roman law and practice is supported by any specifically related to arbitration.

DISPUTE RESOLUTION

A fragment of a bronze tablet found near Padua contains legislation, from as early as 76BC, a century before Britannia began, which gave colonial governments authority to appoint arbitrators:[60]

---

58. *Digest* 28.3.6.7.
59. *Digest* 49.15.6. This case's English origin is argued in E Birley *Roman Britain and the Roman Army* pp51–2 and 87–103; the chapter 'Roman Law and Roman Britain', pp48–57, is still of primary value. He suggests, p57, that Gaius, author of the most influential law textbook of classical times, was the P Cornelius Gaius who served in Maryport, Cumberland, in the reign of Hadrian. Gaius's many references to arbitration are dealt with in *Roman Arbitration*, with excerpts pp207–9.
60. Found in 1880 in Italy in Este; MH Crawford ed *Roman Statutes* I pp313–24, which gives a word-for-word translation, *Roman Arbitration* p9.

3.17 In any municipality, colony or prefecture, in which any *duumvir* or other person, according to statute, treaty, plebiscite, or decree of the senate or custom…, had jurisdiction and authority to appoint or confirm a *judex* or *arbiter* or *recuperatores* in respect of whatever was in dispute between private persons, nothing is proposed by this law to give a private person a right… to take away from whoever was in charge of jurisdiction there before the statute etc… that jurisdiction over whatever matter or authority to appoint or confirm a *judex*.

Moreover, the Lex Irnitana of the emperor Domitian in AD91, a generation after the birth of the province of Britannia, dealt with delays in proceedings before arbitrators and may be assumed to have extended throughout the empire.[61]

3.18 Nor shall any *judex* or *arbiter* or *recuperator* adjudicate upon any private matter on those days above written, nor assess the value of the suit, nor on those days do any work on its adjudication, nor render any award by way of adjudication, unless the *judex*, *arbiter*, or *recuperatores* and all the parties to the claim want it to be heard then and it is not a [specially prohibited feast day].

In Latin a *judex* (or *iudex*, plural *iudices*) is anyone who adjudicates, who speaks the law, *ius dicit*. There were no judges in Rome until well into imperial times. There a *judex* was a private person chosen by the parties but appointed by the *praetor*, the elected politician with authority over the legal system. The Romans sometimes distinguished a *judex* from an *arbiter* but just as often used the words interchangeably. Festus, the lexicographer, writing in the second century AD, gave this definition:[62]

3.19 A *judex* who has the arbitration and control of the whole matter is called an *arbiter*.

And the *Digest* itself says:[63]

3.20 A person is taken to have accepted appointment as *arbiter* if he has undertaken to be *judex* for the parties and promises to put an end to their disputes by his award.

The imperial civil service employed some *judices* who had more of the characteristics of a modern judge, the *legati juridici*. They were full-time judicial officers and were first employed in the provinces.[64]

---

61. 92 lines 39–46, found in Spain, from a lost town Irni, near Seville, *Roman Arbitration* p44.
62. Festus *On the Meaning of Words* s.v. 'arbiter' in Bruns *Fontes Iuris Romani Antiqui: Scriptores* 3.
63. *Digest* 4.8.13.2.
64. The *recuperatores* were officials who dealt with some kinds of dispute which involved the public interest, some requiring them to make assessments and valuations; though they sometimes formed a court, they were not arbitrators, *Roman Arbitration* pp31–2. There is no evidence of their use in Britannia.

If the different provinces offered similar systems for parties seeking arbitration of their disputes, two questions then arise. What was the 'colonial legal system' of arbitration law and practice? Were any changes made to adapt it to English circumstances?

The first question is easier to answer and *Roman Arbitration* sets out the sources and makes the arguments. It was possible for any free person, citizen or not, male or female, to make a binding arbitration agreement, called a *compromissum*, submitting most kinds of existing dispute to the arbitration of a single arbitrator, chosen by the parties, always called *arbiter*. Slaves could not make binding agreements and those who did not have legal capacity needed the cooperation of their tutor or guardian. Criminal matters and questions of status were usually excluded. Both parties to the *compromissum* agreed to pay the same penalty each to the other if they failed to submit to and participate fully in the arbitration and to comply with the award. The provincial authorities would enforce payment of the penalty against a party who defaulted. We have no direct evidence of how this worked in Britannia or of how widespread arbitration was.

Nor is there any evidence of the old Roman procedure before a *bonus vir*, whose function was to bring the dispute to a satisfactory conclusion. That would be done best by mediating a settlement – 'best to reconcile!' as the Greek tradition taught.[65] As Horace said:[66]

3.21 Who is the *bonus vir*? The one who serves the senate's decrees, the statutes and the laws. Many a mighty suit is settled by his arbitration. His surety confirms matters and his testimony determines cases.

The *bonus vir* settled disputes. Today we draw a line firmly between arbitration, in which third parties adjudicate like private judges, and mediation in which they do not. The Romans were well aware of the distinction but required their arbitrators to use all the techniques available to them to produce a settlement which the parties would accept. Though sometimes they used the terms *arbiter* and *judex* indiscriminately, or perhaps with a difference which is lost to us, the Romans always required that a third party decision maker should act as a *bonus vir*.

Arbitration by a *bonus vir* may well have been founded in the trust which Romans of the old republic could place in their chosen arbitrator's honesty (though not his skill) and the social pressures on all parties to conform. There would have to be some evidence before it could be assumed that the institution was imported into the quite different societies of Britannia.[67] It is unlikely that a Roman citizen would have been happy to have a

---

65. *Ancient Greek Arbitration* pp319–31; Roebuck 'Best to Reconcile'.
66. *Epistles* 1.16.40.
67. Ausonius's epigrams against a Briton who had annoyed him suggest that he, at least, had no doubts about the unsuitability of any Briton, *Epigrams* 107–12, below **4.4**.

non-Roman arbiter. A Vindolanda tablet reveals a typically colonial view of the colonised, calling them '*Brittunculi*' – 'little Brits'.[68]

One incontrovertible fact which may be of some tangential relevance is the presence in Britannia of a well-known authority on the Roman law of arbitration, that jurist Javolenus Priscus who was quoted above on the chief pilot's will, **3.15**.[69] He was probably born in what until recently was Yugoslavia. Provincial governors were both commanders-in-chief of the army and heads of the judicial system. While they could usually be expected to know something about war, in law they might well be quite unskilled. Vespasian, emperor AD69–79, created the office of *legatus iuridicus*, a kind of chancellor if such an anachronistic Common Law analogy is permissible, with the rank of *praetor*. The emperor, not the governor, appointed him. When Agricola was governor of Britannia, Javolenus Priscus was his *legatus iuridicus*, acting not only as his legal adviser but his deputy in charge of the administration of justice. After he left Britannia he had an outstanding career, in Rome as consul AD86, then governor of Upper Germany, then of Syria, and later as proconsul of Africa. Most relevant for arbitration, though, is his status as a jurist. He is one of the earliest authorities represented in Justinian's *Digest* of AD533, which quotes him often, including his most profound insight into the nature of legal thinking, indeed of all scholarship:[70]

> **3.22** Every definition in the civil law is dangerous because it is rare that it cannot be overturned.

He would have needed all his legal acumen to deal not only with the application of Roman law to the different realities of the province but also with disputes involving British law and custom. He may well have practised as a jurist during his time in Britannia.

It is clear that he was considered an expert on the law of arbitration. Most disputes submitted to arbitration in Britannia may be assumed to have arisen out of unperformed obligations. Roman law classified obligations in three categories: to pay a debt, to perform an act, or to fulfil some other contractual duty. The *Digest* quotes Javolenus's treatise *From Cassius* as authority:[71]

> **3.23** The penalty provided for in the *compromissum* is not incurred in every case where the arbiter's award is not obeyed but only in those which pertain to the payment of money or performance of a service. The arbiter could punish the wilful disobedience of a party by ordering him to pay money to the other side. Failure to provide the names of witnesses as required by the arbiter's [interim] award should not count [as wilful disobedience].

68. Potter and Johns *Roman Britain* p54.
69. AR Birley *Roman Government*.
70. *Digest* 50.17.202
71. *Digest* 4.8.39 preface, quoting Javolenus Priscus *From Cassius* 11.

If a party had a good excuse for not appearing, or some other reason required that, for equity's sake, there should be a postponement, the arbitrator must make the necessary order. A party who failed to appear at the adjourned hearing was liable at once to the penalty, even if the adjournment had been made for the benefit of the other party. The *Digest* quotes Javolenus on this point, too:[72]

> **3.24** When an arbiter has ordered a postponement of the day in the *compromissum*, if he is allowed to do so, the delay of one party advantages the other, to whom the penalty is incurred.

That is, the innocent party has the immediate advantage of an action for the penalty. Such an action must have been available from the provincial governor in Britannia (or his *legatus iuridicus*) as it was in Rome from the *praetor*. Whatever else this evidence proves, it shows that the man in charge of the legal system of the Roman administration of Britannia in the AD80s was an arbitration expert. His skills were available. We have no evidence of how or even whether they were ever called on to play any part in arbitration.

There is nothing from Britannia like the arbitration agreements and awards that survive on papyrus from Egypt at the end of the Roman Empire.[73] But just one stilus tablet has been found which floods with light what had previously been almost total darkness. It has been edited and published with such skill that it has transformed our knowledge of dispute resolution among the Roman citizens in Britannia.[74]

During excavations in 1986 in the City of London, at the corner of Throgmorton Avenue and Austin Friars, archaeologists from the Museum of London found a stilus tablet. It is one page of a document originally written in wax on a wooden base. The wax has long since gone but the writer's stilus scratched through it and unintentionally left signs on the wood beneath. The extraordinary skills of the editor have produced the drawing which appears with his permission on pxviii. If you can read the cursive script, with the help of the editor's reconstruction of the text and his translation, you will see that it says:[75]

> **3.25** In the consulship of the emperor Trajan Hadrian Caesar Augustus for the second time and Gnaeus Fuscus Salinator, on the day before the Ides of March. Whereas, on arriving at the property in question, the wood Verlucionium, fifteen *arepennia* more or less,[76] which is in the canton of the Cantiaci in Dibussu[ ]

---

72. *Digest* 4.8.39.1, quoting Javolenus Priscus *From Cassius* 11.
73. *Roman Arbitration* pp1–10, 201–6. So far nothing about disputes has been found among the Vindolanda tablets, Vindolanda Tablets Online http://vindolanda.csad.ox.ac.uk.
74. RSO Tomlin 'A Five-Acre Wood'.
75. I have broken my own rule here and adopted Dr Tomlin's translation; it would have been impertinent to do otherwise and he has generously agreed.
76. About 4.6 acres.

parish, [ ] neighboured by the heirs [of...] and the heirs of Caesennius Vitalis and the vicinal road, Lucius Julius Bellicus said that he had bought it from Titus Valerius Silvinus for forty *denarii*, as is contained in the deed of purchase. Lucius Julius Bellicus attested that he [ ]

And there it ends. The date is 14 March AD114. The parties are Lucius Julius Bellicus – Dickens could not have invented a better name for a claimant – and Titus Valerius Silvinus. The subject matter is a wood in Kent, called Verlucionium, whose boundaries are fixed in the technical way later described in the *Digest*.[77] We are not given the name of the single arbitrator appointed, by the parties or the authorities, to go to the property and view it presumably to identify its limits and perhaps to hear evidence. Somehow T Valerius Silvinus had acquired the ownership of a substantial wood in Kent and sold it to L Julius Bellicus, who now claimed it.[78]

Caesennius Vitalis, Iulius Bellicus, Valerius Silvinus. These three landowners of Roman Kent, the first ever recorded, are otherwise unknown. All three were Roman citizens. The name Caesennius suggests an Italian, perhaps Etruscan, origin... Iulius and Valerius suggest provincial origins, particularly Cisalpine or Transalpine Gaul, or Spain, the descendants of provincials enfranchised in the late Republic... The cognomen Bellicus is of Celtic etymology... None of these persons, to judge by his name, was of British origin.

This is part of an award. It shows that arbitration in the Roman fashion was alive in Britannia early in the second century, at least for Roman citizens, and followed the Roman form. Moreover:[79]

... this is a legal document which implies a judicial authority and a secretariat to record its deliberations and decisions.

The technical terms *arepennium* for a square measure of land and *via vicinale* for a minor road are some evidence that the profession of land surveyor was not unknown in Britannia then. We are fortunate to have a substantial body of professional writing by Roman surveyors.[80] They start about AD100. They reveal not only that there was a profession of surveying but that its members, called in Latin *mensores*, measurers, or *agrimensores*, land-measurers, were active in the arbitration of disputes about land, especially boundaries. They acted, then as now, both as arbitrators and experts.

---

77. *Digest* 50.15.4 from Ulpian's work on the census, written early in the third century AD, at least a century after this award.
78. Tomlin 'A Five-Acre Wood' 214.
79. Tomlin 'A Five-Acre Wood' 215.
80. We are fortunate too to have the manuscripts newly edited and translated with a rich commentary by Brian Campbell *The Roman Surveyors*; I have followed his translation closely; *Roman Arbitration* pp83–6.

Probably the first writer on surveying whose works have survived was Julius Frontinus, who wrote early in the second century AD, about the same time as our London fragment. He began the categorisation of land disputes, first into boundary and site, which later writers elaborated:[81]

> **3.26** The subject matter of disputes is twofold: boundary and site. One or the other of these contains whatever disagreement arises from land. But since even in these categories individual disputes have different characteristics, they ought to be defined specifically. Therefore, as far as I have been able to comprehend them, there are fifteen varieties of dispute: about the position of boundary markers, about a straight line boundary, about a boundary, about the site, about area, about ownership, about possession, about alluvial land, about the right of territory, about bits of cut off land, about public places, about places omitted and not enclosed, about sacred and religious places, about control of rain water, and about rights of way.

Frontinus also distinguishes between disputes which belong to the ordinary law, *ad ius ordinarium*, and those which are appropriate for a surveyor to settle. Boundary disputes are for the surveyor, rainwater for the law:[82]

> **3.27** A dispute arises about the passage of rainwater which accumulates and then cuts across a boundary, flowing on to someone else's farm, and the parties disagree. That will belong to the ordinary law. But, if the dispute is about the alignment of the boundary itself, that requires the intervention of a surveyor, and the dispute is settled.

This suggests that it was usual for surveyors to act as mediators and for the parties to settle on the surveyor's expert advice, while other arbitrators might be needed for legal differences. Hyginus, perhaps contemporary with Frontinus, wrote:[83]

> **3.28** Disagreements often arise about a road, right of way for cattle, right of way, right of way around a building, access, streams, valleys, ditches, and springs. All these categories require not our work but the legal process, that is the civil law. We are only involved in them when there is something to be marked out after investigation or something to be recovered after examining what is written on some map.

A later writer expressly advised that it was better to get the surveyors and the lawyers together at the outset, before the dispute was submitted to any tribunal, to work out the best way to deal with it.[84]

There is nothing to show how the use of Roman arbitration changed over the four centuries of Roman rule. We know nothing, either, of the procedures which the indigenous people used who had no access to the Roman system

---

81. Julius Frontinus *On Disputes* Campbell p5 lines 4–10.
82. Julius Frontinus *On Disputes* Campbell p8 lines 8–11.
83. Hyginus *On Kinds of Disputes* Campbell p98 line 37 to p100 line 3.
84. Agennius Urbicus *On Land Disputes* Campbell p40 lines 19–20.

or chose not to take advantage of it. Some insights may be gained from language use, discussed in Appendix A.[85] Recent scholarship, particularly in genetics rather than historical linguistics, suggests that throughout the four centuries of Roman rule it is likely that, while some of the indigenous people of Britannia spoke the language which now survives as Welsh, with a few on the fringes speaking its Irish version, others may have spoken Germanic languages. Nothing survives in those tongues from this period.

Not only the nobility spoke Latin; so did many others,[86] the spread and the fluency varying according to class and need, and from place to place and time to time, and dwindling after the Romans left. They did not write as they spoke. Writing was almost exclusively in a Latin as near to classical as the scribe could manage. In the towns it cannot have been too difficult to find someone to pen a *compromissum*, the standard agreement to submit an existing dispute to arbitration, if the parties wanted one and were prepared to pay for it. Plenty of stili have been found by archaeologists and some inkwells, and papyrus was known in Britannia even before the Roman conquest, though wax tablets seem to have been in most ordinary use, like those found at Vindolanda, which are only a tiny part of the hundreds of thousands which must have been created by the accounting and administrative needs of the army alone. It is not impossible, with the increasing requirement of preliminary archaeological enquiry as a condition of planning permission, that more tangible evidence of Roman arbitration may be found.

THE LEGAL PROFESSION

There were indigenous lawyers then in Britannia, or at least trained advocates. Juvenal, as early as the second century AD, wrote of them:[87]

3.29 Fluent Gaul has taught the British advocates.

By that he meant that those who wished to plead in English litigation went to Gaul to the schools which famously taught rhetoric there. Rhetoric was the third and final part of the liberal arts curriculum in which Juvenal's older contemporary Tacitus said Agricola 'educated the sons of the leading men', **A.1**. There is plenty of evidence that elementary legal studies were part of courses in rhetoric later, in the Middle Ages,[88] when rhetoric was

85. Charles-Edwards 'Language and Society'.
86. Peter Schrijver 'Rise and Fall of British Latin' and 'What Britons Spoke around 400AD'; JC Mann 'Spoken Latin in Britain as Evidenced in Inscriptions' pp218–24.
87. Juvenal *Satires* XV 111: *Gallia causidicos docuit facunda Britannos*. The schools ranged from Marseilles in the south, where Tacitus says Agricola himself was educated, *Agricola* 4, to Toulouse, Bordeaux and Trèves; JEB Mayor *Thirteen Satires of Juvenal* cites the authorities pp433–4.
88. *Auctor ad Herennium* II I, quoted by Hastings Rashdall *The Universities of Europe in the Middle Ages* I p102 fn1.

divided into three categories – demonstrative, deliberative and judicial – and no reason to doubt that Juvenal was implying that some knowledge of legal argument was included in what Britons went to learn in Gaul in his day. Learning the techniques of advocacy – and even practising them – may not, of course, require much knowledge of the law. There is no evidence of indigenous professional lawyers in Britannia.[89] But Tacitus, who cannot be accused of bias in this, said the Britons showed aptitude, **A.1**, and it would be surprising if none of them ever worked as a lawyer in the Roman system.

Ausonius, the teacher, poet and statesman (and sometime *judex*) from Bordeaux, at the end of the fourth century AD wrote obituaries of professors of rhetoric there.[90] He says that some were also advocates and hints that one or two gave advice, perhaps legal. He lists the subjects they taught: not only history, poetry and eloquence but medicine and Platonic philosophy; but he does not mention law. He thinks it worth listing the odd subjects which Victorius, only an assistant lecturer, found in worm-eaten and peculiar volumes: the code of the *pontifices*,[91] treaties, decrees of the old Romans (*Quirites*) and of the senate, the laws of the ancient Greek lawgivers Draco, Solon and Zaleucus, before them the mythical Minos the first lawgiver, and Themis (customary law) before him. But no mention of contemporary law at all. Surely he would have mentioned law if it had been taught in his time by professors of grammar (the second stage) or rhetoric (the third).

Yet there can be no doubt that there were lawyers practising in Britannia from quite early in the Roman period and the evidence grows as time goes on. The later cases already discussed, **3.15**, **3.16**, and the stilus tablet from the City of London, **3.25**, show that there were lawyers drafting documents and working on the appeals which went from the province to the emperor, and even some with a knowledge of Roman law and practice working on arbitration.

MUTATIS MUTANDIS

The second question has not yet been attempted. What changes were made to accommodate local needs? There is no direct evidence from Britannia. There is a great deal, though, from one other province, Egypt, where the climate and other conditions preserved the records on papyrus. There the practice was heavily influenced by what already existed when the Romans

89. Detlef Liebs *Römische Jurisprudenz in Gallien* can identify not a single one of any provenance. I have Professor Honoré to thank for this reference.

90. HG Evelyn White *Ausonius* (Loeb) I, 5 *Commemoratio Professorum Burdigalensium* II, XV, XVII, XXIII, XXIV and XXVI; Liversidge *Britain in the Roman Empire* pp202–3. Ausonius had himself acted as *judex*, *Personal Poems* IV 14.

91. We know he means the old Roman pontifex, not the Pope, because he is cribbing from the pre-Christian Quintilian here.

came.[92] That itself was partly indigenous Egyptian but predominantly Greek from the time of the Ptolemies.[93] There was no such regular, recorded and replicable tradition in Britannia, which before the Romans had no literate law.

Most of what has been suggested here is the product of inference from scraps of evidence. It is reassuring to find that a standard history of Roman Britain supports and summarises these tentative propositions:[94]

> It is not unreasonable to assume that in his everyday affairs the ordinary inhabitant of the empire enjoyed such protection as the law afforded his particular class and circumstance and, perhaps in day-to-day matters more important, that his transactions with his neighbours were governed by rules that had the backing of a developed legal system. The very fact of the existence of such a system must of itself have transformed the relationships between individuals and often made the settlement of business, even disputes, a matter of discussion and agreed settlement where it might once have led to armed conflict. But it also, particularly if the individual had a patron, meant access to legal arbitration.

Yet I know of no evidence that 'the settlement of business, even disputes... might once have led to armed conflict'. What little has survived is of land disputes. There is not a scrap of evidence of business disputes ending in violence.[95] I think it unlikely in all but the most unusual cases and more recent scholarship confirms that it would be unwise to ignore the resilience of indigenous custom to the end of the Roman period and after. For example, Michael Jones, whose comprehensive study has provided many of the sources as well as the ideas for this section, writes:[96]

> ... conditions in Roman Britain seem to have favoured the survival of native legal custom. Because Britain was never completely conquered by Rome, a zone of independent British kingdoms survived between the Pictish territories of the far north and the frontier of the Roman diocese. Within this zone native British Celtic law persisted ... Within the area under military government, the habits and practice of Roman civil law may never have become strongly rooted. During the fluid but obscure conditions of the fourth century and after, areas of the military zone including the Pennines, mid-Wales, and the south-western peninsula may even have passed from effective Roman government into the hands of native dynasties. If so, these areas may also have returned to the practice of native law and custom – if, indeed, they ever really left it.

On the other hand, where it is clear that the Romanised British adopted so many aspects of metropolitan behaviour, there is some justification for

---

92. *Roman Arbitration*, particularly Chapter 1; Detlef Liebs *Römischer Jurisprudenz in Africa*.
93. *Ancient Greek Arbitration*, particularly Chapter 14.
94. Salway *Roman Britain* pp526–7 but remember Mattingly's caution, *Imperial Possession* p43.
95. Unlike among the Germans, Thompson *Early Germans* p21 fn2.
96. ME Jones 'The Legacy of Roman Law in Post-Roman Britain' pp61–2.

suggesting that they made use of Roman techniques of dispute resolution. A careful study by Neil Faulkner, archaeologist and historian, provides a fruitful suggestion:[97]

> Archaeology cannot give direct testimony to the thought-world and social round of this elite. This is the stuff of literature. But they were mimicking their Italian peers so closely in the design of their buildings and their taste in art that we can assume the relevance of some contemporary Latin writing. The letters of Pliny the Younger (AD61–113)... Pliny pursued a traditional and highly successful senatorial career at Rome: he pleaded cases at the bar, held a series of junior magistracies... The aristocratic culture of Pliny the Younger is probably that to which the Romano-British gentry aspired.

If that were true, it would allow us another insight into arbitration in Roman Britain, because we know something of Pliny as arbitrator.[98] About AD104–7, he wrote in his *Letters* that he had acted as arbitrator in a substantial and difficult inheritance dispute, made no easier in that he was a potential beneficiary. There was no *compromissum* and he acted as a *bonus vir*. Indeed, though he perhaps makes too much of it for effect, he seems to have been burdened with more disputes to settle than he had time for. The prevalence and ordinariness of arbitration by a *bonus vir* are shown by other letters, where he tells of the duties of the conscientious landowner, distracted from his scholarly pursuits by having to deal with the complaints of his tenants and servants:[99]

> **3.30** I was going the rounds of my little properties, hearing the farmers' many complaints and checking their accounts – reluctantly and cursorily because I am a devotee of other kinds of manuscripts, of other literature.

Hearing complaints is not the same as arbitrating disputes but this letter refers specifically to arbitration:[100]

> **3.31** Town business chases after me even here. There are some who would make me their *judex* or *arbiter*. And then there are the complaints of the farmers, who exhaust my ears on the grounds of my long absence.

Those complaints he heard orally but the next letter shows that not only the farmers' accounts but some of the disputes may have been presented to him in written form, not unlike what now would be called 'documents only' arbitration:[101]

> **3.32** I took refuge in Tuscany so that I could do what I liked. But not even in Tuscany, so greatly am I put about everywhere by the farmers' petitions and

97. Faulkner *Decline and Fall* pp95–6.
98. *Roman Arbitration* pp62–6, particularly John Barton's footnote, which compares Pliny's arbitration with that of a great lord in medieval England.
99. Pliny *Letters* 5.14.8.
100. Pliny *Letters* 7.30.
101. Pliny *Letters* 9.15.1.

complaints, which I read much less willingly than I do my own papers, and I do not welcome even them.

He must have decided those disputes 'on the papers'; it is unlikely that his tenant farmers would have had the means and leisure to follow him on holiday to plead their cause before him.

Pliny arbitrated both as *bonus vir* for his tenants in the country and in a more formal role as *judex* or *arbiter* in matters arising in Rome. Not much straw from which to make the bricks for any sort of solid structure; but enough perhaps to encourage the imagination to run, as it can in contemplating a ruin. Aulus Gellius's *Attic Nights* was written cAD180 as a light-hearted diversion – just the book that a homesick colonial official and his wife might be reading in the posting at the end of the world. What background, what experience must they have had to comprehend this quotation from his friend Favorinus, the philosopher:[102]

> **3.33** It is often asked whether it is fit and proper for a *judex* after the case has been heard, if there seems to be a chance to settle, to postpone his adjudicatory function for a little while and play the part of a mutual friend and a kind of peacemaker.

CHRISTIANITY AND THE CHURCH

In AD306 the emperor Constantius died in Britannia on campaign in the north. His army acclaimed his son Constantine as emperor and he ruled first in the West and then over the whole empire until 337. In 312 he ordered his soldiers to paint the cross on their shields and they won the battle of the Milvian Bridge. In 313, with his eastern counterpart Licinius, he issued the Edict of Milan, which made Christianity legal. The church was an essential ally in the imposition of totalitarian rule. Its ideology was both proselytising and exclusive. You had to be in or out. It had its own well-trained bureaucracy which it was prepared to put at the service of the state and in return it was rewarded by the direction of wealth to its use.

The military elite, in Britannia as elsewhere, was to some extent supplanted by the bishops. Each *civitas*-capital had its bishop, who was given the responsibility of handling civil disputes. The hearing before the bishop, *episcopalis audientia*, overlapped the jurisdiction of the secular authorities. Constantine even legislated to give precedence to the decisions of bishops:[103]

> **3.34** We have sanctioned... that the awards given by bishops, of whatever kind, shall be kept inviolate and ever uncorrupted without any distinction of age: that

---

102. Aulus Gellius *Attic Nights* 14.2.13–16, *Roman Arbitration* p69; Leofranc Holford-Strevens *Aulus Gellius*.

103. *Sirmondian Constitutions* 1; *Roman Arbitration* pp35–6. Doubt has been cast on the validity of this *Constitution* but the latest study accepts it in substance: AJP Sirks *Theodosian Code*. I have Tony Honoré to thank for bringing it to my notice.

is, that whatever award has been concluded by the bishops shall be held forever holy and venerable. So that, whatever has been decided by the bishops, whether between minors or adults, we wish to have enforced by execution by you, who hold the highest jurisdiction, and all other judges. Therefore, whoever shall have a suit, whether as plaintiff or defendant, whether at the commencement of the action or after the statutory periods have expired, or during the final arguments, or even when the *judex* has started to pronounce his judgment, may resort to the jurisdiction of the holy law of the high priest and there and then without any quibble – even if the other party objects – the parties in person shall be directed to the bishop. For there are many things which the captious fetters of technicality do not allow to be laid bare in litigation which the authority of sacred religion seeks out and makes public. Therefore, all causes which are dealt with by praetorian or civil law, having been determined by the awards of the bishops, shall be confirmed by the perpetual law of stability. No matter, which has been decided by the award of the bishops, shall be allowed to be reviewed later.

I have found no evidence of the use of bishops to resolve disputes in Britannia and Christianity was never widespread.[104] It was one of the religions of the army officers, some landowners like St Patrick's grandfather, and some merchants. There is far more evidence of pagan temples of all sorts than churches in Britannia. Theodosius II, emperor AD408–50, gave back jurisdiction in most civil and criminal matters to the provincial lay authorities in his Code of AD438:[105]

3.35 Whatever is the concern of religion concerns the bishops. But other claims, which belong to provincial governors or to the application of public law, ought to be heard according to law.

But by that time Roman legislation had ceased to be enforceable in Britannia.

THE END OF ROMAN BRITAIN

In the last years of the fourth century Britannia, though still considered by the emperors to be part of the Roman Empire, was slipping out of Roman control. Great prosperity seems to have spread throughout the four provinces, though the South-East, the southern Midlands and the West Country have most of the remains of the more than a hundred country mansions now known. Those for example at Brading in the Isle of Wight and North Leigh in Oxfordshire may have been the largest private dwellings ever built in England, as big as Blenheim Palace; and: 'some poor men's timber cottages were equipped with window glass and door keys, evidence of property worth stealing'.[106]

---

104. There is a hint that Victricius, bishop of Rouen, came to mediate a dispute among the clergy in England in AD390, *De Laude Sanctorum* 1, Potter and Johns *Roman Britain* p205.
105. *Theodosian Code* 16.11.1; *Roman Arbitration* p35.
106. Morris *Londinium* p300.

The almost contemporary historian, Ammianus Marcellinus, wrote that the Romans had a treaty with the Scoti, the Irish whose colonies were to the north of Hadrian's Wall; that in AD360 the Scoti broke it and in alliance with Saxons attacked in 367, and that two years later Count Theodosius (father of the emperor Theodosius I) drove them back and carved a new province, Valentia, out of the existing colonies.[107] Whether any or all of that is true or not, the Roman administration was feeling the strain of military ambitions both in Britannia and in Western Europe. In AD383 the military leader Magnus Maximus claimed to be emperor in Britannia, took his army across the Channel and conquered both Gaul and Spain, defeating and killing the emperor Gratian, but dying in battle against Theodosius in 388. In 395 Theodosius died and the Empire was again divided East and West. In 409 the emperor Honorius briefly recognised as ruler in Britannia Constantine III, who had taken his army to Gaul, leaving the administration in Britannia without military support. In 410 the Goths sacked Rome and Honorius told the British administration of the *civitates* that they would have to fend for themselves, so they expelled Constantine's officials and set up their own administration as far as they could.

And so, by the second decade of the fifth century, the Roman provinces in Britannia looked no longer to Rome for resources. After Constantine's death in 411 Rome never regained control. But the parts of Britannia that had been Romanised remained so. The authorities, the Romano-Britons in the *civitates*, still thought of themselves as Roman citizens and no doubt the professional administrators continued to administrate in a provincial Roman way, the Romano-British teachers still taught in Latin, and the lawyers, presumably left behind at least for a while, carried on business within some kind of Roman legal system.

From the start of the fourth century:[108] 'Britain probably witnessed a progressive shift of governmental functions from public to private hands, with increasing control vested in an aristocracy which had relocated to the countryside.' They were able to organise administrations which defended their interests against foreign attack. The rulers were the same landowners who had governed in the Roman Empire. But they lacked the legitimacy which that Empire had given them and on which stability depended. There was no external sovereign power to appoint, confirm and defend those who exercised authority. Until the return of imperial power, which the British leaders no doubt at first expected to be imminent, some means had to be found to resolve the claims of the ambitious. For a while that seems to have been possible but eventually what the Romans had left fell apart.

The great majority of the inhabitants must have maintained (or reverted to) the old customary ways of dispute resolution. Indeed, the final downfall

107. JC Rolfe *Ammianus Marcellinus* 21.1, 27.8.
108. Higham *Rome, Britain and the Anglo-Saxons* p61.

of Roman power may have been achieved partly by popular uprisings, not so much against the distant Roman emperor as his former colonial servants, the indigenous and tax-gathering aristocracy.

CONCLUSIONS

Can a history be written of arbitration in what is now England when it was a part of the Roman Empire? Perhaps there is evidence enough to show that Britannia was like other provinces in general, and specifically in a few instances. It is likely that a Roman legal system similar to that described in *Roman Arbitration* applied here contemporaneously and with it Roman practices of mediation and arbitration. To what extent we cannot safely say. Any attempt to show that it might have influenced the later development of arbitration in Anglo-Saxon Britain will have to withstand the mighty scepticism of Maitland, the greatest historian of English law:[109]

> It has been maintained at various times, and sometimes with great ingenuity,[110] that Roman institutions persisted after Britain was abandoned by the Roman power, and survived the Teutonic invasions in such force as to contribute in material quantity to the formation of our laws. But there is no real evidence of this... within the sphere of law, everything that is Roman or Romanized can be accounted for by later importation... there is no trace of the laws and jurisprudence of imperial Rome, as distinct from the precepts and traditions of the Roman Church, in the earliest Anglo-Saxon documents. Whatever is Roman in them is ecclesiastical.

As we know almost nothing of how disputes were resolved outside the Roman law and practice, it will be harder still to show survivals of that British customary law in Anglo-Saxon England. But we must first trace the progress of dispute resolution in the customary laws and practices which survived during the next two centuries, until written sources provide the first evidence of the legislation of Anglo-Saxon kings.

---

109. Pollock and Maitland *The History of English Law* 2nd edn 1968 I ppci–ciii.
110. No doubt a reference to Coote *Romans of Britain*.

4 ROMAN TO ENGLISH: THE FIFTH AND SIXTH CENTURIES

Those who wish for certainty in history and who like to feel the ground firmly under their feet are best advised to study another period. For those who care to venture into a quagmire, the archaeological evidence, and the truly remarkable intellectual effort of archaeologists to make sense of it, are of basic importance.

James Campbell in Campbell, John and Wormald *The Anglo-Saxons* p29

Such is the unity of all history that anyone who endeavours to tell a piece of it must feel that his first sentence tears a seamless web... The web must be rent; but, as we rend it, we may watch the whence and whither of a few of the severed and ravelling threads which have been making a pattern too large for any man's eye.

Frederick Pollock and FW Maitland, *The History of English Law*

INTRODUCTION

What a marvellous Maitland metaphor! No wonder it is quoted so often. Having made the first cut and tried to follow the whence and whither of as many as possible of the severed and ravelling threads, what are we to do when there seems to be a gaping hole, not only in the history of arbitration but in all our legal history? The gap is of two centuries, from the end of the Roman Empire in Britain, about AD410, to the dooms of Aethelberht about AD600, after which the tapestry starts to be more detailed. To substitute a duller but contemporary metaphor, we are like devotees who have missed episodes of a serial but do not know how many. We know where we were at the end of the last instalment and we know how the story develops later, but we are not going to be satisfied until we find out enough of what we missed to allow us to pull the ends together.

To return to Maitland's web, first we need the strands left free when the story was interrupted. Later we may find threads from when we can take up the story again. Care must be taken not to put too much strain on the ones from both ends which we hope to weave together. Best of all to weave a patch. For dispute resolution in these two centuries there is just enough material to allow that, though it will have less colour and pattern than we would like.

Just because there are so few sources which speak directly of arbitration, it is all the more necessary to be sure of the background into which to

61

weave them. Controversies abound and there is little scholarly consensus on which to rely. I must therefore show all the workings of my arguments to allow the greatest opportunity and encouragement to those who can correct me. In the general unravelling, we must keep our eyes on the two threads that most concern us: the Roman legal system and the various customary laws. If we keep hold of them they will allow a little embroidery of the plain cloth of life from which disputes arose. We may even find a bead or two of evidence of mediation and arbitration.

Lack of evidence is not evidence that something did not exist. In particular, lack of literature is not evidence of a crude culture. The lives of the many people in England today who cannot read or write are not necessarily qualitatively different from those who read the gutter press. Quite apart from radio and television, which have transformed their lives, all have a wealth of non-literary stimuli and the means of expressing orally whatever they want to tell, in ways they find satisfactory. Our lack of written sources for this period makes writing its history hard but says little about the quality of life then. The darkness of the 'Dark Ages' is in our eyes; there was plenty of light for those who were there.

It must not be forgotten that what is now England – and will be called England from now on – had been inhabited by settled communities for thousands of years before the Romans arrived, each with its own laws and systems for resolving disputes. There is no evidence that they managed disputes in ways less refined, sensitive or effective than ours today. The Romans added a layer of administration in some parts. As they left, gradually that layer was replaced; elsewhere life no doubt went on much the same.

THE BACKGROUND

The End of Britannia   Archaeologists do not agree on whether England remained Roman in any significant way when the Roman administration left.[1] What can we be sure stayed the same? There was no immediate change in geography or climate, though it gradually got colder and wetter.[2] Those who worked the land still had to grow enough to live on and may well have worked much as they did before the Romans came.[3] They may not have been too concerned who exploited them and took any surplus,

1.   Most chastening (and amusing) for the non-archaeologist is the recent debate between Neil Faulkner 'The Case for the Dark Ages' pp5–12 and Martin Henig 'Remaining Roman in Britain, AD300–700: the Evidence of Portable Art' pp13–24, in Rob Collins and James Gerrard *Debating Late Antiquity in Britain AD300–700*. A quotation from each gives the flavour: Faulkner p6: '[The decline of towns] cannot be compared in importance with the more superficial phenomena – such as the use of Latin or a taste for Mediterranean wine'; Henig p18: 'It makes no sense to speak or write of Roman Britain being in terminable decline: only superficial features like the economy had shrunk out of recognition....'
2.   Petra Dark *The Environment of Britain in the First Millennium AD*.
3.   'The evidence that disproves the idea that the post-Roman period witnessed a widespread rural economic and environmental "collapse" is overwhelming', Francis Pryor *Britain*

whether they were Britons or Romans or Anglo-Saxons. Given a chance, they would no doubt have refused to hand over their surplus to anyone. If they were relieved to be free of the Roman imperialist yoke they had no modern ideology in which to express their feelings. They are unlikely to have sought other exploiters until they had to pay for protection. Then they paid in produce, for they had no cash, and as tribute not rent, because chiefs did not then see themselves as lords owning all the land.

No doubt that accounts for nine out of ten of all the people of Britannia. The rest, able to live a more comfortable life with some education and the opportunity to acquire different tastes, adapted themselves to the loss of Roman protection in different ways, depending partly on where they lived and partly on whether they had become Christian, as increasing numbers did, at least of the better-off, throughout the fifth and sixth centuries.[4] Most of the inhabitants of England, the native Britons, were presumably still 'Celtic', though some speaking Latin and others a Germanic tongue may have been among those who welcomed or vainly tried to repel the new German invaders, who were to become known collectively as the Anglo-Saxons.[5] Not only the parts outside what is now England survived those invasions unconquered but all of the present counties of Devon, Cornwall, Somerset, Gloucestershire and Wiltshire, with Cumbria in the north. There were other large areas which stayed 'Celtic' long after the Anglo-Saxons came, including that part of the North-West which much later became Lancashire but could only be described until after the Norman Conquest as 'between the Ribble and the Mersey'.[6]

It may be helpful to recapitulate here what is known or guessed (but not much disputed) about England from the first breakdown of Roman rule to final collapse. In AD285, Carausius, commander of the British fleet, set himself up as emperor, just of Britannia, at the time Diocletian was dividing the Empire between East and West. In 293 Alectus killed Carausius and claimed to be emperor. In 296 Constantius crushed Alectus's revolt, succeeding Diocletian as emperor of the West in 305 and dying in York the next year, succeeded by his son Constantine. In 312 Constantine reunited

---

AD p197, citing Petra Dark *Environment* and Peter Murphy 'The Anglo-Saxon Landscape' pp23–9; 'the clear break between Roman settlement patterns and early English settlements has gone... the farms of the period which witnessed the English migration were closer in style and distribution to those of Roman Britain than to the nucleated settlements of the medieval Midlands... land use continued at Roman levels into the fifth and sixth centuries, without a check', Nicholas Higham *Rome, Britain and the Anglo-Saxons* pp10, 79.

4. Henig 'Remaining Roman' p18.
5. The question of what languages were spoken, where and when, is too large to fit within this chapter and has been dealt with in Appendix A. '*Germani* is itself more likely to have been in origin a Celtic word to describe new neighbours than a German word for which there was no need.' JM Wallace-Hadrill *The Long-Haired Kings* p148.
6. Ken Dark *Civitas to Kingdom: British Political Continuity 300–800.*

the eastern and western parts of the Empire, tolerating Christianity in 313. In 367 the Picts and Scots invaded over Hadrian's Wall and in 369 Emperor Theodosius drove them out. In 383 Magnus Maximus made himself emperor in Britain and conquered Spain and Gaul but was killed in 388. Theodosius died in 395 and the empire was again divided East and West. By 418 the Franks[7] (who were Germans) were settling in Gaul, taking power from the Gallo-Romans. The last legions were leaving England. By 450 there were incoming Germans settling in Kent. That much history can probably be relied on. There are few other facts to be found in the literary sources. Much must depend on hypotheses based on the interpretation of the findings first of archaeologists but now increasingly of experts in other sciences, notably genetics.[8]

The archaeological evidence has to be supplemented by Continental literary sources.[9] One drawback is that they tend to speak of the bit of Britannia with which they were familiar as if it were the whole, when it is clear that it broke up into various communities and administrations, most of which we know little or nothing about, as soon as the Imperial Government of the Britannias fell apart. In some there may have been peasant uprisings; some no doubt retained their traditional British chiefs and structures; in others those in power may have tried to keep the Roman system working as far as they could. There must have been power struggles within those communities and between them.

Archaeological research shows that, even before the Romans left, in many towns the forum was no longer the centre of life and the colonnades of the basilica had been turned into shops.[10] There are signs that the élite first built more elaborate town houses and they may have performed their public functions within them, including resolving disputes. But there is evidence, too, that some of the large Romano-British landowners in the more southern, civilised parts had moved from town to country, which:[11]

> implied a dispersal of pseudo-governmental functions and patronage from the centre to the hinterland, where many great households probably became the centres of estate-centred societies with many of the attributes of a medieval lordship... [By AD400] wealth, land and power were concentrated in the hands of a comparatively small number of great landholders (often absentee), state officers, and officials responsible for the interface between state and population.

Population and production may have declined, though it seems that standards of food and health did not. The quality of life for the majority may even have

7. The name Franci, the Free Men, was given to them by those who wrote about them in Latin.
8. Higham *Rome, Britain*; his last chapter pp209–36 is uncommonly measured and most convincing. The following footnotes do not sufficiently reveal my reliance on it.
9. Ian Wood 'The End of Roman Britain' pp1–2, who discusses those sources.
10. Potter and Johns *Roman Britain* pp199–200.
11. Higham *Rome, Britain* p213.

improved: 'Stature increased dramatically in the fifth and sixth centuries, having hardly altered during the Roman Empire. Few locals saw the benefits of Roman rule and the Empire facilitated the transmission of disease.'[12]

In the rest of the country the old tribal groupings grew more pronounced. Roman armies had had a monopoly of arms. When they functioned no longer, in some communities their place was taken by home-grown forces led by warrior-chiefs. Where that had been made impossible by the introduction of a Roman culture of rich landowners and poor peasants, with no one trained to fight, the administration of landowners or the petty kings who grabbed power had three alternatives. If they wanted temporary relief from pirates and other raiders they could buy them off, as the Roman authorities had sometimes done. If they needed an armed force to provide more permanent protection, or to establish their own authority, they could try to raise their own militia, employing the remnants of the Roman army if they could[13] or they could employ mercenaries, who may have expanded the role which they had always had in Britannia, first as hired auxiliaries to legions then, when the legions left, in some places as the dominant warrior class. But:[14]

> It is sometimes argued that Anglo-Saxons, serving as mercenaries, were already present in fourth-century Britain, bolstering up the by now weak Roman army. This view is based mainly on the occurrence, especially in towns and villas, of distinctive types of belt-fittings. However, it is now recognised that these were insignia worn by both soldiers and by civil servants at this time, and their so-called 'Germanic' characteristics are in fact typical of late Roman art generally.

Roman colonial civil servants had always worn military uniforms.

Who Were the People Left Behind? If we are to argue that there were Germanic people living in England in large numbers before AD400, we shall have to rely on the genetic evidence:[15]

> The genetic evidence shows that three quarters of our ancestors came to this corner of Europe as hunter-gatherers, between 15,000 and 7,500 years ago... Another wave of migration arrived during the Neolithic period, when farming developed

---

12. Nicola Köpke and Jörg Baten 'The Biological Standard of Living in Europe During the Last Two Millennia'.
13. It is clear that there were still troops at the Birdoswald fort on Hadrian's Wall long after the end of the Roman occupation, Pryor *Britain AD* p202.
14. Potter and Johns *Roman Britain* p214.
15. The most radical rethinking has come from Stephen Oppenheimer *The Origins of the British: a Genetic Detective Story*. Its arguments are so important that no one should now form an opinion on any aspect of what it covers without reading every word of it with care and an open mind. Oppenheimer has, however, provided an accessible précis, 'Myths of British Ancestry', from which I have sometimes, as here, preferred to quote a succinct statement of his conclusions. His is not the only very recent contribution from substantial genetic studies, considered above in Chapter 2, including Chris Stringer *Homo Britannicus*; Brian Sykes *Blood of the Isles*; Robin McKie *Face of Britain*.

about 6,500 years ago. But the English still derive most of their current gene pool from the same early Basque source as the Irish, Welsh and Scots. These figures are at odds with the modern perceptions of Celtic and Anglo-Saxon ethnicity based on more recent invasions. There were many later invasions, as well as less violent immigrations, and each left a genetic signal, but no individual event contributed much more than 5 per cent to our modern genetic mix.

I can find no fault with Oppenheimer's thesis. His arguments are convincing and such of his detractors as I have read do not shake either his methods or his conclusions.[16] What are we then to make of the literary evidence which has been all that historians could draw on until a few generations ago and which some scholars still assume to have historical value. How important are the archaeological discoveries and their conflicting interpretations?

Gildas, a Romano-British Christian, had written his *On the Ruin of Britain* by about AD540.[17] He says (in Latin) that he had to rely on foreign sources because all the British documents (which can only have been in Latin) were burnt in the upheavals which followed the end of Roman rule. He relates that a king, whom he does not name but calls 'the proud tyrant', succeeded to the authority once exercised by the Roman administration and later by the landowning aristocracy which had tried to continue in its place. He says that he recruited German mercenaries, '*Saxones*' as he calls them. They, or the remnants of the Roman army, may have seen how the tyrant extracted the surplus from the agriculture and other industry he controlled and realised that they did not need him to do it for them but that he needed them. Perhaps they took over – 'rebelled' as it is usually called. The dispossessed aristocracy either fled or perished or – in most cases much more likely – collaborated. No doubt the slave traders who had always been busy in England would have got a better price for those with some education like St Patrick and, if there had to be human sacrifices, it made sense to get rid of aristocrats rather than workers. There is evidence that some entire British communities became part of Anglo-Saxon kingdoms and that, if they could, their British leaders took on the attributes necessary for them to be treated as Anglo-Saxon. This process is hard to date:[18]

> Careful analysis of the available literary sources suggests that the nature of the 'Saxon' presence changed in about 440, though archaeological finds indicate that there was already an increasing number of specifically Germanic artefacts in cemeteries in eastern England from about 425. What we may be dealing with

16. There is a very recent but burgeoning accumulation on the internet, e.g. from Mark Liberman who extrapolates his criticisms as a historical linguist to Oppenheimer's scientific method as a whole: http://itre.cis.upenn.edu/~myl/languagelog/archives/004346.html
17. Michael Winterbottom ed *Gildas: The Ruin of Britain and Other Works*. The disputed dates of Gildas's birth and book are discussed in DN Dumville 'The Chronology of *De Excidio Britanniae* Book I' in Lapidge and Dumville *Gildas: New Approaches* pp61–84.
18. David Mattingly *Imperial Possession* p536.

here is a gradual tilting of the scales as the balance of power shifted from the British communities to the Germanic groups.

When money from Rome to pay the troops and civil servants stopped, some no doubt left; but most would have been local recruits or Germanic mercenaries. Even those at the top were appointed from the Gallic prefecture. There was no home for any of them in Italy. In AD406 the Vandals, Suevi and Alans had crossed the Rhine. In AD410 the Visigoths sacked Rome. By AD418 the Franks had settled in Gaul. Where could the refugees go? Most of them came originally from western Europe, with some from farther afield. They were colonials with nobody to welcome them where they or their ancestors had come from.

The population of Britannia when the Romans left was at least two million and may have been more than three.[19] How many left and how many stayed? It is hard to imagine more than a few thousand emigrating without their influx making enough of an impact to be recorded where they settled. There are no records from England, though there are hints from abroad. Some who fled joined their kin in Armorica, now Brittany.[20] Moreover, not only were there always Britons/Bretons on both sides of the Channel, there were British soldiers in the Roman army in Armorica/ Brittany as in the rest of Gaul from the late third century and many retired there.[21] Gildas himself may have emigrated to Brittany, perhaps from what we now call Wales.[22]

What sort of people stayed? There was a North–South, East–West division:[23]

> The distribution of monument classes illustrates that there were two very different native cultures in Roman Britain, one of which was able to adopt and adapt Roman values and symbols, and one which apparently was not. These two cultural expressions had their roots in the tribal society of pre-Roman Britain... and strong continuity has been identified from the late pre-Roman iron age among the native population: in the north and west this may have been more pronounced and have extended throughout society.

This archaeological evidence is supported by the old authority of Julius Caesar and the new genetic evidence of an age-old separation of sources of population from Gallia Celtica and Gallia Belgica.

19. Edward James *Britain in the First Millennium* p56.
20. Pierre-Roland Giot, Philippe Guigon and Bernard Merdrignac *The British Settlement of Brittany: The First Bretons in Armorica* is the fullest treatment of emigrants to Brittany from Britain. Cunliffe *Facing the Ocean* p462 suggests that Irish invasions of the south-west coast may have caused the emigration.
21. Britons also established a colony in Galicia, in what is now Spain, EA Thompson 'Britonia' pp201–6.
22. Merdrignac in Giot, Guigon and Merdrignac *British Settlement* p101.
23. Andrew Sargent 'The North–South Divide Revisited'.

If there were, say, two and a half million and 10 per cent of them were well-off and 'Romanised', that would mean that there were about a quarter of a million 'Romano-Britons' to exercise privilege and influence and to carry on such parts of the Roman way of life as they could afford, if they wanted to.[24] The resources and ambitions of the Church may have kept alive and renewed both scholarship and legal practice.

TRADE

There is also plenty of evidence that the Romano-Britons preserved their trade and cultural links with their friends and kin on the Continent.[25] The archaeological evidence shows that even in later centuries there were still some who wore showy clothes and jewellery in the late Roman fashion.[26] Trade and travel never stopped between them and their counterparts on the Continent and both were quicker and easier by sea than by land. It took 'a day and a half with oars' wrote Procopius cAD550 – at second hand and from Constantinople it is true.

It was not only in the 'Romanised' parts that trade and other exchanges continued with the rump of the Roman Empire. Many Roman artefacts – brass bowls and wine jars from Byzantium, glassware from Spain, oil jars and fine pottery from North Africa, imported in the fifth and sixth centuries – have been found in Tintagel in the South-West, which was never part of Britannia. Too many beads have been found to have been made from amber washed up on English beaches. There must have been trade between the Baltic and many different parts of Britain, not only where Roman lifestyles lingered. Purses have been found, fitted with rings of elephant ivory, and shells from India in seventh-century graves.[27]

The evidence of this trade in luxuries is not evenly spread, however. The western parts provide the most. Mattingly sums up the divide:[28]

> By the end of the fifth century, Britain was divided between a northern Pictish kingdom, an 'eastern' zone (with its western limits running through Hampshire, eastern Gloucestershire, Leicestershire, Lincolnshire and Yorkshire) characterized by Germanic cremation and inhumation cemeteries, and a series of western zones (Dorset, Somerset, Devon, Cornwall, Wales, north-western England) where a Christian and Latinate British culture survived in part, though

24. 'Presumably the old élites still maintained a degree of control, perhaps aided by the Church, especially in and around towns. We have some evidence for such control at the Roman city of... Wroxeter... The 'Dark Age' buildings of the fifth and sixth centuries are remarkable... because they were built in a Roman style and laid out using a Roman system of measurement', Pryor *Britain AD* pp167, 171.
25. Michael McCormick *Origins of the European Economy*.
26. Henig 'Remaining Roman' p22. In *The Heirs of King Verica: Culture and Politics in Roman Britain* Henig shows how a powerful imagination applied to the archaeological evidence can bring the Romano-Britons to life.
27. John Hines 'Society, Community and Identity' p84.
28. Mattingly *Imperial Possession* p537.

also affected by Irish migrations into parts of Wales and Scotland. The Germanic groups had thus seized control of the productive heartlands of the Roman provinces. The future lay in their hands and those native Britons who lived under their authority evidently soon shared the cultural agenda they set. We should not envisage the complete replacement of one ethnic group by another... Late antique imports from the Mediterranean world and Gaul are predominantly clustered along the western seaboard of Britain... The lack of trade between the Continent and the Germanic areas suggests a dramatic repudiation of Roman culture by the incomers in eastern Britain and the acceptance of this new un-Roman identity by the eastern Britons under 'Saxon' suzerainty.

That is the latest and most convincing contribution of archaeology to solving the problem of what was going on in England when the first Saxon invasions are recorded.

THE COMING OF THE ANGLO-SAXONS[29]

The Literary Tradition The traditional story comes from Bede's *Ecclesiastical History*, written in Latin about AD730, three hundred years after the events.[30] He tells us that the first forces of Angles and Saxons came in just three long ships, which could in all have carried a hundred men or so, and that they were followed by great waves of migrants – 'Angles, Saxons and Jutes' – who invaded different parts of Britain and replaced the British population.

4.1 They came from three of the more powerful peoples of *Germania*, that is the Saxons, Angles and Jutes. Originating from the Jutes are the *Cantuari* and *Victuarii*, that is those kin who occupy the Isle of Wight and those who today are still in the region of the West Saxons called the nation of the Jutes, which is situated opposite the Isle of Wight. From the Saxons, that is that district which is now called 'of the Old Saxons', came the East Saxons, South Saxons and West Saxons. Besides them, from the Angles, that is from that country which is called *Angulus*, originated the East Angles, Middle Angles, the Mercians, and the whole stock of Northumbrians, that is of those peoples who live north of the River Humber, and also the rest of the people of the Angles.

Bede's source for the facts of the invasion was Gildas, the only substantial written source to have survived from within a generation or two of the events. England then was still divided between a British north and west

---

29. The name 'Anglo-Saxon' was not coined until much later and then first, as one would expect, by foreigners. It is first found in the late eighth century on the Continent and only in the ninth century in England, W Pohl 'Ethnic Names and Identities in the British Isles' pp21–22.
30. Bertram Colgrave and RAB Mynors eds *Bede's Ecclesiastical History of the English People* is the best edition. Hunter Blair's assessment of Bede's reliability is a warning, all the firmer for its gentle tone: 'Bede's genius resides not so much in the registration of fact as in his subtle subordination of history to the didactic purposes of a well-hidden agenda', *Anglo-Saxon England* pxxii.

in which Christianity was dominant and a south and east partly ruled by
pagan Anglo-Saxons. Gildas's religious tract, *De Excidio Britanniae*, On the
Ruin of Britain, is not history but some facts seem to be discernible which
his readers, educated Christians, would have had their own knowledge of,
not at first hand but certainly from talking in their youth to those who had
been there. He says that the trouble started when Saxons were invited in
as mercenaries, at first only three boatloads, which may seem few but may
well have been all that their employers needed or could afford. Gildas liked
to make his points forcefully:[31]

> **4.2** Then all the counsellors, together with the proud tyrant,[32] are struck blind.
> The safeguard which they invent for our country – or rather its destruction – was
> that the most ferocious Saxons – abominable name! – loathed by God and man,
> should be brought into the island like wolves into the fold to keep out the peoples
> of the north. Nothing more destructive, nothing more bitter, has ever been done to
> it than that. The absolute height of folly! What utterly desperate, crude stupidity!
> They feared these people worse than death when they weren't there, and yet of their
> own free will they invited them, I might tell you, to share the same roof! As the
> saying goes: 'Foolish princes of Tanis, giving unwise counsel to Pharaoh'.[33]
>
> Then from the lair of the barbarian lioness burst out a pack of cubs, in three
> keels, *cyulis*, as they say in their language, which we call long ships, with the
> winds, omens and auguries behind them. They foretold, in what was for them a
> sure prophecy, that for three hundred years they would occupy the land to which
> their prows turned and for half that time, a hundred and fifty, they would harry
> it again and again.

And so he rants on. The Saxons first 'fixed their claws on the eastern side
of the island'; but when 'the aforesaid dam had found that the first throng
had prospered, she sent a more copious slave-market of henchman dogs'.
These 'godless easterners' then set fire to 'almost the whole island' and
battered to bits every major town. If that were so, then there would be
evidence for the archaeologists to interpret. There is none. Even Gildas's
few facts must therefore be counted untrustworthy. No doubt his readers
would have put his exaggerations down to religious fervour and condoned
them if they shared it.

For more than seventy years historians have found this story
unconvincing:[34] 'One thing is certain – that for the time being the Germanic
conquest of Britain cannot be told as a narrative. How then are we to treat it?
There is no choice. It is a great enigma.' There is so little evidence, and what
there is is so confusing, it is tempting to speculate as if there were none.

31. Gildas *De Excidio* 23.4.
32. Gildas is careful here to avoid calling Vortigern *rex*, which would imply legitimate
    authority. In Gildas's eyes that still belonged to Rome.
33. Isaiah XIX 11,13. Tanis is the Greek name for the biblical Zoan.
34. Thomas Hodgkin *A History of the Anglo-Saxons* I p75.

Who were the new German immigrants, when did they come, and who did they find here? These questions are fundamental to all work on the Anglo-Saxon period and every element of them is in dispute. Not only do scholars in different disciplines take opposite views. The debate goes on within the disciplines.[35] They now include not just historians and archaeologists but natural scientists, geneticists, linguists and those drawing on interdisciplinary research.

Anthropology There is anthropological support for the minimal position:[36]

> As for the 'three ships' in which 'the race of the Angles or Saxons' came to Britain called by the Britons, this figure may be not so far off the mark: Bede specifies that they were 'warships'. Each warship may have transported as many as thirty soldiers for a total of about one hundred, not a mean force for those days... The likelihood that the contingents of migrants were small is supported by the fact that, well into the eighth century, Continental Saxons, and most probably Angles and Jutes, had a clan structure.[37] Within a clan, except in case of immediate danger from enemy raids or when a raid would be considered attractive because of the possibility of easy plunder, it would have been quite difficult to raise a contingent of more than a hundred.

That may explain Bede's numbers but there were many other incursions and undoubtedly some settlements. What about the women? However many women immigrated, the invading men must have taken advantage of the surplus of British women their raids had produced. They were well known for selling slaves so they would perhaps have had to choose between the money and the mate. They would also have had to decide whether to keep a man as an agricultural slave or sell him. They would usually kill him if he was a noble. As they settled, later generations would not have had the same choices.[38]

It should not surprise anyone to find that the more privileged you are the more likely to have children who produce children. The archaeological

35. Francis Pryor's conclusion (*Britain AD* p196) from studies of land use is at one extreme: 'if there actually were any incomers, they must have been few in number, and have settled within existing communities'. Nicholas Higham does not go so far (*Rome, Britain* pp15, 234–5): 'By the late sixth century, the Anglo-Saxon world was peopled by a cross-bred community with far more British than Germanic genes.' On the other side is MG Welch 'Rural Settlement Patterns' pp13–14: 'The minimalist view of Anglo-Saxon settlement... flies in the face of the combined available evidence from linguistic, historical and archaeological sources.' Also Janet Nelson 'Our Forefathers?' and most entertaining Pryor 'Invasion, What Invasion?'.
36. Giorgio Ausenda in Hines *The Anglo-Saxons* p419, where a bracing discussion follows Ian Wood's paper 'Before and After the Migration to Britain' pp41–64.
37. Bede *Ecclesiastical History* 5.10.
38. Don Henson *The Origins of the Anglo-Saxons* is, as I write, the latest attempt to summarise the evidence. It is particularly helpful on the 'material culture', artefacts and coins, pp153–61 and the summary which follows pp161–75.

evidence shows that the German incomers were a highly privileged group. There is some literary evidence that they were clannish and preferred to take their legal spouses from their own group, no doubt with less formal relations with slaves and conquered women.[39] The children of their wives would be more likely to survive than those of their slaves or concubines. Some recent scientific research blends anthropology with genetics:[40]

> Under a model of cross-generation ethnic apartheid it is expected that the chromosomes of the advantaged ethnic group would increase in overall frequency. However, intermarriage between ethnic groups would serve to homogenize the genetic makeup of those groups… Computer simulations indicate that a social structure limiting intermarriage between indigenous Britons and an initially small Anglo-Saxon immigrant population provide[s] a plausible explanation of the high degree of Continental male-line ancestry in England.

Archaeology   The archaeological evidence does not now support the traditional account:[41] 'The simple view of a wholesale or near wholesale replacement of a British population with a German one is inconsistent with the evidence which derives from a wide spectrum of research.'

Travel between parts of England and parts of the Continent has never been too difficult. Therefore, even the ornaments worn by the dead are not a reliable guide to ethnicity. Fashions travel more easily than populations.

New methods of radiocarbon dating and other scientific testing have made all kinds of new checks possible. Farming practices, buildings, burials and pottery provide no persuasive evidence of mass migration. Perhaps they may show that many Germans brought their wives with them but the present evidence suggests that is unlikely.[42] Studies of teeth by stable isotope analysis may show that their owners started off in a place with a different German kind of water from that where they were buried in England. A cemetery in West Heslerton in Yorkshire was found to contain the remains of people buried not long after the first Anglo-Saxon settlements. Stable isotope analysis was applied to 24 bodies from there and to eight from Early Bronze and Iron Age sites nearby. All of those eight were found to come from East Yorkshire. So were ten of the 24 from the 'Anglo-Saxon' cemetery. Another ten came from over the Pennines. It is true that four came from Scandinavia, north of where the Anglo-Saxons are supposed to have come from (and where other things found in the cemetery originated). Those four were buried over a period

---

39. William Stubbs *Constitutional History* p46, quoting Rudolf *Translatio Sancti Alexandri* of cAD863, on the Germans in Francia: 'they scarcely ever allow themselves to be infected by any marriages with other or inferior races'.
40. MG Thomas, MPH Stumpf and Heinrich Härke 'Evidence for an Apartheid-Like Social Structure in Early Anglo-Saxon England'.
41. Higham *Rome, Britain* p15.
42. C Capelli and 14 others 'A Y Chromosome Census of the British Isles'.

of 250 years. Were they invading warriors? Hardly. All were female and one a child.[43]

Genetics The most radical rethinking has been in historical genetics. Geneticists do not agree among themselves and recent research has not convinced the sceptics.[44] For one thing, the difference in genetic make-up of the two groups to be compared, invaders and invaded, is quite insignificant in the larger scheme of things.[45] Stephen Oppenheimer has attacked not only the old assumptions but also recent research in his own field, in particular that which suggests that the invaders were guilty of 'genocide followed by a social-sexual apartheid that enhanced Anglo-Saxon reproductive success':[46]

> The problem is that the English resemble in this way all the other countries of northwest Europe as well as the Frisians and Germans... I have found greater similarities of this kind between the southern English and Belgians than the supposedly Anglo-Saxon homelands at the base of the Danish peninsula. These different regions could not all have been waiting their turn to commit genocide on the former Celtic population of England. The most likely reason for the genetic similarities between these neighbouring countries and England is that they all had similar prehistoric settlement histories.

There are those connections to Gallia Belgica again!

Suggested Answers Some answers must be found, however tentative, to the three questions: who were the new German immigrants, when did they come, and who did they find here?

To take the last question first, my preference is for the conclusion that the British were not wiped out or driven into the fastnesses of Wales and that fewer new immigrants of German origin settled in England in the fifth and sixth centuries than was traditionally believed, in misplaced and over-enthusiastic reliance on Gildas and Bede. There were many different groups, some the invaders called, in their language, 'Welsh'. There is plenty of evidence for that, as later chapters will show. What evidence is there for groups of another kind, speaking Germanic languages? Not much, as Appendix A shows. Ine's laws speak of payment of taxes in Welsh ale as distinct from 'clear ale'.[47]

43. Pryor *Britain AD* pp212–13. There may have been communities of Romano-British and Anglo-Saxons co-existing separately but side by side, with different burial customs but using the same pottery, as late as the second half of the sixth century: Martin Henig and Paul Booth give a careful account in *Roman Oxfordshire*, particularly Chapter 7 pp179–98.
44. Cf Oppenheimer *Origins* with M Richards et al. 'Archaeology and Genetics: Analysing DNA from Skeletal Remains'.
45. Sam Lucy *The Anglo-Saxon Way of Death* pp176–8 has an admirably clear analysis of ethnicity and what it means (and does not mean) to belong to a group.
46. This summary is taken from Oppenheimer 'Myths of British History'.
47. FL Attenborough *Laws* Ine 70.1.

4.3 XII ambers of Welsh ale, XXX of clear....

It seems unlikely that bands of fighters or even settlers would have brought their own brewers. So some ale was Welsh and some was not. Who brewed that other? The laws relating to the Welsh, which come from Wessex but not from Kent, and their use as evidence for separate Celtic and Germanic groups, will be dealt with when those laws are discussed in later chapters.

Who were the incomers? They were not homogeneous but everyone who invaded Britain after the Romans left had one thing in common, though they arrived piecemeal and many would not have known it. They were all Germanic, part of a great long diaspora, whether they came directly from what is now Germany or Scandinavia, or indirectly from Normandy or elsewhere in Francia. And when it suited them, for example when they had to flee into exile, usually because of murderous family squabbles, they relied on family ties to find a home.

David Miles gives a fair summary of all the evidence:[48]

> No one has yet quite won the argument, but on present evidence it seems that Germanic warriors did attack Britain and then migrate and begin to settle, some with families while others intermarried with the British. The number of Continental immigrants probably varied in different regions with most in the south and east and far fewer in the north and west. Gradually, over about two centuries, the Germanic Anglo-Saxon culture became dominant.

The last word has not been said. My opinion, for what it is worth, is that the new colonials whom we call Anglo-Saxons replaced or transformed the British upper classes. They cannot have wished to destroy the people who provided the labour, skilled and unskilled, with which they would not have wanted to soil their hands. After all, an apparently amicable treaty was made with the British border people, the Dunsaete, in the time of Athelstan, **8.2–9**, and there were still British communities among the Anglo-Saxon as late as 1086, as *Domesday Book* shows.[49] Yet it is possible to generalise: 'the material culture and language of the British lowlands, and the group-identity of the population which emerged, were the property of immigrants'.[50] But that can be safely said only of the Lowland Zone. For much of the rest, they were invisible until they adopted the ways and language of the Anglo-Saxons.[51]

48. David Miles *Tribes* pp172–7, 176 and compare now Alex Woolf 'Apartheid and Economics' p129: 'many individual Britons may have found themselves drifting into Anglo-Saxon households, as slaves, hangers-on, brides and so forth... such households would have become ethnic sausage machines, recycling stray biological material....'
49. Discussed below in Chapter 10. See now CP Lewis 'Welsh Territories' and the sources he cites p130 n1 and n2.
50. Higham *Rome, Britain* p15.
51. Heinrich Härke 'Invisible Britons' p60.

LANGUAGE

The problem with rejecting one or more overwhelming influxes of Germans is how to otherwise explain the replacement of the British languages by Anglo-Saxon. I have done the best I can to answer that question so far as it is essential for understanding the background to dispute resolution in England. To avoid the distraction here of what must be an extended treatment, I have shown my arguments and the work of others in Appendix A. The result is inconclusive. More work may well show that that is because we are looking for too simple an answer.

Because much of the background, not only linguistic, is still so controversial, greater effort than usual must be put into getting it right. There is still more to do to place dispute resolution in the foreground. So far there have been no signs of it at all. But first something must be sketched in the middle ground, as much as possible of what is known about the whole legal system.

ROMAN LAW?

When the Roman administration left, some Romano-British lawyers are likely to have stayed in England. No doubt there were many of the better-off who took their status as Roman citizens seriously and hoped to retain its privileges, and indeed looked for a return of the Roman forces. But there was no colonial state power to enforce the Roman law. The courts of the Roman administration must have ceased to function, though some of the successors to Roman power may have preserved simulacra. Litigation of the Roman kind cannot have remained available for very long, though in AD418, eight years after he is said to have told the administration there to look after itself, Honorius passed legislation for Britain to protect papal interpretation of doctrine against the British followers of Pelagius; and in AD429 the Pope is said to have sent Germanus, bishop of Auxerres, to England to enforce it.[52]

Those Romano-British generations followed nearly four centuries of Roman rule. Probably as late as 440, in England as in Brittany, they were still looking to the Roman authorities to come back and help them against insurrection and incursion. It was about that time, according to Gildas, that Britons appealed to Aëtius, a Roman general in Gaul, for help against German invaders.[53] If there was an appeal it was unsuccessful.

52. FR Hoare ed *Constantius: The Life of St Germanus*. Germanus had been *dux*, in charge of Armorica. Pelagius (Latin for the British name Morgan), though born in Britain, worked in Rome and Africa, Giot 'British Settlement' p105. Higham 'Rome, Britain' pp74–5 says: 'It was, though, very much in the interests of the land-holding classes that Roman law be maintained, and courts seem to have survived... The jurisdiction of Roman-style courts was subject to the geography of the Roman provinces and *civitates* would have tended to perpetuate them.'
53. Gildas *De Excidio* 20.

That would not mean that what was left of the Imperial authorities had given up the province. It is even less likely that the Roman senators and others who had large landholdings in the British provinces had willingly abandoned all hope of regaining them.[54] We, with Gildas and all the foreign sources, look back with hindsight and see the Romans gone forever, though Gildas **4.2** denied the 'proud tyrant' any title but *tyrannus*. The Romano-British might have been *déclassé* and expendable *Brittunculi* to the Romans, and even comical upstarts to a fellow-colonial in Burgundy like Ausonius, writing towards the end of the fourth century, but there were some who took their status as Roman citizens seriously. A Romano-Briton might write Latin verse and even aspire to be a literary critic. Ausonius in Bordeaux cAD400 made quite a meal of one whose name we know but not his works, date or place. Silvius Bonus had dared to criticise Ausonius's verse:[55]

4.4 That Silvius Bonus, who lacerates my verse,
Deserves my distichs all the more, good Briton.
This Silvius is Bonus. What Silvius? That Briton!
Either this Briton is not Silvius, or he is a bad one.
Silvius is called Bonus and called Britannus too:
Who would credit that a good citizen, *civis*, could sink so low?
There is no good Briton! If simple Silvius he starts to be,
Let the simple man desist from being Bonus.
This Silvius is Bonus but the same Silvius is a Briton;
It's a simpler thing, believe me, that the Briton is bad.
Hey, Silvius good Briton! Yet you claim a man not to be good
But you must not link Briton and Bonus.

The text of the last line is incomplete but the meaning has been repeated too often for it to be in doubt. There is no such thing as a good Briton. Ausonius may have had a low opinion of Britons, but he did not think they capered about in woad. They had Roman names and might have to be acknowledged, like Silvius, to be 'good citizens', and therefore full Romans, even though you should not believe a word they said. At least they were not like the Picts and Scots, whom Gildas said were:[56]

4.5 ... readier to cover their villainous faces with hair than their private parts and neighbouring regions with clothes.

In their own eyes, some of them were still citizens of the Roman Empire. Both Gildas and Patrick called themselves *civis*, which to them could

54. Ian Wood 'End of Roman Britain' p6.
55. Ausonius *Epigrams* 107–12. One can detect a touch of Polonius but not much Horace here.
56. The matchless translation of Michael Winterbottom *Gildas* 19 p23. The Italian poet Venantius Fortunatus, writing in Francia in the sixth century, called the Britons in Brittany barbarians, Charles-Edwards *After Rome* pp6–7.

only have had, I believe, the connotation of *Roman* citizen.[57] And, though some preferred to give their sons British names, they kept their Roman haircuts.[58]

It would be surprising if the Romano-Britons did not handle their disputes among themselves in the ways they had inherited, according to Roman law, not now that of the state but as their own customary law in whatever assemblies their communities provided. What other legal system could they have had by which they would all abide?[59] Probably there were not so many lawyers who practised Roman law. There would be little work for them. They had all been trained not in law but in rhetoric, as they still were until the twelfth century. They have left no obvious traces; there is no direct reference to the continuation of Roman law and practice in any surviving source. Indeed, there is almost no literature from England which has survived from the fifth and early sixth centuries, other than the Romano-British saints Gildas and Patrick.

As Samuel Butler saw: 'God cannot alter the past, historians can: it is perhaps because they can be useful to Him in this respect that He tolerates their existence'.[60] There is no doubt that these two Christian writers were eager to help their god by their writing. Nor were they the last to believe that truth is what it ought to be. From the earliest charters it is clear that clerical writers were adept at improving the evidence of their god's ownership of land against those who might claim a superior title. But, provided their purpose is kept in mind, and they are not treated as if they were historians, they may inadvertently disclose the truth even when they are trying to further their cause.

Gildas wrote that Magnus Maximus had put an end to the rule of Roman law when he grabbed power from the authorities as early as AD387. For then Britannia was:[61]

4.6 keeping the Roman name but not the custom and law.

57. Gildas *De Excidio* XIX 3 and XXVI 1 and 2; Patrick *Letter to Coroticus* 2 in Hood p35; contra Wood 'End of Roman Britain' p22. Professor Higham, whose generous criticisms have saved me from many errors and greatly improved this chapter, wrote to me: '*civis* is an interesting problem; both seem to be referring to a sense of Britishness. Gildas is reasonably clear that he thinks of the Britons as analogous to the Israelites of the Old Testament. I don't think this necessarily means Roman citizen.' Wood and Higham are much more likely to be right than I am (and we are reviewing the same evidence) but I cannot bring myself to accept that Patrick or Gildas had such 'a sense of Britishness'. See now Higham's extended argument in 'Historical Narrative as Cultural Politics' in Higham *Britons in Anglo-Saxon England* pp72–5.
58. Charles-Edwards *After Rome* p6; Higham 'Historical Narrative' p74.
59. It may be relevant that 31 deeds of sale survive from about AD493–96 of land on the border between what are now Algeria and Tunisia. They are all drafted according to the requirements of the Lex Manciana which by then was nearly 500 years old, H Wessel *Das Recht der Tablettes Albertini*.
60. Samuel Butler *Erewhon Revisited* Chapter 14.
61. Gildas *De Excidio Britanniae* 13.1: *nomen Romanum nec tamen morem legemque tenens*.

That seems to be a straightforward enough assertion. We have seen that it was common enough to keep a personal Roman name[62] and Britannia was still called that in Latin, and its people *Britones*. But what Gildas and Patrick say cannot be true; both Roman law and Roman custom survived, as they themselves inadvertently reveal.

Until the Romans left, the state ran schools for boys where the learning was all in Latin. After primary school, where they learned the elements of reading, writing and arithmetic to the age of eleven, they were taught by a *grammaticus* until they were fifteen or so. With him they concentrated on learning the correct Latin style from intense study of a narrow selection of classical authors, particularly Virgil. At about sixteen, they graduated to the school of a *rhetor*, to learn rhetoric, public speaking, including forensic advocacy. For this they studied some Roman law.[63] There is no direct evidence for the teaching of rhetoric in England after the Romans left, though the works of Ausonius reveal how it was taught in Gaul, where civil law does not seem to have been part of the curriculum.[64] There is, however, enough indirect evidence.

We do not know when Patrick was born or died but we can be fairly sure that he was alive in the fifth century.[65] By great good fortune we have his own words, which say that he was taken as a slave at the age of sixteen,[66] just when a privileged youth like him would have been expecting to graduate from the *grammaticus* to the *rhetor*, and he was conscious of his lack of a tertiary education.[67]

> **4.7** I have not been educated as others have, who have soaked up the law and the holy scriptures in the best way and never changed their languages since infancy but have been continually perfecting their Latin, for my speech and talk have been translated into a foreign language... So stand in awe you great and small who fear God, Sunday rhetoricians! He who roused me, a fool, from the midst of those who seem to be wise and the professional jurists and the powerful speakers....

Now the law in which those 'Sunday rhetoricians'[68] were expert cannot have been canon law. From Patrick's text is is clear that it can only have

---

62. Like Aurelius Caninus in Gildas *De Excidio Britanniae* XXX 1 and Silvius Bonus, **4.7**.
63. Michael Lapidge 'Gildas's Education and the Latin Culture of Sub-Roman Britain' p28.
64. Ausonius makes it fairly clear that the study of rhetoric in Gaul did not include Roman law, Chapter 3 above at fn75; Lapidge 'Gildas's Education' pp28–9 gives the slight evidences of the teaching of rhetoric in Roman Britain.
65. EA Thompson *Who Was Saint Patrick?* ppxiii, 166–75 and Colmán Etchington's preface pxx.
66. ABE Hood ed *St Patrick: His Writings and Muirchu's Life*, *Confessio* 1.
67. Patrick *Confessio* 13.
68. *Dominicati rethorici*. *Dominicati* is a doubtful reading but is to be preferred here to the equally possible *domini cati rethorici* – 'clever rhetorician masters', not only because it makes such a good point but just because it is unusual and therefore less likely to be a scribal error. Moreover, it is rare in the sense of 'on Sunday' but I believe the point Patrick is making is clear: these are the men who put the skills of rhetoric into their Sunday sermons, unlike poor uneducated Patrick whose only advantage is that God tells him what to say.

been Roman civil law. But they were not taught that in any of the religious schools, which banned the study of civil law. Moreover, Patrick said God picked him out 'from the midst of the professional jurists', despite his inferior eloquence. Who were they if not practising lawyers, still functioning in the second half of the fifth century? They were not what we would classify as canon lawyers, as distinct from those practising the civil law, because that distinction had yet to be drawn in England.

Gildas says that Latin is his language, calling it *lingua nostra.*[69] The most careful linguistic analysis of his writings shows that 'Gildas did not derive his Latin vocabulary at second-hand from glossaries, but rather from first-hand knowledge of Latin as a living language.'[70] That may be evidence enough of his education by a *grammaticus*. Is there evidence he was taught rhetoric? Analysis of Gildas's *On the Ruin of Britain* shows a similar structure and even language, including technical legal terms, to that of a forensic oration in the style of Cicero.[71] He speaks directly of the legal process and even of arbitration:[72]

4.8 Britain does have kings, but they are tyrants; it does have *judices*, but they are wicked... They do defend and protect, but the guilty and thieving... They sit in the position of one who is to arbitrate, *arbitraturi*, but rarely do they look for the rule of correct judgment.

The word *judices* has no overtones of 'judges' as distinct from 'arbitrators'. In Roman law it can as easily mean either, indeed the distinction was not relevant to Gildas here. It means nothing more specific than 'decision-makers'. The *judices* perform adjudicatory functions. In doing so they are immoral. As arbitrators they do not apply the right rule of law. How would Gildas know that and of what law should they be seeking the right rule? 'It is not easy to see how such familiarity can be explained except on the assumption that Gildas had undergone training at the hands of a *rhetor* in preparation for a career in the law-courts.'[73] Twice he uses a technical term, *condebitores*, joint debtors, which does not seem to be found elsewhere.[74] But Gildas lived a century after the Romans left. There is no suggestion that he was trained in England for a career abroad. He was educated to work in England, not perhaps in 'law-courts', for which we have no evidence in his

---

69. Gildas *De Excidio* 1.23. Indeed his grasp of British seems weak: even a modern English speaker who knows almost no Welsh can guess that *cynoglas* means greyhound, not red butcher.
70. Michael Lapidge 'Gildas's Education' p37.
71. Lapidge 'Gildas's Education' pp43–50. Gildas's use of such words as *respondeo* and *comprobo* in relation to calling witnesses is legal jargon, 2.37 and 2.34.
72. Gildas *De Excidio* 2.27: *iudices habet, sed impios*; Paul Schaffner 'Britain's *Iudices*' in Lapidge and Dumville pp151–5.
73. Lapidge 'Gildas's Education' p47.
74. Gildas *De Excidio* I 15 and XIX 1.

time, nor in the Roman civil service, which no longer survived, but none the less for some kind of career in law.

These arguments support the case that in the time of Gildas there was still education in rhetoric, necessarily private now that the state schools had closed, and that families were prepared to pay for it, presumably in the hope that their sons would be able to use it. Moreover, Gildas had a mission by the time he wrote. He had become a religious enthusiast, perhaps because he could not get a secular job. He rants not against the warrior chiefs of the uplands but the new 'tyrants', from the landowner class who had taken power in the lowlands. They were supposed to be Christian but their behaviour fell far short of what he thought their religion required. Who was he addressing? In theory the tyrants but in practice his audience of Latin-readers, who could appreciate, or so he thought, the rhetoric of the classical orators. He must have hoped there were enough of them to make it worthwhile. In a gnomic sentence, he tells one of the tyrants, Maglocunus, that he should know better because he had been taught by a *rhetor*, elegant master of almost all Britain.[75] Presumably it would not have been too difficult to be teacher of rhetoric to most of Britain if there were dwindling numbers of students you could attract. We know that Faustus, who became bishop of Riez cAD460, was a Briton apparently taught by a *rhetor* in England well into the fifth century but the evidence of Gildas takes the practice of Roman civil law in England into the middle of the sixth. It is also important to remember that both Patrick and Gildas were Romano-British, and that none of our sources turned much of their attention to ordinary people.[76]

CUSTOMARY LAWS

Zosimus, probably a lawyer in Constantinople, was a contemporary of Gildas. He wrote an unreliable history of the Roman Empire in Greek, in which he purported to describe what happened when the Romans left.[77]

4.9 Gerontius... won over the soldiers who were there and got the barbarians among the Celts to rise up against Constantius. When Constantius offered no resistance to them, most of his forces being in Spain, the barbarians from over the Rhine attacked as they liked those who lived in the Britannic island as well as some of the peoples among the Celts and forced them to withdraw from the

---

75. 2.36: *cum habueris praeceptorem paene totius Britanniae magistrum elegantem*; Lapidge 'Gildas's Education' p50.
76. Merdrignac and Guigon in Giot p284 stress 'the eternal divorce between the true country and the ruling classes... When one speaks of "Romans", "Bretons", "Saxons" or "Franks", we should understand this refers only to the families of the mighty or the leading ecclesiastics.'
77. Zosimus *New History* 6.5. The text is edited by François Paschoud. The translations relied on in ME Jones 'Legacy of Roman Law' p66 and EA Thompson 'Zosimus on the End of Roman Britain' p130 are unreliable. JJ Buchanan and HT Davis: *Zosimus: Historia Nova* is misleading.

government of the Romans and make a life for themselves, no longer obeying their laws.

So those from Britannia took up arms and, recognising the danger to themselves, liberated the cities from the occupying barbarians. All of Armorica and the other provinces of the Gauls copied the Britons and freed themselves in the same way and established as they wished a government of their kin.

It is not easy to be sure what all that means, even if it is accurate. Who were these 'Celts'?[78] Did barbarians from over the Rhine really attack the island of Britain then? Even if the 'non-Romans' reverted to some British customary law, some Romano-British could not have known any non-Roman customary law to which they could revert. In a personal communication, Professor Higham has made it clear:

> Roman law was imposed under Roman rule in the *coloniae* and *municipia*, but Britain had very few of these. Local customary law would have been the norm in the *civitates* and to an extent in the large areas beyond civil government, in the military zone. When the provincials became citizens under Caracalla, in theory Roman law would have applied to all but in practice this may well have been very partial. In other words, local assemblies may well have still been operating a not particularly Roman set of customary laws in the fifth century, as had been applied even under Roman jurisdiction.

We do not need the testimony of Gildas, **4.6**, or Zosimus, **4.9**, to persuade us that, after the Roman imperial administration left Britain, all those who were left behind relied for the resolution of their disputes on their customary laws and practices.[79] What else could they do? Apart from the Romano-British, those were the laws by which all of them had always governed their affairs. The Roman administration had in most respects and for most people been happy for them to do so and routinely assisted when occasionally called upon to enforce them, thereby providing the necessary encouragement to use them.

Every community must have some system of dealing with disputes if it is to be a community. It has its own law, which is customary until its ideology insists that nothing is law which is not set by the state. The individuals which make up the community expect their customary law to apply and to be used. That is what it is there for, for all those who have the power to make it work for them. It is potentially comprehensive, like the Common Law, so that the community could just about survive if it were the only law

---

78. Giot *British Settlement of Brittany*.
79. To deny the status of law to customary law is to impose the self-serving distinction of nineteenth-century imperial powers (and their Roman counterparts, of course) and scholars who thought as they did.

and all legislation were abolished. All this goes without saying and none of the surviving sources mention it anywhere.[80]

There is no evidence, of archaeology or literature, that England was not made up of communities. We may therefore accept as truisms the statements of Gildas and Zosimus that the Britons who had not been 'Romanised' reverted to their British customary laws. There is no direct evidence of their substance or procedure. We cannot be sure without further enquiry whether they were specific to each clan or were local, varying from place to place.[81]

There may have been a revolt against Roman colonial rule, starting perhaps in AD409, which drove many of the Romano-British upper class and their followers to Brittany, where the people are said to have risen against both the immigrants and their own upper class and unsuccessfully rebelled against the Empire. Rutilius Namatianus in a contemporary poem[82] says that a general called Exuperantius put down such a revolt in Aquitaine in 417, but the job had to be done again by Aëtius in Armorica in 435 and in 445.[83] There are stories of ordinary farmers sitting under oak trees to resolve their disputes but nothing reliable can be deduced from them about what was happening in Britain.[84] Procopius, writing in the sixth century, said that some British emigrated to Gaul.[85] There, by 500BC, as British colonials have done ever since, they: 'established a little Britain beyond the sea, with a Cornwall and a Dumnonia of its own (Cornouaille and Dumnonée), and a distinct and still enduring identity and language'.[86] It is possible that Breton customary laws were not unlike those of some clans in Britain. Later Breton written laws may therefore have included provisions similar to some Celtic counterparts in Britain.[87] But all this is speculative at best.

KIN OR KING?

With no evidence at all to tell us the content of the customary law of any of the British communities, Celtic or not, can nothing at all be known? Perhaps something can be deduced by analogy from scraps of knowledge

---

80. Roebuck 'Customary Law before the Conquest'. This is discussed in Chapter 2 above and in HP Glenn *Legal Traditions of the World* Chapter 3.
81. SL Guterman *From Personal to Territorial Law*.
82. Rutilius Namatianus *De Reditu Suo* 1. We know there had been connections for more than 2,500 years, as shown by the buried dagger in Chapter 2.
83. Thompson 'Zosimus on the End of Roman Britain' p165; Giot *British Settlement of Britanny* pp61, 105.
84. Faulkner *Decline and Fall of Roman Britain* p257.
85. Procopius *History* 8.20 and 6.10.
86. Campbell, John and Wormald *Anglo-Saxons* p22.
87. Soazick Kerneis 'L'Ancienne Loi des Bretons d'Armorique' and 'The Ancient Law of the Armorican Bretons' in Giot *British Settlement of Britanny* pp115–18, discussed below in Chapter 5.

of somewhat similar German kinship groups on the Continent, in the same way that a better understanding of the edicts, or dooms, of the earliest Anglo-Saxon kings can be won from a comparison with the contemporary edicts of Germans there.

All the members of a clan or kin (the terms used here generally for a kinship group whose members believe they are related by blood), from their first conscious moments, start to feel a special relationship with other clan members, almost as strong and all-pervasive as those they feel with their parents and siblings. Outsiders may characterise those feelings as rights and duties, as elements of a legal system even, but they are not like that. My experience is of modern clans, in Papua New Guinea, where clan ties predominate, and to some extent in Hong Kong and China, where they cannot be ignored with impunity. Clan members know what truth is, just like anyone else, but the obligation they feel to tell it is much stronger when they are speaking to a member of their clan than to an outsider. Wallace-Hadrill has done much to reveal the nature of kinship in Francia. He writes: 'Every German felt this. He had the sense of being himself within a kin-structure; for his kin embraced the living and the dead; outside it was no honour, no luck, no peace, no life.'[88] I am sure he did not intend to restrict that to males. I would add: not only the living and the dead but all those yet to be born. Within a family, disputes can be settled or contained by the mediation and arbitration of a father or mother; within a clan by a chief, if it has one, or by a number of clan members, often elders. All members of a clan believe they know their customary law, though they may be unhappy how chiefs or elders declare and interpret it in their own interest.

Between individuals from different clans, or between clans themselves, however, there must be another acceptable process. That is the feud. Those who have concentrated their attention on Europe in the early Middle Ages may be forgiven for thinking that there is something especially Teutonic about the feud but experience elsewhere shows that it is widespread in space and time, if not an integral element of the world of the clan. Certainly it was equally a part of the lives of Germans on both sides of the Channel. What can be said of the Germans in Francia can be assumed generally to apply in England, though care must be taken to spot the differences:[89]

> We note the development from the private feud-settlements of the Germans to public and royal arbitration and intervention, even if we do not always see the corollary, that the legal processes of the *Volksrechte*[90] succeeded just because they derived from feud-processes and closely followed them.

88. JM Wallace-Hadrill *Early Germanic Kingship in England and on the Continent* p14.
89. JM Wallace-Hadrill 'The Bloodfeud of the Franks' in *The Long-Haired Kings*, on which much of what follows is based.
90. This is the term which German scholars have used in this context to describe the early written laws of western Europe, for example the *Lex Salica* of the Franks.

It is easy to misunderstand the feud if it is thought of first as a private war. It may come to that, just as a dispute between modern businesses may end in litigation. Not one in a hundred does. The feud is a formal process recognised by law, the law of the parties in dispute. If they share the same customary law, its substance and procedure prevails; if not, as is likely if the dispute is between members of different clans, some means must be found to deal with the conflict of laws. The purpose of the feud is settlement, to find a solution acceptable to both sides. The threat of violence is basic and taken for granted, as is the convention that a transfer of value may buy it off. That value is assessable by customary law. It must be enough for the injured party to accept it honourably as a substitute for retaliation but not more than it would be honourable for the offending party to pay. Someone other than the parties must say what amount is right according to customary law and in the circumstances. The wronged kin's blood is cooler than that of wronged individuals, unless they are dead. The kin will include wiser, more dispassionate heads, less interested in every sense, or at least with more of an interest in a settlement than bloody vengeance.[91]

The amount depends not just on the severity of the wrong but also on the status of the wronged and sometimes the wrongdoer. You cannot buy off the customary duty to retaliate for an injury to the mighty as cheaply as you can an injury to a slave. Honour is at stake and its value varies with status. The wrong may be so great that no payment will suffice, though that is rare. What is finally offered may not be accepted, at least at first, which is not uncommon. But only then does violence follow. How the amount is assessed and how payment enforced are directly relevant to the history of arbitration; as Wallace-Hadrill saw: 'The world, private and official, stood ready to arbitrate'.[92]

By the fifth century, the ties of kinship had slackened. Migration creates new communities. The *Lex Salica*[93] already provided a method by which individuals could choose and change their kinship group. Movement from one to another, new or long-established, must have been common for it to have legislation provided to deal with it. Moreover some societies were bound together not by ties of blood but loyalty to the same lord. Christians considered themselves members of a distinct community and bound by their own laws and procedures. The Frankish Church encouraged arbitration and composition, though within the system of the feud:[94] 'Without the sanction of blood, composition would have stood a poor chance in a world lacking

---

91. A present-day example of mediation in the feud is elegantly and movingly presented by Sarah Rainsford 'The Turkish Peacemaker'.
92. Wallace-Hadrill 'Bloodfeud' p125; PR Hyams *Rancor*; Richard Fletcher *Bloodfeud* pp9–10.
93. 46 and 60, of cAD500.
94. Wallace-Hadrill 'Bloodfeud' pp126, 129; he gives many examples of feuds and of arbitration to resolve them, pp126–45, but none from England.

not simply a police-force but the requisite concept of public order.' Feud
was not outside the law, just the opposite. It was the procedure provided
by customary law. Kings could usually offer no alternative and did not see
it as their job to do so. When they did they acted as arbitrators, and only
sometimes were prepared to enforce their awards, rather than leaving it to
the feud to handle enforcement.

The king's role in the feud was therefore not primary. A king may at first
have been the representative of the kin, as the Anglo-Saxon word *cyning*
suggests. But the German and later the Anglo-Saxon kings were from the
start what we now call warlords, leaders of warrior bands. Of course they
would hope that their descendants would succeed them. That seems to
be a natural phenomenon even today, not only for the Kims and Assads
but also the Gandhis and Bushes. They needed to be able to control their
peoples – there were usually more than one kinship group – not only by
force when they were physically present themselves or by deputy but by
their authority without force. By a system of laws they could provide for
exceptional challenges to their 'peace'. At the end of the fifth century,
the kings of the Burgundians and the Visigoths had established laws for
their Gallo-Roman subjects. At the beginning of the sixth, Clovis, king
of the Franks, laid down the *Lex Salica* not for the Gallo-Romans in his
kingdom, whose customary law was some remnants of the Roman, but
for his various Frankish groups. To be bound by the *Lex Salica* was to
be Clovis's Frankish subject. It included some rules brought from the
German homeland and others created for the Frankish kingdom. Before
it was written its contents had been in force in their oral form. Now it
became law because Clovis said so. He made it, only he could change it,
and he interpreted it when he enforced it as judge or arbitrator. It applied
throughout his realm over all kinds of kin: 'he has collected his Frankish
followings into a people that accepts the law that he says is their own'.[95] It
is theirs now because he says so – a revolutionary idea for those traditionally bound by customary law. And it is his law, too, which his sons and
grandsons promulgate again, as part of their heritage. By AD592 when
Gregory of Tours wrote his history, the distinction between Roman and
Frank had gone and all were subjects of a Frankish king in Francia, the
kingdom of the Franks.

The first laws the kings made, whether in Francia or England, were
attempts to refine the practice of the feud. They included the technical
improvement of a list of payments or tariffs of payments, fixing what was
to be paid and accepted to buy off retaliation. The amounts were what was
considered appropriate, both for the wrong and the status of the victim.[96]

95. Wallace-Hadrill *The Long-Haired Kings* p181 and *Laws of the Salian Franks*.
96. Pollock and Maitland *History of English Law* I pp7–8.

There was nothing to stop the parties agreeing different amounts in settlement. In England they, and the feuds to which they brought order, continued for generations after the Norman Conquest.

THE LAW OF THE CHURCH

Many of those who emigrated from England were Christians who fled as pagans took control. Some of those left behind were also Christian and probably considered themselves, within the church community, to be governed by church law and required to submit their disputes with one another to the bishop. The Church must have been quite well established in some parts of England when the Romans left, because the emperor Constantine had summoned British bishops a century before, in AD 314, to a council in Arles to sort out problems of the Church in Africa.[97] Even in the fifth century the Pope thought it worthwhile to send Germanus to put a stop to the Pelagian heresy. At the end of the sixth, Augustine found he had to deal not only with the paganism of the Anglo-Saxons but the shrewd, sophisticated and suspicious questions (no doubt put to him in Latin) of the representatives of the British church.[98]

Christianity was more likely to be adopted first by the upper classes in the more civilised south than by their peasants or anyone in the tribal areas. But, after the Romans left, the British tribal chiefs, in consolidating and enlarging their power, converted to Christianity as they began to see themselves as kings.

Patrick describes one distinctive element of Christian Roman Gallic custom, in a letter to someone he calls Coroticus, contrasting its qualities with the brutality with which Coroticus had treated fellow Christians baptised by Patrick:[99]

> **4.10** The custom of the Gallo-Roman Christians: they send appropriate holy men to the Franks and the other peoples with so many thousands of *solidi* for the ransom of baptized captives. But you would rather kill them or sell them to a foreign people ignorant of God.

Wherever and whenever and to the extent that it could do so, the Church has exercised worldly authority. Church law has always said, as Jewish law does, that disputes between the faithful should be settled with love if possible not law, but if necessary by procedures provided by the Church. The Church was part of the administrative establishment when the Romans left and there is no evidence to show any sudden collapse in its authority

---

97. Pollock and Maitland *History of English Law* I p4.
98. Bede *Ecclesiastical History* 1.25.Though Augustine expresses them as 'doubts which have occurred to him', their nature reveals that some of them arose from the different practices of the British church, e.g. in relation to consanguinity.
99. Patrick *Letter* 14: *Consuetudo Romanorum Gallorum Christianorum.*

over Christians.[100] It may have co-operated with the larger landowners and those who continued to try to exercise authority inherited from the Romans. There is a suggestion that it may have given its blessing to the continuance of Roman forms of tax gathering and been a means of providing tax avoidance schemes: you could perhaps avoid tax by taking holy orders, as St Patrick's deacon father and priest grandfather did, or by turning your landholding into a religious endowment. So far as it could it no doubt exercised jurisdiction or, put another way, offered its processes to those with disputes. Of course, its power was curtailed for a while when pagans ruled.

If the bishops in England played similar roles to their brothers' in Francia, some of them must have taken seriously the biblical encouragement, 'blessed are the peacemakers', and tried to bring disputing Christians to a settlement. Gregory of Tours writing at the time gives many examples[101] and 'is at pains to emphasize the habitual role of the Church, especially the bishops, in arbitration and making peace'.[102] That does not mean that the Church opposed the feud; on the contrary it relied on the feud to enforce its awards and threatened God's vengeance when necessary to protect His kin.[103]

What seems clear, even in this obscurity, is that property disputes between clergy, and between cleric and lay, were at this time, as for long afterwards, heard in the assemblies of hundred and shire, rather than in church courts. The councils of Orléans and Auxerres in the later sixth century, which required clergy to submit all their disputes to their bishops, did not prevail in England.[104]

CONCLUSIONS

Has sufficient thread been found to weave a patch in the story of the development of dispute resolution? The material is customary law and there are

100. EG Stanley 'The Administration of Law in Anglo-Saxon England' describes the Church's influence.
101. Edward James '*Beati Pacifici*', in John Bossy *Disputes and Settlements* pp25–46, gives examples from Gregory of Tours, writing in the sixth century. The Germanic East Goths were in power in Italy when Justinian's *Corpus Juris* was completed in Constantinople (AD534); Dionysius Exiguus created his *Collectio Dionysiana*, the foundation of the first *Corpus Iuris Canonici*, in Rome in troubled times cAD500, Pollock and Maitland *History of English Law* I p9.
102. Ian Wood 'Disputes in Late Fifth- and Sixth-Century Gaul' in Davies and Fouracre pp7–22; there is little evidence in England of the *episcopalis audientia*, bishop's hearing, though it was formal and well established elsewhere and has produced a considerable literature: JN Bakhuizen van der Brink, *Episcopalis Audientia*, Vratislav Busek, 'Episcopalis Audientia, eine Friedens- und Schiedsgerichtbarkeit', Paul Caspers, 'Der Gute- und Schiedsgedanke', Gino Masi, *L'Udienza Vescovile*, Giulio Vismara *Episcopalis Audientia* and *La Giuridizione Civile dei Vescovi (Secoli I–IX)*, and in Anne Lefèbvre-Teillard 'L'Arbitrage en Droit Canonique'.
103. Wallace-Hadrill *Long-Haired Kings* pp126–7.
104. This was simply a matter of status, *ratione personae*, in the Roman church, enforced by the state, e.g. the edict of Clothar II AD614; Lefèbvre-Teillard 'L'Arbitrage en Droit Canonique' p7, fn3.

four or five strands of different colour: Romano-British, Celtic vernacular, Anglo-Saxon, ecclesiastical (for the Church had its own unwritten law as well) and possibly Germanic. We know that the Roman administration respected and perhaps took advantage of the customary laws of its people in the provinces. No doubt there were idiosyncratic governors and magistrates, but it suited them all to encourage those of the governed who had disputes, if they were not citizens subject to Roman law, to settle them among themselves. They would choose to interfere only if a dispute caused trouble, as it could if an award were not performed. So we may infer that the Roman governments, while no doubt unwilling to enforce the mere agreements of barbarians, would see that the adjudications of customary bodies were enforced. We have the story of Pontius Pilate enforcing a decision of a customary court, the Sanhedrin.

Once the imperial administration had collapsed, the resolution of disputes and enforcement of settlements and other solutions were dealt with according to the customary laws of the different communities. By the end of the sixth century they were the Anglo-Saxon kingdoms, the surviving British chiefdoms and the Church. Within a century, most but by no means all of the British kingdoms had fallen under the rule of one or other of the Anglo-Saxon overlordships.

There is nothing to show that the earliest Anglo-Saxon authorities were concerned with disputes between the British or that they respected their customary law. In a dispute between an Anglo-Saxon and a Briton, the Anglo-Saxons presumably imposed their own customary law, if any legal solution was possible. But once the edicts of Anglo-Saxon kings were reduced to writing they show that, though they drew many distinctions and recognised many different categories of person, they were directed not just at those of recent German stock but at everyone within their jurisdiction, including the Germanic British, and those called Welsh, who were dealt with separately and expressly. That power did not extend over the whole of England. The Anglo-Saxons made much more of an impression, and much earlier, in the south and east than they did in the north and west. In many parts the ancient patterns of land allotment continued and elements of ancient rituals show that the old beliefs survived.

The next chapter will try to answer the question: 'Is it fanciful to see, in the pacts and edicts of this time, a growing disposition to settle differences by arbitration and by royal initiative?'[105] The sources relied on there to answer that question and to throw light on dispute resolution more generally will provide the clues with which this chapter's few threads must be joined if there is any continuity to be shown.

---

105. Wallace-Hadrill *Long-Haired Kings* p202.

5 AETHELBERHT

It was not that *the* organic order of custom was replaced by *the* artificial rule of law, it was not a case of one system supplanting another. The new law was not merely confronted by custom but by a conglomerate of overlapping heterogeneous elements: some concerned with standards of social behaviour, others with moral ideals; some concerned with dispute settlement, others with the breach of norms; some with compensation, some with revenge, some with punishment, some with guilt, some with purification or placation; some concerned with gods, spirits or ancestors, others with mankind, society, the group, individuals, relatives, strangers, objects, powers or symbols.

The wand which was to turn this soft iridescent mess into a rigid black and white system was the idea of law enforcement, the kingpin of the legal order, the idea which set the stage and created the belief that in the end all pieces of the puzzle would fall into place...

This is how the alliance between the new law and the state came about; it is the authority of the state which anchors the hot-air balloon of the new law to the ground, and it is the shadow of the law floating above it which gives the state the cool air of legitimacy.

Peter G Sack 'The Cult of the Eight-Foot Yam' pp325–6.[1]

I have a special dread of those theorists who are trying to fill up the dark ages of medieval history with laws collected from the barbarian tribes that have been observed in modern days... If I see a set of trucks standing on a railway line from week to week, I do not say, This is the main up line to London. I say, This must be a siding. The traveller who has studied the uncorrupted savage can often tell the historian of medieval Europe what to look for, never what to find.

FW Maitland 'The Body Politic' *Collected Papers* III p300.

INTRODUCTION

Earlier chapters have discussed the systems of customary dispute resolution in prehistory, in Roman Britain and later, though there was not much hard evidence of mediations or arbitrations to discuss. Roman law either ignored or accommodated whatever customary law there was. Roman law was not modified by the custom it took for granted; nor did it try to change it. After the Romans left, there was nothing but the various customary laws

---

1. My understanding of customary law has come not only from Dr Sack's extraordinary insights but from our common experience in the different legal world of Papua New Guinea. Everything that follows is indebted to the manifold ideas and arguments of Patrick Wormald.

(including, for the Romano-British, what was remembered of Roman law) to provide the framework for the resolution of disputes.

If a society has a hierarchy, in which status determines legal rights and duties, it is likely that disputes between those of lower status will be determined by or with the help of those one or two steps up. Disputes between slaves of the same master will be settled by him, or sometimes her, as a father or mother settles disputes between members of the same family. As the timeless Anglo-Saxon proverb has it:[2]

5.1 Good man shall make dooms in his home.

Dooms here means both rules and judgments. Only when the dispute escapes from these accepted or imposed processes will there be need for outside intervention. If the dispute is between parties who have the same customary law, of family, clan or kin, that law will apply. If not, they must either agree to accept the customary law of one of them, or submit to some third party. If the dispute is between two high-status parties, who do not accept any other mutual superior, they may be able to persuade the ruler to intervene, to mediate and arbitrate their dispute, perhaps with the help of a sweetener. A system of royal intervention in dispute resolution may be regularly provided, which becomes more refined and replicable as the state is established. Some higher body of rules is needed and that may appear as legislation by the ruler, at first oral and recorded later in writing when that technology becomes available. The dooms are potential judgments, sometimes based on actual ones. Wherever there is evidence, that seems to be what happened in the Anglo-Saxon kingdoms.

The king's rules, though superior, were no more than a particular interference in (or perhaps a new expression and later a confirmation of) the general and all-embracing customary law or laws of his people and there is no evidence that any Anglo-Saxon king ever intended them to be. Each king's successor needed in practice (and there was no theory) to republish them. At least that is how it was presented then, though Alfred seems to have made it a subterfuge to disguise royal intervention into customary law.

The first law-making was no doubt oral in the form of royal adjudications in specific cases, in which the king declared the law on which he or some delegated body would make or had made a decision on the facts. The British kings may have declared their decisions publicly and intended them to have an effect wider than just between the parties but they have left no evidence. The Anglo-Saxons called those statements *demas*, or *domas*, judgments, which translators have given their own word: dooms. These were statements of whatever law was necessary to decide an actual case.

2. '*Til sceal on eðle dōmes wyrcean*'. Does *til* equal *bonus homo*? From 'Gnomic Verses' lines 20–1 in Dorothy Whitelock *Sweet's Anglo-Saxon Reader* p175.

But the statement of law might be expressed (or could be taken) more widely, as a principle.[3] These judgments would be kept in the memory for future use by those who knew about them. Later, they were written down by those who wanted them kept. The successful party would want a record. Anyone who wanted those dooms to have a wider reach than the original parties would make use of writing to establish and publish them, if they had access to that technology. That might be the king, using clerics as clerks when they became available, for the use of those he deputed to mediate and arbitrate and judge on his behalf. The clergy, too, had an interest in establishing their new privileges which the dooms proclaimed. This first English legislation, of Aethelberht king of the Kentish people, was intended for use by those who applied the law, not those who were expected to abide by it. Few could read. There was no ready access to the written law. It was a matter of governmental indifference whether those who were ruled knew of its existence before their dispute fell to be settled. They were assumed to know right from wrong according to the customary law, later from Christian teaching, and the sources reveal no sign of ignorance of the law being offered as a defence or even in mitigation.

In seeking evidence of mediation and arbitration in England at the beginning of the seventh century, two things can be assumed and must be kept in mind: all disputes which were not settled informally were dealt with publicly by some system of mediation and arbitration provided by the community; and the law which applied was customary law, until it was supplemented by royal dooms.

LAWSPEAKERS

In societies which do not rely on writing, all members of a clan or kin are assumed to know the law to which they are subject but often there are those, either elders generally or someone given the task specifically, who can be called on, when a dispute is heard, to tell the tribunal (and incidentally the parties) what the law is. Gildas, **4.8**, criticised the unsatisfactory 'tyrants' who did not seek the correct rule to apply. There must have been some repository, oral or written, to which they ought to have resorted. Is Gildas referring here to Roman law? If so, it could possibly have existed in writing but that is hardly likely. What else could he have meant? If he was referring to whatever British customary law applied to the parties, where would a good king find it? Gildas's tyrants were British, not Anglo-Saxon.[4]

'Lawspeakers' are known to have functioned in many German customary groups on the Continent and continued in Iceland until modern

3. AWB Simpson 'Laws of Ethelbert' pp3–17; this is, of course, what made up the *Codes* of Theodosius and Justinian and the laws of the kings in western Europe who succeeded the Romans; it is also how the Common Law has always worked.
4. Robin Stacey's *Road to Judgement* offers interesting comparisons from Wales and Ireland.

times.[5] There is not much to suggest that there were men – and it seems to have been an exclusively male job – with such a regular function in the German societies of Anglo-Saxon England but there is a little. In *The Gifts of Men*, an Anglo-Saxon poem of unknown date which lists the various talents which God distributes, there is mention of such 'lawspeakers' in England:[6]

> **5.2** One in a meeting, prudent of mind,
> Calls up from his memory the rules of the people,
> Where wise ones are gathered, crowded together.

That is the man who is called on to declare the customary law, *folcriht*, the 'right of the people'. Thirty lines later in the poem, separated by men of many different talents, comes another lawspeaker:[7]

> **5.3** One knows dooms, *demas*, where the retainers
> Work out their counsel.

That is the man whose memory can be called on for the dooms, which included the king's own declarations of law, in an assembly where the king's men are meeting to work out what advice they should give or what decision to make.[8]

Though no one knows when that poem was composed nor even when it was included in the tenth-century collection now known as the *Exeter Book*, such experts must have belonged to an early stage of the development of Anglo-Saxon kingdoms in England.[9] The first kind is relied on to remember and state the customary law and predates the second, expert in the legislation, presumably before the dooms were written down and easier to get at for anyone who could read. They are not together in the list. Their roles were different. No other source provides further evidence but there is none to gainsay it. There is evidence of other remembrancers, of

---

5. MT Clanchy 'Remembering the Past and the Good Old Law'. When Iceland was settled from Norway, by cAD930, the story goes that Ulfljot was sent from Iceland to Norway for three years to learn the customary law and returned as the first lawspeaker, *lögsögumaðr*, in the annual assembly, the *alðing*, Johannes Brøndsted *The Vikings* p84.
6. GP Krapp and E van Kirk Dobbie eds *The Exeter Book* p138 lines 40–3; Lisi Oliver *The Beginnings of English Law* p35.
7. Krapp and Dobbie *Exeter Book* p139 lines 72–3.
8. The word 'doom' means 'decision' in general and, in this context, would include any decision, whether of the king or not, which the assembly considered relevant and helpful.
9. This may help, therefore, to fix the time when the poem was first composed. It must have been before it was common to have ready access to written dooms yet the man called on for the customary law is still known to the poet. Does this show that it comes from no later than the end of the seventh century? There is perhaps a distant echo of this ancient procedure when Bishop Aethelric was summoned to give evidence of old customary law in *Lanfranc v Odo* (1072) in (1990) 106 *Selden Society* 8, see Chapter 10 below and JH Baker *Introduction to English Legal History* p6.

genealogies, needed perhaps not only to protect property and succession rights but also to fix kin responsibilities in feuds. The decision-makers were not judges. They were arbitrators, sitting for that dispute, sometimes chosen by the parties but more often provided by customary law or appointed by the king, and occasionally the king did the job himself.[10] The lawspeakers declared the rules for the decision-makers to apply. Once the law had been revealed, the parties had a chance to settle their dispute before a decision was pronounced which applied it to the facts.

ASSEMBLIES

The British who still lived in communal groups resolved their disputes in their customary assemblies. The Christian clergy do not seem to have been involved in secular assemblies until the missionaries from Rome arrived in Kent; nor is there evidence of bishops regularly hearing disputes in civil matters in the Celtic church where it existed in the British chiefdoms which had not been taken over by Anglo-Saxons.[11] There was little room among them, or indeed among the Anglo-Saxons, for any other kind of arbitration, private, ad hoc, arranged by the parties according to their own unreplicable rules and procedures, without the involvement of the group in an assembly. If there were any such arbitrations, perhaps among merchants or similar to the arbitration by *bonus homo* of the Romans, we know nothing of them.[12] All our sources are about public arbitration, which became the regular process of dispute resolution of the new Anglo-Saxon kingdoms. It is not possible for us to make a distinction between royal justice and this public arbitration, nor did the Anglo-Saxons, at least at first, as far as we know. They thought of their assemblies as meetings where it was appropriate for men, and sometimes women, of high status to discuss a dispute and resolve it either by their decision or by referring it to the king or his delegate or to an arbitrator agreed by the parties. As far as we can tell, their first thought was to produce a settlement which would restore the community to harmony. The decision was put to the assembly, the whole *folc*, for approval.

10. JM Wallace-Hadrill *Early Germanic Kingship* p43 on Aethelberht's laws: 'though it is not stated, we can suppose that royal agents were already being used, as on the continent, to act as arbitrators'.

11. There is a large literature on the *episcopalis audientia*, the bishop's audience, in Continental Europe at the time, e.g. Edward James '*Beati Pacifici*: Bishops and the Law in Sixth-Century Gaul'; Giulio Vismara *La Giurisdizione Civile dei Vescovi*; Derek Roebuck 'Sources for the History of Arbitration' pp251–2. A mediation of Archbishop Theodore is discussed in the next chapter.

12. Perhaps the *til* in fn2 above, but though Anglo-Saxon phrases appear, some in examples quoted later, they refer to thegns who took part in the assembly, public not ad hoc arbitrators.

The assembly met at a place determined by immemorial tradition, still made use of for many more purposes than dispute resolution, as perhaps many had been for centuries, for weddings and funerals and feasts and trade.[13]

Writing between 840 and 864, the biographer of Leofwine, an English missionary to the Continental Germans of a century before, described the ancient Saxon legal system:[14]

> **5.4** The ancient Saxons had no king, but counts, *satrapas*, appointed by their community (*pagus*); and it was by custom that, once every year, they held a general council in the middle of Saxony, by the River Wisura at a place called Marklo. There all the counts used to gather together, with twelve nobles elected from each community and the same number of free men and of *lati*.[15] There they confirmed the laws anew, decided the outstanding matters, and whatever each year there was to be done, either in war or in peace, they decreed by common consent.

This picture of a folk-moot attended by the great and other representatives may be accurate for the Germans on the Continent. It would be unwise to rely on it or on the analogy of the Frankish *mallum publicum* illustrated in the case of the runaway slave, below at **5.7**. While they may throw some light on the practice and procedure in Kent, there are obvious differences. In Kent the basic unit of decision-making was the assembly, *gemot*, of the hundred.[16] All free men were expected to attend. That was their right and their duty. They would not have far to travel, within walking distance. They may also have had the right to attend the *gemot* of the shire but it could not have been the duty of all. Apart from the difficulties of getting there if you had no riding horse, few ordinary people would have had a view much wider than first their extended family and then their wider kin and the immediate neighbourhood. These assemblies had a long history, perhaps from before the Romans, though there are no written sources and the archaeological evidence is not always clear.[17] Certainly there seems to have been no bar to those of British ancestry attending and making claims, as late as the time of Cnut, **9.36**.

There must be a recognised system of enforcement, without which litigation and arbitration, indeed settlement of any kind is useless. In

---

13. Wendy Davies 'Local Participation' p48; 'such places are suggested as microcosms', Sarah Semple 'Locations of Assembly' p150. A burial ground was often adjacent even in medieval times.
14. A Hofmeister ed *Vita Sancti Lebvini Antiqua* p793.
15. A *latus* is always said to be a person with a status intermediate between a free man and a serf. I believe the term originally applied, like the Anglo-Saxon *læt*, to an incomer, one not of the clan but a freeborn permanent resident.
16. It is possible that the English hundred was itself an import from Francia, discussed later in this chapter.
17. Discussed above in Chapter 2, 'Assemblies and Dispute Resolution'.

seventh-century England there was no handy means of enforcing a simple contract, such as an agreement to arbitrate and stand by the award of the appointed arbitrators. There is plenty of indirect evidence of customary assemblies where settlements were secured and imposed by the will of the group. It will be discussed in more detail in the next chapter. The king would not ordinarily play any part in enforcement, though he might if it could be shown that he had an interest, either his personal advantage or the preservation of order. His intervention was necessary when the parties were from different kin groups with different customary laws. Then there was nobody common to both to declare the law for them. There were at that time no courts with professional judges or lawyers in England nor were there any to come for some centuries.

LANGUAGE

It is not at all clear what languages were in use in England in this period. Many people must still have spoken different Celtic dialects. The Anglo-Saxon incomers spoke their own tongue. There were those who spoke Latin, and for some of them it may have been their mother tongue. The problems are discussed in Appendix A, though there are few unchallenged solutions. Latin was at first the only literary language. Some could write Anglo-Saxon in runes, but all that remains is in the form of inscriptions, coins and fragments, with just a few scraps of literature.[18]

In AD597 Pope Gregory sent Augustine with a team of clergy to Aethelberht.[19] Within a few years they had produced a collection of dooms, which are of great linguistic interest, because they are almost the first body of Anglo-Saxon prose. Their language reveals much about how they were used. There are, for instance, formulas which show that they were intended to be remembered. That may show that they were not created by Aethelberht's team but copied down from oral tradition. Many of those who needed to know them, those who had to apply them in the management of disputes, would not have been able to read them.

The first mention of Aethelberht's laws is by Bede, **5.7**, writing cAD731. There is no reason to doubt his assertion that Aethelberht had them written down but he does not tell us when. The first and only manuscript we have is the *Textus Roffensis*, a miscellaneous twelfth century collection, which also contains the laws of Hlothere and Eadric and of Wihtred.[20] A manuscript written more than five hundred years later is unlikely to represent accurately the words as they were first written. The first problem

18. Susan Kelly 'Anglo-Saxon Lay Society' p37.
19. DR Howlett *The Celtic Latin Tradition of Biblical Style*: AS Gratwick '*Latinitas Britannica*'.
20. PH Sawyer *Textus Roffensis* provides a facsimile. Ine's laws survive as attachments to mss of Alfred's. Aethelberht is not named in the text and the attribution of these dooms to him starts with Bede, Patrick Wormald '*Inter Cetera Bona*' p192.

is that they started off as the earliest surviving written Anglo-Saxon, as far as we know.[21] It would therefore be the best evidence we have of the language at that time, if what we have is what was written. But we know it is not:[22] 'the dialectal origin of a share of Old English texts has been established and now for many works it is also possible to follow the steps of the re-writing in West Saxon'. So, though there are traces of the Kentish dialect in the laws, they had been largely rewritten over the centuries.[23] And we must remember that Bede himself said that Aethelberht's laws were written in *sermone Anglorum*, which could mean 'the speech of the Angles' (as opposed to the Kentish) rather than that of the Anglo-Saxons generally, though Bede does use Angli comprehensively elsewhere.

After a careful analysis of the text, Lendinara's conclusion is that:[24]

> All these features show that the laws were used somehow, or at least circulated, for more than four centuries, being copied repeatedly and probably undergoing several changes, perhaps not only as far as their content was concerned, but also as regards their language.

If their content was changed, we cannot be sure what it was that Aethelberht decreed.

SOURCES

Like every other scholar who approaches these texts, I have gone first to the great three-volume edition of the doyen of Anglo-Saxon editors Felix Liebermann, *Die Gesetze der Angelsachsen*.[25] It was published at the beginning of the twentieth century and, despite its pre-eminence, it must be used with some caution. As Richard Dammery has written:[26]

> There are three fundamental flaws in Liebermann's treatment of the manuscript sources: the first is his handling of the textual transmission; the second is his naming and classification of the law-codes; and the third is his division of the texts into chapters. These problems necessarily affect the utility of his edition, for the manuscripts form a cornerstone upon which any analysis of the laws themselves must be constructed.

I have used Liebermann's text and divisions because others commonly use them, and shown when I have differed. The complexities of his presentation

---

21. Caedmon's hymn found in mss of Bede is probably somewhat later.
22. There is a clear statement of the problems, followed by a lively discussion, in Patrizia Lendinara 'The Kentish Laws' in Hines *Anglo-Saxons* pp211–43, citing Elmar Seebold 'Was ist Jutisch? Was ist Kentisch' and 'Kentish and Old English Texts from Kent'.
23. JR Schwyter *Old English Legal Language* and 'Syntax and Style in the Anglo-Saxon Law Codes'; Dorothy Bethurum 'Stylistic Features of the Old English Laws'; Lisi Oliver 'The Language of the Early English Laws' and *Beginnings of English Law*, particularly pp120–3; MP Richards 'The Manuscript Contexts'.
24. Lendinara 'Kentish Laws' pp218–19.
25. A reprint by Law Book Exchange was promised for December 2007.
26. Richard Dammery 'Editing the Anglo-Saxon Laws' p257.

are formidable. Even Maitland found the layout: 'like the full score of an opera... and the natural man sighs for the simplicity of a pianoforte arrangement'.[27] Liebermann's arrangement has influenced scholarship ever since. His education prized orderliness. He draws on manuscripts from mid-tenth to the seventeenth century, from collections in which the laws are mixed up with other material of historical interest to those for whom they were compiled.[28] Many of the laws bear the names of kings, so it was natural for Liebermann to extract them and put them in the chronological order of their reigns. That process has obscured contemporary realities. Whoever used them and whatever their purposes, when they were first written they represented current law, with the more recent grafted on to the still applicable old. Alfred's laws contradicted Ine's in places but they continued to be copied together. There were no express repeals, as far as we know, and, in a version of the laws of Alfred and Ine simply known as the doombook, they survived the Conquest.[29]

THE PEOPLE OF KENT

The dooms of Aethelberht are the first and almost the only evidence that has survived of Anglo-Saxon state intervention in law-making before the last years of the seventh century. They can be explained only if the prevailing customary laws are understood. The fact that those laws are plural is the key. The first law was created to deal with their plurality.

Tribes did not have kings, still less did clans. At that time, only a people had a king or queen. A people can seem to us and to its members, if they ever thought about it at all, like a 'natural inherited community of tradition, custom, law and descent',[30] but in reality it was not exclusive. Non-kin could join by invitation or long residence (or rather cohabitation) and regularly did so through marriage, as they joined clan and kin. Kings were rulers of peoples not places and only when they became nations did they lose their formal generic self-definitions. One man might be king of peoples with different customary laws. Aethelberht was king of one kingdom and overlord of another. There was a place called Kent and at least one kingdom there before the Romans came. When they left, the first German immigrants took over a Romano-British *civitas*, with its centre in Canterbury, probably some time in the fifth century.[31] That became the eastern part of an Anglo-Saxon kingdom which also came to include a west Kent kingdom, the former *civitas* with its capital Rochester.[32] At the start of the fifth century all the British in the *civitates* may well have been subject to Roman law. Outside

27. FW Maitland 'Laws of the Anglo-Saxons' p152.
28. Wormald *Making* pp244–53, particularly figures 8 and 9, analyses the text.
29. MP Richards 'The Manuscript Context of the Old English Laws'.
30. Susan Reynolds in Edward James *Origins of the Barbarian Kingdoms* p41.
31. DP Kirby *The Earliest English Kings* p15.
32. Patrick Wormald 'Bede, the *Bretwaldas* and the Origins of the *Gens Anglorum*'.

the *civitates* they no doubt were subject to a body of customary law which varied at least in detail from one community to another.[33]

It is possible but unlikely that the people of the new Anglo-Saxon kingdoms, if they ever considered the matter, believed that they all lived under the same customary law but, even if the customary laws of all the Anglo-Saxons were identical, they could not have been the same as that of the native British and in particular the Romano-British. As there must have been more than one customary law, though the peoples governed by them were intermingled and may rarely have noticed it, anyone who had the task of resolving disputes needed guidance, particularly where there was a conflict of laws because the parties claimed to be subject to different laws and could not agree which should govern their dispute.

Only the highest authority could be relied on to answer these questions and that was the king. In Kent Aethelberht, king of east Kent, was 'overking'. The king of west Kent accepted his overlordship.[34] Two letters dated AD601, from Pope Gregory to 'Aethelberht, king of the Angles' (in Latin, of course) and to his wife Bertha, daughter of the Frankish king of Paris,[35] are the first clear evidence of foreign recognition of an English king. For what it is worth, Bede certainly had no doubts. He would have given him more:[36]

5.5 [Aethelberht] was the third of the kings of the English peoples of all the southern provinces, which are separated from the northern ones by the River Humber and the contiguous boundaries.

FRANKISH INFLUENCES

Where did the Germans come from who took over Kent? What legal traditions might have influenced Aethelberht? It was long thought that Kent was colonised by Jutes but:[37]

33. Kent's idiosyncratic customary laws survived into modern times: gavelkind inheritance (all sons equally rather than primogeniture); no escheat for felony ('father to the bough, son to the plough'); hue and cry to recover land from a widow who married again and bore a child; and the presumption that all Kentish men were born free, see WS Holdsworth *History of English Law* III pp260–1; Paul Brand 'Local Custom' pp155–9.

34. DN Dumville 'The Terminology of Overkingship in Early Anglo-Saxon England' in Hines *Anglo-Saxons* and the following discussion pp345–73.

35. P Ewald and LM Hartmann *Monumenta Germaniae Historiae: Epistolae* II xi 35 and 37; Lewis Thorpe tr *Gregory of Tours: The History of the Franks* p219, IV 26: 'King Charibert's daughter married a man from Kent'.

36. Bede *Ecclesiastical History* 2.5.

37. Hills *Origins* p104, citing Pernille Sørensen's DPhil thesis 'A Reassessment of the Jutish Nature of Kent', which makes a detailed study of the archaeological evidence and draws these conclusions: '"migration streams" are the most likely scenario for fifth century Kent, where the initial immigrants play an important role for the area of destination of the subsequent migration. The process of migration provides an opportunity to renegotiate the social order, and for the initial immigrants to take advantage of the "Founders' Effect" by establishing themselves as apex families... richly furnished burials may therefore be seen as the graves of an aspiring elite in the establishment phase.' Conspicuous consumption and display are not unknown among colonials in modern times.

... more recent excavations in Jutland do not confirm this comparison... 'there is no evidence of large-scale Jutlandic immigration to Kent' but that an elite which did believe its origins to lie in that region perpetuated the dynastic tradition... Much of the distinctive jewellery worn by women in sixth- and seventh-century Kent is Frankish in character, not Scandinavian. Proximity and possibly close political ties including dynastic links explain this, not migration.

How close were those 'political ties'? Were they close enough for the practices of the Franks to have influenced their English cousins? We have seen that there were no great language problems: 'less difficulty probably than a Londoner today experiences in grasping Lowland Scots'.[38] Frankish coins circulated in Kent. There was plenty of trade. London under Aethelberht was: 'a marketplace for many peoples coming by land and sea' according to Bede.[39]

Bede provides a clue, apparently unambiguous though scholars cannot agree what it means:[40]

5.6 So King Aethelberht died on 24 February [AD616]... Among the rest of the good things he bestowed on his people, caring for them, he also established for them, with the counsel of wise men, decisions of judgments close to [or following] examples of the Romans, *decreta iudiciorum iuxta exempla Romanorum*. These were written in the speech of the Angles and to this day they are kept and observed by them [his people].

It is just possible that *iudiciorum* should go with *Romanorum*, rather than with *decreta*, so that the translation would read: 'decrees, following the examples of Roman judgments'. That would make better sense than the apparently tautological 'decrees of judgments'. I believe the meaning to be that Aethelberht established laws by having judgments he had made written

38. HG Richardson and GO Sayles *Law and Legislation* p157, from Appendix I, 'Kent under Aethelberht'.
39. Bede *Ecclesiastical History* 2.3.
40. Bede *Ecclesiastical History* 2.5. A translation can determine how questions asked of the text are answered. Patrick Wormald '*Exempla Romanorum*' 15 gives: 'a *code* of laws after the Roman *manner*'. There is no word in the Latin which represents a code (in any sense), no word for laws, and *exempla* means 'examples', not manner. Nor can I accept his argument (p18): 'it is *prima facie* plausible that laws set out in a neatly logical sequence will be codifying what already exists (so in this case orally preserved material), whereas those with no detectable system in their arrangement should be laws responding to random contingencies, and so in this context laws more likely to have been made in writing'. The opposite is more likely: the oral customary law that 'already exists' is in no scheme other than mnemonic and was only ever voiced in response to 'random contingencies'. I have attempted the experiment of trying to remember a section of the laws of Aethelberht and compared the results with my attempt to remember the same amount of a modern statute. Aethelberht's win – they go with more of a swing – but others with better memories should try for themselves. David Daube had the insight in his linguistic study of *Forms of Roman Legislation* p6: 'This change reflects an evolution from what we might call folk-law to a legal system.' Wormald's linguistic analyses are fascinating and will be considered again in relation to the later laws.

down, as was the practice from Theodosius and Justinian to Clovis. They would be based on legal principles either arising from particular judgments or extrapolated for more general application. It has been suggested that the Romans were Clovis, King of the Franks and the other successors to Roman rule who had created written laws, and that Aethelred's laws could be said to be *iuxta exempla Romanorum* because they followed their model to some extent in content. But they did not.[41] There are similarities of structure; the subject matter and its division are much the same. But the careful analysis of Wormald's comparative tables convinces me no more than his arguments that there was anything other than a common heritage. Borrowing was easy and natural but not exact.

When Charles the Bald, king of the Western Franks dAD877, imposed compulsory work on fortifications, he said it was 'according to the ancient custom of other nations', *iuxta antiquam et aliarum gentium consuetudinem*.[42] That most English of institutions, the hundred, may have been influenced, at least in name, by its Frankish forerunner, in Latin *centena*. As Bishop Stubbs insisted:[43] 'the parallels between Frank and English law must not be pressed without allowing for the similarity of the circumstances which prompted them and the common stock of common custom and principle which underlay them'. No doubt the king's Frankish scribes followed Frankish practices; it is not so easy to be certain of Frankish influences on the king and his advisers who voiced what the scribes wrote down.[44]

It has also been suggested that 'according to the examples of the Romans' means no more than that the scribes copied the Roman practice of writing laws down. That is possible, though they were written in a form of Anglo-Saxon, whereas all the continental examples were in Latin.[45] Perhaps it is

---

41. *Pace* Wallace-Hadrill *Early Germanic Kingship* p38; Giorgio Ausenda, however, shows a definite similarity between the laws of Aethelberht (which he dates AD601–04) and the *later* Lombard laws of Rothari (AD643), Hines *Anglo-Saxons* p235. Bruce O'Brien, in his generous criticisms of the ms of this chapter, writes: 'Patrick Wormald's view derives from a consideration of continental early medieval legislation – esp. that of the Lombards – and from the fact that none of the continental Germanic codes was written down in isolation from written Roman codes – and so was always formed in a Roman image, if not necessarily in content.' I do not suggest that the last word has been said on this controversy, whose importance makes us all try perhaps too hard to resolve it.

42. James Campbell *Essays in Anglo-Saxon History* p161.

43. William Stubbs *The Constitutional History of England* I pp223–7, 224. When Alfred required a general oath to the king of all males above the age of twelve, he may have known of the same earlier Frankish law, James Campbell *Essays* p162.

44. Wormald *Making* p97 and table 2.3. Just how different the dispute resolution methods were in England from the Continent then is incidentally revealed by PJ Geary 'Extra-Judicial Means of Conflict Resolution' and the sources he cites.

45. Isidore in the seventh century said of the Goths in the fifth: 'Under this king [Euric 466–83] the Goths began to have the institutes of laws in writing. For before that they were bound only by customs and customary law (*moribus et consuetudine*).' Isidore *Historia Gothorum* 35 quoted by Wallace-Hadrill *Long-Haired Kings* p40; Guido Donini and B Ford *Isidore of Seville's History* p18.

unwise to look for precision in expression where none existed in the mind of Bede. We do not know how good his knowledge was of the *exempla*. The point he was making was that Aethelberht became a good king when he was converted. That is good evidence at least that Bede thought the dooms came later. We have no direct evidence of what form the dooms were in when Bede saw them, if indeed he ever did, though he notes the first clause protecting the interests of the Church and generally sought records and information where he could, including Canterbury.[46]

There were many groups of Germans in western Europe in the sixth century. The Burgundians and Visigoths had written laws – two sets, one for themselves, the guests as they were dubbed, and one for their subject hosts, the Gallo-Romans. There is nothing in them which throws light directly on what later happened in England. But in the laws of the Franks, who had lived alongside the Romans on the Rhine for centuries and by that time had defeated both the Burgundians and the Visigoths, Clovis their king (cAD482–511) laid down rules for all his peoples, whatever kin they belonged to.[47] Though they contain nothing that can be shown to be connected in any way with Aethelberht's laws, the *Pactus Legis Salicae* of about AD508–11 includes a provision which has been said to establish the closeness of the Franks with the Anglo-Saxons across the Channel, presumably the *Angli* in Kent. This is a good example of an edict which is so complicated and specific that it must surely have started life as the decision of an actual case:[48]

> **5.7** If any slave of another person has been kidnapped and that slave has been taken across the sea and been found there by his master, and [the master] has named in a public court (*in mallo publico*) him by whom the slave has been kidnapped in his native land, [the master] shall bring together three witnesses to the same (*ibidem*). Then, when that slave has been summoned back [or perhaps 'recovered', *revocatus*] from across the sea, he shall name him [the kidnapper] yet again before a second court and there three appropriate witnesses shall be brought together at the same time; in the same way it shall be done before yet a third court, so that nine witnesses swear that they heard that very slave give the same evidence against the kidnapper before three courts. And so afterwards he who kidnapped him shall be adjudged guilty in the folkmoot (*mallobergo*) and liable to an indemnity on top of the compensation and damages 1,400 denarii (which make 35 solidi). If the slave's confession is admitted against up to three

---

46. Someone with greater skills, particularly in the quantitative analysis of Latin texts of Bede's time, may be able to produce evidence from a close study of Bede's syntax which would support or destroy my arguments for his meaning here.
47. Ian Wood 'Roman Law in the Barbarian Kingdoms' p14: 'All the successor states were influenced by Roman lawyers and borrowed from Roman law.'
48. KA Eckhardt *Pactus Legis Salicae* 39.2; Katherine Fischer Drew *The Laws of the Salian Franks* p101; TJ Rivers *Laws of the Salian Franks*. AC Murray *Germanic Kinship* pp133–50 is generally enlightening.

kidnappers, he [the master] shall name, but in the same suit, the names and addresses always against each of them equally.

'Across the sea' could only mean one thing for someone in Francia then. There was no sea other than the Channel and no country across it other than England. So it seems that it was worthwhile for the Franks to legislate to provide a means for a master to get back a slave who had been taken out of their jurisdiction to a part of England whose authorities would assist the master, which could only have been Kent then. The master first had to find where the slave was. Then he had to make a claim before a *mallum publicum*.[49] It has been argued that this was in England, not necessarily a court or 'folkmoot' or other gathering of the Frankish type but whatever analogous traditional meeting had jurisdiction in Kent. But the text does not say that directly. It says that the master must name the kidnapper, *plagiator*, with three witnesses to hear the slave's story. The second and third courts are clearly in Francia. What evidence is there to support the contention that the first is 'across the sea'? Because that is where the slave is. Now it is obvious that neither the kidnapper nor a person who had bought or was protecting the slave would have been willing to return to face a court in Francia. Somehow they and the slave have to be got back to appear in the Francian courts. That could be accomplished by force, by the self-help of the master. But that is hardly something that would give rise to this legislation, which is only relevant and only conceivable if it relates to the English authorities extraditing the accused and the slave, the essential witness. That required some kind of 'court' in Kent to hear the slave's evidence. At least this is evidence that the legislator in Francia believed that such an assembly existed then in Kent, which the Francian authorities could call on to assist them. This legislation presupposes that there were such close ties between the two kingdoms that cooperation could be relied on. Presumably it had been in the actual case which gave rise to this part of the *Pactus Legis Salicae*.

With some kind of order from the assembly in Kent the master could return with the slave to Francia and make a claim against the kidnapper. There the slave had to tell the story again with three witnesses. This edict states what the kidnapper must pay if found liable on the claim. The parties then had a chance to settle. If they did not, then at a third hearing with the slave and three witnesses again, the Frankish court would make a decision ordering the return of the slave and awarding payments according to the law, both a fixed sum and what is clearly compensation, an amount calculated to recompense the master for the slave's lost services. All this a century before the laws of Aethelberht.

---

49. *Mallum* (neuter) is sometimes found as *mallus* (masculine) in the same sense but usually, as here, it is impossible to tell the gender.

There is no other evidence of such cooperation between the judicial systems of different nations at that time or for centuries to come. Of course absence of evidence is not evidence of absence; but such sophisticated collaboration would be incredible if it were not for the other hints that the German *Angli* in Kent were close to the German *Franci* in Francia.[50] Procopius tells of a Frankish embassy to the emperor in Constantinople cAD553, half a century before Aethelberht's laws, in which certain *Angli* were included to show that the Frankish king claimed some kind of overlordship of them;[51] and Aethelberht married the Frankish king's daughter, Bertha, great-great-granddaughter of Clovis; and Pope Gregory's letter dated July AD596 to the Frankish kings Theuderic and Theudebert speaks of some *Angli* as 'your subjects'.[52] And Hlothhere, king of the Kentish, shares his name with Clothar, the contemporary king of the Franks. Of course, 'it is wiser and safer to allow the coincidences to speak for themselves; and to avoid a positive theory that the first independent investigator may find means of demolishing'.[53] Safer, certainly, but wiser? Stubbs himself put a limit to caution: 'No amount of analogy between two systems can by itself prove the actual derivation of the one from the other.'[54] But there are plenty of other scraps of evidence and Stubbs is not afraid to build on them, for example on insisting that the later English law was not influenced by the British:[55] 'The Cantred of Howel Dha may answer to the hundred of Edgar, but the hundred of Edgar is distinctly the hundred of the Franks, the Alemannians, and the Bavarians.'

THE DOOMS OF AETHELBERHT

It is not surprising that Aethelberht was called on to speak, not yet to lay down principles but to give guidance which would apply to the disputes of all his subjects where uniformity was preferable. Perhaps he wanted to encourage an existing trend:[56]

> Kentish culture was a cross between Frankish and northern cultures, with perhaps some mingling of a British strain in its remoter ancestry; but it was a new type,

50. Ian Wood 'The End of Roman Britain' in Lapidge and Dumville *Gildas* pp23–4.
51. Procopius *Wars* 8.20.10.
52. Quoted in Wallace-Hadrill *Early Germanic Kingship* p25, who believes that Aethelberht's laws were influenced by Continental models and like them were 'to have his people's customs written down and attributed to him' pp33–6. He asks the right question: 'Can we determine what they were for?' but his answer is unconvincing (despite finding favour with Wormald '*Lex Scripta*' pp2–3): 'that fraction of custom that seemed enough to satisfy royal pride in legislation. This was their immediate practical use.' Wormald, *Inter Cetera* p181, asks the same question: 'just what they were *for*'. His footnote there is a rich source of recent scholarship.
53. Stubbs *Constitutional History* I p226.
54. Stubbs *Constitutional History* I p227.
55. Stubbs *Constitutional History* I p68.
56. RH Hodgkin *A History of the Anglo-Saxons* I pp98 and 101.

a native growth... made like the 'English', and so many other hybrid nations, out of different elements.

It has been suggested that Aethelberht wished to show he was overlord of all Kent and proclaimed his laws to bolster his position or satisfy his pride but that is unconvincing. There were few to get the message and more direct ways to dissuade anyone who might challenge him. Moreover, to proclaim laws which were not enforced would hardly enhance a king's reputation. It has also been assumed that his dooms offered a gentler system than the old feud, exacting money payment rather than blood, and that this shows a Christian influence. Such pleasant thoughts are quickly dispelled not only by the evidence of the Church's practical adoption of the feud, at that time with enthusiasm, but also by the cruelty with which it treated its opponents in this world and its promises of even nastier suffering in the next. Perhaps there is a simple answer: there were many kinds of dispute which could be left alone but not those which were new and for which no customary law existed, for example those which arose from recent conversion to Christianity and the presence of powerful clergy. An even simpler one may be that Aethelberht issued many other decrees orally, which were never written down and of which we can know nothing. Perhaps the ones which were written down and have survived are just the ones which the masters of the clerical scribes chose to preserve.[57]

When Aethelberht adjudicated in a dispute, he first had to find the right rule of law. Gildas could rely on his audience's support when he objected that a tyrant failed to do so, **4.8**. The king must then apply it to the facts or give that task to someone else. When the king spoke, his decree laid down the law not only for that matter. He would not intentionally be inconsistent. He could not handle all disputes himself. His delegates, customary or appointed by him, would want to be consistent, too, and he would expect them to be. Disputants themselves could reasonably expect replicability. When Augustine converted him to Christianity, Aethelberht found himself with literate administrators, including the interpreters who could speak the language of the Franks and probably write it. They could please the king by writing in his own language, which could not have been so different, which we now call Anglo-Saxon. It may have been quite a novelty for him to see such writing for the first time. We do not know whether he was himself literate. If he was, it was in Latin. He would not have been able to read what the scribes wrote for him in Anglo-Saxon. They gave priority to their own privileges, setting them high. Then they and anyone else who had to apply them could refer to them and have them read out in their own tongue, the language of the ruling class, though few at first could have read it.

57. The earliest surviving reference to Aethelberht's laws is Bede *Ecclesiastical History* 5.2. We cannot be sure that he is referring to what we now have in the twelfth-century ms. He tells us nothing of their content.

Historians have called these collections codes but that is misleading. In modern English a legal code is a systematic collection of laws arranged in order. *Codex* does not mean that in Latin.[58] There is no such Anglo-Saxon concept.[59] No Anglo-Saxon king attempted any such task. They are heterogeneous collections of edicts.[60] Indeed there is no convincing evidence that Aethelberht promulgated his dooms as a collection at all, let alone intended them to be systematic. We have no direct evidence of the form in which they were first written, though the form of the text as it has survived is some evidence of its original form and the archaic Kentish dialect forms are evidence of a Kentish origin. In their present state the laws are a series of lists, each with its own internal logic of a sort.[61] At the back of Aethelberht's mind and those of his advisers, there must have been the notion:[62]

> Contradictions that in an oral culture are quietly erased or elided through the natural processes by which social memory is constructed and reconstructed over time cannot be as easily overlooked once they take written form.

58. It originally, as *caudex*, means a tree trunk, then a block of wood, which came to include one divided into tablets lined with wax on which one could write; the meaning 'law book' first appears in England in AD1291, RE Latham *Revised Medieval Latin Word-List*.
59. By this I mean there is no contemporary term, no periphrasis, no attempt to describe such a concept, which is itself modern and invented for use here by historians, who not infrequently have fallen into the trap of anachronism which they have set for themselves.
60. This disposes of the difficulty Wormald had with all the collections, 'What does it signify that the remit of legislation remained so limited?', *Making* p28 and: 'Throughout northern Europe, the issues selected for legislative record sometimes seem to have been dictated by arbitrary obsession rather than rational choice', '*Lex Scripta*' p12. That is how it must always seem when the needs of the parties dictate what is dealt with by the lawmaker. Even today it is hard for a non-lawyer to understand why it may take a generation before the House of Lords has a chance to correct a mistake of the Court of Appeal. Wormald seemed surprised that, in an exhaustive survey of 'judicial decisions... there is not a single direct reference to, still less a quotation from, the extant texts', *Making* p21. No one at the time would have been. They had no idea of the modern functions of legislation. Moreover, charters rarely deal with the same subject matter as lists of *gylde*. Nor did decision-makers have to distinguish between matters of fact and law. Wormald *First Code* is his last word on this. Bruce O'Brien chides me: 'I think this does not represent Patrick's views fairly. The reason he notes this discrepancy is the obvious one – why produce written laws if no one cites them as authoritative? And there are examples of such citation on the continent during the period – esp. among the Visigoths, their successors in the north, and in Italy. Furthermore, if written laws mattered, they could have appeared in any number of descriptions of suits, cases, trials, whatever, that come from many genres of evidence from the Anglo-Saxon period. Cf. Wormald's articles on lawsuits and on dispute settlement. Wormald only raises the "difficulty" in order to resolve it, which is the main task of *Making*.'
61. Wormald *Inter Cetera* pp184–5 table 7A is a neatly divided list under the heads: '1 compensation of church property in grades; 2–12 compensation of king's property and dependants; 13–14 compensation of *eorl*; 15–25 compensation of *ceorl*; 26 compensation of *læt*; 27–32 enclosures; 33–72 injury list [which runs from hair to toenails]; 73–84 women; 85–8 *esne*; 89–90 slave.
62. Thomas Charles-Edwards *After Rome* p250.

The language of the dooms is simple. It had to be. Even after they were written down, they still had to be kept in the memories of most of those who needed to use them. It was probably as different from the way people spoke at that time – the real Anglo-Saxon language – as a recipe is today from the conversation at the dinner which follows its use.

Many decision-makers would not have been able to read in Latin, let alone the newly created Anglo-Saxon script, and all would be used to memorising whatever rules they needed. Simple in expression they are but their meaning is neither obvious nor uncontroversial. To avoid incorporating assumptions which would affect the argument, excerpts are given here in a translation which retains their ambiguities. They start with a group of provisions, probably a later written addition to the oral canon, inserted perhaps when they were first written down. Indeed, they could have been included at any time after Augustine but before Bede, who mentions them.[63] They apply to the Church and clergy, who appear nowhere else:[64]

5.8 God's property and the Church's 12 payment, *gylde*
    Bishop's property 11 payment
    Priest's property 9 payment
    Deacon's property 6 payment
    Cleric's property 3 payment
    Church's peace 2 payment
    Assembly's peace 2 payment

The word *gylde* simply means 'payment' or, better still, 'transfer of value' if payment connotes coin. It is usually translated 'compensation'. That is technically incorrect and this is not a legal or semantic quibble. It is important for the understanding of arbitration, mediation and settlement to get the meaning right. Compensation means payment of a sum (or transfer of other value) calculated according to the decision maker's assessment of the value of the injured party's loss – damages, as we would say. But the *gylde* was from a different tradition of customary law, based on feud. The fundamental premise of the feud was that, if an individual's person or property was harmed, it was up to him, or her, or their kin, to retaliate – to use self-help. Customary law provided some guidance about how that could be done, including what it was appropriate to accept to buy off the retaliation, which may be called 'retaliation payment', or better still in the Anglo-Saxon context 'reconciliation payment'.[65] That payment had to be enough to make it honourable for the recipient to accept it and forgo violence but not so much that it was beyond what a reasonable kin would

63. Richardson and Sayles *Law and Legislation* pp3–4.
64. *Aethelberht* 1; I cite first by the number of the collection (if there is more than one for that king), then by the name of the king and then the number of the doom.
65. I set out my arguments in *Ancient Greek Arbitration* pp61–4, discussing the arbitration on the Shield of Achilles in Homer's *Iliad*.

demand. If the king were involved in the process, and the award had his approval, then there could be no argument about whether it was honourable to accept it. And always the purpose and preference of any tribunal was to produce a settlement. Feud was real and necessary but was not intended to end in violence.[66]

That is not to suggest that the concept of compensation was unknown. It had existed in Roman law and a clear example is that of the payment for loss of the slave's services in **5.7**. But the *gylde* was not compensation. Moreover, there was nothing to stop the parties negotiating a different sum. That is quite common today: the parties use the award as a basis for further negotiation and the sum finally paid is determined according to other criteria, particularly the urge to do further business – now as then to restore harmony. The parties also know all kinds of things which for whatever reason they did not want to tell the tribunal.

'Payment' assumes that coin is used. At the time of Aethelberht, who did not mint his own but made do with Frankish money, it is more likely that it was used more for calculation than payment. Customary legal processes require great discrimination and expertise on the part of the assessors, especially where coin is not available, or not customarily acceptable for this purpose, as in the Highlands of Papua New Guinea. When I practised law there in the 1980s I saw pigs being attached to 400 stakes in a 20x20 grid, each an individual of different value, which the mediator-arbitrators had to assess before deciding whether a fight between two clans should continue. There had been a lack of coin in Britain since the Romans left. By Aethelberht's time shared money values may have reduced but could not have eliminated the difficulties of assessment when payment might still have to made, for example, in pigs.

The existing oral customary laws of all Aethelberht's peoples would have provided for reconciliation payments. What his collection of dooms was intended to do was not only to cope with differences between the customary laws of his different peoples and to extend them to new offences, particularly against new categories of victim, the churchmen; he was also astute to ensure that his own interests were properly protected. As king he could retaliate at any time in any way he liked for any wrong, real or imagined, though it might not be politic to do so too arbitrarily, too often. But, when his deputies had to adjudicate or assist in a settlement, or when an assembly or other arbitral body was faced with an injury to the king's interest, he was letting them know in some detail what payment to exact on his behalf. That might depend on the value of the servant or slave harmed, for example:[67]

---

66. Paul Hyams *Rancor and Reconciliation* is a full treatment of the feud in medieval England.
67. *Aethelberht* 10–11. I have deliberately and consistently translated *gebete* as 'is due' without more.

5.9 If a man lies with the king's maiden, 50 shillings is due; if she is a corn-grinding slave 25 shillings; if third [rank] 12 shillings....

In these cases the payments went to the king, of course, not the woman.

The amount would be multiplied according to the status of the injured party. The rules for the clergy have been discussed. It is interesting that for theft the multiple for the king is nine, that of a priest, and not so high as the bishop's eleven, and in later documents preserving dooms it is usual for the scribe to put the bishop before the king.[68]

The amount might also depend on the injury. There was a standard tariff:[69]

5.10 If a person kills a person, 100 shillings is due as the ordinary person yield.
5.11 If an eye be gouged out 50 shillings is due.

There is a long list of payments for physical injury: causing deafness in one ear 25 shillings; different amounts for damage to different teeth and different fingers, with a shilling for any fingernail. The most interesting provision, however, and the most mysterious, relates to a broken thigh:[70]

5.12 If a thigh be broken, 12 shillings is due.
If he becomes lame, then friends (*freond*) should (*motan*) arbitrate (*seman*).

Who are these friends and why are they brought in for this injury alone? It is easier to answer the first question. From the earliest times the third party asked to arbitrate was not someone who could be relied on to be objective because he was unconnected with either party and had no previous knowledge of the case, in modern jargon a 'neutral'. Just the opposite. There were no such people in a community where everyone knew everyone else, at least through their family. Ideal third parties were not those with nothing in their heads or hearts to start with. They were those who could be trusted to be equally well disposed to both sides not neither. In other words, friends of both. The more they knew of the parties, their kin and the subject-matter of a dispute, the better.[71] That they could be relied on to know the same shared customary law was taken for granted. *Freond* is plural, which means that a number of such positive people would be asked to make an assessment of the amount necessary in such a case to buy off retaliation appropriately, in such a way as to reconcile the parties and their kin. They would not, of course, perform the function of a modern judge, following the advice of the parties' medical experts in assessing the monetary equivalent of a broken femur. They would not distinguish questions of fact and law. Who today

68. *Aethelberht* 1. This must cast doubt on the interpolation dating from Aethelberht's own time.
69. *Aethelberht* 21 and 43.
70. *Aethelberht* 65, 65(1).
71. *Ancient Greek Arbitration* p349: *koinos*, the Greek equivalent, meant 'friend not of one side only but of both sides (perhaps equally)'. Oliver *Beginnings* p75 note e.

would be bold enough to say which is the more realistic and efficient method of resolving such disputes?

The meaning of *motan* extends from 'may' to 'must'. There would be no point in saying that arbitration was allowed to fix the payment: it always was. Then as now, there was nothing to stop the parties arbitrating liability for an injury. Nor was it then compulsory. The best translation therefore is 'should', in the sense 'the best course is'.

The second question, 'why just for lameness?', can be answered only if the origin of the doom is kept in mind. It started off as the king's statement of law to whoever was charged with resolving a particular dispute in which a person's thigh had been broken. When the dooms about broken limbs came to be written down, it was remembered that in one case the king had ordered a particular manner of assessment rather than leaving that to the parties or their kin. The reconciliation payment was to be assessed by 'friends'. That became the law. There was a victim, lame as the result of a wrong, and the amount of the reconciliation payment had to be determined. According to what principles? Those were not stated. Was the concept of compensation in mind? The idea may have been creeping into Anglo-Saxon consciousness. The 'friends' would have to decide such matters as whether the lameness was likely to be permanent or get gradually better. Would they also consider the victim's job? The disability should matter more for a fighter than a priest but the victim's status was only one of the criteria.

Just because this method of fixing the quantum of a claim was prescribed in this doom for a broken leg does not mean that it was not similarly available, or common, or even the regular practice, for any broken limb, all personal injuries, or an even wider range of wrongs. There is no evidence so we just do not know.

CONCLUSIONS

If we are to believe a manuscript created half a millennium later, supported by a statement in Bede,[72] who may never have seen the version which existed in his day or known much about its contents, the seventh century began with the first English legislation, a collection of dooms, statements of law with royal approval. They provide the best evidence we have of how disputes were resolved then. But it is important to keep their context in mind: they were declarations of, and sometimes additions to, the customary law which provided the comprehensive whole of the system of justice. Everyone of sound mind and past infancy, regardless of origin or kin or status, knows you should not steal. What they do not necessarily know is what their response should be if they are called on to deal with a dispute arising from theft, particularly if they are not familiar with the parties' own customary law or if the parties do not share the same law. The very

72. But note the arguments of Wormald *Making* pp93–103 and '*Inter Cetera Bona*'.

language of Aethelberht's laws shows clearly that they are meant for those who resolve problems rather than those who create them. The first part is just a list of payments, **5.8.** Thereafter they are not directed to the people. They do not say: 'Thou shalt not kill' or 'If you kill, you will be hanged' but 'if a person kills a person, a hundred shillings is due', **5.10.** The amount must vary with the status of the injured because it is more shameful for a noble family to accept a modest sum than it is for an ordinary person's, and it is that shame which will lead to violence unless bought off.

There is no trace of a code in these collections.[73] Most of the provisions are meant to reform the law only in the sense that they fixed the amounts to be paid to avoid self-help, once liability had been determined. It is clear from the sources that the tariffs were guidelines, as common law rules on damages still are. Those who decided disputes according to customary law aimed to provide a solution to fit the particular case, whatever was necessary to resolve it. The methods they chose were those of mediation and arbitration. Though the better educated people in England in the seventh century knew well enough what courts and judges and lawyers were, if only from the Bible certainly and from the classical Roman authors probably, those who ran the new Anglo-Saxon kingdoms seem to have seen no need to replace the established customary legal systems.

They had the chance. There were teachers in Canterbury from cAD670 who could well have included Roman law in their curriculum. St Theodore of Tarsus, archbishop of Canterbury, taught there with Hadrian, the abbot from North Africa. The only learned law was that from the Roman heritage. There is just one source which puts the matter beyond doubt.

Aldhelm, born cAD640, was a contemporary of Bede. He was educated first in Malmesbury, in Wiltshire, in an Irish-founded school, from where he went to study in Canterbury. While there, he was invited by the bishop of Winchester to spend Christmas with him at Malmesbury. This is part of his letter in reply, apologising in magniloquent Latin that the demands of his legal studies were too great:[74]

---

73. Citations of Frankish law in Frankish capitularies is of customary not written law, Hermann Nehlsen 'Aktualität' p463.

74. Aldhelm *Opera* 476: *legum Romanorum iura medullitus rimabitur et cuncta iurisconsultorum secreta imis praecordiis scrutabitur*; JW Adamson *The Illiterate Anglo-Saxon* pp1–2; Frank Stenton *Anglo-Saxon England* pp180–2. When I first read his overdone Latin, it reminded me of James Joyce's *Finnegans Wake*, as later I found it did Peter Hunter Blair *Anglo-Saxon England* p311, but now, having had to translate some, it is more like *Ulysses*. By a second coincidence it also struck Michael Lapidge as 'Joycean' in his entry for Aldhelm in the Oxford *DNB*. Also Michael Lapidge and Michael Herren tr *Aldhelm: The Prose Works*. MR James *Two Ancient English Scholars* pp13–14 suggests that Aldhelm must be referring to one Roman law book only, *Alaric's Breviary*, which Frank Stenton *Anglo-Saxon England* p181 said was still there in Canterbury, but that did not contain the opinions of jurisconsults in such a form as to substantiate the brilliant student Aldhelm's complaint of unravelling mysteries and prolonged memorising. There is no evidence that Canterbury had a copy of Justinian's *Digest*.

5.12 ... because they are not at all small spaces of time that must be stretched out in this study of the text. To be sure, someone like me whose keenness has been kindled for reading, in the marrow of my mind I'll remembrance the rules of the Roman laws and I'll cross-question all the arcana of case law from the law books' veriest vitals.

But there is no more trace of that learning in the dooms of the later kings of the Kentish people than there was in Aethelberht's collection. The Anglo-Saxon kings, and the Normans after them, were content to rely on the legal system as they found it, making only the changes they needed.

There may be just a glimpse of the administrative machinery available to early Anglo-Saxon kings in the earliest surviving manuscript source of the Anglo-Saxon language, a bilingual Latin and Anglo-Saxon glossary.[75] It has *commentariensis*, the Latin word for a recorder, the clerk of a law court, glossed with *giroefa*, more commonly *gerefa*, the word for reeve or more generally agent. That was written for use about AD675.

The independent creation of written law, apparently quite autonomous however much it may have been thought to have followed the 'examples of the Romans', is all the more surprising when set against the background of the life of the wealthy in Kent at that time, which not only had regular and extensive links with Francia, just across the Channel, but occasionally with Constantinople and even Africa:[76]

> It is curious to think that at the very time when Gregory was writing to the patriarch of Alexandria to tell him of the success of his mission, bronze vessels from Alexandria were being imported into Kent. Objects of ivory are not very rare... English missionaries going abroad sometimes just paid their fares and got on a ship.

Trade was brisk, with imports paid for especially by the export of slaves, as the old story of Gregory and the blond boys in Rome's slave market attests. Nothing has survived from this time, though, to tell us how the disputes were resolved which must have arisen from England's flourishing commercial life. We must wait for the eighth century to provide the first documents which contain evidence of arbitrations and mediations of any kind.[77]

75. JD Pheifer *Old English Glosses in the Épinal-Erfurt Glossary* p13, line 223.
76. Campbell, John and Wormald *The Anglo-Saxons* p64.
77. There may be faint traces of a lingering idea of England as still in some way part of the Roman Empire in Charlemagne's role in the negotiation of settlements of two disputes between kings of Northumbria and Mercia early in the ninth century, Deanna Forsman 'An Appeal to Rome'.

6 THE LATER KENTISH KINGS AND INE OF WESSEX

> Written laws and legal documents, being written for present use and not for the purpose of enlightening future historians, assume knowledge on the reader's part of an indefinite mass of received custom and practice. They are intelligible only when they are taken as part of a whole which they commonly give us little help to conceive. It may even happen that we do not know whether a particular document or class of documents represents the normal course of affairs, or was committed to writing for the very reason that the transaction was exceptional.
>
> Frederick Pollock 'Anglo-Saxon Law' 239[1]

> If, instead of pursuing the myth of reason triumphing over unreason, we accept what appears to be a perennial factor in observable human societies, namely, a sustaining tension between cognitive and affective processes, the rational and irrational elements in medieval judicial procedures, as in our own, can be treated as constituent parts of one system and explained in terms of their particular social context.
>
> Rebecca V Colman 'Reason and Unreason in Medieval Law' 572

INTRODUCTION

The last chapter concentrated on Kent and the dooms of Aethelberht. It may be that Kent was more settled earlier than other Anglo-Saxon kingdoms but the emphasis was determined by the sources. After Aethelberht there is just no evidence from elsewhere about the legal systems in general or dispute resolution in particular until the end of the seventh century. When Aethelberht died in 616 (or 618) there were many other kingdoms in Britain, large and small, Anglo-Saxon and British, distinguished primarily by their peoples rather than place. Their kings were kings of the Mercians or the Angles, rather than of Mercia or Anglia, but it is easier here to identify them by place. Starting from the north and moving south, and west to east, the Anglo-Saxon list would include the kingdoms of Bernicia, Deira, Elmet, Lindsey, Mercia, Middle Anglia, East Anglia, Maegonsaete, Hwicce, Essex, Wessex, Sussex and Kent. To the north and west of them were the British kingdoms: Gododdin, Rheged, Gwynedd, Powys, Dyfed and Dumnonia. Their boundaries fluctuated, alliances merged them and splits divided them. Many smaller chieftains bobbed up and down among them and some called themselves kings. There was frequent fighting between peoples and murderous struggles within royal families for power. Our

---

1. Reprinted in Chapter 2 of Pollock and Maitland *History of English Law* I p26.

sources are inadequate to produce a dependable still picture at any time of this changing scene.[2]

For most of the seventh century, too, all our sources come from Kent. (Only with the dooms of Ine, king of Wessex at the end of the century, can we begin to find out what was happening in other legal systems.) Aethelberht's son Eadbald succeeded and ruled until 640, when he was succeeded by his son, Eorcenberht, who ruled until 664. No evidence has survived of lawmaking under Eadbald and the only reference to Eorcenberht's laws is limited to the destruction of idols and enforcement of the Christian fast of Lent.[3] His son Egbert ruled until 673 and was succeeded by his brother Hlothhere,[4] who appears to have named Eadric, son of Egbert, as co-ruler, perhaps 'underking' of West Kent. Eadric rebelled and succeeded when Hlothhere was killed in 685 but lasted only till the next year. His brother Wihtred ruled to 725.

The same *Textus Roffensis* which preserved Aethelberht's dooms contains texts of the laws attributed to Hlothhere and Eadred jointly, as well as those of Wihtred. It may be that Hlothhere acted jointly with Eadred, or that Eadred added his own laws to Hlothhere's. As there is so little other evidence for the working of the law, these two sets of dooms provide the start for an enquiry into dispute resolution at the end of the seventh century. Ine's from the same period allow a comparison with laws and procedures outside Kent. But it must always be kept in mind that:[5]

> The legal collections are highly individual with respect to the particular selection of laws, the choice of non-historical accompanying materials, and the purposes for which they were made.

THE DOOMS OF HLOTHHERE AND EADRIC

If we could be sure that the words of our twelfth century manuscript accurately represented those used when the laws were first declared, the rubric with which they begin would be revealing:

> **6.1** These are the dooms which Hlothhere and Eadric, kings of the Kentish people, set. Hlothhere and Eadric, kings of the Kentish people, added to the laws which their ancestors had made before, by these dooms hereafter stated.

Those words, however, may have been put there by any of the scribes who copied the manuscript over the next four centuries and there is no evidence

---

2. DP Kirby *Earliest English Kings* is clear and helpful.
3. Bede *Ecclesiastical History* 3.8.
4. The name Hlothhere is the Anglo-Saxon equivalent of Clothar. Clothar, King of Francia, was Hlothhere's contemporary. Clothar's mother, the extraordinary Bathilde, came from East Anglia, see David Keys 'Erotic Ring Sheds Light on Slave Queen'.
5. MP Richards 'The Manuscript Contexts of the Old English Laws' p171.

to tell us when. Yet there is no reason to believe that they are untrue. The natural sense would be that the two kings added these, their own decrees, to the existing general laws – the plural may be significant – and we can accept them as such. They certainly read like addenda. The first four sections deal with killing, 5 and 7 with theft and 6 with care of a child on the father's death.[6] Sections 11–15 deal with various breaches of the peace. Section 16 provides for the purchase by a person from Kent of chattels in London. Presumably the greater opportunities for fraud in the city already required this special treatment.

Sections 8–10[7] are of most interest for the development of dispute resolution, including as they do procedural rules from which we can get the first direct glimpse of what went on in an assembly as disputes were mediated and arbitrated. Their meaning has been obscured by misreadings of the text. My arguments are set out in Appendix B. As I read the text it says:[8]

> **6.2** If a person makes a claim against another in a dispute and lays a claim against him in a moot, a medley, or a meeting, the one always gives surety to the other and does the right to him which the decision-makers of the Kentish people award.

These are laws of and for the Kentish people. They are to be applied in the assemblies where those people or their representatives make decisions. Anyone with any claim, so the doom seems to say, can bring it before a 'moot, medley or meeting'. Both claimant and defendant must give surety of some kind and each must perform what the decision-makers award. Any attempt to distinguish separate meanings for the three kinds of meeting is almost wholly speculative. If forced to make an attempt, bearing in mind that etymology is unlikely to show how they were used at that time, I would venture that *mot* may mean any kind of meeting, *medle* has a hint of violence (perhaps the feud has already begun), and *þing* may be a 'formal meeting to resolve a dispute' as the dictionaries suggest, that is a meeting called specially for that purpose rather than a general periodical assembly at which hearing disputes might be only one of its activities. It is quite possible that these near-synonyms came from different dialects and refer to the traditional gatherings of different kin-groups included in the kingdom of the Kentish people.[9]

The next sections deal with the procedure before the mediator-arbitrators.

6. Following the numbering of Felix Liebermann *Gesetze*, generally used elsewhere. Lisi Oliver *Beginnings* has different numbers.

7. Oliver's s6.

8. Liebermann *Gesetze: Hlothaere und Eadric* 8; Oliver *Beginnings: Hlothhere and Eadric* 6, p131 and commentary pp134–46.

9. Oliver *Beginnings* p140.

Because the Anglo-Saxon does not use pronouns in a way which distinguishes the parties clearly enough, I have put X after the claimant and Y after the defendant.[10]

6.3 If he Y then refuses [to provide] surety, twelve shillings payment, *agylde*, to the king, and the dispute shall be as open as it was before.

If one person X makes a claim against another Y, after Y has given X surety, let them look for a mediator-arbitrator, *sæmend*, within three nights unless X who makes the claim would rather it were longer. After the dispute has been arbitrated [or settled], *gesemed*, in seven nights the person [against whom the award has been made] shall do right to the other. Let that person make satisfaction either with chattels or with an oath, whichever he [presumably the loser] prefers.

If [the loser] refuses [the winner] that, 100 payment to [the winner] without an oath, within one night after the arbitration, *gesem*[?].

X, the person who believes he, or she, has a claim, may begin the process by attending the assembly, whether moot, medley or meeting, and stating a claim. Women can bring a claim in their own right, or defend it, **8.61, 8.63**, apparently in any assembly, though a thegn may speak for them, **9.35**. X must support the claim by giving surety, to show serious intent and to ensure that if Y wins, X will abide by the award, whatever the decision-makers decide. If the other party Y will not give similar surety, Y must make a payment to the king. If X wants to continue, he or she can bring the claim again, as if nothing had happened.

If, however, Y does give surety, then the matter can go forward. Together X and Y must find someone to mediate and arbitrate for them, the *sæmend*. It is clear that the parties choose their own arbitrator, and that there is just one. They have three days in which to do it, though X can allow longer. The range of meanings within the noun *sæmend* and the verb commonly spelt *seman* includes mediate, arbitrate and settle. They were all one in the minds of those concerned, though no doubt they could have distinguished the separate functions had they wished. The point is that they did not.

No doubt this procedure was well known and was not new. It was not the royal intention to create a new system of resolving disputes by arbitration. That system existed and was governed by customary law. Its purpose was simply to fix numbers, at least as a starting point for negotiation: the amount of surety, the period for performance, and the penalty for non-performance. The arbitrator would try to help the parties to a settlement and, if unsuccessful, would make a decision. The parties had seven days in which to comply with the award. It must not be assumed that there would be a winner and a loser. No doubt a clever *sæmend* would try to bring about a settlement which both sides could accept. A party against whom all or part of the award had been made could satisfy it either by transferring property forthwith or by

10. Liebermann *Gesetze*: *Hlothaere und Eadric* 8; Oliver *Beginnings*: *Hlothhere and Eadric* 6.1–3, p131.

an oath to comply. If he simply refused, he must pay 100 within one day. The unit of currency is not stated but is presumably Kentish shillings, a substantial sum, the same amount as the *wergeld*, the fixed reconciliation-payment, for an ordinary free man. Moreover, the sum of the sureties lodged by the parties would presumably be at the arbitrator's disposal.

There is more than enough evidence here to show a developed system of public dispute resolution. It is not possible to say how long it had operated but it is unlikely that this new law set up the scheme. It has all the marks of a well established customary procedure and could well predate the dooms of Aethelberht. This was the way the Anglo-Saxons knew of preventing the feud ending in violence. By the time of Hlothhere and Eadric the central authority, the king of the Kentish peoples, was prepared and presumably powerful enough to declare that he had an interest in how ordinary disputes were handled. No doubt feuds continued which kings could not prevent but there is clear evidence here of royal interference. Still the feud provides the structure of enforcement but the king has declared an interest in assisting the traditional arbitrators or, put another way, was bringing ordinary claims within his jurisdiction. There was still no distinction in legal theory between civil claims and criminal prosecutions and still no other courts.

THE DOOMS OF WIHTRED

Wihtred probably became undisputed king of all the Kentish peoples in 694 after some years of power struggles. His dooms probably date from the following year. The rubric and prologue with which they begin, no doubt added later, state:[11]

> **6.4** These are the dooms of Wihtred, king of the Kentish people… at Berghamstead… [perhaps 6 September 695[12]]… there was gathered a deliberative assembly of the fortunate.

The 'fortunate' are then listed, first Birhtwald, 'archbishop of Britain', then 'the aforesaid king', then 'Gybmund, bishop of Rochester', and every order of the church unanimously with the 'subject people'. It is the 'fortunate' – *eadigan*, what a lovely word for the privileged, clerical and lay – who:

> **6.5** devised these dooms with the consent of all and added them to the lawful customs of the Kentish people.

So it was clear to the writer of the prologue that this was a legislative assembly at which the 'fortunate' together devised the dooms but that it was the whole assembly that made them law by adding them to what was already the law: 'the lawful customs of the Kentish people'. The two kingdoms of east and west Kent, joined by Aethelberht and together again in the hands

---

11. Liebermann *Gesetze* p12; FL Attenborough *The Laws of the Earliest English Kings* p24.
12. Oliver *Beginnings* p165.

of his great-great-grandson Wihtred, had been two dioceses, represented by their bishops, of Canterbury 'archbishop of Britain' and Rochester.

The content of the dooms says nothing of dispute resolution. They are concerned in the main with religious matters, the first being to relieve the Church of all taxes.

THE DOOMS OF INE

Ine was king of Wessex and his dooms are the first to survive from outside Kent.[13] They were probably made just before Wihtred's.[14] They therefore provide the first opportunity for comparative analysis. The Kentish dooms show a legal system which resolved disputes at gatherings, sometimes called for that purpose but sometimes with a more general agenda of which arbitrating disputes was just one part. Though there is no direct evidence, it seems most likely that in Kent decisions were taken collectively in some way, with the king's representative, if one were present, presiding rather than deciding. The king was not usually involved directly. Ine's laws, however, show that in Wessex the ealdorman, the king's deputy, was given a more individual and decisive role, with the assembly still responsible for exercising any discretion as to payment or punishment, as was still the case in Alfred's day.[15]

Ine's prologue is not unlike Wihtred's:[16]

6.6 I, Ine, by God's gift king of the Wessex people, with the counsel and with the teaching of my father Cenred, of Hedde my bishop and of Eorcenwold my bishop, with all my ealdormen and the most senior counsellors of my people, and also with a great congregation of God's servants, have been making inquiry for the salvation of our souls and for the security of our kingdom, so that right law and right government should be established and secured throughout our people, so that no ealdorman or associate of ours shall henceforth depart from these dooms of ours... we command that the customary law, *folces aew*, and dooms, *domas*, of all the people be obeyed.

This is a programme of law reform. It makes it clear that, in Alfred's time at least, from which our sources originate, it was recognised that those whom the king asked to act as his deputies, whether as ealdorman or other agent, were expressly obliged to apply not only the customary law represented by the words *folces æw* but also the dooms, *domas*. The same distinction was drawn between them as has been observed throughout this and the last chapter: the underlying customary law and the specific dooms made in the form of legislation to supplement and become part of it. This

---

13. They survive only in mss of Alfred's laws, Patrick Wormald *Making of English Law* pp103–6.
14. Liebermann *Gesetze* p88; Attenborough *Laws* p34.
15. Alfred *Biblical Introduction* 21 discussed below, **7.1–6**.
16. Attenborough *Laws* p36.

prologue is expressly addressed to those who are in charge of the legal system, the ealdormen and other 'associates of ours'.

Ine 8 also makes it clear in what circumstances these procedural rules are necessary and apply:[17]

> **6.7** If anyone asks for justice before any shire official or other decision-maker, *dema*, and he cannot get it, and he [the defendant] will not give him security, thirty shillings payment and within seven nights do him the justice he deserves.

That places on the officials and those required to make decisions an obligation to do justice to whoever asks for it. It also fixes the penalty to be paid by a recalcitrant defendant.

Ine 9 makes the necessary complementary provision to stop self-help and compel all those who want justice to follow the procedures now established:

> **6.8** If anyone resorts to self-help, before asking for justice, he shall give back what he has taken, and recompense, *forgielde*, and thirty shillings payment, *gebete*.

There are other provisions that give more detail of the ways in which disputes were heard. One of them, Ine 62, which is so complicated and specific that it looks as if it arose from the decision of an actual case, introduces the ordeal. That was a process by which defendants who had sworn they were innocent could call on divine support for the validity of their oath. It was not surprising that claimants and the assembly should doubt the veracity of an exculpatory oath, which relieved the swearer of the penalty of death. But if God could be called on to vouch for it, by some magical intervention, then that was that.[18] Ine's ordeal is by hot water, which is called here 'the basin'. If the defendant is required to endure the ordeal because he has nothing with which to buy it off, another may stand surety by pledging goods to the required amount for him. The surety may then make the defendant submit himself into the surety's hands until he has paid back that amount. If however the defendant is accused again of a further wrong, and put to the ordeal, and the surety refuses to continue to stand surety for him, the surety loses the pledged goods.

The prospect of a scalded hand must have been an inducement to settle. There is little evidence of the use of the ordeal, except in what we would call criminal prosecutions, until much later in Norman times.[19]

The miscellaneous nature of this collection of dooms is shown by this detailed provision standing between one which could hardly be more general – church dues are payable according to where you reside at midwinter – and a mysterious interference with normal life and individual choice: 'If

---

17. Attenborough *Laws* p38.
18. JH Baker *An Introduction to English Legal History* p5; Derek Roebuck *Background* p23.
19. Chapter 10 below; Robert Bartlett *Trial by Fire and Water*.

a nobleman goes on a journey he should take his reeve with him and his smith and his children's nurse'. They follow two provisions which seem too trivial to justify the intervention of such an august assembly:

6.9 58. An ox's horn is worth ten pence.
6.10 59. A cow's horn is worth twopence.

Ine's laws are still recognisably dooms; as Wormald wrote: 'Though preserved as a single statement, his laws in fact look like a *series* of successive pronouncements, each responding to problems confronting him and his subjects.'[20]

There are a number of sections which provide separately for the British, which show that, though considered to require separate treatment and reckoned at half the value of an Anglo-Saxon, they were probably numerous in the kingdom and still not without importance. Ine's laws call a Briton a *wealh*, from which the English word Welsh[21] is derived. But it was never used then to denote just the Britons who lived in what centuries later would come to be called Wales – the separate kingdoms of Gwynedd, Powys and Dyfed. The term *wealh* still included the inhabitants of Gododdin and Rheged in the north and Dumnonia, what is now Devon and Cornwall, as well as those who lived among the Anglo-Saxons.

There were British landowners, some called *horswealh* – perhaps of higher rank because they were horse-riders in the service of the king. There were free and slaves. Not surprisingly, the amounts necessary to buy off their retaliation were not so high as those for Anglo-Saxons. They could not aspire to be so proud but they still had disputes which could cause trouble:[22]

> It could be equally likely that what Ine's Code represents was not an attempt to placate British interests as such, but rather to set a framework for settling disputes between Saxons and Britons who had kin and lords within Wessex capable of waging vendettas and disturbing the peace, making it essential for him to include them in the Code.

And it may well follow that 'the presence of a Welsh nobility within Wessex implies the existence of British-dominated districts within West-Saxon jurisdiction'.[23]

There is a hint of the state of trade in 25:

6.11 If a merchant trades up country among the people, he shall do so before witnesses.

20. In M Lapidge and others *Blackwell Encyclopedia* p279.
21. In VI *Aethelstan* 6.3 the adjective is *Wylisc*. Other Anglo-Saxon laws do not use the word, which in Latin remained *Britonus*.
22. Martin Grimmer 'Britons in Early Wessex' in Higham *Britons in Anglo-Saxon England* pp102–14, 107; with full and valuable footnotes.
23. Alex Woolf 'Apartheid and Economics' in Higham *Britons in Anglo-Saxon England* p128.

This presumably refers to trade outside the major centres, perhaps any trade which was not in a recognised market, the forerunner of what later became known as market overt.

Ine 52, it has been suggested,[24] deals with preventing an out-of-court settlement. But that is not what it says:

> **6.12** He who is accused of secret agreements (*geþingum* dative plural), shall clear himself by 120 hides of those agreements (*geþingea* genitive plural) or 120 shillings payment.

It is true that in Roman law, and perhaps in contemporary German law elsewhere, and indeed in much later English law, once parties had placed their dispute before the tribunal they could not settle it without the arbitrator's or court's consent for which they had to make a payment. Though the meaning of Ine 52 is by no means clear, there is just nothing in it to allow the introduction of such concepts from other systems or to anticipate the evidence for England. Clandestine contracts of any kind were viewed with suspicion until modern times. If you wanted to buy and sell, you should do so out in the open with witnesses.[25] How else could you prove ownership before there was paper in some conventional form, with the parties' signatures? The prohibition in Ine 52 is general; there is nothing to link it with settlements, which assemblies of all kinds did all they could to foster, as far as the sources reveal.

One thing is clear from Ine's laws. This king has a different approach from Aethelberht to the feud. While the feud is necessary still to underpin all law enforcement, it is not enough. Some infringements also carry a fine to the king, the *wite*. As Wormald says, with due caution:[26] 'If this is the innovation which extant evidence makes it seem, it is as good a marker as any of how Anglo-Saxon royal power grew in the course of the seventh century.' It may also exhibit a difference between the customary laws of the peoples of Kent and those of other Anglo-Saxon communities, Wessex for example.

ASSEMBLIES

There is evidence from another Anglo-Saxon kingdom that the regular procedures for resolving disputes were based on customary law applied in general assemblies. The most illuminating evidence comes from archaeological discoveries at Yeavering in what is now Scotland. Forty miles north of Hadrian's Wall, high in the Cheviots, Edwin, Anglian king of Bernicia, built a palace on what had been a gathering place since the Iron Age.[27]

24. Attenborough *Laws* p90.
25. If not, the contract would not be binding, as Plato provided, *Laws* 11, and Charondas before him in Sicily in the sixth century BC.
26. Wormald *Making* p105. The word *wite*, which is used often in Ine in different compounds, appears only once in Aethelberht.
27. Brian Hope Taylor *Yeavering*.

What appear to be the remains of a massive corral for cattle, with its own defences, lie close to a succession of great halls, built about the first half of the seventh century. Edwin's hall is likely to be the grandest of them, 80 feet by 40.

But the assemblies were not held there. As always they were in the open air, in a specially constructed meeting place, which in Edwin's time could accommodate 320 people. In front of its tiered seats stood a platform:[28]

> Even more remarkable is the 'grandstand'. Its only purpose can have been for meetings; and of a kind where one man on the platform, presumably the king, faced many. It gives a kind of reality to Bede's description of Edwin consulting his *amici, principes* and *consiliarii* (friends or relations, great men and counsellors) on the adoption of Christianity... That 'grandstand' is the oldest item in the constitutional archaeology of England.

No doubt Edwin did consult his nobles there. But the place was in use for assemblies of a more regular and ordinary kind for centuries before him and for long after.

No doubt Edwin, on the few occasions he visited Yeaverton, lived, dined and slept with his closest associates in the great hall, as the poet describes in *Beowulf*. But neither he nor any other king in Northumbria before or after him had 320 close associates. Nearer 300 than 200 places must have been for more ordinary people, even after conversion to Christianity added clergy to those attending. What was the platform for then? It was quite big enough for all the leading men, the thegns, to have sat there, listening to the evidence and argument, with one or more of them making suggestions for a compromise or other means of resolution which would be put to the whole assembly for formal ratification, after which it would become law, enforceable by the community.

THE CHURCH

The influence of the Christian church in Anglo-Saxon England begins at the start of the seventh century and grows much stronger in the next. Augustine and his missionaries or their successors ensured the privileges tacked on at the front of Aethelberht's dooms. There is not much to show how they worked in practice. Nor is there evidence that clerical influence was strong at first in the secular assemblies where they were represented. No doubt the higher clergy had control over disputes and wrongs which those assemblies dealt with if they were of a religious nature, such as breach of the sabbath or fornication. No records have survived from England.[29] As men of learning with the skills of literacy in Latin, and some perhaps in

---

28. Campbell, John and Wormald *Anglo-Saxons* pp56–7.
29. Rob Meens 'Sanctuary, Penance and Dispute Settlement under Charlemagne' is a rich source of contemporary Continental material.

Anglo-Saxon, they would have been listened to. Once adherence to Christian beliefs became widespread and more pervasive into private life and thought, no doubt fear of transgression added to the clergy's influence, backed as it was by religious sanctions such as excommunication and other avenues to the fires of hell.

There is no mention of penances in the laws of Aethelberht, Hlothhere and Eadric, or Ine. But Wihtred provides for excommunication in default of penance:[30]

> **6.13** Men who have unlawful sexual intercourse shall adopt a lawful life with penance for sins, otherwise they shall be separated from the fellowship of the Church.

He also gives privileges to the word of the clergy, making a bishop's unsworn testimony, like the king's, incontrovertible.[31] Priests could exculpate themselves merely by reciting in Latin: 'The truth I tell in Christ; I do not lie.'[32]

There is good evidence that the Church took the feud's system of enforcement so much for granted that it based its own system of sanctions upon it. Theodore of Tarsus, archbishop of Canterbury c668–90, wrote a *Penitential*, not long before Ine's dooms, which shows the Christian response to customary law's obligation to kill:[33]

> **6.14** If anyone kills a man in vengeance for a kinsman, let him do penance as a homicide, seven or ten years.

The penitentials show the Church's acceptance of the reality. Like the royal dooms, they were addressed to those who had to impose the penance, not to the wrongdoer. The uncertainty of 'seven or ten years' is more evidence that tariffs were only ever guidelines.

Penitentials were also like royal dooms in form, lists of tariffs which added religious sanctions to the secular reconciliation payments and punishments. But they did more. They supplemented the efficacy of the secular procedure by way of oath. Theodore's *Penitential* has detailed provisions for perjury, with the period of penance greater, three years, if the oath was sworn on the hand of a bishop, priest or deacon, or on a consecrated cross; less, only one year, if sworn on an unconsecrated cross or on the hand of a layman.[34] It would seem then that the clergy took part in some, perhaps most, though not in all legal proceedings. In Alfred's reign a distinction was drawn between the exculpatory oath of the defendant and the oath of a witness but there is no evidence for that in the seventh century.

---

30. Liebermann *Laws*: *Wihtred* 3.
31. Liebermann *Laws*: *Wihtred* 12.
32. Liebermann *Laws*: *Wihtred* 15; other privileges are granted by 17–19.
33. *Penitential of Archbishop Theodore* 3.3, TP Oakley *English Penitential Discipline* p169.
34. *Penitential of Archbishop Theodore* Book 1.

Although there are no surviving records of clergy acting as arbitrators in ordinary disputes, nor of the bishop's audience, *episcopalis audientia*, in England in the seventh century, there is a reference to the bishop's jurisdiction in Ine 13:

> **6.15** If anyone lies in giving witness or a pledge before a bishop, 120 shillings payment.

Archbishop Theodore himself relied on the legal system of the feud to facilitate a settlement.[35] Bede tells how he mediated between the warring kings of the Northumbrians and the Mercians in AD679:[36]

> **6.16** In the ninth year of the reign of Ecfrith a great battle was fought between him and Aethelred, king of the Mercians, close to the River Trent. King Ecfrith's brother Aelfwine was killed. He was a young man of about 18, much loved in both provinces because King Aethelred had married his sister, called Osthryth. There seemed to be potential for more bitter fighting and longer-lasting enmity between these fierce kings and peoples but Archbishop Theodore, beloved of God, trusting in God's help, by his salutary encouragement extinguished at its roots the great and dangerous fire that was breaking out. So much so that kings and peoples on both sides were pacified. No man's life was paid for the killing of the king's brother but only the wergeld that was owed in money to the king his avenger. His peace treaties lasted for a long time after that between those kings and their kingdoms.

Bede was born in AD672, so these events happened in his lifetime. Despite his propensity for exaggerating the works of the clergy, there is no reason to doubt the simple facts in this story. Theodore, who came from St Paul's birthplace, Tarsus in Cilicia, was not made archbishop of Canterbury until he was 65 years old but then spent the next twenty years knocking the English church into shape. He was an interfering old autocrat in ecclesiastical matters but it is not likely that he would have taken the risk of failure in acting as mediator between warring kings unless he had been invited to do so. His success depended on the existence of a traditional tariff, which even included the reconciliation-payment appropriate for causing the death of the brother of a king, killed by the soldiers of his sister's husband. The duty to avenge his brother fell on Ecfrith – 'the king his avenger (*ultor*)'. The skill Theodore showed was to persuade Ecfrith that he could honourably accept a wergeld fixed by customary law or some doom that has not survived, for it can hardly have been Aethelberht's Kentish law. Mercian or Northumbrian? Perhaps Theodore invented or manipulated the customary law until he found the

---

35. There is evidence of a wergeld (probably of 30,000 sceattas, six times that of a thegn) paid in 694 by the people of Kent for the killing in 687 of the brother of a West-Saxon king in the *Anglo-Saxon Chronicle*: GN Garmonsway *The Anglo-Saxon Chronicle* pp38–41; Michael Swanton *The Anglo-Saxon Chronicles* p41.
36. Bede *Ecclesiastical History* 4.21.

sum which both sides could accept. Not only did he dispose of the problem of revenge in the feud, apparently he negotiated 'peace treaties, *foedera pacis*', which lasted for a long time. So here we have an early English example of both private and international mediation. And its success depended on the acceptability, particularly to the nearest kin but generally to their communities, of the customary procedure of the feud with a tariff of reconciliation payments. Nothing could be clearer than the integral role of the mediator in the resolution of disputes then.

Another excellent example of mediation comes from the second half of the next century, from which evidence is otherwise sparse. It had its origin in a transfer of land at some time between 670 and 676 by Ine's father, Cenred king of Wessex, to Abbot Bectun, and confirmed by a charter.[37] Bectun was succeeded by Catwali, who transferred part of the land, let us call it Fontmell for convenience, by charter to Abbot Wintra. Generations later, the successors of Catwali and Wintra each claimed Fontmell and produced those charters as evidence of ownership. In later times, the sale to Wintra would have been recorded on the original grant, showing the subtraction of Fontmell from Catwali's title, but this all took place long before that practice had been invented. There was no one left who remembered the transactions 90 years later when a dispute came before Bishop Cyneheard. He mediated a settlement which, gratifyingly for us, he recorded:[38]

6.17 † I, Cyneheard, unworthy bishop, have impressed this sign to confirm and strengthen this charter which I declare to have been drawn up as follows: the successor of the above-named Abbot Bectun, called Catwali, sold the land of ten hides described above to Abbot Wintra for money, and he wrote another deed confirming the sale and the possession described above. But he retained the charter of the original gift, and the subscriptions of the kings, bishops, abbots and leading men, because it could not be easily separated, because this part of the land had been enrolled among the other testimonies of their lands, and it still cannot be. And so, after the original witnesses were dead, a lengthy dispute arose between the communities of the two monasteries and it still continues. From the time it was given to Wintra by the above-named abbot his successors have held this land. But the successors of the other community kept the original deed, confirmed by the hands of the witnesses named above.

So now I and our king and all the others who bear witness and subscribe below have brought about a peaceful reconciliation between them, partly by means of the payment of money and partly by the making of an oath,[39] so that the successors of Abbot Wintra, namely Ecgwold and his community of the

37. The story is told by Robin Chapman Stacey 'Texts and Society' pp247–9. The documents are translated in Dorothy Whitelock *English Historical Documents* 55 pp441–3. The earliest charters survive from the 670s.
38. Whitelock *English Historical Documents* pp441–2, on which this translation is closely based.
39. Compare **7.17**.

monastery called Tisbury,[40] with the permission of the other community of which Abbot Tidbald is head, shall henceforth have and hold for ever the land over which there has been a dispute for a long time. I have transcribed this present deed and made excerpts from the one which was originally given to Abbot Bectun, with the agreement of Abbot Tidbald and his community. I have given this document to Abbot Ecgwold, with the consent and confirmation of the witnesses named below, but I have rejected the other documents that have been prepared concerning this land.

These things have been done 759 years from Our Lord's incarnation, the twelfth interdiction.

† Cynewulf the king

† Herewold the bishop... [and other witnesses]

The clarity and confidence of this document do not look like the product of an unpractised mediator-arbitrator but there are no others like it which have survived as evidence of the practice of bishops in dispute resolution at the time. This was, of course, a dispute between religious communities. We do not know whether bishops offered their help in civil disputes between lay parties.[41]

CONCLUSIONS

In the seventh and eighth centuries there were no judges, lawyers or royal courts as we would define them. The history of public arbitration at that time is therefore the history of the whole of legal procedure. The sources are fragmentary, little more than the collections of dooms from the beginning and end with nothing in between, but the small fragments can be fitted together to provide a partial picture, reliable as far as it goes and suggestive of more. The old bonds of the clan had been loosened by widespread intermarriage between the different groups of German incomers and with some indigenous Britons. So long as there were kin groups which automatically accepted common responsibility for all their members, central government could rely on them to provide a system for the resolution of conflicts, which seems to have worked in many cases, even when a prince was killed, though not in the internecine struggles by which chiefs fought one another to be king. There were no legal limits to the kinds of dispute which could be settled by mediation and agreement. The concept of arbitrability, which certainly existed in Roman law, seems not to have troubled the Anglo-Saxons, whose assemblies had no restrictions on their jurisdiction. Not only the title to land but the killing of a prince could be managed by compromise.

40. Tisbury, *Tissanbyrig*, is mentioned in **7.17** and in the *Burghal Hidage*: 'To Tisbury 500 hides', AJ Robertson *Anglo-Saxon Charters* p246.

41. In England as in Francia, however, it is as well to keep in mind that: 'Churchmen are far more often to be found... asserting rights to dues... or worrying away at old property claims... than as the peace-makers of clerical ideology', Janet Nelson 'Dispute Settlement' p63; Edward James '*Beati Pacifici*'.

The later dooms show the growing influence of the king, using legislation and royal officers but still within the framework of the customary legal system operating in traditional assemblies and occasionally ad hoc, like the mediation of Archbishop Theodore. There are no collections of dooms from the eighth century and little documentary evidence of dispute resolution other than Bishop Cyneheard's mediation. Such as it is the evidence shows continuity of the customary processes rather than development, except perhaps for the greater involvement of royal officials, the ealdorman and reeve, at least in Wessex, and the beginnings of the responsibility of local groups, the tithing and hundred, taking over from that of the kin, the group defined by ties of blood.

By the end of the eighth century, trade was flourishing and London was a busy centre:[42]

> **6.18** ... the province of the East Saxons, who are separated from Kent by the River Thames and are bounded by the eastern sea, whose metropolis is the city of London, on the bank of that river, and it is an emporium for many peoples who come to it by land and sea.

No sources have yet been found to tell us anything at all about the way in which disputes were resolved there.

---

42. Bede *Ecclesiastical History* 2.3.

7 ALFRED

The Anglo-Saxon laws themselves, and the rulers who framed them, had little
call to enter into theoretical discussions or abstruse speculations; instead, they
saw all around them what seemed to be the results of the system of blood-feud.

TFT Plucknett *Edward I and Criminal Law* p21

Beneath his [Alfred's] preoccupation with duties, often of desperate urgency,
there was always a sense of imponderable values.... His conviction that a life
without knowledge or reflection was unworthy of respect, and his determination
to bring the thought of the past within the range of his subjects' understanding.

Frank Stenton *Anglo-Saxon England* p266

INTRODUCTION

We have seen that Aethelberht's laws were intended to deal with the
problems of different peoples with different customary laws being brought
within one kingdom and that similar problems of uniting their peoples
faced the later Kentish kings and Ine of Wessex. The biggest task by far
though fell to Alfred, who struggled for the whole of his reign to fight off
the Vikings and hold on to Wessex when they had killed the rulers of all
the other Anglo-Saxon kingdoms. He seems to have been just the man for
the job.

The eighth century was a time of internal wars, not only between kingdoms
for supremacy but between rivals within the kingdoms. Though their grip on
power might not have been as secure as that of some earlier kings, eighth-
century rulers began to intrude more into the ordinary affairs of their people,
encouraged by the Church. They took on more of what we now consider to
be the attributes of kingship. If they proclaimed laws, however, they have
left little trace. They seem to have been content to leave the resolution of
most disputes to customary assemblies and customary law.

The kings of the Kentish peoples lost control over much of the territory
they had once had. The kings of Mercia expanded their realm. When Wihtred
died in 725, Kent fell under Mercian control. Aethelbald, 716–57, styled
himself: 'King not only of the Mercians but of all the provinces called by
the general name Southern English'. But Wessex and Northumbria remained
independent, even when Offa succeeded Aethelbald in 757 and established
Mercian superiority everywhere else throughout the Anglo-Saxon parts of

the country.[1] Offa corresponded with Charlemagne about one matter of trade, and links with Francia shifted to Mercia from Kent.[2] Charlemagne's early and late coinages were influenced by the designs of Offa's new silver coins and there were communities of Frankish merchants in the major ports.

When Coenwulf died in 821, Mercia's power declined and that of Wessex rose. By 829 Ecgberht, king of Wessex, dominated the kings of Mercia and had forced Northumbria to acknowledge him as overlord. The Vikings first attacked England and Ireland in 793 and 795. For forty years the Danes had been intermittently attacking the east coast from north to south. Then in the 850s, not only did armies from what are now Denmark and Norway continue to invade England's east coast, but also Norwegians, sailing round the north of Scotland, landed in the Western Isles, the Isle of Man, Ireland, the British kingdoms of what is now Wales and the west coast of England. The Danes captured York in 867. It took them only three years to take Northumbria and East Anglia.

Ecgberht's son Aethelwulf had seen what happened when sons fought to succeed and he arranged for his kingdom to pass to his four sons by seniority.[3] When the Danes attacked Wessex in 870, Aethelred the third son was king. He and his brother, the fourth son Alfred, defeated the Danish army in the first battle but lost the second. The Danes were reinforced. Aethelred died and in 872 Alfred (reigned 871–99) had to buy the Danes off. For five years they turned their attention to settling Mercia but in 876 they attacked Wessex again. They had little success and withdrew until 878, when they overwhelmed Alfred's forces and drove him to take refuge in the marshes of Somerset. Yet within a few months he was able to rally an army and defeat the Danish forces, compelling their king Guthrum and other leaders to accept Christian baptism and terms which allowed the Danes to keep much of what they already had.

Alfred used his respite well, building up his fleet and fortifying towns. By 886 he was able to capture London and fend off further Danish invading

1. Charters confirmed by a king are often the best evidence at this time of his sovereignty over the place and the parties involved. There are British charters from this time, and legal documents written on Gospel manuscripts in Latin and British (Welsh), which record settlements from what is now Wales, David Howlett *Sealed From Within* pp62–73.

2. The leading scholar and adviser at Charlemagne's court was Alcuin, from Northumbria; Rob Meens 'Sanctuary, Penance and Dispute Settlement under Charlemagne' is enlightening. Dispute resolution developed differently on the Continent, however, under and after Charlemagne, PJ Geary 'Extra-Judicial Means of Conflict Resolution' and the wealth of sources he cites.

3. Most of what we know about Alfred comes from the contemporary biography written by Asser, a British bishop from Powys, whom he invited to work with him in his programme for the advancement of learning. Simon Keynes and Michael Lapidge *Alfred the Great: Asser's Life of King Alfred and Other Contemporary Sources* is a translation with ample notes and an introduction which is a model of how to present the results of exemplary scholarship to non-specialists, cheaply and attractively. The information about dispute resolution to be found in Asser's *Life* is discussed below.

forces. His kingdom was secure over Wessex and Mercia. The north-west remained under the Danes, now permanently settled, its old cultural and literary world destroyed for ever.

It may just be by accident that so little survives to tell us what the intellectual and cultural life of Mercia was like. A stroke of luck has left the first evidence of people's assemblies there. A memorandum of the Mercian king Coenwulf expressly frees the granted land from the responsibilities of attendance at *popularia concilia*.[4]

Even from the other great kingdom of Wessex there is little or nothing to be found which tells of lawmaking or of dispute resolution in the two centuries between Ine and Alfred.

What is clear, though, is that, despite the internal strife, this was a period of economic growth. England's commercial centres, *emporia* in Latin, *wics* in English, continued to trade widely, not just with Francia but even as far as the Caliphate, exporting slaves, captured in civil wars, and importing luxuries and, perhaps, knowledge. Trade flourished in England, too, in the eighth century, between what would become great towns:[5]

> Middle Saxon southern England was about more than just trade in objects from foreign parts: these networks were about people living their daily lives – selling their wool, making their clothes and growing their food… a significant proportion of the population must have spent all their time being merchants or artisans.

They must have been able to resolve the inevitable disputes but we don't know how.

ALFRED'S LAWS: THE BIBLICAL INTRODUCTION[6]

Alfred was unusual and admirable in many ways. He was determined to improve learning in his realm. He learned Latin at the age of 38 and, having carefully chosen the books he thought of greatest educational value, is said to have translated the most important of them into English himself, encouraging a team of scholars whom he invited to his court to translate others. They came not only from Mercia but Dyfed, Francia and Old Saxony, so most did not have Anglo-Saxon as their mother tongue.

Alfred's aim was to improve the quality of the clergy and then to prepare his lay officials to carry out their various tasks, including presiding at decision-making assemblies. He therefore began his educational programme, about AD890, by translating Pope Gregory's *Pastoral Care* into Anglo-

4. WdeG Birch *Cartularium Saxonicum* 201; Frank Stenton *Anglo-Saxon England* p298.
5. Francis Pryor *Britain in the Middle Ages* pp47, 38–9, 42. These towns are not the fortified *burhs* which Offa built in Mercia and Alfred later in Wessex, which were 'fundamentally different from the *wics* that preceded them because of this new element of planned location, administration, security and control', pp105, 147.
6. EG Stanley 'The Administration of Law in Anglo-Saxon England' pp56–62; EG Stanley 'On the Laws of King Alfred'.

Saxon, no doubt with the assistance of his experts.[7] He deplored the decline of scholarship. There were few, he wrote, who could translate a letter from Latin to Anglo-Saxon, not one south of the Thames. None could follow the divine service even in Anglo-Saxon. He could not at first understand why none of the earlier scholars had bothered to translate the essential books but then he realised that they could not have foreseen how Latin learning could be lost so quickly and completely:[8]

> **7.1** Then I remembered how the law was first made in the Hebrew tongue, and then the Greeks, when they had learned it, translated it all into their own language, and all other books as well. And so did the Romans, once they had mastered them, getting learned translators to translate them all into their own language. All the other Christian peoples translated part of them in the same way into their own tongues.

The law he is referring to there is, of course, the law of the Bible, not the Anglo-Saxon customary law or the royal dooms but, having dealt with the shortcomings of the clergy, he turned his attention to his civil service. Even then he set his reforms in a Biblical context, prefacing his compilation with what Wormald calls the 'Mosaic Preface' but I have called his *Biblical Introduction*.[9] He starts with a version of the Ten Commandments and continues with quotations from Exodus and from the New Testament,[10] showing how the law of Moses was applicable to Christians. He occasionally does a bit of adaptation, going far beyond his own exhortation to translate sense for sense, not word for word. For example, in relation to an ox which has gored someone to death, Alfred says that the amount to be paid by its master to avoid the death penalty should be 'whatever the *witan* finds to be correct'.[11] The Anglo-Saxon word *bot* is introduced and with it the concept of reconciliation payments. He avoids the technicality of the Roman law phrase *convictus noxae* by addition and subtraction:[12]

> **7.2** He who steals a free man and sells him and it is proved so that he cannot clear himself, let him be put to death.

Somebody had to explain to Alfred what the technical phrase meant. Was there a Roman lawyer in his team? There is nothing to tell us. But we know where the concept of clearing oneself, by oath or ordeal, came from. It was already Anglo-Saxon.

7. Henry Sweet ed *King Alfred's West-Saxon Version of Gregory's Pastoral Care*.
8. Sweet, Preface to *Pastoral Care*.
9. Following Richard Dammery 'Law-Code of King Alfred the Great'. MH Turk *The Legal Code of Aelfred the Great* pp68–81 has the Anglo-Saxon text and facing it the passages from the Latin Bible. Benjamin Thorpe *Ancient Laws* pp20–6 faces the Anglo-Saxon with an English translation.
10. *Acts of the Apostles* xv, 23–9.
11. *Biblical Introduction* 21.
12. *Biblical Introduction* 15. Similarly at 26 he translates the technical term *pro damni aestimatione restituet* as 'give *bot* as it may be valued', '*gebete swa hit mon geeahtige*'.

Alfred makes it quite clear who he is addressing. He is not speaking to his people generally but to his officials, especially those who have the responsibility for making decisions in disputes. He is happy to claim divine support for his laws. He does not distinguish God's word from his own insertions, which are shown here in square brackets.[13]

> **7.3** Take no notice of the word of a liar! [Do not accept his dooms nor any witness or statement from him!] Do not prefer the ill-advised counsel and wishes of the people, in their speech and clamour, against your own better judgment, nor follow the teaching of the least wise!... [Judge very fairly! Do not give one doom to the rich and another to the poor! Do not give one doom to friend, another to foe!] Reject false witness! ... Do not accept payment for favours, which blinds even the eyes of the wise and corrupts their words! Do not be unkind to foreigners [or outsiders nor do them injustice]!

Alfred says that 'These are the dooms which Almighty God himself spoke to Moses', and that Christ said that he came not to break them but to implement them. He adds, from the Acts of the Apostles, that:[14]

> **7.4** From this single doom one should remember to judge everyone according to right. One needs no other doombook, *domboca*. Let him keep in mind that he deems to no man what he would not have him deem to him, if he sought a doom from him.

He then explains that, as Christianity spread, synods were held, including among the 'Angle-kin, after they had received the faith of Christ'. These meetings ordered secular lords to allow feuds to be settled by payment of *bot*, for the first offence, except for treason against a lord:[15]

> **7.5** In many synods they set a *bot* for many human misdeeds and in many synod-books they wrote one doom in one place and another in another.

Next Alfred explains how he worked in compiling his own collection of dooms:[16]

> **7.6** Then I, King Alfred, gathered these together, and I ordered to be written down many which our forebears kept, which seemed good to me; and many of them which did not seem good to me I rejected, with the counsel of my *witan*, otherwise I ordered that they be kept; because I did not dare to presume to set down in writing many of my own, because I did not know what would be acceptable to those who would come after us. But those which I found, from the days of my kinsman Ine, or of Offa, king of the Mercians, or of Aethelberht, who was the first of the Angle-kin to be baptised, those which I considered most right I gathered together here and left out the others. Then I, Alfred, king of the West Saxons, showed them to all of my *witan*, and they said that it pleased them all to keep them.

13. *Biblical Introduction* 43 and 46.
14. *Biblical Introduction* 49.
15. *Biblical Introduction* 49.8.
16. *Biblical Introduction* 49.9 and 49.10

There are deductions to be made from this statement of intentions, some with confidence. Alfred knew of a collection of dooms attributed to Aethelberht which may be that which has come down to us. He says he has preserved some in his collection, and traces can be found, though none verbatim. The dooms of Ine have been preserved by Alfred himself as an addendum to his own. He has taken what he wanted from them without subtracting those parts from Ine's text.[17] Offa's laws have not survived.[18]

Alfred had no doubt of his right to repeal the dooms of his forebears and to proclaim dooms which would change the customary law. He was cautious, however, about putting into writing – perhaps a significant phrase – any dooms of his own which his successors would find unacceptable. That reads more like Alfred's good sense than his habitual formal humility. As Liebermann wrote:[19]

> English monarchy, by no means absolute, required the consent of a very conservative nobility for the slightest legal alterations from time-honoured custom. For three centuries longer new laws were never permitted to be instituted in England without being masked as mere re-enactments of some older constitution.

Alfred was careful to stress that everything was done with the agreement of his counsellors in the *witan*. They had had their say. They were the ones who would have to carry out his instructions. Now they had no excuse for failure to do so.[20]

In one respect above all Alfred's Christian teaching was intended to be revolutionary. No longer was the basic moral law the simple Anglo-Saxon imperative: to support one's friends and to harm one's enemies. Royal officials carrying out their duties as makers of decisions in disputes were instructed to do right to friend and foe alike, taking no gifts and giving preference to nobody's evidence. That this counsel of perfection was not always heeded is not surprising and there is plenty of evidence of influence which Alfred would have considered improper. The Fonthill letter discussed below itself contains enough, **7.17**, and there is plenty more evidence of corruption in the Ely of Edgar's day, seventy years later.[21]

ALFRED'S LAWS: THE ADMINISTRATION OF JUSTICE

Nothing could be clearer than Alfred's intention to collect together the dooms he considered right and instruct his civil servants to make decisions

17. Richard Dammery 'Editing' p255.
18. It is not certain that Offa ever created a discrete collection of dooms; the question is discussed in a full footnote by Keynes and Lapidge *Alfred the Great* p305 n5 and Patrick Wormald was firmly in favour in 'In Search of King Offa's Law-Code'.
19. Felix Liebermann 'King Alfred and the Mosaic Law' p23.
20. Meetings of chieftains to confirm laws and make judgments had been a tradition in the Anglo-Saxon homelands for centuries, A Hofmeister ed *Vita Sancti Lebvini* p793, cited by DP Kirby *The Earliest English Kings* p16.
21. AG Kennedy 'Law and Litigation in the *Libellus Aethelwoldi Episcopi*' p153.

in accordance with them. They are still not a code. They do not pretend to subvert the comprehensive customary law but, in Christ-like fashion, to supplement and implement it. They are not comprehensive. They say nothing about those areas of law where different customs might still be expected to prevail in different parts of Alfred's new extended kingdom: rules of inheritance, for example. They do not disturb the most basic law of all, which determines rights to family or kin land. But they deal with new questions which have arisen in respect of land which is not held in that way but by the new technique of written conveyance – bookland:[22]

> **7.7** A man who holds bookland, which his kin have left him, we order that he shall not give it away out of his kin if there is written or other evidence that that was forbidden by those who first acquired it or who transferred it to him and that that shall be declared before his kin with the king or a bishop as witness.

The laws say nothing directly about arbitration, which was still the province of the assembly. But the very first clause shows the importance Alfred gave to procedure there:[23]

> **7.8** First of all we instruct that it is most necessary that every man keep his oath and his pledge carefully.

Alfred knew that the whole administration of justice which he was about to elaborate relied on oaths being kept and pledges honoured. Arbitrations before the assembly depended on testimony given on oath and the effectiveness of pledges given to ensure performance. The laws say little of the law or legal procedure of the Church, except for fixing holidays and extra punishment for offences committed in Lent. But the procedure of the assembly had come to rely on the Church's co-operation:[24]

> **7.9** On God-pledge. If anyone accuses another on a God-pledge, and wants to make a claim that he has not fulfilled any of them he gave him, he shall make a fore-oath in four churches; and if the other wants to show that he is speaking the truth, he shall do that in twelve churches.

The formal procedure for the determination of a dispute could begin by the claimant stating the claim on oath, the fore-oath. The defendant then took an oath that his denial was the truth. The outcome of the hearing before the assembly might be that a party, in normal circumstances the defendant, made one or more promises, for example to make a reconciliation-payment, the *wergeld* or *wer* for short. He might support the promise with a pledge made in church, a God-pledge. If the promisee then claimed that the promisor had not performed the promise, the promisee had to make a new fore-oath to that effect in four churches. If the promisor wished to deny his breach, he must take an oath in twelve.

22. *Alfred* 41; AG Kennedy 'Disputes about *Bocland*'.
23. *Alfred* 1.
24. *Alfred* 33.

The other mainstay of the legal system was still the feud:[25]

> **7.10** On Feuds. We also command: the man who knows his adversary to be staying at home shall not fight before he asks him for justice. If he has the power to keep him trapped at home, he shall keep him there for seven days and shall not fight him if his adversary is prepared to stay inside. If after seven days he is willing to surrender and hand over his weapons, he shall keep him unharmed for thirty days and give notice to his kin and friends.

That is all very well if the claimant has the necessary force of arms. But what if his forces are just too weak to take the prescribed measures of self-help?

> **7.11** If he has not enough power to trap him in his home, he shall ride to the ealdorman and ask for his assistance. If he will not lend his aid, then he shall ride to the king before he fights.

The king appears to intend to take control. He allows no fighting in the feud without his approval, which he will not grant except under the supervision of his ealdorman. The king proclaims his intention to step in if the ealdorman fails. None of this undermines the feud itself as the rock on which the legal system still stands. Further clauses provide more detailed procedures postponing the fight and defining who may become involved in the feud. If the defendant escapes to a church, he may claim sanctuary. And none of these statements proves that reality followed purposes.[26]

The assembly – the moot, *gemot*, or *folcgemot*, folkmoot or people's assembly – could only work if order was kept. In particular, the disputes which were presented to it for resolution must not be allowed to turn violent there:[27]

> **7.12** If anyone fights in an assembly before the king's ealdorman, he shall pay *wergeld* and fine, *wer* and *wite*, whatever is the right amount, but first he shall pay 120 shillings fine to the ealdorman.
> 1. If he disturbs the *folcgemot* with a drawn weapon, he shall pay a fine of 120 shillings to the ealdorman.
> 2. If something like this happens before an assistant of the king's ealdorman or before the king's priest, 30 shillings fine.

The *folcgemot* was the right place to make a claim for a debt – but not lightly:[28]

> **7.13** If anyone makes a claim for a debt in the *folcgemot* of the king's reeve, and afterwards wants to withdraw it, he shall bring it against the right person, if he can; if he cannot, he shall lose his right to payment.

25. *Alfred* 42.
26. Hyams *Rancor* pp98–110.
27. *Alfred* 38.
28. *Alfred* 22.

This is not to say that, once a claim was before the assembly, it could not be settled without some payment of a fine. It merely shows that the assembly must not be burdened with frivolous claims. Once a dispute had been brought before it, which required solemn oaths to be sworn by both parties, the claimant would lose the right to bring another claim on the same subject matter, but against a different defendant. The claimant must substitute the new defendant in the same proceedings. This provision would not inhibit settlement, which would still be the best reason for withdrawing the claim. Of itself settlement would ensure that the same claim could not be made again.

OTHER LAWS

Most of the rest of the text of Alfred's laws is given over to tariffs for injuries, after the fashion of the earlier collections of dooms, setting the amounts payable for injuries of all kinds and to all parts of the body. This one still shows clear signs of its origin in the decision of a specific case:[29]

> **7.14** It is also established: if someone has a spear over his shoulder and someone is pierced by it, he shall pay *wer* without *wite*. If pierced front on, he shall pay the *wer*. If it is claimed he did it deliberately, he shall make an oath equivalent to the *wite* and by that the *wite* abates. That is, if the point is more than three fingers' width higher than the end of the shaft. If they are both level, the point and the end of the shaft, it is not dangerous.

However concerned he was for the welfare of his people, it is hard to imagine how Alfred could have thought of the need for such a specific law unless he had been stimulated by the challenge of a particular incident or he had taken it from some earlier laws.[30]

The last clause has general significance for dispute resolution. Having dealt with the amount of *bot* for an injury which severs the tendons of the neck, but not fatally, it concludes by saying:[31]

> **7.15** one hundred shillings be given as *bot*, unless the *witan* grant him a more just and greater amount.

This is further evidence of the role the assembly played in fixing the amount of *bot*, once the ealdorman, reeve, or other royal officer had made a decision on liability, if that was his function at that time, which may well not have been the invariable reality. The tariff was intended as a guide. The amounts awarded could be varied to suit the circumstances and changes in the value of coin. They were all means to promote settlement of the dispute.

29. *Alfred* 36; Rosamund McKitterick ed *The New Cambridge Medieval History* 2 p418; Patrick Wormald '*Lex Scripta*' p113.
30. The author of the *Leges Henrici Primi* says that this law survived for another two hundred years or more, until his own time, Downer *Leges Henrici Primi* 88.3, 3a, 3b. Compare Cnut's law on spears, **9.20**.
31. *Alfred* 77.

ASSER

About 890, Alfred invited Asser to join his team of scholar-advisers from his home in St David's at the far west of what is now Wales and was then in the British kingdom of Dyfed. He may well have already been a bishop. He wrote his *Life* in Latin, probably in 893 when Alfred was at the height of his powers.[32] There is much to be found in it to illuminate the administration of justice and not a little about dispute resolution. What is strange is that it does not mention Alfred's collection of dooms at all, even by implication. If the weight of expert evidence were not so strong that they date from c890, it would be tempting to suggest that they were promulgated later. That would still not explain, however, why one who was in Alfred's inner circle of advisers did not think it important to write about what must surely have been a subject of discussion among them.[33]

Asser says much about Alfred's determination to improve the quality of the system of justice, in particular through the education of his judicial officials, the ealdormen and reeves, whom he calls in Latin *iudex*, though there were no professional or even regular judges in the Anglo-Saxon legal system.[34]

7.16 He also used to concern himself in judicial decisions, in order to be helpful to both nobles and commoners, because they often stubbornly quarrelled among themselves at assemblies of ealdormen and reeves, so that scarcely any of them would concede that anything that had been decided by the ealdormen and reeves was right. Most obstinately driven by such stubborn disagreement, the parties would submit to the decision of the king, which both parties would hasten to implement forthwith. But if a party reckoned that there would be some injustice from his point of view, although he might have been obliged to attend by force of law or by agreement, he would be unwilling to agree to the decision of such a *iudex*, against his will. He knew that there was nothing arising out of his ill-will that would not be revealed without delay.

That is no surprise because the king was a very clever hunter in judicial matters as in everything else. He would very shrewdly enquire into all the decisions made in his absence almost everywhere in his jurisdiction, whatever they might be, to find whether they were just or unjust. If he was able to discover anything unfair in those decisions, gently (according to his usual practice) he would question those very *iudices*, either himself or through someone or other he could trust, asking why they had decided so unfairly. Was it through ignorance or some sort of ill-will, or fear or favour, or enmity, or because they wanted money from somebody? If eventually the *iudices* confessed that they had made their

32. The translation and notes of Keynes and Lapidge are indispensable. The Latin text is in the scholarly edition of WH Stevenson, reprinted 1998 with Dorothy Whitelock's updating essay.

33. Asser's first language was presumably British and his second Latin, and so he may not have been quite at home in Anglo-Saxon. We saw (at **7.2**) a hint that Roman law was not unknown, if only through the Latin Bible.

34. Asser *Life of King Alfred* 106. I see no reason to emend the first word *studebat* to *sedebat*.

decisions for such reasons, because in the circumstances they did not know any better, then he would discreetly and moderately point out their inexperience and lack of wisdom. He used to say: 'I am surprised by this lack of understanding of yours, because by God's gift and mine you have taken on yourselves the office and rank of the wise, yet you have ignored the study and effort of wisdom. So, in those circumstances, I order you either to give up the offices of earthly authority which you hold, or give much more devoted study to the learning of wisdom.

Asser writes that as a result the ealdormen and reeves were quick to try to learn to read, as well as trying harder to understand how to do better justice to the parties. They preferred the hard work of study to losing their jobs. If they could not learn to read, because they were too old or too slow, the king would instruct their sons to take over. The king would appoint one of his own people, free or slave Asser says, to read books to them in Anglo-Saxon, night and day, so that they wished they had learned to read in their youth.[35]

Alfred wrote letters with instructions to his officials,[36] and intended them to read his written dooms. In that way he could exercise some control over their decisions.

THE FONTHILL LETTER

By a stroke of luck a contemporary account has survived from the hand of an ealdorman who was an arbitrator in an arbitration which Alfred instituted and whose award he enforced.[37] It is a letter written about AD920 to Alfred's son and successor, Edward the Elder, by old Ordlaf, whom Alfred had appointed ealdorman for Wiltshire in 897.[38] Ordlaf wanted to ensure that Edward would not overturn Alfred's decision of twenty years before. It has so much to say about how arbitration fitted into the legal system that it deserves to be set out here in full:[39]

7.17 Dear Lord, I will tell you how it was about the land at Fonthill, the five hides which Aethelm[40] Higa is talking about. When Helmstan did the wrong by stealing Aethelred's belt, Higa immediately began to make a claim against him, with other claimants, and wanted to recover the land. Then he [Helmstan] sought me out and asked me to speak on his behalf because I had been his

35. Asser *Life of King Alfred* 106.
36. Alfred's translation of Augustine's *Soliloquies* (Keynes and Lapidge *Alfred* pp141 and 300 n10); Asser *Life of King Alfred* 79 'he sent me letters'.
37. It has understandably generated scholarship of impressive quantity and quality. I have taken special advantage of Mechthild Gretsch 'The Language of the Fonthill Letter' for linguistic help and Simon Keynes 'The Fonthill Letter' for everything else. Between them they refer to the many other works on different aspects of the letter, which it would be supererogatory to list here, though there are many in the Bibliography. EG Stanley 'The Administration of Law in Anglo-Saxon England' pp62–3 makes comparisons with Einhard on Charlemagne and Suetonius on Augustus. I have drawn my own conclusions and made my own translations, confident only that my failure to show all my workings and those of the experts will ensure that my errors will be corrected.
38. Mark Boynton and Susan Reynolds 'The Author of the Fonthill Letter'.
39. Canterbury, Dean and Chapter, Chart. Ant. C.1282.
40. His name was Aethelhelm but the manuscript always calls him Aethelm.

sponsor at his confirmation, before he did the wrong. Then I did speak on his behalf and put in a word for him with King Alfred. Then – God reward his soul! – because I spoke for him and my testimony was accepted,[41] he allowed him to show his right to the land against Aethelm. Then he ordered an arbitration, and I was one of the ones appointed to it, with Wihtbord and Aelfric (who was then keeper of the wardrobe) and Byrhthelm and Wulfhun the Black from Somerton and Strica and Ubba and more men than I can name now.

Then each of them told his story and we all thought that Helmstan ought to produce his documents and make his claim to the land on the ground that Aetheldryth had transferred it to Osulf at an appropriate price [i.e. market value?] and that she had told Osulf that she had every right to transfer it because it was her morning gift when she first went to Athulf. Helmstan put all this in his oath. When Osulf bought the land from Aetheldryth, King Alfred gave him his signature so that it would stand, and Edward his and Aethelnath his and Deormod his and each of those whose they wanted to have.

When we were arbitrating between them at Wardour the document was produced and read. All the signatures were there on it. Then all of us who were at that arbitration thought that Helmstan was 'nearer the oath'.[42] But Aethelm would not give his full assent until we went in to the king and told him everything about how and why we had come to our decision. Aethelm was standing there with us. And the king was standing – washing his hands – in his room at Wardour.[43] When he had finished doing that he asked Aethelm why he thought that what we had decided for him did not seem right to him, saying that he could not imagine anything fairer than that Helmstan should have to take the oath if he could. Then I said that Helmstan wanted to make proof and I asked the king to fix a day for it and then he did so.

On the appointed day Helmstan produced the oath in full. He had asked me to support him and had said that he would prefer to transfer the land to me than that the oath should go wrong or it ever [gap in text]. Then I said that I would help him to get justice but never injustice, on condition that he granted his land to me, and he pledged he would surrender it to me. We rode there on the appointed day: I and Wihtbord rode with me; and Byrhthelm rode there with Aethelm. We all heard him take the oath in full. Then we all said that the dispute was over as the doom had been performed.

Dear Lord, when will any dispute be ended if you cannot finish it either with a payment or with an oath?[44] Or, if one wants to change every doom which King Alfred declared, when shall we have done with assembling to hear disputes?

41. Gretsch 'Language' p78 explains this technical term.
42. That is, that Helmstan should first be allowed to swear that he was telling the truth, thereby establishing his claim.
43. EG Stanley 'The Administration of Law in Anglo-Saxon England' pp64–6 sees a reference here to Pontius Pilate, *Matthew* 27:24, and makes much of it, misunderstanding the significance of the technical phrase 'nearer the oath'.
44. Compare **6.17**. As early as 825 in Mercia, King Beornwulf and a full council, *sinodlic gemot*, heard a dispute between Earl Eadwulf and the Bishop of Worcester over pasture for pigs. The dispute was resolved by the bishop giving a pledge to produce an oath. That was done 30 days later and the earl's representative was present and did not challenge it, Robertson *Anglo-Saxon Charters* V pp8–9.

Then Helmstan gave me the land-charter, *boc*, as he had earlier pledged to surrender it, as soon as the oath had been given. And I promised him that he should have enjoyment of the land for as long as he should live, if he would keep himself from disgrace. Then – I don't remember whether it was a year and a half or two years after that – he went and stole the wretched oxen at Fonthill, thereby utterly ruining himself, and drove them to Chicklade, where he was apprehended. His goad-man recovered the goad-driven.[45] As he ran away a bramble scratched him across the face; when he wanted to deny it, this was given as evidence against him.

Then Eanulf Penearding – he was the reeve – swept in. He took from him all the property he owned at Tisbury.[46] When I asked him why he did so, he said: Helmstan was a thief; all his property was adjudged to the king because he was the king's man; and Ordlaf succeeded to his land because Helmstan could not forfeit it because he occupied it under his life interest (loan, *læn*).[47] And then you declared him an outlaw. He then went to where your father is buried and brought me a seal,[48] which I gave to you when I was with you at Chippenham. Then you let him go home[49] to the estate where he is still living.

I succeeded to my land and then transferred it to the bishop with you and your *witan* as witnesses, five hides for the five hides at Lydiard, and the bishop and his household granted me four of them but one other was subject to tithe.

Now, dear lord, it is absolutely necessary for me that it should stand as it is now done and has been for a long time. If it is going to be otherwise, then I shall and I will be obliged by your charity, whatever you think right.

The endorsement reads:

• Aethelm Higa withdrew from this dispute when the king was at Warminster, as witness Ordlaf and Osferth and Odda and Wihtbord and Aelfstan the Bald and Aethelnoth.

The letter was written by Ordlaf in his own hand. The endorsement is in a different hand, which would be unlikely if it were a copy. Moreover, it is in his own words. It is not an official document. It follows no form. It includes words that are taken from ordinary speech and appear nowhere else in surviving manuscripts. It shows Ordlaf's careful handwriting: he was not a professional scribe. But it also reveals his grasp of legal terminology: he was a professional judicial officer, the nearest there was to a judge in his day. The language is exactly as you would expect from one of the ealdormen who had benefitted from Alfred's educational reforms: he wrote as he spoke but could switch to what he thought was the proper

---

45. The meaning of this clause is unclear, Gretsch 'Language' pp84–8.
46. By coincidence this seems to be the same place as the subject of the dispute at **6.17**.
47. This interpretation gets rid of the problem that Ordlaf suddenly appears in the third person.
48. Presumably this means that Helmstan went to Alfred's grave and brought back some token to show he had been there.
49. By revoking his outlawry.

language when he remembered or thought it important enough. His choices of register were not necessarily conscious.[50]

THE SIGNIFICANCE OF FONTHILL

Of course, we cannot assume that the story of the arbitration of Fonthill was representative or that there were many others like it:[51]

> There is no such thing as a typical Anglo-Saxon lawsuit. But the Helmstan saga is altogether out of the ordinary... It raises in acute form the early medievalist's eternal problem, whether the curtain has merely parted by chance to give a rare glimpse of the normal, or has been blown briefly open by some abnormal disturbance.

It is not too difficult, however, to gain some insights with confidence, and they help to illuminate the background of dispute resolution then.

The assembly had other kinds of business to transact than the resolution of disputes: it was responsible for licensing the movements of traders, for example. But it was still the normal place where justice was administered.[52] It is noticeable that Alfred intervened in the administration of justice in many more ways than his forebears, from what we know of them. He appointed ealdormen, whose responsibilities for the administration of a shire included the decisive role in the *gemot*. He collected dooms and published them in writing and taught the ealdormen to read so that they could take instructions and he could control the quality of their performance.

For the first time we can see a clear distinction between arbitration and the judicial work of the assembly, the *gemot*. Arbitration, always preceded by and intermingled with mediation, was intended to produce a settlement with which both parties, indeed all parties, ought to be satisfied. Alfred ordered it after claims had been made in the Fonthill dispute and Ordlaf's letter shows how arbitration and what may now be called litigation fitted together. Alfred expected the team of mediator-arbitrators to work out a settlement, partly by sorting out the legal rights of the parties. For this dispute there were many arbitrators appointed, including at least one, Ordlaf, with a direct interest in the outcome. Byrhthelm seems to have been Aethelm's appointed arbitrator. Perhaps there were others suggested by each side. They would be there as 'friends to both sides', in form if not reality, rather than dispassionate outsiders with no connection to either party and no prior knowledge of the facts of the dispute or the interests of the parties. But Ordlaf was there to protect his own interests, as well as Helmstan's, however much he might be careful to appear to

---

50. Simon Keynes 'The Fonthill Letter' pp57–8 shows that Edward the Elder granted land to Ordlaf in 903 and that Ordlaf was dead by 925.
51. Patrick Wormald *Making* p145.
52. RA Adkins and MR Petchey 'Secklow Hundred Mound'.

be disinterestedly ensuring that justice was done, according to Alfred's laws, exhortations and education, in the shire for which Alfred had made him responsible.

The arbitrators decided that the matter should be resolved in the traditional way by an oath. But who should have the advantage of winning by swearing an oath? Helmstan. Why? Because he had a document of title. That was why he was, in the technical jargon of the day, nearer the oath.[53] The process, ordered as here by the judicial authority, is not far from what is nowadays called 'early neutral evaluation'. It is intended to lead to settlement by showing the parties at an early stage which way the legal wind is blowing. But here Aethelm never had a chance. No doubt he argued that Helmstan had forfeited his advantage by his criminal conduct. He may well have argued, too, that Helmstan had come by the deeds in some illegal way, simple theft perhaps. Aethelm's arguments, if they were ever recorded, have not survived.

Ordlaf controlled the outcome. He did not do all this for nothing. The transfer of ownership from Helmstan to Ordlaf, with a life interest back to Helmstan, was an obvious device to avoid Helmstan forfeiting his land on conviction. A neat bit of chicanery, almost an early analogue of 'money-laundering', and clearly a 'payment for favours' which Alfred had been so keen to forbid, **7.3**. Ordlaf got the disputed land and quickly swapped it for other land with the bishop, taking care to have Edward himself and his *witan* there as witnesses when he completed the exchange. Alfred, the 'very clever hunter', **7.16**, might have seen through all this but Edward agreed to enforce the award.

It was just as well that Ordlaf had had such foresight. He must have known his Helmstan as well as his law. When Helmstan stole the cattle, Ordlaf was not quick enough to stop the reeve Eanulf Penearding confiscating Helmstan's *yrfe*, which presumably meant here his personal property, everything other than land, but including 'loans', that is the life interest. Ordlaf had authority to ask Eanulf to explain his actions. Nothing Eanulf had done had affected Ordlaf's ownership of what would later be called the freehold. It would have reverted to Ordlaf anyway, he says, because of the oral condition he had put on the 'loan': that it lasted only until Helmstan disgraced himself again.

It is easy to see why Edward the Elder asked for an explanation and why Ordlaf himself took great pains to pen one. Ordlaf was an old man by then. He may have had a genuine feeling for the scapegrace Helmstan, himself a youth no more. He may have used up the last of his influence to get his outlawry revoked. His final sentence reveals his insecurity. He asks not for

53. Simon Keynes *Royal Government* p250 on *Libellus* 35; AG Kennedy 'Law and Litigation' p171 quoting from the *Liber Eliensis* ch. 5: 'the person who had the charter was nearer [to the oath] that he should have the land, than the one who did not have it'.

law but charity. But the endorsement, written later in another hand, shows that old Ordlaf won. For whatever reason, Aethelm withdrew his claim. Perhaps it had at last been amicably settled.

CONCLUSIONS

Alfred had always been concerned more generally with law and order and specifically with the responsibilities of men in groups. Genuine traders could move freely within the kingdom, with the royal licence granted by the assembly, but they must take responsibility for the behaviour of those they included in their group if a feud arose. Few other people moved about much except to fight or cause other kinds of trouble. All were subject to the law of their place. There was not much peace in Alfred's reign. He had prevailed because he could create fighting forces out of those groups. He had the idea of having them serve in shifts, six months on, six months off. Those groups were less identified by their bloodline than they had been, less by kin than place.

Alfred died at the age of fifty on 26 October 899, king of the West Saxons, overlord of the Mercians.[54] Some parts inhabited by the old British remained independent, in Devon and Cornwall and what is now Wales. Danes and Norsemen who were not yet assimilated lived among the English and spoke mutually comprehensible dialects in the east, north-east, north-west and what is now Scotland.

The Vikings were at first raiders, who plundered for the goods they sold. They did not buy them and what they did was not trade. They took money and anything precious and, of course, prisoners they sold as slaves. But they came to be traders, too:[55]

> A hoard of coins found at Croydon in 1862... consisted not only of Mercian, East Anglian and West Saxon pennies, but also of Carolingian *deniers*, and of the sort of Arabic coins from central Asia which appear to have flooded into Scandinavia from about 800 as a result of contacts established along the Russian rivers.

So, despite their destructive past, when they settled in England they had another history, of seafaring and selling from the Caspian to the Mediterranean, which may have influenced the future of the country they came for a time to rule. For all their reputation for violence, there is no evidence that they dealt with disputes among themselves and with those they traded with by cruder means than the Anglo-Saxons.

More than any earlier ruler, Alfred used his legislative powers to issue dooms to reform the law, as we would now characterise his efforts. Yet everything he did presupposed a foundation of customary law. His own

54. Keynes and Lapidge *Alfred* p219 n79.
55. Campbell, John and Wormald *Anglo-Saxons* p145; but the chapters in DM Hadley and JD Richards *Cultures in Context* tell a fuller story.

will makes that clear. He wrote there that he had brought the will of his father Aethelwulf before an assembly of the whole *witan* and asked them to decide freely to recognise its validity:[56]

> **7.18** I urged them all to... declare what was right, and that none of them, from love or fear of me, should hesitate to apply the customary law.

Not only in testamentary matters, where there were no dooms to rely on, but as a general principle, customary law still provided the norms and we shall see in the next chapter how kings took pains expressly to preserve it.

56. FE Harmer *Select English Historical Documents* pp15–19.

8 THE TENTH CENTURY:
EDWARD TO AETHELRED

Law is not in the king's mouth, but so surely in the voice of the nation that it matters little how it finds utterance... This legal popularism, elastic, practical, tolerant as to the composition of its assemblies, yet unyielding in its demand that lawful men shall pronounce right law, is the first and most far-reaching rule which united England inherited from the embryo states....

JEA Jolliffe *The Constitutional History of Medieval England* pp136–7

It is on the cards that the extant material will not be *direct* or *immediate* evidence of the decrees that Aethelred promulgated, because the law itself was pronounced by word of mouth and the written version could be influenced by the special preoccupations of his servants, as well as the carelessness of their scribes... Not only may manuscripts have been lost but many important legal decisions may never, for one reason or another, have found their way into writing at all. We have no good reason to doubt that Anglo-Saxon law-codes tell the truth, within reasonable limitations, about Anglo-Saxon law. But we have every reason to doubt that they tell the whole truth.

Patrick Wormald 'Aethelred the Lawmaker' p49

INTRODUCTION

How far is it possible to find in the sources from the tenth century any evidence to support Jolliffe's 1937 romantic presentation of England's infancy? Some is to be found in the surviving manuscripts of laws. They show something of how disputes were intended to be resolved, so that it is essential to determine whether and how they can be trusted. There are other sources, more helpful still because they tell of the practice. They are mainly charters, some genuine, some forged, with many whose authenticity is disputed.[1] Even a forged charter may reveal much about the time when it was forged.

For nearly fifty years after Alfred's death his three successors as kings of Wessex, Edward the Elder (899–924), Aethelstan (924–39) and Edmund

---

1.   There are over 2,000 charters, writs and wills from Anglo-Saxon times. Most of the charters are in Latin, with Anglo-Saxon 'bounds', statements of the boundaries of land; AJ Robertson *Anglo-Saxon Charters*; PH Sawyer *Anglo-Saxon Charters* 1968; now *The Electronic Sawyer* www.trin.cam.ac.uk/chartwww/eSawyer.99/eSawyer2.html; MT Clanchy *From Memory to Written Record* p28.

(939–46), concentrated on recapturing territory from the Danes. Edward was supported by his sister Aethelflaed, lady ruler of Mercia, until her death in 917. Soon thereafter all the people of Mercia who had owed her allegiance, English and Danish, submitted to him; the British kings of Dyfed and Gwynedd accepted him as overlord and then the Northumbrians and the Scots and the Britons who remained in Strathclyde, says the *Anglo-Saxon Chronicle*.[2] Edward was then in control of all of England and more besides, though the British and Scots retained their independence under his overlordship. A treaty of c926 between Aethelstan's *witan* and a British nation, the Dunsaete, gives a glimpse of how overlordship worked, **8.2–9**.[3]

In 918 Raegnald and his Norsemen invaded from Ireland and set up their kingdom in the north-east, with the capital at York. Raegnald accepted Edward as overlord. When Edward died, his successor Aethelstan took York and from 927 could claim to be king of England. When he died in 939, Olaf invaded from Norway and the new king Edmund had to accept him as ruler of the north-east. When Olaf died in 941, Edmund took his territories, only for another Norseman, Eric Bloodaxe, to regain them after Edmund died in 947. Edmund's successor Eadred finally drove out the Norsemen in 954. Edwy succeeded him in 955 and Edgar him in 959, ruling all England until 975. The collection of his laws known as IV Edgar proclaims his rights and those of his various peoples:[4]

8.1 In every borough and in every shire I have my royal rights as my father had, and my thegns have their status during my time as they had in my father's. I will that secular rights continue among the Danes according to the good laws, the best that they may choose. But among the English, the additions I and my *witan* have made to the dooms of my ancestors are established for the benefit of the whole people. Nevertheless, this decree applies to the whole of the people, whether they are English, or Danish, or British, as far as my power stretches, so that poor and rich may keep what they have legally acquired.

So the old laws prevailed; Edgar said so.

Later kings until after the Norman Conquest looked back to Edgar's laws as the foundation on which they built their own. After Edgar's death and the short reign of Edward the Martyr (975–78), Aethelred the Unready ruled for 35 years, well into the next century. He was forced to make

---

2. This rich source started in the reign of Alfred. GN Garmonsway tr *The Anglo-Saxon Chronicle* is the translation which has been most commonly used but it has been superseded by Michael Swanton *The Anglo-Saxon Chronicles*, new edn 2000. They say nothing about dispute resolution.

3. A Cornish charter from the reign of Aethelstan is in a distinctive (and elegant) Latin, DR Howlett *Sealed from Within* pp75–8.

4. IV *Edgar* 2. From this time the Danish parts of England had their own customary laws, as well as dooms and legal vocabulary.

payments to buy off the Danes, with huge amounts of gold and silver in return for uncertain truces. His ordinances show the desperation in his efforts to impose order in those perilous times.[5]

Nearly all the Anglo-Saxon rulers of this period issued dooms which have survived, often more than one collection. Some were exclusively directed to the concerns of the Church. Some were treaties with the Danes, fixing boundaries and setting reciprocal rights and responsibilities and sometimes recording the enormous payments in gold and silver the Anglo-Saxon kings had to make to pay the Danes off.[6]

One strange survival from Aethelstan's time, c926, but not in his name, is now known as *Dunsaete*, a British people:[7]

8.2 This is the ordinance which the *witan* of the English people and the counsellors of the British people have set down among the Dunsaete.

It provided rules for the resolution of disputes arising from cattle-rustling over the border, a river now accepted to be the Wye, between Hereford and Wales.[8] Those who were following the trail, whether English or British, had to stop at the border and hand over the search to men on the other side. It would have caused too much strife if they had invaded the other's territory. Those who were thus compelled to take up the chase had to give a pledge. There were provisions for the resolution of disputes:[9]

8.3 1.2 If it is said that the track is being followed wrongfully, then the man who is tracking the cattle must stop at the bank. Then he, with five other good men, not chosen by him, must swear that he is claiming according to customary law against that land because his cattle went across there.

8.4 2. Always after nine days right must be done between the two banks, both in respect of the charge and all other disputes between them.

8.5 2.1 Between British, *Wealas*, and English there is no other method of clearing oneself of a charge than by ordeal, unless the other side allows it.

8.6 2.2 A pledge should be taken from the other bank unless right can be got in some other way.

8.7 3.2 Twelve lawmen, *lahmen*,[10] six English and six British, shall declare the law to the British and English.

5. II *Aethelred*; a fine new book is Ann Williams *Aethelred the Unready: The Ill-Counselled King*.
6. The treaties between Alfred and Guthrum and Edward and Guthrum are in FL Attenborough *Laws* pp98–109. Attenborough contains the texts and translations of the laws from Aethelberht to Aethelstan; AJ Robertson has those from Edmund to Henry I. They are cited here without the page numbers in those two collections. One payment could be as much as £22,000 then in gold and silver and later it could be much more.
7. Felix Liebermann *Gesetze* I pp374–9; Benjamin Thorpe *Ancient Laws* pp150–2; F Noble (ed Gelling) *Offa's Dyke Reviewed* has a facsimile and translation pp104–9.
8. Patrick Wormald *Making* pp381–2.
9. *Dunsaete* 1, 2, 3, 8 and 9.
10. The body of twelve men to decide disputes is a feature of Danish rather than English assemblies but Edgar provided for such a number of 'witnesses' in the hundred, **8.14**.

8.8 3.3 They shall forfeit all they have if they declare it wrongly, unless they clear themselves by showing they knew no better.

Although the purpose of this treaty was to deal with cattle theft, it included a matter of what we would now call 'public law', the status of the people of Gwent, formerly a British nation and later Welsh:

8.9 9. Formerly the *Wentsaete* belonged to the *Dunsaete*, but it is more right that they belong to the West Saxons. That is where they send tribute and hostages.

There are four essential lessons to be learned from these sources, all of which enlighten the processes of dispute resolution, though not all directly. The first is that, though all judicial business was still done in and by the assemblies, their nature was changing. Secondly, royal representatives came to play a different role in the greater assemblies, less presidential and more judicial. Thirdly, though the kin remained essential in the system of the feud, local groups determined geographically according to residence were given greater jurisdiction. Last and by far the most misunderstood is the continuing fundamental importance of customary law, which at first the laws reveal only by implication but by the end of the century reiterate expressly, sometimes recognising the differences between Danish and English, in the dooms of Edmund, Edgar, Aethelred and, as the next chapter shows, Cnut.[11]

GROUP RESPONSIBILITY

All the evidence shows that Alfred's attempts to change deep-seated attitudes to the feud, **7.3**, had not prevailed.[12] There is no evidence that any part of the legal system treated friend and foe alike. The responsibility of the kin in the feud remained fundamental, though it was supplemented by new institutions.

In the Ordinances of the City of London of Aethelstan's reign, the 'bishops and reeves, nobles and commoners' swear that, in avenging wrongs done to all, they would all stand together:[13]

8.10 That we were all in one friendship, *freondscype*, and one enmity, *feondscype*, whichever it should be.

But Edmund's dooms show that times were changing. Violence was widespread and, though responsibility for a killing still lay with the kin, they could shift the feud from kin to individual:[14]

11. This misunderstanding may arise partly from mistranslation, see the discussion in Chapter 1.
12. Patrick Wormald 'Giving God and King their Due' is full of insights and his footnotes give access to the modern arguments; pp336–42 on feud.
13. VI *Aethelstan* 7.
14. II *Edmund* 1.1.

8.11 If henceforth anyone kills another, he shall himself be subject to the feud, unless he with his friends' help within twelve months pays the full *wergeld* according to his birth. If his kin give him up and are unwilling to make a payment on his behalf, then I will that all the kin except for the wrongdoer be free from the feud, provided thereafter they give him neither food nor shelter.

Any kinsman who later protected the wrongdoer forfeited all his property to the king and became subject to the feud again. Anyone from the victim's kin who took vengeance on anyone other than the wrongdoer forfeited all his property to the king.

The *witan* were enjoined to settle feuds and a procedure was laid down by which the wrongdoer appointed a mediator. Edmund declared that this was according to customary law:[15]

8.12 The *witan* shall settle feuds. First, according to customary law, the killer shall give a solemn promise to his mediator, *forspecan*, and the mediator to the kin, that the killer will give *bot* to the kin. Then after that the victim's kin shall give a solemn promise to that mediator that the killer may approach under truce and pledge for the *wergeld*. When he has made that pledge, then he finds a surety for the *wergeld*. When that has been done it sets up the protection of the king; within 21 days *healsfang* is to be paid; 21 days after that *manbot*; 21 days after that the *frumgyld* of the *wergeld*.

It is not entirely obvious what *healsfang* means but probably it was the first reconciliation payment, which would be just enough to stop the injured kin taking immediate retaliation on the wrongdoer, so long as they knew there was more to come in instalments. It might also equal the most that the killer's kin could raise in the time. *Manbot* was the *bot* paid to the dead man's lord. *Frumgyld* was the first instalment of the balance of the *wergeld*.

If that procedure was, as the doom says, what customary law required for a killing, could it have been more general? Was it common, if not obligatory, for the defendant in a feud first to appoint a mediator, who would then go to the kin of the victim (even if it were a lesser wrong and the victim were still alive) and make an offer of *bot*? If the procedure had to be insisted on by royal doom for killings, could it have been common and general for other kinds of claim?

Edmund was taking greater control, not only over the procedures of the feud but also of the traditional bargaining between the kins over the amount of the *bot*, not only for death but for fighting, too:[16]

8.13 I am not willing that any fighting-fine, *fyhtewite*, or *manbot* be forgiven.

---

15. II *Edmund* 7, with the later title 'On Feuds'. Paul Hyams reads the first sentence 'to mean something like "wise men (i.e. elders, even arbitrators) should work to reconcile vendettas"'.

16. II *Edmund* 3.

Moreover, it was no longer open to affronted kin to take the law into their own hands. They must go with the king. If the king's men pursued their kinsman, no right to vengeance arose. Anyone who refused their help must pay 120 shillings to the king and 30 shillings to the hundred.[17]

Later kings created or gave greater importance to new communities defined by place rather than descent, which later became known as the shire, the hundred (or wapentake in the Danelaw) and the tithing. But the feud still applied, even to a member of the clergy, who still had to look to his kin to be part of the feud and pay his *bot*. If he were a monk and therefore legally without kin, he could look first to his religious brethren for support[18] and, failing them, to the ordeal – but of the blessed morsel. It was not seemly for clergy to be tested by hot iron or cold water. They had to take an oath, swallow the holy bread and ask God to let it choke them if they were telling a lie.

SURETY AND PLEDGE

The requirement to provide a surety, *borh* or *borg*, had been stated in dooms from as early as Hlothhere.[19] Surety grew out of the feud and the corporate responsibility of the kin for each of its members. The tenth century kings made wide use of different kinds of surety, starting with Edward, who required a lord to stand surety for his man accused of theft.[20] Edgar repeated the requirement, adding a system by which every transaction should have witnesses chosen from a previously established panel:[21]

> **8.14** Furthermore, I will that every man be under surety, whether within a borough or without. And witnesses shall be established for every borough and every hundred; 36 witnesses shall be chosen for each borough; twelve for a small borough and each hundred unless you want more. And everyone shall buy and sell before these witnesses all the goods he buys or sells in either borough or wapentake. And each of them, when first chosen to be a witness, shall swear an oath that he will never, for money or love or fear, deny anything to which he has been a witness, nor state in his evidence anything other than what he has seen or heard. At every sale two or three sworn men shall be witnesses.

Aethelred, too, provided in an ordinance enacted 'at Woodstock in Mercian territory' for a system of sureties 'for the security of all people according to the law of the English':[22]

---

17. III *Edmund* 2. This is the first reference to the hundred which has survived. III Edmund is in Latin; but the word for hundred, *hundreto*, is adapted from the English rather than the word used by the Franks, *centena*.
18. Until VIII *Aethelred* 25 made it clear that a monk loses his kinship when he accepts the rule.
19. Oliver *Hlothhere and Eadric* 6, in Chapter 6 above.
20. II *Edward* 3.
21. IV *Edgar* 3.1.
22. I *Aethelred* 1.

8.15 That is, that every free man have a trustworthy surety who shall stand surety for him for every right, if he shall have been accused. If he has a bad reputation, he shall go to the threefold ordeal.

OATHS, PERJURY, ORDEAL AND EVIDENCE

There is a tradition[23] that credits Alfred with the creation of the tithing, and later law required every male when he reached the age of twelve to swear an oath of allegiance and provide surety when he was enrolled in a tithing.[24] That may be one of the many reforms that have been attributed to Alfred for no better reason than that he was a 'good king' but there can be no doubt that he put great emphasis on the oath.[25]

8.16 First of all we decree that it is most important that everyone keep his oath and his pledge carefully.

That was general and included every kind of oath. Aethelstan confirmed this and provided sanctions:[26]

8.17 If he swears a false oath, and it is revealed he did so, his oath shall evermore be worthless, and he shall never lie in consecrated ground.

Different kinds of oath were used for different purposes – promissory, exculpatory and the oath that decision-makers swore when they made their determination. Every claim was formally instituted by a fore-oath. Moreover, Edmund made it compulsory for everyone to swear an oath of allegiance to him, to do what he wanted without reservation, creating between him and them the same relationship as between lord and man, which all Anglo-Saxons well understood and had treated as holy long before they became Christians. Specifically, he insisted that that bond overrode the duties of kin.[27]

Evidentiary oaths were common. But the sources are incontrovertible: rather than rely on oaths, the assembly was interested in the best evidence of facts. Edmund's doom on stolen cattle provides:[28]

8.18 If it is not possible to follow that track from that land, a search shall be made wherever there is suspicion or doubt. And if anyone is accused there, he shall clear himself as appropriate there, and that will stand as an overriding oath, *pro superjuramento.*

Liebermann and Robertson, who have edited this text, suggest that the 'that' in the last phrase means 'the track itself', and that the meaning of

23. First found in William of Malmesbury *De Gestis Regum Anglorum* of the first half of the twelfth century.
24. II Cnut 20, **9.23**.
25. *Alfred* 1.
26. II *Aethelstan* 26.
27. III *Edmund* 1 and 2.
28. III *Edmund* 6.

the clause is that, if the track can be found, it will be sufficient evidence to convict.

The facts could usually be found simply by asking those most likely to know them:[29]

> It is in the nature of localised societies to have local experts, and there is nothing specially significant about the use of an oath to make them do what local experts are usually glad enough to do anyway, namely discharge their copious store of knowledge about local characters and conditions. What does matter... is the extent to which local communities are under central direction, and to which local disputes are the business of the king.

Local experts may well be trusted to know the facts but not to agree on them when their own interests are at stake. Their judgment of whether someone was of good character may not always have been objective. That must have been specially so in a society where kin mattered as much as it still did in England in the tenth century. The oath was important because fear of the punishment for its breach could be even more effective than the sanctions of kin and it gave its swearer some excuse for speaking against kin.

It was every landowner's responsibility to ensure that the oaths of all those who lived on his or her land were credible. Many women held land then, though the sources regularly use the masculine gender and the dooms always. An ordinance of Edmund provided:[30]

> **8.19** Every man shall ensure that his men are credible and all those who are within his protection or on his land. All those of ill repute or charged with accusations shall be put under pledge. A reeve or thegn, noble or commoner, who is not willing to do this or ignores it, shall pay 120 shillings and be subject to the above-mentioned penalties.

If a man's exculpatory oath could not be trusted, then he might have to prove his innocence by submitting to the ordeal. Aethelred's Woodstock ordinance sets out the relationship between oath and ordeal and the detailed provisions for the procedure.[31] His Wantage ordinance provides:[32]

> **8.20** And what is declared with witnesses, that may not be contradicted, whether by the quick or the dead. And every man shall bear witness only to what he dares to swear to on the sacred things given him in his hand.

It is a mistake, though one shared by many of the finest scholars until recently, to assume that procedure in Anglo-Saxon assemblies was rigidly formal. In the nineteenth and early twentieth centuries, some may have

29. Patrick Wormald 'Aethelred the Lawmaker' p69.
30. III *Edmund* 7.
31. I *Aethelred* 1.
32. III *Aethelred* 2. Charlotte Neff 'Scandinavian Elements in the Wantage Code of Aethelred II' is an exhaustive analysis of this law, with comparisons with the laws of other Scandinavian kingdoms.

been misled by their reverence for Roman law, which though unquestionably more 'modern' was formalistic in classical times; or by their vision of those whom they considered to be their Teutonic ancestors; or perhaps by the fashion for the misnamed 'social-Darwinism', or progress ever upwards until we reach us.[33] The evidence is otherwise. Possession of a title deed was not of itself conclusive but, as we saw in the Fonthill case, it prima facie gave the holder the right to swear the oath which formally clinched the matter. Assemblies took documents seriously, as the many forgeries prove:[34] 'One does not fabricate superfluous written evidence if one expects to win by out-swearing or out-remembering one's opponents.'

Apart from the establishment of the facts, it seems that there was plenty of opportunity for argument of a more general kind, with compurgation in only the most intransigent disputes:[35]

> It would seem that disputes were regularly resolved on the basis of the rational presentation of known facts, and one must assume that the parties often, or perhaps on the whole, acquiesced in such resolutions. Arbitration and judgment were not concepts which were carefully distinguished, and it may be that some disputes were more in the way of references to arbitration than adversarial contests. But it would appear that parties intent on pursuing their grievances to the bitter end might have recourse as a last resort to compurgation... Disputes where the parties do appear to accept the worth of documentary evidence impress with a sense of genuine conciliation.

Compurgation was an oath by a party whose supporters also swore oaths that their party's oath was reliable. A party whose oath was supported in this way by sufficient oath-helpers was given the verdict.

The prospect of having to submit to the ordeal, whether it was holding hot iron or being submerged in water must have been a powerful incentive to settle a dispute.[36] That has been recognised from the earliest times in the records which survive from Babylon from roughly 1100BC:[37]

> Occasionally the ordeal was declined, the party concerned declaring 'I will not go'. The effect of this was that either a compromise was agreed or his opponent won the case.

33. Patrick Wormald 'Charters, Law and the Settlement of Disputes' pp149–68 is convincing: 'full analysis of the whole range of specific and descriptive evidence, largely drawn from charters, compels radical reappraisal of the conclusions drawn from prescriptive law codes about Anglo-Saxon litigation'.
34. Wormald 'Charters, Law and the Settlement of Disputes' p157.
35. AG Kennedy 'Law and Litigation' pp169 and 172. Timothy Reuter 'Assembly Politics' sets assemblies in a wider perspective, with many comparative examples.
36. Paul Hyams 'Trial by Ordeal: The Key to Proof in the Early Common Law'; Robert Bartlett *Trial by Fire and Water: The Medieval Judicial Ordeal*; Colin Morris '*Judicium Dei*'.
37. The River Ordeal is described, with supporting texts, in OR Gurney *The Middle Babylonian Legal and Economic Texts from Ur* pp10–12.

The choice of 'composition or the cauldron' (of boiling water) was known to Salic Law[38] and later developments of the ordeal in Europe seem to have a Frankish origin, apart from the separate development in Ireland.[39] There are two mentions of the ordeal in the laws of Ine[40] and a manual of procedure for the ordeal, *Ordal*, from the time of Aethelstan.[41] The importance of ordeals for the resolution of what we would now call civil disputes may not have been great in Anglo-Saxon England but the procedure seems to have gained popularity in criminal process under the Normans and it survived until the involvement of priests was forbidden by the fourth Lateran Council 1215.

ASSEMBLIES

Every free individual had responsibilities to groups at different levels. By the end of the tenth century, every free man over twelve years of age had to belong to a tithing. At the next level, a hundred was made up of several tithings, with no symmetry to their distribution or equivalence of size, though the word 'hundred' is commonly used for a geographical district as well as its assembly. Each shire was made up similarly of hundreds, which in the Danelaw were called wapentakes. Some shires were divided into regions, as Yorkshire was into ridings and still is. Though examples have been given above of separate law for the Danes, the expression 'Danelaw', meaning that part of England subject to that law, dates only from the time of Wulfstan.[42]

All justice was done in an assembly, *gemot*, of some kind. At the highest level the king had his council, *witan*, who met in the *witenagemot*.[43] An ealdorman or a shire-reeve attended every *sciregemot* and usually the local bishop. Every hundred had its own *gemot*. There was no hierarchy, however, of control or appeals. Edward provided in his first collection of dooms that every matter should have a date fixed for hearing and for judgment, **8.1**, and repeated and reinforced it in his second:[44]

> **8.21** I require that every reeve shall hold an assembly, *gemot*, every four weeks; and they make sure that everyone shall have the benefit of customary law, *folcriht*;

38. *Pactus Legis Salicae* 53.1; Katherine Fischer Drew *The Laws of the Salian Franks* pp33–7.
39. Bartlett *Trial by Fire and Water* pp4–5; fn5 for Ireland.
40. Ine 62 discussed in Chapter 6 above and Ine 37 on which FL Attenborough *Laws* has an extensive footnote at pp187–9.
41. Patrick Wormald *Making* pp373–4.
42. Ann Williams *Aethelred* p119. Neff 'Scandinavian Elements' argues convincingly that Aethelred's Wantage Law applied only to the 'Five Boroughs': Lincoln, Stamford, Leicester, Nottingham and Derby.
43. A good example of such a meeting is JM Kemble *Codex Diplomaticus Aevi Saxonici* VI 1258; Robertson *Charters* LIX, where the king, Edgar, sat with his *witan* in London on a land dispute in Kent cAD980 in which Edgar had an interest and took the land.
44. II *Edward* 8.

and that every matter shall have a conclusion and a date when it shall proceed. Anyone who neglects this shall pay the *bot* we have earlier decreed.

Aethelstan provided for seven days' notice of an assembly and dealt severely with failure to turn up:[45]

8.22 If anyone is absent three times from an assembly, payment to the king for disobedience.

Eadred who succeeded Edmund in 947 and Edwy who followed in 955 made no decrees which have survived. But by the time of Edgar (959–75) the hundred had clearly become the unit of royal control:[46]

8.23 This is the ordinance for the holding of the hundred.
8.24 1. First, they shall assemble about every four weeks, and shall do right to each other.
8.25 2. That they go in pursuit of thieves. If the need is immediate, the head of the hundred shall be told and he shall tell the heads of tithings…
8.26 3. Anyone who ignores this and does not obey the hundred's doom… shall pay 30 pence to the hundred…
8.27 5. … if one hundred pursues a track into another hundred, notice shall be given to the head of that hundred and he shall take part. If he fails to do so, he shall pay 30 shillings to the king.
8.28 6. If anyone evades justice and escapes, anyone who has helped him in the wrong shall pay the fixed amount for the damage. If he is charged with aiding the escape, he shall exculpate himself as required in that place, *swa hit on lande stande*.
8.29 7. In the hundred, as in other assemblies, we require that customary law be applied in every matter and a date be fixed for its resolution.

Edgar's second collection of dooms relates to Church matters. His third, however, is the first to set out a recognisably modern set of rules of procedure for all assemblies:[47]

8.30 1. This is my first requirement, that everyone shall have the benefit of customary law, whether poor or rich, and be deemed right dooms. And that there should be such forgiveness of *bot* as is fitting before God, and the world will allow.
8.31 2. No-one shall seek the king about any matter unless he is unable to get justice at home or he may not ask for justice.[48]
8.32 2.1 If that justice is too heavy, afterwards ask the king to lighten it.

45. II *Aethelstan* 20.
46. I *Edgar*. It is likely that some of Edgar's legislation has not survived, e.g. for his Anglo-Saxon subjects similar to IV Edgar for the Danes, Dorothy Whitelock 'Wulfstan *Cantor*' p87.
47. III *Edgar* 1–7.
48. The distinction here is unclear and the second part is omitted when the provision appears again in II *Cnut* 17, **9.24**.

8.33 2.2 No-one shall be liable to pay what can be atoned for by *bot* greater than his *wergeld* [provides].

8.34 3. The decision-maker who makes a bad doom to another shall pay 120 shillings *bot* to the king, unless he dares to declare on oath that he did not know how to make a better and he shall give up for ever his thegnship, unless he buys it back from the king for whatever he consents to...

8.35 4. If anyone makes a false accusation against another... he shall forfeit his tongue unless he pays for it with his *wergeld*.

8.36 5. Attendance at the hundred assembly shall be as before.

8.37 5.1. The borough assembly shall be held thrice a year and the shire assembly twice.

8.38 5.2. The bishop and the *ealdorman* shall attend the shire assembly and there shall apply both God's justice and the world's.

8.39 6. Everyone shall find themselves a surety and that surety shall produce him and keep him to every right. If anyone commits a wrong and gets away, the surety shall bear what he should bear...

8.40 7. If he has a bad reputation and people cannot trust him, and is absent from the assembly three times, then three men shall be picked from the assembly to ride after him, and then he may still find a surety if he can....

The last section provides for one coinage throughout the realm, for standard weights and measures and a minimum price for wool.

Aethelred provided for meetings in the Danelaw:[49]

8.41 An assembly shall be held in every wapentake; and the twelve most senior thegns shall go out with the reeve and swear on the sacred things which are given into their hands that they are unwilling to accuse any innocent person or to protect any guilty one.

The evidence to be found in the charters shows that most disputes brought before shire moots ended in compromise settlements. One reason was that the decision of the shire moot was final unless a party could show that it was 'too heavy' and could persuade the king 'to lighten it'. That would be possible if the disappointed party could prove that one or more of the thegns who decided it had 'made a bad doom'. From this it is clear that it was the thegns who decided. The royal officer, ealdorman or reeve, or the bishop presided and after evidence and argument left the verdict to the assembled thegns. That is not to deny the possibilities for the presiding officer to influence the decision or to take the lead in fashioning a compromise.[50] Moreover, it is clear that the amount to be paid had to be assessed by the assembly and not by its president, whether *bot* the reconciliation payment, *wite* the fine, or *angyld* when that became the term for restitution

49. III *Aethelred* 3.1.
50. Whitelock 'Wulfstan *Cantor*' p92; Kennedy 'Law and Litigation' pp173–4.

of the equivalent amount for the object stolen.[51] It was to the assembly that the tariffs in the royal dooms were addressed.

The decision seems always to have been expressed as unanimous, the will of the whole assembly. Sometimes that is expressly stated in a charter but, even where it is not, it is clear that any dissenters were expected to go along with the majority, or perhaps the dominant voices. Aethelred's legislation shows the policy:[52]

> **8.42** The doom stands which is that of the thegns united. If they dispute it, that stands which eight declare; and those who are defeated in this, they shall each pay six halfmarks.

That was the law in the Danelaw, where twelve thegns were chosen to decide the dispute. A minimum of eight votes was set for a verdict of any wapentake, the assembly to which this legislation relates. Any dissenter who persisted in the minority was heavily fined.

Supervision of the proceedings in the assembly of the hundred, and the revenues which flowed from it, could be granted as if they were the king's property, as Edgar did apparently in 970:[53]

> **8.43** I grant ten thousand eels which every year in the vill called Wellen are rendered for expenses,[54] to the brothers for victuals now and hereafter; and with goodwill for the needs of the brothers and with penal sanction I bestow the secular claims of the two hundreds within the marshes and the five hundreds outside the marshes in Wicklow in the province of the East Saxons,[55] and furthermore all claims or reproofs for transgression of the right law in secular speech of all lands and vills rightly belonging to the said monastery and also those which in future by God's providence may be bestowed on the said place, whether by purchase or gift or any rightful acquisition. Secular claims shall be emendable under the kind supervision of the brothers living there who minister to the requirements of food and clothing.

Because the decision of the shire assembly was final, it could be asked to legitimate transactions and there is evidence of its use to convey land to a monastery, subject to a life interest,[56] and to make formal a marriage contract.[57]

---

51. Julius Goebel *Felony and Misdemeanour* p351.
52. III *Aethelred* 13.2.
53. *Liber Eliensis* II 5, EO Blake p77, Janet Fairweather p101.
54. Fairweather has 'instead of military service', perhaps reading *pro expeditione* for Blake's *pro expenditione*.
55. A scribe's mistake for East Angles.
56. Robertson *Charters* CV p200.
57. There is an analogous requirement not only for *boni homines* but also for neighbours who knew the facts, for the final decision of a land dispute in a Frankish assembly in AD857, even though the title deeds had been produced, JL Nelson 'Dispute Settlement in Carolingian West Francia' p56.

THE KING'S REPRESENTATIVES

The legislation of the tenth century shows how the ealdormen and reeves grew in importance and the range of their duties. Most of the dooms are in the form of instructions to the king's officials and say so expressly. They were not directed to the people.[58] To start with Edward the Elder:[59]

8.44 Edward's Decrees
[On dooms, *dome*, and decisions][60]
King Edward commands all the reeves that you deem right dooms as most right as you can and base them on the *dombec*, doombook. But do not neglect in any matter to take the customary law, *folcriht*, into consideration. And that every matter shall have a date, when it shall be dealt with, on which judgment is given.

Reeves were not the highest royal officers. Those were the members of his own council, the *witan*, to whom II Edward is directed.[61]

8.45 King Edward exhorted his *witan* when they were at Exeter that they should all consider how their peace could be kept better than it was before, because he thought that the orders he had previously given had not been carried out as well as they should.

Edward's successor Aethelstan directed his dooms more widely:[62]

8.46 Aethelstan's decrees
I, King Aethelstan... tell the reeve in every borough... And the bishops... and my ealdormen and my reeves...
8.47 I, King Aethelstan,... tell all my reeves....

And he provided for the punishment of reeves who disobeyed him.[63]

Edmund, Aethelstan's successor, addressed his officials directly, telling them that he expected their support in keeping order.[64]

8.48 The *witan* shall bring about reconciliation: first, according to customary law, *folcriht*, a killer shall give a solemn promise....

Edgar was the first king to give express instructions for the publication of his ordinance, and he makes it clear that it is addressed not just to his officials:[65]

---

58. Patrick Wormald 'Uses of Literacy' p111 followed by Hanna Vollrath 'Gesetzgebung' pp28–54 thought that, because literacy was so limited, the laws were not formally published by the king with the intention they should bind, Simon Keynes 'Royal Government' p229, but no general literacy was needed when they were addressed not to the people but to assemblies or to royal officers who, if they could not read, had others to read to them.
59. I *Edward* preamble.
60. An addition by a later scribe.
61. II *Edward* preamble.
62. I *Aethelstan*, on church matters, preamble.
63. II *Aethelstan* 25.
64. II *Edmund* 5.
65. IV *Edgar* 15.1.

8.49 Many copies of this shall be written and sent both to Ealdorman Aelfhere and Ealdorman Aethelwine, and then in all directions, so that this ordinance shall be known by poor and rich alike.

There were no poor royal officials. These poor are ordinary folk. This is the first English legislation in the modern mode: addressed to all the king's subjects for them to obey.

No doubt many assemblies of the hundred met without a royal officer but his attendance would be specially useful when more than one hundred assembled together, as often happened, or when the parties were from different hundreds. Then the reeve might have mediated, armed with royal dooms of which he had knowledge, even if the parties and the decision-makers did not. But this is speculation; I have found no evidence in the surviving charters.

All this legislation makes it clear that the kings were concerned to ensure that their officials were acting according to their wishes. What it does not show is any evidence that those kings wanted to have anything to do themselves with the administration of justice in individual cases. Indeed, such evidence as there is denies that.[66] They were quick to intrude only when they saw their interests at stake.

FOLCRIHT AND DOOMS

Throughout this period the infrastructure of all decision-making remained the various assemblies, all of which applied the customary law.[67] In earlier chapters the fundamental place of customary law has had to be argued but the royal dooms of the tenth century expressly insist on its application as the basic law. It applied always and everywhere, unless overruled by specific dooms, though there were differences particularly between English and Danes, **8.1**. As Edward the Elder decreed, **8.44**: 'base your decisions on the doombooks but do not neglect in any matter to take the customary law into consideration'.[68] And he makes clear that one of the functions of the dooms was to set tariffs. They shared that function with other kinds of legislation including treaties:[69]

8.50 ... he shall pay the *bot* which the doombooks provide for... he shall pay the *bot* that the doombooks declare if it is within [our kingdom]... if in the eastern or in the northern, the *bot* shall be what the treaties declare.

66. AG Kennedy 'Law and Litigation' p149; AG Kennedy 'Disputes about *Bocland*' pp175–95.
67. Derek Roebuck 'Customary Law before the Conquest'.
68. Janet Nelson 'Dispute Settlement' provides another analogy, quoting Hincmar of Reims: 'when they hope for profit of some kind they invoke [customary] law, but when they reckon there's no advantage to be had there, they seek refuge in capitularies: thus it comes about that neither capitularies nor law are properly observed'. Capitularies are the Frankish kings' equivalent of the Anglo-Saxon dooms, legislation publicly read out, with written copies disseminated.
69. II *Edward* 5.

Aethelstan also stressed the importance of the customary law's general application. He would not allow anyone to escape its grasp, even if it meant manufacturing an artificial customary law by making the kin responsible for assigning a place of residence to a man who had no lord:[70]

> **8.51** We decree that lordless men from whom one may not obtain justice, their kin find them a residence so that they are domiciled within the customary law and arrange a lord for them in the assembly.

What is specially relevant there is that kin were made responsible for one aspect of the shift from blood to place, and thereby to a lord.[71] There was no excuse for a man being lordless, if he was '*lathleas*', that is he could prove that he had committed no crime, because Aethelstan provided:[72]

> **8.52** If he is guilty of no crime, he may, with those witnesses, choose any lord he likes, for I allow anyone who is free from guilt to follow any lord he wishes.

In the time of Aethelstan, a thief found guilty 'according to customary law' should be put to death[73] and an accused about to undergo the ordeal had to swear that he was 'not guilty of the charge according to customary law'.[74]

In the law which set out the procedure to be followed at the assembly of the hundred, **8.28**, Edgar requires one who abets an escape to: 'exculpate himself as required in that place, *swa hit on lande stande....*' That phrase is surely connected with the earlier provision for one hundred to collaborate with another. The doom is specifically required to show how the potential conflict of customary laws is to be resolved. That little proto-code of procedure for the assembly of the hundred ends with the general decree: 'In the hundred, as in other assemblies, we require that customary law be applied in every matter.' That last phrase in Anglo-Saxon, '*mon folcriht getaece aet aelcere spaece*', is a jingle, something roughly like:

> Give folklaw a place
> In every case.

I cannot believe that anyone with an ear can doubt that this is the sort of phrase that all native Anglo-Saxon speakers learned in childhood.[75] Edgar

70. II *Aethelstan* 2.
71. II *Aethelstan* 9 requires an oath that an intended attachment of cattle is according to customary law.
72. V *Aethelstan* 1.1.
73. VI *Aethelstan* 1, of the ordinances which applied to London.
74. II *Aethelstan* 23.
75. Had this been decreed in the time of Wulfstan (archbishop of York 1002–23), who had a big hand in later drafting, it might have been one of his characteristic rhyming and alliterative phrases; **8.68** is another example. 'Anglo-Saxon law had a fondness for rhymes, jingles and the like', TFT Plucknett *Early English Literature* p92 fn4; FE Harmer *Anglo-Saxon Writs* pp85ff; M Daunt 'Old English Verse and English Speech Rhythm' p57.

stated the basic principles even more plainly and generally in his third collection of dooms, **8.29**:[76] 'Everyone shall have the benefit of the customary law, whether poor or rich, and be deemed right dooms.'

Though Edgar gave the Danes the right to choose the best laws they could, he insisted that the rules for preventing cattle theft be the same for all. The Danes may fix the penalty for them killing 'a reeve of mine or any other man' or for even offering any resistance to those investigating a theft but 'for the English, I and my *witan* have chosen what the penalty should be'. As for the procedure:[77]

> **8.53** It shall apply to all of us who live in these islands.
> Furthermore, Earl Oslac and all the armed forces[78] living in his earldom shall ensure the observance of these laws, for the love of God, and for the good of all our souls, and the peace of the whole *folc*.

The idea of customary law as the basis for the control of everyone's relations, supplemented where the king thought necessary on the advice of his *witan*, was no longer merely tacitly understood. It was the fundamental constitutional principle on which the kingdom of England was being expressly settled.

MEDIATION AND ARBITRATION

The *Liber Eliensis* is a history of the monastery at Ely written by a monk there towards the end of the twelfth century. One of its purposes was to sustain the monastery's ownership of a large amount of land of various kinds and extents which had come into its hands over four centuries or more. His descriptions of acquisitions from donors, some quite unwilling, include stories of disputes which ended in settlements in favour of the monastery.[79]

After Edgar's death in 975, there were those who would have liked to overturn his grants to religious houses. One of them, Aelfwold, tried to get back land he had sold to Aethelwold, abbot of Ely, on the grounds that the sale was forced on him. Presumably the land had risen in value. This was a matter for the shire moot:[80]

> **8.54** Then Abbot Byrhtnoth went and brought a claim against him at Hertford and, in the presence of everybody in a general assembly, he told him how his wife and sons were born slaves on St Aethelthryth's land at Hatfield, and how he had sold the land in question so that he might have them free and without challenge,

---

76. III *Edgar* 1.
77. IV *Edgar* 14 and 15. Compare III Aethelred, the Wantage Law, in Neff 'Scandinavian Elements' pp288–97.
78. *Here*, which literally means 'enemy army' is used conventionally for the Danish people.
79. EO Blake *Liber Eliensis* (text); Janet Fairweather *Liber Eliensis* (translation). The surviving manuscripts of Book II, the part relevant here, are Latin translations of an Anglo-Saxon original, the *Libellus Aethelwoldi*.
80. *Liber Eliensis* II 10, Blake p83; Fairweather p107.

having accepted twenty mancuses [gold coins] from the bishop. Therefore, having listened to this argument, Aelfwold started to go back on his presumption and, when a final settlement had been made, Abbot Byrhtnoth added forty shillings to the aforesaid gold and gave it to him.

Having shamed Aelfwold, Byrhtnoth clinched the settlement by giving something to him as a sweetener, forty shillings being a nicely-judged sum, not too little to be taken seriously, not so much as to cast doubt on the Abbot's confidence in his own claim.

The authority of the shire moot was considered necessary to authenticate the settlement, if a dispute were of sufficient importance. Another claim arising out of an attempt after Edgar's death to recover land granted to the Ely monastery started in London but ended in the shire moot at Northampton:[81]

8.55 A general assembly was called in London at a time when commanders, chiefs, governors, orators and pleaders, *duces, principes, satrape, hrethore et causidici*, had gathered together there from all parts. The Blessed Aethelwold summoned the said Leofsige to law, *in ius*. Before them all in an orderly way he set out his claim... When the matter had been discussed by all, well and properly and openly, they all by their judgment gave back Peterborough and Oundle and Kettering to God and the Blessed Aethelwold. They also adjudged that Leofsige should compensate the bishop for the whole of his loss and restore to him his *mund*, and for the violence make amends to the king by forfeiture of the amount of his *wergeld*. A week later they met again at Northampton. All the province or shire was gathered there. They set out the aforesaid claim again and when it had been set out and explained, those at Northampton decided as had been the earlier judgment in London.

Even though all the leading men had been involved in the unanimous decision of the London assembly, it was considered necessary to have it formally ratified by the assembly of the relevant shire.

There is direct evidence that arbitration in the shire moot had the blessing of Aethelred. Bishop Godwine sought to recover land from Leofwine:[82]

8.56 When the dispute became known to the king, he sent his writing and his seal to Archbishop Aelfric and instructed him and his thegns in East Kent and West Kent to arbitrate it according to law, *onriht gesemdon*, comparing claim and defence. Then it was that Bishop Godwine came to Canterbury to the Archbishop and the sheriff Leofric came and with him Abbot Aelfun and thegns of both East Kent and West Kent, all men of substance. Then and there they declared what they had

---

81. *Liber Eliensis* II 11, Blake p84; Fairweather p108.
82. Rochester Cathedral *Textus Roffensis* f155; Robertson *Charters* LXIX, text and translation pp140–3, notes pp384–5. Paul Fouracre, 'Disputes in Later Merovingian Francia' p27 and Appendix V, provides a comparable instruction of Clovis III in Francia at the end of the seventh century, which also required the decision-makers to know the local law: '*quicquid lex loci vestri de tale causa edocit*', 'whatever the law of your place provides for such a case'.

discussed for a long time, after Bishop Godwine had produced his evidence. They all humbly asked the bishop to grant Leofwine possession of the land at Snodland with his blessing for his lifetime. The bishop granted this to the satisfaction of all the *witan* there assembled. Leofwine gave his solemn promise that after his death the land would revert to the foundation from which he had been given his life interest, *læn*, and he gave up the documents concerning the land, which had previously been alienated from the foundation, together with all the dwellings he had to the west of the church. These were the mediators, *ærendracan*, of the settlement: Abbot Aelfun, Abbot Wulfric, Sheriff Leofric, Siweard, Wulfstan of Saltwood and Aelelm Ordelm's son.

Then follows a list of witnesses beginning with the archbishop, then Bishop Godwine the claimant himself, the communities of Christchurch and of St Augustine's, the citizens of Canterbury and 19 others. The settlement required Leofwine to give up his claim to ownership of the land and in addition to convey to Godwine other dwellings he had near the church. In return Godwine granted him a life interest, called here a loan as in **7.18**. In this matter there were six mediators. But it is clear that it was the assembly of the thegns of the shire who approved the settlement.

The shire moot's preference was for the dispute to be settled by a compromise acceptable to both parties, as the quoted examples show, **8.54**, **8.56**, **8.57**, **8.62**. Sometimes the process by which agreement was mediated seems contrived. A charter drawn up by Wulfstan at Aethelred's command recites that Leofric had sold land at Inkberrow to Bishop Aethelstan, with a full title: 'unopposed and unquestioned, to give and to transfer in his lifetime or at his death, to kin or friends however he wished'. Many years later, a different Wulfstan and his son Wulfric claimed part of the land. Bishop Aethelstan took the matter before the shire moot at Worcester. There Earl Leofwine presided and he and Leofric and 'the whole shire' granted him full title to the land because he had taken it 'unopposed and unquestioned' and they set a date for the boundaries to be inspected and confirmed by those who had confirmed them in the first grant. Bishop Aethelstan took Leofric with him and Wulfstan and Wulfric and 'their friends' joined them and inspected the boundaries. Then Leofric and all who were there held that Bishop Aethelstan was the rightful owner. But that was not the end of it; negotiations continued:[83]

8.57 Then Leofric's friends and Wulfstan's friends said that it would be better if they were to come to an agreement rather than to keep up any dispute between them. So they worked out this settlement. Leofric was to give one pound to

83. Robertson *Charters* LXXXIII, p162; Sawyer *Anglo-Saxon Charters* 1460; Kennedy 'Disputes about *Bocland*' p185. It cannot be entirely fortuitous that the Britons in contemporary Brittany followed similar processes, five hundred years after they had emigrated there, Wendy Davies 'People and Places in Dispute' p76. The essays in this collection give many examples of mediated settlements, from fifth-century Gaul to sixteenth-century Scotland.

Wulfstan and his son. Leofric and two thegns were to swear an oath that Leofric would have been satisfied with that amount if the decision had gone against him as it had for Wulfstan. This was the agreement of all of us. Wulfstan and his son then transferred to Leofric full title to the land; and Leofric and Wulfstan and Wulfric gave full and unquestioned title to the bishop to grant in his lifetime or at his death to whomever he wished.

The names of the witnesses and sureties present are set out, with Bishop Aethelstan, Leofric and Wulfstan first, then fourteen others. Wulfstan's injured pride and fear of shame were assuaged by Leofric's oath that he would have been happy with the compromise if their roles had been reversed.

Aethelred legislated to ensure that such mediated settlements had the force of law, equating an agreement with an adjudication, 'love' with 'law':[84]

> **8.58** Where a thegn has two choices, love or law, *lufe oþþe lage*, and he then chooses love, that stands as fast as a doom. And he who contrary to that allows exculpation or he who himself yields, payment six half-marks.

So you could continue to negotiate after an adjudication but once you had agreed to a settlement which the assembly had approved, that was that. You must pay a substantial fine before the assembly could be asked to approve any alteration. Of the six half-marks, four went to the king and two to the ealdorman.

In an ordinance said to have been made in 1008, among many provisions dealing with Church matters, Aethelred included this one encouraging settlements:[85]

> **8.59** At the holy festivals, as is right, there shall be conciliation and reconciliation, *som 7 sib*, for all Christian men, and every dispute settled.
> **8.60** And if anyone owes surety or *bot* to someone else, about worldly matters, let him discharge it gladly, before or after.

A charter from the end of the tenth century records a mediation which failed in Berkshire.[86] In 990 a dispute arose between Leofwine and Wynflaed about land which they had exchanged. Wynflaed went to Aethelred and proved her right to possession by producing witnesses to the transaction, which included not only the archbishop, Sigeric, and Bishop Ordbriht and Earl Aelfric but also the king's mother, Aelfthryth. Aethelred forthwith sent

---

84. III *Aethelred* 13.3 and 13.4. For the history of the expression 'love-day': MT Clanchy 'Law and Love' pp47–67 and JW Spargo 'Chaucer's Lovedays' pp36–56. By tradition, debts must be settled at the Chinese New Year.
85. V *Aethelred* 19 and 20; the same provisions appear in VI *Aethelred* 25.1 and 25.2.
86. British Museum Cotton Augustus II 15, Robertson *Anglo-Saxon Charters* LXVI, text and translation pp136–9, notes pp379–82; translated and fully discussed in Patrick Wormald 'Giving God and King their Due' pp343–51 and 356–7.

a message with the witnesses to Leofwine, who insisted that the matter be referred to a shire moot. Aethelred sent his seal to a meeting of the whole shire, with instructions to arbitrate:[87]

> **8.61** He ordered and instructed them that they should arbitrate, *geseman*, fairly between Wynflaed and Leofwine in the fairest way they could. Archbishop Sigeric sent his written testimony and Bishop Ordbyrht his. Then Wynflaed was told she should prove her ownership. Then she brought forth her ownership with the support of Aelfthryth the king's mother, and then the first was Abbot Wulfgar, [then ten other named men, two abbesses and eleven other named or identified women] and many a good thegn, and good women – we cannot list them all – so that the full number was made up, both of men and of women.[88]
>
> Then the *witan* there present declared that it would be better to let the oath go than for it to be given, because after that there would be no friendship. Leofwine would be ordered to give back what he had plundered and make a payment and pay his *wer* to the king. Then he let the oath go and transferred possession of the land to Bishop Aethelsig without further contest and [agreed] that he would make no further claim on it.
>
> Wynflaed was ordered to produce the gold and silver of Leofwine's father, all that she had. Then she did what she dared to save her oath. Leofwine would not accept that in satisfaction unless she would swear that that was the whole of his property. She said she could do not that on her part, nor could he on his. Aelfgar the king's reeve was witness to this, and Byrhtric and Leofric of Whitchurch and many good people as well.

When Wynflaed proved her right to possession by producing the required witnesses, all she needed to do to gain the assembly's formal recognition of her ownership was to swear the oath, with the necessary number of oaths from her supporters. She was persuaded not to do so because Leofwine had a claim against her for withholding gold and silver belonging to his father. She did 'what she dared to save her oath', that is the oath she had sworn to the king at the start of the proceedings. She was not prepared to swear that she had produced all Leofwine's father's property in her possession. She then pleaded that she could not do that any more than Leofwine could swear to the contrary. And there it is – a plain example of a dispute which the king wanted settled but which the parties could not resolve despite such powerful mediation. We can guess that the ultimate outcome was some kind of compromise which avoided the oath, the verdict in favour of Wynflaed which would have had to follow it and, the telling factor, the

---

87. Robertson *Charters* LXVI; Wormald 'Giving God' pp343–54, with a translation in the Appendix pp356–7.
88. Perhaps 36 in all. The emphasis here on the presence and involvement of women is quite marked. It almost suggests that there was a full number for women, as well as and separately from men. I know of no other source which suggests that women witnesses were necessary, perhaps where a woman was a party. It would be nice to think that this is an early example of sisterhood rather than a custom peculiar to Berkshire.

imposition on Leofwine of payments of *bot*, *wergeld* and a fine to the king, *wite*, with the – at least theoretical – possibility of the death penalty as the sanction for non-payment.

What is striking here is that Wynflaed tried to take the matter to the king without following the procedures the dooms, and indeed customary law, required. She should first have gone to the shire moot. Leofwine took that procedural point, without citing the relevant law. It was not the practice then to do so, neither dooms nor customary law. They were taken as read, or, if they were cited, it was not considered necessary to record it. Alternatively it has been argued that those involved in dispute resolution did not know of the written dooms' existence.[89] But they certainly knew the relevant law, whether it was customary or royal. In any event, Aethelred's response was to submit the matter to the mediation and arbitration of the shire moot.

It would hardly be possible for all the assembled thegns to act as mediators. A leading role must surely have been played by whoever presided, or possibly an attendant bishop. Where the ealdorman was a dominant local landowner and political leader, his own authority would overcome the recalcitrance of most parties. In any case, he was the king's representative and acted with royal authority, sometimes expressed by the king sending him his seal, necessarily on a document, an early form of writ.[90]

The process was similar in the assembly of the hundred:[91]

8.62 Then the abbot bought 200 acres at Witchford from Sumerlida for eleven pounds in the presence of the whole of the hundred as witness in the time of King Edgar. But when he died and the kingdom was in disorder, that Sumerlida reverted to tricks and treated as invalid the agreement which he had with the abbot, saying that he had been forced to make it and had wanted many times to return the money he had received. Meanwhile Ealdorman Aethelwine came to Ely and below the churchyard at the north gate of the monastery he held an assembly with the whole hundred and there he put an end to the dispute or case which was between the abbot and Sumerlida, like this: that the abbot gave Sumerlida thirty shillings and so paid in full twelve pounds for the 200 acres.

The sums do not add up. The original price was eleven pounds. The abbot, if he originally paid eleven pounds and now paid another thirty shillings, had paid in all £12.10s. It is possible that the copyist made a slip, xxx for xx, but would nobody have noticed? Surely at that time there would be people who were greatly concerned about the accuracy of this record and would have checked it. The error was most likely introduced by a later scribe. Even so, the abbot is now required to pay twelve pounds though the price was eleven. How can that be explained? There is no difficulty. That is just what might be expected of a settlement mediated by an *ealdorman* and

89. Simon Keynes 'Royal Government'.
90. Campbell, John and Wormald *Anglo-Saxons* p238.
91. *Liber Eliensis* II 12, Blake p91; Fairweather p115; Kennedy 'Law and Litigation' p173.

given legal force by the assembly of the hundred. Both sides have to give a little to have a settlement which has the backing of the assembly, whether of shire or hundred, and thereby is made legally binding.[92]

That is shown expressly by a matter settled before an assembly of three hundreds:[93]

> **8.63** So when the witnesses were produced before the three hundreds they gave testimony for the abbot, that is, that at a certain time, when the three hundreds had assembled, Ulf, with Aelfwold's wife also present, had made his defence before them all in relation to that land, six months before the abbot sought to buy that land from her. And they affirmed that they were witnesses and sureties between the abbot and the woman, that the abbot would pay her fifteen pounds if she would release to him three hides clear in Chippenham; but if she was not able to do that, the abbot would pay her a price according to the value of the land.
>
> So Ealdorman Aethelwine, seeing that the abbot had been considered to be in the right on the evidence, asked him, for love of him, to give a little bit more than the aforesaid amount, i.e. seven pounds and a half. In response the abbot gave her thirty shillings....

Then the monastic scribe lets his feelings show:

> **8.64** What a sacrilegious time! What a selfish world!... That hide cost 100 shillings and the 24 acres twenty shillings and the six and a half properties sixty shillings, which nobody in his right mind would have valued at more than twenty shillings!

THE CHURCH

Edgar's grant of jurisdiction to the monks of Ely was discussed above, **8.43**. The *Liber Eliensis* sets that jurisdiction out more fully later:[94]

> **8.65** These are the honours and customs of the church of Ely, granted and confirmed by King Edgar and all the kings of England who succeeded him up to this day, of St Aethelthryth within the Isle [of Ely] and within the two hundreds of the Isle, i.e. all assemblies and rights which belong to the Crown. All the men of the two hundreds of the Isle must assemble every fortnight at Ely or at Witchford, which is called the head of the hundreds of the Isle, or at Modich, which is a fourth part of the hundreds, for the rights of St Aethelthryth to be decided. No one holds land or any right within the Isle except St Aethelthryth. None of the king's barons holds his court within the two hundreds of the Isle. Claimant and defendant shall come to the aforesaid places and be judged there. Similarly in the five-and-a-half hundreds of Wicklow and the one-and-a-half of Dereham and the trithing of Winston. And if anyone on the land of St Aethelthryth, whoever he owes homage to, whether he is a native or outsider, shall have been the defendant

---

92. Kennedy 'Law and Litigation' p172 comes to the same conclusion: 'it may be significant that the account gives the impression that Aethelwine was a mediator as much as a judge in this dispute, *Libellus Aethelwoldi Episcopi* 15, *Liber Eliensis* II 12'.
93. *Liber Eliensis* II 11; Blake p90; Fairweather p115.
94. *Liber Eliensis* II 54, Blake p124; Fairweather p150.

to a claim and sentenced to the water and fire, nowhere else but in Ely shall he get what God vouchsafes to him. No person, lay or cleric, shall exact a right over this, but the Church alone may release him, by the hand of the sacrist, who performs the function of archdeacon in the Isle....

I have derived these from writings and letters of the Church, not from my own ideas as opinion.

There is nothing there or anywhere else to tell us what procedures were followed. There is no reason to believe that the Church intervened in any way other than to ensure that the profits of this jurisdiction went to the monastery, through the hands of the sacrist, the official in charge of the valuables.

CONCLUSIONS

By the beginning of the eleventh century, some aspects of the legal system look quite modern. The preamble to VI *Aethelred* shows the king's council's self-conscious understanding of their role as legislators:[95]

8.66 This is the legislation which the legislators of England have determined and decreed gladly enjoining that it should be obeyed.

The provisions at the end set out general principles of law and show that there was a clear and now express distinction in the minds of the legislators between intentional and unintentional wrongs and for the need for discretion both in judging liability and fixing penalties.[96]

8.67 If it should happen that someone involuntarily or unintentionally does some wrong, that is not the same as if he did it willingly and intentionally of his own will; similarly an involuntary agent who does some wrong should always be spared and have the benefit of better dooms because he acted as agent involuntarily. Every act should be carefully distinguished and the doom be made to fit the act justly and proportionately.

And this is right, this decree concludes, because all of us need God's mercy good and often.

These are huge steps forward in the development of the law from where it stood with Aethelberht or even in the age of Alfred. VIII *Aethelred* looks back to the earlier laws of the secular *witan* of Aethelstan and Edmund and Edgar[97] but it proclaims again the widest principle of justice:[98]

8.68 Law shall be with right judgment according to the deed and be made with due measure.

And the Anglo-Saxon phrase *Rihte dom aefter daede 7 medmung be maeþe* is another moral jingle:

95. VI *Aethelred* preamble.
96. VI *Aethelred* 52.1 and 53.
97. VIII *Aethelred* 43.
98. VIII *Aethelred* 5.2.

> Right doom after deed
> And according to meed.

That was in the language of the ordinary people, who by then could be expected to understand this royal grant to Ely, when it was read out to them:

> **8.69** And we have also given instructions that our edicts shall be written down in ordinary language so that they may be heard in the ears of the common people, so that it may be clear that they are not bedevilled with jargon but, by the royal authority and power given to us by God, let every opposite opinion be utterly annulled.

No wonder that Edgar's laws were looked back on with affection! Not only were they directed to his people rather than officials, he directed that they should published, in language which all would understand. They were always expected to know the customary law. Now they were deemed to know their duties under the new legislation. But subjects can also begin to think about their rights when they know what the law is supposed to grant them.

Moreover, X *Aethelred* makes it clear that, though it is the king who is legislating, it is the *witan*'s decree that general principles of justice, *rihte laga*, prevail, of which everyone shall have the benefit. Indeed, VI Aethelred is a set of ordinances which purports to be made by the *witan* itself, with no mention of the king, speaking first as an ordinance of the bishops only and thereafter of the whole council. Perhaps it was never more than a draft.[99] But, even before that, in the time of Aethelstan, *Dunsaete*, **8.2–9**, is a treaty with no mention of the king.

Wulfstan, when he became Cnut's draftsman, did not announce his dependence on the laws of Aethelred but there can be no denying their influence, or the fact that Aethelred's laws lasted through Cnut without legislative reform until the Conquest. Even thereafter they remained 'the staple and the starting-point for further endeavour'.[100]

Moreover, it has been suggested that the legislative activity evidenced by the surviving manuscripts is nowhere near the whole: 'The various flotsam and jetsam of fragments, interpolations and obscure references to lost codes suggest the production during this period of much royal legislation that is no longer extant.'[101] But the better opinion may be Wormald's:[102]

> While it may, on the one hand, be right to deduce that there were many written laws which are now lost, it may, on the other, be that some laws inevitably left few or no traces, because they never proceeded beyond the spoken word....

99. Wormald *Making* pp132, 191–2.
100. Williams *Aethelred* p149.
101. Kennedy 'Law and Legislation' p174.
102. Wormald *Making* pp127–8, 414.

What reason is there to think that the pre-conquest legislative tradition ran to many codes that are now lost?

Of course, it is not only the written laws which applied then, or are of interest to us now. But we are less likely to know of those, just as valid, which were never written down.

A comprehensive study of whatever evidence can be found in the charters leads to the conclusion:[103] 'The prevalence of conventions among the cases cited warrants the observation of Adams [*Essays in Anglo-Saxon Law* p26] that a compromise was always effected in the Anglo-Saxon courts when one was possible.' That bears out the message drawn here from all the sources cited: most disputes which could not be resolved informally were brought before an assembly, where if possible they were mediated, if not then submitted to the arbitration of a body of leading men who, often with the help of a royal officer or bishop, applied the customary law of that assembly, subject to any relevant royal dooms. That was public arbitration, of course, and there is little evidence of private ad hoc arbitration or mediation. It was still the only formal system of resolving disputes.

---

103. Zinkeisen 'Anglo-Saxon Courts of Law' 136 fn2.

9   CNUT TO THE CONQUEST

In the twelfth century, some time after the Conquest, it was the established theory
that England was or had been divided between three laws, the West-Saxon, the
Mercian and the Danish. The old laws themselves notice this distinction in a casual
way; but we have little means of telling how deep it went. It is highly probable,
however, that a great variety of local customs was growing up in England, when
the Norman Conquest checked its growth.

> FW Maitland *The Constitutional History of England* p3

INTRODUCTION

Is it true that by the time of the Conquest the efforts of central government had been successful in simplifying the various regimes of customary
law? Was that ever an aim of government? Or was a 'great variety of local
customs' growing? This chapter may help to answer these questions but it
will be left for the next to decide whether the Conquest checked the growth
of customary law and with it the development of the established methods
of dispute resolution.

The eleventh century starts with England subject to recurrent internal
strife and regular invasion. Aethelred never felt secure at any time in his
long reign. Indeed, he lost his kingdom to the Dane Swein Forkbeard for
a year in 1013, when he took refuge among his kin in Normandy. There,
Scandinavians had been settled for five generations, since they invaded
in 911, in what James Campbell calls 'the French Danelaw'.[1] From there
their leader would within a little more than half a century lead the last of
the Germanic invasions.

But first England was to be taken by other Germanic invaders, the
Vikings again. The Danes who had come first as raiders, fighters organised
by their inclusion in the ship they came in, had settled by this time among
both Anglo-Saxons and British. Some had bought the land they now
farmed.

The *Anglo-Saxon Chronicle*'s annals[2] are full of the verbs *hergian* and
forhergian, to harry. It is easy to miss the full consequences of such an
unfamiliar word. Harrying was a military attack, sometimes punitive by
English kings on their own subjects but more often for plunder by invaders.

1. Campbell, John and Wormald *The Anglo-Saxons* p194.
2. Swanton *Anglo-Saxon Chronicles*.

The process was not a form of warfare between trained soldiers. It was the destruction of crops and homes and the killing of defenceless workers and their families, unless they were spared to be sold as slaves. A place that had been harried stayed dead for a while, burnt and barren, until it could be revived to be harried again.

A modern myth is that England has always been easier to defend because it is an island. But travel by sea with an armed force was easier than by land, where every mile might be met by armed resistance. Most parts of England were at risk. Not only the eastern shores and inland to York and Cambridge but midlands Oxford and Bedford and even Cheshire were harried in the last years of Aethelred. Much of that harrying was done by Cnut. When he became king of England in 1016 he governed by the ultimate threat of death and destruction. Indeed, it was more dangerous to be a noble Englishman on the wrong side than a commoner. And it must be kept in mind that it was not only the ordinary people who preferred a strong foreign king, who brought peace, to rule by an unsuccessful Anglo-Saxon with constant unrest. Many of the Anglo-Saxon aristocracy sided with Cnut. His empire came to include not only Anglo-Saxon England, with overlordship of the British kingdoms of Gwynedd, Powys and Dyfed,[3] but also Denmark, Norway, parts of Sweden, and lands further east.

How far he had become familiar in his own country with some of the components of the administration he inherited in England is disputed.[4] We do not know enough about the legal system of contemporary Denmark, where there were no written records, or indeed of England, to make close comparisons. It is hardly likely, though, that society was organised completely differently in Denmark from the systems Cnut found in the various parts of England. He chose both Anglo-Saxons and Danes to exercise authority under him.[5] After his time the chief men's title changed from ealdorman to earl. The evidence shows that people from the various language groups were able to communicate with one another well enough for the exercise

3. Gruffydd ap Llewelyn became ruler of all Wales in 1055 but the kingdoms fell apart again on his death in 1063. Though this book makes no attempt to discover how disputes were resolved in Wales, it is important to remember that until well after the Conquest the Welsh retained their own British laws and considered themselves the true remaining Britons. The chronicle *Brut y Tywysogion* p45 calls Gruffydd 'the most noble king of the Britons'. About 1200 Walter Map, himself Welsh, wrote his *De Nugis Curialium* 'Courtly Trifles', translated by MR James. At p101, Gruffydd is said to have boasted to Edward the Confessor c1056 that he was the senior king because: 'his people had gained all England, with Cornwall, Scotland (?Ireland), and Wales, from the giants'.
4. MK Lawson *Cnut: England's Viking King* is a recent, comprehensive and accessible text for the background to this chapter. JD Richards *Viking Age England* is a judicious survey of the archaeological evidence. Henry Loyn *The Vikings in Britain* shows the significance of what the Vikings were doing elsewhere in Britain. Johannes Brøndsted *The Vikings* has an even broader view with its centre in Scandinavia.
5. SD Keynes 'Cnut's Earls'.

of power, for the most part peacefully, once Cnut had shown it did not pay to cross him.[6]

There are hints that under Aethelred there had been much unjustified confiscation, sometimes as a result of unpayable taxes, and other forms of corruption.[7] Cnut took care to announce that he was different from Aethelred and would be a just and Christian king.

Cnut died in 1035. His stepson, Edward the Confessor, may well have proclaimed similar sentiments seven years later in his coronation oath[8] and in his charters[9] but these aspirations were political, introduced by religious interests, and cannot be relied on to describe anything that was happening in practice. It must always be kept in mind, too, that central government did not yet attempt to administer the whole of England. Much was left to local government and local assemblies. It is said that Edward never strayed north of Gloucester.[10]

SOURCES

The written evidence for this period is patchy. In addition to the laws there are a few relevant charters, a letter attributed to Cnut, the *Liber Eliensis* and the *Anglo-Saxon Chronicle* which is neither regular nor informative, though some parts of some of the texts seem to be almost contemporary.[11]

Some recent scholarship suggests that many of the later dooms were not meant to be enforced as they stand, or, even if they were meant to be, they failed.[12] That may be partly because more is made of them than their creators intended. Modern writers who characterise them as codes, statutes, or even legislation without some qualifying adjective, run the risk of anachronism. It is true that by this time they are no longer mere collections of dooms, they increasingly show an orderly structure and are approved more formally by councils of great men, but they should not be judged by criteria appropriate

6. Matthew Townend *Language and History in Viking Age England*. The *Liber Eliensis* II 79 tells of St Dunstan's prophesy to Aethelred that: 'your kingdom shall be handed over to another kingdom, whose tradition and language the people you govern do not know'. Prophesy is easy with hindsight and the writer knew that Cnut was going to come later, but he also knew a great deal about the differences in 'tradition and language'. Cnut spoke the language of the people of Ely well enough to compose a song in it and sang it to them, *Liber Eliensis* II 85; language is discussed in Appendix A, the song at **A.9**.
7. Aethelred considered it sufficiently important to state on his restoration that he would see to it that the laws were imposed justly, V *Aethelred* and VIII *Aethelred* 43, **8.34** and Lawson *Cnut* pp48–9 and 'Archbishop Wulfstan' pp148–52.
8. Richardson and Sayles *Governance* p137.
9. A Latin royal charter of 1063, probably spurious, granting land in Devon, has Edward say: 'everywhere there is the threat that law and justice will be overthrown', JM Kemble *Codex* 814; PH Sawyer *Charters* 1037. Frank Barlow *Edward the Confessor* p176 gives a full and accessible description of the background and assessment of the sources.
10. Barlow *Edward the Confessor* p169.
11. Lawson *Cnut* pp53–79 is full and helpful on all the sources.
12. In different ways Wormald *Making of English Law* pp330–60 and 449–65 and Lawson *Cnut* pp59–65.

only for modern legislation. They remain exhortatory, and Wulfstan who drafted most of Aethelred's and Cnut's liked to preach in them, sometimes incorporating parts of his previous sermons. In his *Institutes of Polity* of 1008 and in 1014 in his *Sermon of the Wolf to the English*, he denounced the shortcomings of the times:[13]

> **9.1** The customary laws, *folclaga*, have got very much worse [since Edgar died][14]... Too often now a kinsman has not protected a kinsman any more than a stranger... Many are forsworn and have greatly perjured themselves and pledges are broken oft and again... breaking oaths and pledges... And what I say is true: we know of worse acts among the English than among the Britons... Let us... punctiliously keep both oath and pledge....

These moral sentiments are reconstituted in the laws of Edgar and Aethelred and most clearly in those of Cnut, for whom Wulfstan was not only archbishop of York (and bishop of Worcester at the same time) and religious adviser but also law reformer and legal draftsman. A letter from Cnut in 1019, preserved in the York Gospels, also shows Wulfstan's hand.[15] It calls for decisions and penalties to be fair and for Cnut's Oxford promise to apply Edgar's laws to be followed.

A few charters have survived. There are 36 in all of Cnut, of which just one or two reveal something of how public arbitration was conducted in the assemblies, e.g. **9.35, 9.36**. There are writs, too, which at that time means no more than letters, some eight from Cnut bearing the royal seal, and what have been called 'writ-charters', letters sent to shire assemblies to inform them of royal acts.[16] It is in the descriptive parts of these documents that information about dispute settlement can be found. Even forgeries, supposing they can be spotted, may tell us something. For every document which has survived, hundreds must have been lost.

THE LAWS

As soon as he could, Cnut sought to establish law and order on a foundation of the old legal systems, for English and Danish alike but not identical. His first decree is a set of laws declared in 1018 at a meeting in Oxford of Danes and English, shortly after the fighting had ended and Cnut had become king.[17] They begin:

> **9.2** 1. In the name of the Lord. This is the decree which the *witan* decreed and considered according to many good examples. And it was done as soon as King

13. Dorothy Whitelock ed *Sermo Lupi* pp23–42 and *English Historical Documents* pp854–9.
14. This phrase is in ms E.
15. Lawson *Cnut* p66. It was perhaps originally an oral message from Cnut, committed to writing by an ecclesiastic for circulation to the shire courts, and then redrafted into its present state by Wulfstan.
16. Lawson *Cnut* pp66–7.
17. This decree differs from I and II *Cnut*. It is in a manuscript in Corpus Christi College, Cambridge 201 pp126–30; Dorothy Whitelock 'Wulfstan and the Laws of Cnut'. AG

Cnut, with his *witan*'s advice, fully established peace and friendship between Danes and English and settled all their former disputes.

This is the first decree of the *witan*: that above all other things they would ever worship one god and with one mind keep one Christendom, and love King Cnut with justice and with truth, and zealously follow Edgar's laws....

So Cnut used Edgar's laws when he 'settled all their former disputes'. 'Settled' not adjudicated. Edgar's laws not Aethelred's. To have renewed the laws of Aethelred would have been unpopular with both the Danes and the English who formed Cnut's *witan*. Everything of Aethelred's was discredited. And anyway he had copied from Edgar, whose name had a resonance and an acceptability to both sides, because:[18] 'There is evidence... for Edgar's willingness to grant a measure of autonomy to his Danish subjects. More pertinent still, there are reasons to believe that his policy had been reversed by Aethelred.'

Sir Frank Stenton doubted whether Cnut's legislation introduced anything new:[19]

It is in no sense original. At every change of subject Cnut looks back for guidance to the laws of earlier kings. More than a third of his work is demonstrably based on theirs, and there is every reason to think that texts, now lost, lie behind most of what remains... The men of Cnut's own time valued it as a restatement of the good customs of the past by a king who was strong enough to enforce them.

There is no need to suppose lost texts. Cnut's laws may be the first written expression of long established customary law, including royal dooms, until then transmitted orally.

Cnut may have recognised that he had enough trouble without trying to change the law too much. His Anglo-Saxon subjects would have resented change and his Danes kept the law they had brought with them. Indeed there may have been strong and fundamental similarities in the laws of the Anglo-Saxons and the Scandinavians, as there were among Danes, Norwegians and Swedes. Haakon, king of Norway, who died in 960, had already proclaimed written laws, the laws of the *Gulathing* and the *Frostathing*, though they survive only in much later manuscripts and there is little basis for comparison with Anglo-Saxon laws.[20] Haakon, brought

---

Kennedy 'Cnut's Law-Code of 1018' not only provides a new edition of the text, with translation and commentary, but many insights into the law. My translation differs in substance only rarely. Lawson *Cnut* points out that 'Cnut is not himself said to have had any connection with the document, and it may reveal little of the real business of the Oxford meeting'. That hardly matters when it is clear that Cnut expressly approved I and II Cnut.

18. Wormald *Making* pp132–3.
19. Frank Stenton *Anglo-Saxon England* p410.
20. LM Larson *The Earliest Norwegian Laws*. There have been attempts to find evidence of life in Anglo-Saxon England in contemporary Icelandic texts but a recent monograph

up in England, was the foster-son of Athelstan, king of the West Saxons 924–39 and brother of Eric Bloodaxe, king of England 948–54.

In 1035 Magnus expelled from Norway Aelfgifu, the regent of Swein, Cnut's choice for king. Magnus proclaimed his own laws, the *Grágás*:[21]

> What can be positively asserted about all the Nordic Countries, however, is that Viking law was based on the proceedings of the institution called the Thing – the assembly of free men... A gathering of free men of age and quality to bear arms who met to put the law into effect, pronounce judgments, and discuss matters of interest within the community. The law was a customary one, handed down orally... memory supported by the alliterative formulae.

That would not seem so strange to an Anglo-Saxon, or, indeed to those Britons who were left to take an interest. Even the structure and use of tariffs were similar and easily adapted.

There were many other things on Cnut's mind. He left it to Wulfstan to do the drafting, with plenty of religious exhortation to the whole of his English kingdom to be obedient, while he himself took no notice of the restrictions on behaviour, such as the requirement of monogamy, any more than Wulfstan worried about the religious offence of pluralism. He was content to have existing laws collected, written and re-enacted as the base for his administration.[22]

Prominence was given to the establishment of the basic laws of each community:

9.3 3.1 Henceforth let every one, poor and rich, be entitled to *folcrihtes*, customary laws.

It may be that the last phrase is rendered better as 'customary rights', as Kennedy does, but there is no difference in substance; customary rights are what you get if your customary law is enforced. I think its meaning is clear and quite different: customary laws are in the plural. This recognises at least the two major law groups, English and Danish, or three if we accept Maitland's Wessex, Mercia and Danelaw, or even four if Cnut was legislating, as he seems to have intended, for all his subjects, the British as well. It is most likely that the plural shows that the lawmakers knew there

---

suggests that the stories are mostly 'pure fantasy', Magnús Fjalldal 'Anglo-Saxon England in Icelandic Medieval Texts' p33. *Contra* Matthew Townend *Language and History* pp145–79. Those texts reveal a process which has been called 'self-judgment' or 'self-doom'. The wrongdoer or losing party sought to avoid retaliation by allowing the victim to fix the amount of retaliation-payment. The sources, though ample for Iceland, are not sufficient to establish its practice in England, Fritz Mezger 'Self-Judgment' and generally WI Miller *Bloodtaking and Peacemaking*.

21. Brøndsted *The Vikings* p242; and pp79, 106.
22. Not all agree that he understood what he was doing: 'Cnut the Dane however does not stand in the tradition of Anglo-Saxon law; he had not grown up in it and had to learn it', Hanna Vollrath 'Gesetzgebung und Schriftlichkeit' p53.

were more than one customary law and wanted to include them all, without being more particular. When he wants to be specific, he is, as in II Cnut 12–15, **9.16–18**.

Most of the rest is not hard law, concerning itself with what would now be classified as sin rather than illegality, though there is an attempt to restrict the death penalty in clause 5. Otherwise most injunctions are to watch, pray, abstain and pay the clergy their various impositions promptly. Like Aethelred, Cnut exhorted all Christians to make up their quarrels at the time of holy festivals in the same words as Aethelred had done, **8.59**, **8.60**.[23] Other clauses repeat the emphases of the earlier laws and of Wulfstan's *Sermo Lupi*, **9.1**:

9.4 18. Each friend shall order with justice both words and works; and carefully keep oath and pledge.

So the oath and the pledge are again set firmly in the foundations of Cnut's law. The responsibility to make the legal system work is placed squarely on everybody. First those who make decisions:

9.5 25. Henceforth anyone who promotes bad law, *unlaga*, or deems bad dooms, *undom*, through ill-will or bribery, shall be liable to the king for 120 shillings unless he swears an oath that he knew no better.

Not only must decision-makers apply these laws but the parties to disputes must not challenge their application:

9.6 26. He who disputes, *forsace*, right laws, *rihte lage*, and right dooms, *rihtne dom,* shall be liable to him to whom it happens.
9.7 26.1 If to the king 120 shillings.
9.8 26.2 If to an earl 40 shillings.
9.9 26.3 If to a hundred 30 shillings.[24]
9.10 26.4 If to anyone to whom it happens in English law.
9.11 27. If subject to the just laws of the Danelaw, he pays the *lahslit*.

Lahslit was the Danes' word for a general penalty for any breach of the law, where a more specific fine was not provided for. The Anglo-Saxons adopted the word, having no such concept of their own.[25]

From this it is clear that Cnut was concerned to prevent disputes about what law applied. Anyone who denied that Cnut's dooms applied to their dispute or argued that some other law should apply, whether *lage* or *dom*, thereby committed an offence and was to be punished according to the law of their community, English or Danish. Customary laws were still basic but there must be no mistake: Cnut's dooms ruled. These dooms are directed

23. II *Cnut* 15.1 and 15.2.
24. The scribe makes a wonderfully revealing slip here, writing *unread*, but he must mean 'hundred', as Kennedy suggests.
25. Loyn *The Vikings in Britain* pp92–3.

expressly to those who must obey them, as Edgar's were, **8.49**, not just to those who apply and enforce them. How much more evidence is needed to persuade those who hang on to the belief that Cnut's laws were just Wulfstan's window dressing?

Two years later in 1020, Cnut proclaimed the laws known since as I and II Cnut, referring back to the Oxford decree and taking care again to restore formally the old laws of Edgar, not Aethelred:[26]

> **9.12** 1. King Cnut greets his archbishops and bishops and Earl Thurcyl and all his earls and all his people, nobles and commoners, clergy and lay, in England in friendship.
>
> **9.13** 2. I tell you that I shall be a gracious lord, faithful to God's rights and to just secular laws...
>
> **9.14** 11. I also order my reeves by my friendship and by all that they have and by their very lives, that they keep my people in justice and deem them right dooms...
>
> **9.15** 13. I will that all the people, cleric and lay, hold fast to the laws, *lage*, of Edgar, which everyone has consented to and sworn to at Oxford.

I and II Cnut are much fuller than the Oxford decree. Together they make one set of legislation, the first part ecclesiastical, the second expressly secular yet with much of the Church in it.[27] Wulfstan, who probably drafted the Oxford decree, rewrote as he copied from it and from the laws he had drafted for Aethelred, incorporating material from Edgar and elsewhere, some of which can be traced to earlier surviving documents, some otherwise unknown and some no doubt new. They are quite comprehensive collections, though nothing like a through-composed code.

II Cnut expressly deals with Wessex, Mercia and the Danelaw separately:

> **9.16** 12. These are the rights which the king has over all men in Wessex...
>
> **9.17** 14. And in Mercia he has over all men the same as is before written.
>
> **9.18** 15. And in the Danelaw he has *fyhtawita* and *fyrdwita*.

Fyhtawita are fines for fighting and *fyrdwita* fines for failing to heed the call to military service. Though the rights of the king in these matters are expressed to be the same in Wessex and Mercia, they are different in the Danelaw. Nothing is said here about the customary law in the parts still under British kings, which Cnut may have been happy to leave to their own devices.

At least one section looks like a doom from a real case:[28]

> **9.19** 75. About when a man stands his spear against another man's door: I declare that it is right, if anyone stands his spear against the door of another man's house,

---

26. *Cnut Proclamation of 1020* 13, AJ Robertson *Laws* p143.
27. Dorothy Whitelock 'Wulfstan and the Laws of Cnut' and 'Wulfstan's Authorship of Cnut's Laws'; Richard Dammery 'Editing' pp254–7.
28. II *Cnut* 75; Lawson *Cnut* p189.

and he has an errand within, or if anyone carefully lays down other weapons where they may lie quietly, if let be, and if someone then picks that weapon up and does some harm with it, then it is right that he who does the harm shall make the payment.

This is evidence of what we would now call 'fault liability' replacing 'strict liability'. Payment must be made by the one who had the greater responsibility, the active wrongdoer, rather than one whose careless or even innocent act had made the wrong possible.

Wulfstan's own hand is heavy on these laws. They show the style of the preacher. Often they go with a swing, though his little tricks of language jangle when repeated and make parts of the laws sound like a bad sermon. For some of Aethelred's death penalties, which might be inflicted before the sufferer had a chance to repent adequately, Wulfstan substituted mutilation, which to Christians was an amelioration, providing ample opportunity to avoid the fires of hell.[29]

There is little to show how Cnut's laws were put into practice, though there is much in them that is detailed and specific and there is every reason to suppose they were meant to be. No doubt they were intended to be good propaganda. Wulfstan could be trusted to see to that. But it is beyond belief that Cnut went to the trouble of having these laws proclaimed, consolidating if not elaborating and extending those of his predecessors, unless he meant them to be imposed. He was not a man to be mocked.

After 1023 no king seems to have proclaimed new laws until after the Conquest. None have survived from the reigns of the sons who succeeded Cnut, Harold Harefoot (1035–40) and Harthacnut (1040–42). In the long reign of Edward the Confessor (1042–66), the son of Aethelred and stepson of Cnut, the sources provide nothing more than hints.

A *Life of King Edward*, written about the time of his death by an anonymous monk, says:[30]

9.20 Edward abolished bad laws and established wise ones with the help of his *witan*.

The author cannot be taken at his word. Even if what he wrote was true, there is no trace of any such legislation. Not until shortly before the Conquest is there any further hint, in the *Anglo-Saxon Chronicle* for 28 October 1065, just two months before Edward died:[31]

9.21 The king granted this... and renewed there the laws of Cnut.

---

29. II *Cnut* 30; I *Aethelred* 1.
30. *Vita Aedwardi Regis* 12–13; Barlow *Edward the Confessor* pp178 and xviii.
31. *Anglo-Saxon Chronicle* 27 October 1065; Wormald *Making* pp129–30. The document known as *The Laws of Edward the Confessor* was written in the twelfth century and is dealt with in the next chapter.

ASSEMBLIES

Archaeological work has shown that, even at this late stage of Anglo-Saxon legal development, assemblies often met where they had from time immemorial, still in the open air as they had done before the Romans came.[32]

> Secklow (Buckinghamshire) is one of thirteen meeting places which have been excavated in England. It was found to consist of a mound, 25m in diameter, surrounded by a roughly circular ditch, some 1m deep, constructed in the tenth century.

That was quite natural and indeed inevitable because there were few great public buildings and much more of life was in the open. Most churches were small. Houses were for shelter. By the time of Cnut there was an assembly for every hundred, shire and borough, as well as the king's own council, the *witan*, meeting in the *witenagemot*. Dispute resolution was handled in these assemblies, though they were administrative places, which did not necessarily fit the natural groupings for trade and other social links.

Every man had to attend the assembly of his hundred. Though there is evidence of women attending when they were involved in a dispute, they were not required by law to do so regularly. As far as there is any agreement on what a hundred was at this time, it is probable that, as a geographical area, it represented 100 hides. A hide was a measurement of land, probably according to what in that location would support a family. Whatever it was, the measure was flexible in application and determined by customary law.

The provision that every man shall be sworn into a tithing at the age of twelve, though first found here in II Cnut, is probably taken from much earlier legislation:

> **9.22** 20. That everyone shall be in a tithing.
> We will that every free man be brought into a hundred and tithing if he wants to have the benefit of exculpation or of *wergeld* if he be killed, once he is over twelve years old; or he shall not have the benefit of any free man's rights, whether he be householder or servant, so that each shall be brought into a hundred and into surety, and the surety shall keep him and produce him to every legal duty.

The first level of regular assembly remained that of the hundred. By II Cnut 17:

> **9.23** 17. No one shall bring a claim before the king unless he shall not have had his rights in his hundred.

It is clear that at this time the king was not at pains to extend his jurisdiction. The legal system still depended on the assembly, at its lowest level, the hundred, for the resolution of disputes.

---

32. JD Richards *Viking Age England* p53; Aliki Pantos 'The Location and Form of Anglo-Saxon Assembly-Places'.

9.24 17.1 A man attends his hundred. A man attends the assembly, *gemot*, of the hundred, on pain of a fine, whenever it is right to attend.

That required every adult male to attend every meeting of his hundred on pain of a fine, of unspecified amount. Attendance was expressly required of bad characters, who presumably might expect to have claims made against them there:

9.25 25. Someone who is burdened with charges and is not worthy of the people's trust, *folce ungetreowe*, and who declines to attend an assembly three times, then men shall be chosen from the fourth assembly to ride to him and then he may still find a surety if he can.
9.26 25a. Then if he cannot, they shall overpower him however they can, alive or dead, and take all that he owns.

By Cnut's time, the assemblies of the borough had been added to those of the hundred and shire:

9.27 18. And there shall be three borough assemblies and two shire assemblies, on pain of a fine, according to what is right, unless more frequent are needed.
9.28 18.1 And the bishop and *ealdorman* of the shire shall be there and there each shall apply both God's law and earthly law.

If that means what it clearly says – and there is no argument that it should not – then both the *ealdorman* and the bishop were required to attend every meeting of shire or borough assembly. Whichever of them presided, and perhaps they both did in some way, they were responsible for imposing both church and lay law.

Some idea of how the procedure worked can be gained from the provisions of II Cnut on recovering property. Self-help was forbidden. The lawful way to get back one's property which was being held by another was first to ask the help of the hundred and, if that failed, of the shire.

9.29 19. No one shall make any seizure, either within a shire or outside a shire, before he has sought his rights three times in the hundred.
9.30 19.1 If at the third choice, *cyrre*, he gets no right, then he shall go a fourth time, to the shire assembly, and the shire shall fix him a fourth appointment.
9.31 19.2 And if this fails, then he shall get leave from both this one and that one that he may go after his property.

There are some problems with this doom. What is clear is that any person claiming to be rightful owner of movable property must first seek a decision from the hundred assembly. If the hundred refuses or neglects to help at three meetings, the owner may go to the shire assembly.[33] Delay is a tool used

---

33. The word *cyrre* is not easy to translate. It means a choice, or the free will to make a choice. By coincidence, I believe, it is glossed in Latin, *arbitrium*. *Liberum arbitrium* means 'free will', throughout the centuries of theological controversy. It cannot be translated here by any arbitration word. Perhaps the phrase means 'on the third opportunity (which the hundred has had to deal with the matter)'.

by the law in many times and places to take the heat out of disputes. 'This one and that one' must refer to the assemblies of shire and of hundred. The language leaves no doubt that both must give permission, though the shire could presumably bring sufficient pressure on a recalcitrant hundred which stubbornly refused to do what the shire decided was justice.

Moreover, someone faced with a claim in an assembly was not allowed to prevaricate or complicate the process by bringing a counterclaim. The first claim must be dealt with first:

> **9.32** 27. Anyone who in an assembly defends either himself or his man with a counterclaim has spoken all that in vain and must answer the other in the way that the hundred considers right.

Though there is less evidence for the reign of Edward the Confessor, such as it is it confirms that the legal system continued to deal with disputes in the same way: 'The law courts were popular assemblies; the law was immemorial custom, and each shire had its peculiarities....'[34]

OATHS, SURETIES, ORDEALS AND EVIDENCE

The dooms of Alfred, Aethelstan, Edmund and Aethelred had emphasised the importance of oaths and sureties. Cnut's went further. First they required that everyone over the age of twelve should swear an oath to be neither a thief nor an accomplice to theft.[35] Then they set out how the various oaths fitted into the scheme of procedure at assemblies:

> **9.33** 22. Every trustworthy man who has never been burdened with charges nor has failed in either oath or ordeal in the hundred clears himself with a single [oath].

But defendants, who are 'totally untrustworthy' in the eyes of the hundred and face three claims at the same time, must face the triple ordeal, unless their lord supports them.[36] More complex provisions deal with less trustworthy parties, requiring compurgators to support their oaths and the ordeal for those who could not summon them.[37] In particular, there are strict requirements for those who bring witnesses to prove their legal ownership of animals, the process later to be known as vouching to warranty. If the value of the livestock is more than four pennies, four witnesses are necessary.[38]

Every lord is made responsible as surety for the men of his household.[39] Strangers and 'friendless men' who can provide no surety must defend

---

34. Barlow *Edward the Confessor* p176.
35. II *Cnut* 21.
36. II *Cnut* 30, 30.1; cf I Edward 3.
37. II *Cnut* 22.1 to 22.3, 30.2–9.
38. II *Cnut* 23 and 24.
39. II *Cnut* 31 and 31a.

themselves by the ordeal.[40] A person who swears one false oath is not only barred from swearing another but is liable to lose a hand.[41]

Any person giving evidence, even if not on oath, is to be punished if it proves to be obviously false:

> **9.34** 37. On false witness. Anyone who gives clearly false evidence and is convicted of it, thereafter his evidence shall stand for nothing, and payment to the king or the local lord of *healsfang*.

Healsfang is a penalty mentioned in earlier legislation but its exact meaning is not known.

MEDIATION, ARBITRATION AND SETTLEMENT

There are between thirty and forty contemporary Anglo-Saxon records of dispute resolution in the time of Cnut. At some time between 1016 and 1035, an account of a dispute over land between mother and son brings to life the workings of the shire assembly and its place in the community:[42]

> **9.35** It is declared here in this writing that a shire assembly sat at Aegelnothesstan in the time of King Cnut. There sat Bishop Aethelstan, Ealdorman Ranig, Edwin, son of the ealdorman, Leofwine son of Wulfsige, and Thurkil the White. Tofig the Proud came there on the king's errand. And Bryning the sheriff was there, and Aegelweard of Frome, Leofwine of Frome, Godric of Stoke and all the thegns of Herefordshire. Edwin, the son of Enniaun, had travelled to the assembly and made a claim against his own mother for a piece of land; that was Wellington and Cradley. Then the bishop asked: 'Who should answer for his mother?' Then Thurkil the White answered and said he would if he knew what the claim was, because he did not know what the claim was. Then they chose three thegns from the assembly to go to where she was, at Fawley: Leofwine of Frome, Aethelsige the Red and Winsig the sailor. When they got to her they asked her what the dispute was that she had about the land which her son was claiming. Then she said that she had no land that belonged to him. She became very angry with her son. She sent for her kinswoman, Leofflaed, Thurkil's wife, and said to her in front of them: 'Here sits Leofflaed, my kinswoman, to whom I give both my land and my gold, my clothes and my robes and all that I possess, after I am gone.' And this she said to the thegns: 'Do as thegns should! Declare my errand well to the assembly before all the good men![43] Let them know to whom I have given my land and all my possessions. To my own son never a thing! And tell them to be witnesses to this.' And so they did. They rode to the assembly and told all the good men what she had charged them to do. Up stood Thurkil the White in that assembly and asked all the thegns to give his wife the land clear, which her kinswoman had given to her. And so they did. Then Thurkil rode to St

40. II *Cnut* 35.
41. II *Cnut* 36.
42. Dorothy Whitelock *English Historical Documents c500–1042* 2nd edn pp602–3, no135; Robertson *Charters* LXXVIII; Sawyer *Charters* 1462; Kemble *Codex* IV 755. On the significance of the charters, Pauline Stafford 'Political Ideas' especially pp69–70.
43. *Boni homines*?

Aethelbert's Church with the approval and witness of all the people, *folces*, and had it put in a book of Christ.

St Aethelbert's Church is Hereford Cathedral and that book of Gospels is said to be still there.[44] Presumably the whole proceedings were conducted in much the same dialect of the Anglo-Saxon language as the record, despite the fact that Thurkil was a Dane and Edwin the son of a man with a British name, Enniaun, unlikely to be held by anyone other than a Briton at that time.

There was no inhibition against a woman – whose name is not mentioned – owning land and leaving it away from her heir, by making an oral will. She was represented by a man, Thurkil, the husband of her kinswoman, but that did not mean that she was not the party. Thurkil seems to have acted more in the role of attorney or advocate, perhaps because that was easier for her than making the journey to the assembly. She instructed the thegns about the nature of her defence and the award she proposed, which they accepted. The award had the express approval of all the *folc*.

There was a fine line between the adjudicatory functions of the shire assembly and what might be called its more administrative functions, or rather a gradation, probably with no divisions apparent to those who attended then. An agreement of 1046, between the bishop and religious community of Sherborne, and Care, son of Toki, disposes of their different interests but may have arisen without the parties having fallen into an open dispute. It fits well the latest modern category of 'dispute management':[45]

9.36 Here it is made known in this writing how the agreement was worked out at Exeter before Earl Godwin and before the whole shire, between Bishop Aelfwold and the community at Sherborne and Care, Toki's son, about the land at Holcombe. That was that they would settle it that all the brothers should leave the land but one, called Ulf, to whom it was devised, and he should have it for life and that on his death the land should pass just as it was, with produce and men, undisputed and without conflict, to the holy church at Sherborne.

Witnesses: Earl Godwin, Bishop Aelfwold (and many more).

There are two of this writing, one is at Sherborne and the other at Crediton; both say the same.

There was no adjudicated award here but a mediated settlement. This was soon after Edward the Confessor had become king. A little later, about 1053, a settlement allowed Wulfweard a life interest in land at Hayling Island at an agreed rent and so that it would pass without contest on his death to the Old Minster, Winchester.[46]

---

44. Whitelock, *English Historical Documents c500–1042* p603; Hereford DC P I 2 fo 134 reverse, acc to Sawyer *Charters* p410.
45. Robertson *Charters* CV; Sawyer *Charters* 1474; Kemble *Codex* 1334. Care and Toki are Scandinavian names.
46. Robertson *Charters* CXIV; Sawyer *Charters* 1476; Kemble *Codex* 1337.

In 1060 Edward himself became involved in mediating a settlement rather than adjudicating, as presumably he had the power to do, though in the circumstances he was wise not to do so. Leofgifu had made a will before setting out on a pilgrimage to Jerusalem, on which she died. She left land to Peterborough Abbey, whose abbot Leofric, learning of her death, claimed the land and offered to prove the will by witnesses. Edward's queen Edith, however, claimed that Leofgifu had left the land to her. She was the sister of Harold (later the king who died at Hastings) and Tostig. Her husband and brothers mediated. They got Edith to give up her claim to the land in return for twenty gold marks and the same value of church ornaments. The settlement was formally incorporated in a grant by Edward and Edith to the abbey.[47]

> **9.37** I, King Edward, have decreed, *constitui*; I, Queen Eadgyth, have granted, *concessi*; I, Archbishop Stigand, have joined in the award, *collaudavi*; I, Archbishop Ealdred, have added my approval, *comprobavi*; I, Wulfwig, Bishop of Lincoln, have confirmed, *corroboravi*; I, Duke Harold, have consented to the alienation, *favi* [a technical term]; I, Duke Tostig, have been a witness, *testis fui* [and seven other witnesses].

Whoever were responsible for the drafting, they exhibited a command of technical Latin which enabled them to draw the nicest legal distinctions between the roles of the signatories.

Something can be gained from a study of those awards or settlements which were given formal recognition by the king. By a writ of which happily both parties kept copies, Edward the Confessor gave his approval to an award of their chosen experts.[48] The dispute, which continued in different forms for many centuries, long after Edward and the experts and the original parties thought they had disposed of it, was between the abbeys of Ramsey and Thorney, over the boundaries between them at a ditch known as King's Delph. A memorandum records that the abbot on either side was accompanied by a team of clerical supporters and that other clergy were witnesses. The two sides appointed a group of five laymen, old men, *homines antiqui* in the Latin, to resolve the dispute. They did so by swearing that two thirds of the fen belonged to Ramsey and one third to Thorney. Were they arbitrators, or experts, or some sort of proto-jury?[49] Contemporaries did not feel the need to make such distinctions.

47. Sawyer *Charters* 1029; Kemble *Codex* 808; Barlow *Edward the Confessor* p177.
48. The parties' copies of the various documents, some forged at least in part, are in *The Cartulary of Ramsey* no115 i p188; no544 iii p38; and in *The Red Book of Thorney* ii fo372; RC Van Caenegem *Royal Writs* p69; FE Harmer *Anglo-Saxon Writs* pp252–65; DM Stenton *English Justice* p15.
49. From their names and descriptions they seem to be ordinary men, Harmer *Anglo-Saxon Writs* p254.

In 1049 Edward declared his grant of land which an assembly had 'deemed' to Westminster Abbey:[50]

> **9.38** I declare to you that I have granted the lands… as fully and totally as Alwunn the nun held them from the monastery and Queen Edith delivered them up to Abbot Edwin and the monks and as King Edgar transferred them to the monastery and also as they were deemed in the nine shires in Wendlebury.

At some date between 1053 and 1061, Edward issued a writ confirming an award by thegns of a shire assembly in Kent:[51]

> **9.39** I, King Edward, greet Archbishop Stigand and Earl Harold and Abbot Wulfric and Osweard and all my thegns in Kent in friendship. I declare to you that I will that the land at Mersham, with all that rightly pertains to it shall belong to Christ Church, Canterbury, with sake and with soke, as fully and totally as Sigweard and his wife transferred it to it, because I will that the doom which my thegns deemed shall stand.

These royal confirmations of awards of arbitrators or settlements achieved by other means shows the relationship between the emerging system of state control of dispute resolution and the private agreement of the parties to submit their dispute to their chosen mediator-arbitrators. There was no doubt where ultimate power lay. The king had his men in every shire assembly, not only the earls and bishops which he appointed and who attended by right of their office but the thegns he had appointed specifically to act as reeves, in charge of the suppression of crime and other forms of conflict resolution when they concerned the king.[52]

Yet it is clear that Anglo-Saxon assemblies always preferred the dispute to be mediated to a settlement. Mediation might continue after an adjudication, **8.57**. And 'Where a thegn has two choices, love or law, and he then chooses love, that stands as fast as a doom', **8.58**.

THE CHURCH

Much of Cnut's legislation, in all probability drafted by Wulfstan himself, concerns the clergy. None of it reveals them performing any kind of dispute resolution, other than bishops attending and presiding at assemblies, and performing the roles exemplified by Bishop Aethelstan, **9.35**. There is no sign of bishops sitting as such to hear disputes in any kind of equivalent to the Continental *episcopalis audientia*, though there is of mediation a lifetime later, **10.66** and **10.67**. So much depends on chance survivals that it would

---

50. Harmer *Writs* no79.
51. Harmer *Writs* no35; there are other straightforward royal confirmations of sales rather than awards, e.g. nos69 and 73–8; and others of delegated jurisdiction with or even separate from a grant of land, as in Harmer *Writs* Pt2.
52. Barlow *Edward the Confessor* p177.

be unwise to assume that bishops here did less mediation than they did on the Continent, where more records have survived.[53]

CONCLUSIONS

The kings and claimants of this period were members of extended, ambitious, ruthless and murderous squabbling families, but there is little evidence that they saw their differences as national, let alone racial. They made alliances as easily with their cousins in other countries as they sought refuge with them in exile. There is no sign of any of them allowing nationality to interfere with their self-interest. They made political marriages and swore loyalty to their temporary friends but recognised the primacy of expediency. By this time:[54]

> It is rather simplistic just to speak of Anglo-Saxons and Vikings. Over the course of the Viking Age new identities were being forged, and language and customs were each used to articulate an Anglo-Scandinavian identity. Whether it was through new place-names and new words, new forms of burial, new building types, or simply new dress fashion accessories, the peoples of Viking Age England were constantly re-inventing themselves.

All were comfortable in their common Germanic background.

At the end of Cnut's reign trade was flourishing across the North Sea. Scandinavian merchants had privileges in London. Special assemblies for commercial disputes came to be known by the Viking name *husthing*, an assembly in a house, as distinct from all the other kinds which were still held in the open. Their successors have been known as hustings ever since.[55]

By the end of Edward the Confessor's reign, central government had control over all aspects of the legal system, whenever it wished to exercise it. But that was still the exception. Most disputes were settled, mediated and if necessary arbitrated or otherwise decided by traditional means, according to customary law (paying respect to whatever royal dooms might apply), in the assemblies of hundred, shire and borough. But the parties could now look to the king to enforce awards and settlements, sometimes in exchange for a little gift, even when the king's own interest was not involved.[56]

9.40 King Edward sends greetings to Bishop Wulfwig, Earl Tostig, Sheriff Norman and all his counsellors and liege men, ecclesiastic and lay in Northamptonshire, in friendship. I tell you that Aelfwine, Abbot of Ramsey, and Leofric, Abbot of

---

53. PR Hyams 'Feud in Medieval England' pp3–4. There seems little to be gleaned from the English ecclesiastical records, RH Helmholz *The Oxford History of the Laws of England I: The Canon Law and Ecclesiastical Jurisdiction from 597 to the 1640s.*
54. JD Richards *Viking Age England* p227.
55. Loyn *Vikings* p101.
56. Harmer *Writs* no62 p264 (discussion pp252–6), in Anglo-Saxon (from which this translation) and Latin versions, probably an Anglo-Norman concoction but substantially convincing on these points.

Peterborough, have told me of the agreement and exchange which they have made between them by common consent... So I want you to know that Abbot Aelfwine has spoken with me, and given me so much of his own that I have consented to this agreement and I will that it shall stand firm for ever.

Even a forgery may tell the truth about what it has no interest in lying about. The next chapter will show that, if care is taken, the evidence of later sources, even as late as the middle of the twelfth century, can reveal what was happening in the eleventh century.

Though the Conquest brought great changes immediately, much stayed the same. There were still no professional judges or lawyers, no jurists and no legal education or scholarly writing, for at least another generation.

10   AFTER THE CONQUEST: 1066–1154

But it is slowly that the consequences of the great event unfold themselves, and they are not to be deduced from the bare fact that Frenchmen subjugated England. Indeed, if we read our history year by year onwards from 1066, it will for a long time seem doubtful whether in the sphere of law the Conquest is going to produce any large changes. The Normans in England are not numerous. King William shows no desire to impose upon his new subjects any foreign code. There is no Norman code. Norman law does not exist in a portable, transplantable shape. English law will have the advantage in the struggle – a good deal of it is in writing.

> Frederick Pollock and FW Maitland *The History of English Law* I p79[1]

Anglo-Saxon laws and institutions survived the Conquest and formed a material part of the system of common and local law in later ages.

> HD Hazeltine 'The Laws of the Anglo-Saxons' p391

INTRODUCTION

As a matter of policy, this book progresses by 'reading our history year by year onwards'.[2] Sometimes, however, it is only in later sources that evidence can be found for earlier practice. The final century or so of this work, from the mid-eleventh to the mid-twelfth, produces richer literary and administrative documents which can be used to show not only what happened then. If great care is taken, they can sometimes be relied on to state accurately what had happened in their past. It begins to be true of the law, as Maitland said, that 'a good deal of it is in writing'.

William I was a clever man with a clear objective: to secure control of conquered England. He had won it and held it by force but all the evidence shows that he was determined to complete his dominion by the only method

---

1. Though more recent work has changed what we know, in both substance and detail, Pollock and Maitland *History of English Law* is where everyone must start who wants to understand the development of the law after the Conquest. This chapter shows how impossible it is to keep Maitland out and how ill-considered not to let him speak in his own words, particularly when they reveal presumptions, and even perhaps an ideology, that are no longer uncritically accepted. Marjorie Chibnall *The Debate on the Norman Conquest* shows how the history of the Conquest has changed.
2. The opposite of FW Maitland, *Domesday Book and Beyond* Preface pv: 'I have followed that retrogressive method "from the known to the unknown"... The Beyond is still very dark: but the way to it lies through the Norman record.' But he could not keep that up, John Hudson 'Maitland and Anglo-Norman Law' p21.

which could ensure its permanency: absorbing what he needed of what existed. First he took away the property and power of those who had opposed him. Killing and terrifying when he thought he needed to, all the while he was using whatever means he had of persuading the conquered that they were better off under him. After all, he insisted, he was the rightful heir to the throne of the Anglo-Saxon kings. Everyone might know that he was illegitimate but that was of no importance when set against his express adoption by the man he called his cousin, Edward the Confessor, who he insisted had chosen him to succeed. Provided it took nothing of substance away from his grasp, it was in William I's interest to allow his new subjects what they considered essential to their Anglo-Saxon identity: their Anglo-Saxon laws and legal system.

In any case, there was much he could not change:[3]

> But how significantly could the Normans have changed English society when they could not change its economic base and when, moreover, they themselves, seen in a wider comparative context than medieval historians before this century could see them, had much the same economy, kinship system, religion, legal system, and values in general as the pre-Conquest English?

No doubt the later turmoil in the time of Stephen and Matilda weakened the previously sufficient administrative system of shire and hundred and borough. It may have not only provided an opportunity but created a need for centralisation of the legal system, as of the rest of government. Certainly the honorial courts, those held by the greater lords for the disputes of those who owed them allegiance, regularly ratified and thereby gave force to concords recording the settlement of disputes.[4] But it was not until after our period ends that:[5] 'Under Henry II the exceptional becomes normal. The king concedes to his subjects as a royal boon his own prerogative procedure.' Even then the king's courts and the burgeoning courts of the lords, the seignorial courts, did not take all the traditional work away from the customary assemblies of shire, hundred and borough.[6]

Language is all-important for understanding the relationships between formal and informal methods of dispute resolution in any jurisdiction where the language of litigation is not that of the people. That is a phenomenon discernible in colonies at most times, and England was a Norman colony. There must be some quite special reason before any parties, particularly merchants, prefer to have a dispute resolved in a language other than their own. Disputes between *Francigeni*, the mostly Germanic invaders who are better translated 'Francia-born' than 'French-born' (let alone Maitland's 'Frenchmen') were no doubt heard in the language which has become known

3.   Susan Reynolds *Fiefs and Vassals* p9.
4.   Edmund King 'Dispute Settlement in Anglo-Norman England' p129.
5.   Pollock and Maitland *History of English Law* I p144.
6.   Hudson 'Maitland and Anglo-Norman Law' pp40–1.

as Anglo-Norman or insular French.[7] The Anglo-Normans were subject to a different law of treason from the English, according to the contemporary historian, Orderic Vitalis.[8] All other disputes must surely have been resolved in the English language, not only in the assemblies of hundred, shire and borough, which continued throughout this period, but by private arbitration too, if there was any.

The more English life remained the same, the easier it was for William I to deal with the opposition of powerful opponents. He had many and there was trouble throughout his reign, not just from the defeated English landowners but Scandinavian invaders, Scots, the ambitions of Philip of France and, most dangerous, the rivalry of members of his own family.[9] So he left ordinary life largely untouched. The price of an ox was the same as it had been under Edgar and the thirty London silver pennies to pay for it were struck there by the Englishman, Algar, who was the moneyer before the Conquest, then after him by his grandson in 1100 and still two generations later by his great-great-grandsons in 1154.[10]

Neither William I nor the rulers who followed him, William II Rufus (1087–1100), Henry I (1100–35) and Stephen (1135–54), have left much legislation. Not until the great reforms of Henry II (1154–89) do royal initiatives transform English law, and they are outside the period of this book. But there are important compilations purporting to set out the contemporary law.[11]

The law we seek for our purposes, therefore, is that which remained much the same despite the Conquest. Any discernible changes may help to show how dispute resolution changed. Two types of evidence need to be married: the rather scant legislation of the Norman kings and the literary sources, some of which purport to be collections of laws.

THE LAWS

There are many myths to be dispelled. It has been assumed that, as soon as he could, William I imposed his Norman law throughout the land he took by conquest. Before 1124 Eadmer wrote that William I:[12]

---

7. George Garnett '*Franci et Angli*'; there were many French in England before the Conquest, CP Lewis 'The French in England'. I have put my arguments about language into Appendix A, where the use of and relations between English, Latin and Anglo-Norman are discussed.
8. Chibnall *Debate* p132.
9. Richard Huscroft *Ruling England 1042–1217*.
10. BR O'Brien *God's Peace* p10, citing Pamela Nightingale 'Some London Moneyers' 35–9. The only coins then were silver pennies, though they were counted in pounds (240) and marks (160), Huscroft *Ruling England* pxx.
11. Patrick Wormald *Making* p398: 'The flow of anything that can be called official lawmaking never rose above a trickle for the next hundred years. That of unofficial treatises soon became something like a flood.'
12. Eadmer *Historia Novorum in Anglia* ed M Rule p9; O'Brien *God's Peace* p212 fn41.

10.1 brought with him the customs and laws which William and his ancestors had had in Normandy.

In the 1170s Richard FitzNigel, the king's treasurer, wrote:[13]

10.2 When that famous conqueror of England, King William, had subjugated to his *imperium* the furthest boundaries of the island and overmastered the minds of the rebels by terrible examples… he decided to impose written law and legislation on his subject people. So, having set out the English laws according to their tripartite classification, i.e. Mercian law, Dane law and West Saxon law, he rejected some, approved some, and added to them the laws of Normandy from over the sea which appeared most effective to preserve the peace of the kingdom.

We can understand why FitzNigel got it only half right. William did not import written or even oral customary laws from his homeland. He could not have imported law from Normandy even if he had wanted to, 'most effective to preserve the peace' of his new kingdom generally.[14] In Normandy the administration of Duke William was not based on folk assemblies. The administrative unit of the duchy was the *pagus*, with a *viscomte* in charge. Though that became an inherited office, the duke supervised and controlled it, keeping the most important disputes to his own court. 'Court' still meant then the people round the king. It had few of the connotations of the word in modern use.

There are no contemporary sources from England but, on 18 July 1091, William I's sons Rufus and Robert held an inquiry at Caen to discover the customary rights of the Duke of Normandy. The result was the *Consuetudines et Justicie*, customary laws and jurisdictions, an avowedly incomplete list, concentrating on limiting the powers of the *barones* to build castles and make private war or perpetrate other violent acts. In particular it set limits to violent self-help in the feud:[15]

10.3 These are the customary laws and jurisdictions, *consuetudines et justicie*, which the Duke of Normandy has in that province and King William who acquired,

13. Charles Johnson ed *Dialogus de Scaccario* 1.16, text and translation; notes in Hughes, Crump and Johnson. In 1543 Reginald Pole could still write: 'As it was of the Normans at such time when they ordained all our common laws in the French tongue, to be taught and disputed… Who is so blind that he does not see the great shame to our nation… to be governed by the laws given to us of such a barbarous nation as the Normans'; TF Mayer ed *Thomas Starkey* pp90 and 129, also p82. Indeed, similar misunderstandings survived in New York into modern times, JM Stearns *Germs* p18 (before the Conquest): 'each succeeding conqueror ignored existing laws affecting rights of persons or property, and set up his own arbitrary will'; (on William I) 'He organized the chief courts of the kingdom on the model of the Norman courts of his government on the continent. Even the law language of the Saxons and Danes was repudiated and a barbarous French dialect was made the judicial language of the courts.'
14. O'Brien *God's Peace* p214 fn67.
15. CH Haskins 'The Norman "Consuetudines et Justicie" of William the Conqueror' pp502–8, with full text pp506–8.

adquisivit, the kingdom of England enforced the observance of, in his time with the maximum force.

It ends:

10.4 and if these things were done, the lord of Normandy had there what he ought to have in those places in which he ought to have them and the barons had what belonged to them in those places in which they ought to have them.

What did come in with William was his way of dealing with disputes between his great men. There was plenty of experience for him to draw on.[16] Whether Norman or not, he dealt with them in his own court according to his own rules and presumably in his own language. But it was still recognisable as the *witenagemot*:[17]

William fitz Osbern and Roger of Montgomery, for example, took their place alongside Edwin, Morcar, and Waltheof; Saxon and Norman prelates attended in company; and among the officials present were several who had served the Confessor... in 1080 as in 1050 this court consisted of the monarch and members of his family, the great ecclesiastics and lay lords, and certain officials... By the time of the Conqueror's death, the *curia Regis* had become Norman in personnel... its members attended by reason of military tenure.

Its procedure, though, seems to have continued to be that well known in the Saxon assemblies, including mediation and compromise, failing which arbitrators would be chosen from those there:[18]

By 1066 William's court was established as the place where disputes between the mightiest of his vassals would be heard... Although justice in the sense of deciding greater right was often necessary, a frequent result of a matter coming before the duke was a compromise.... In the event of a compromise being unobtainable, both sides were apparently given the opportunity to present their arguments. If necessary, further evidence was sought... The information in the plea reports suggests that reliance was usually placed on human testimony, but that especially difficult or controversial cases would be decided by the ordeal... The normal procedure was to nominate judges from among those present....

That was the system William and his Norman lords, lay and ecclesiastical, were familiar with. After the Conquest, he had to make new law for England to deal with problems arising from conflicts between the English and the *Francigeni*. The laws of the Norman homeland of most but by no means all of them, no doubt suitably adapted, governed only some of the

16. Jane Martindale 'His Special Friend' describes procedures in 'the Kingdom of the French (Tenth to Mid-Twelfth Century)'.
17. DC Douglas *William the Conqueror* p285.
18. David Bates *Normandy Before 1066* p160, citing the primary sources; David Bates *Regesta Regum Anglo-Normannorum*.

relations between them, particularly the conflicts only the king could end, over landownership and inheritance and relations with the Church.[19] Many conflicts of interest, as might be expected even between military leaders or ambitious churchmen, were concluded by agreements and many of these *conventiones* are preserved in contemporary or later cartularies.[20]

A manuscript from FitzNigel's time shows how William I set about the task, part practice, part propaganda, of establishing the legal system of his new possession:[21]

> **10.5** 7. This I also order and will, that everyone shall have and keep the law of King Edward, about land and everything else, with the additions I have decreed for the benefit of the people of the English.

Note the clever and conciliatory tone and content: 'for the benefit of the English'. Though that evidence of William's intention comes more than a century after the fact, it chimes in with a writ issued in his name soon after the Conquest, of which the Anglo-Saxon original still survives, confirming the customary rights of the bishop and mayor of London:[22]

> **10.6** 1. King William greets Bishop William and Mayor Godfrey and all the burgesses in London, French and English, in friendship.
> **10.7** 2. And I declare to you that I will that you both shall be entitled to all the laws that were in the time of King Edward.

This formula follows exactly that of Edward the Confessor, **9.40**, 'I greet... in friendship. I declare to you that I will that...' and it is written in Anglo-Saxon, though both mayor and bishop were Normans.

William I did as his Germanic cousins had done since the time of Aethelberht: he confirmed the general application of the customary laws and made specific provision for the problems as they arose. He was careful to show who was now in power, not by wholesale changes but by edicts which proclaimed that the old law continued because he said so. It was politically important that he should show that was his government's policy. He wanted to rule by rightful inheritance, as he claimed, not by conquest, whatever the reality was. His successors, too, laid great emphasis on these claims. Perhaps most telling of all, he extended his peace – that English peace which already applied to the English – to everybody, encompassing *alieni*, including those from Francia.[23]

19. There are parallels between the categories of punishments in the *Consuetudines et Justicie* and the developments in twelfth century England, Pollock and Maitland *History of English Law* II p454 and Haskins 'Norman *Consuetudines*' pp504–5.
20. King 'Dispute Settlement' gives a full account with references.
21. Felix Liebermann *Gesetze* I p488; AJ Robertson *Laws* p238, called *Hic Intimatur* or 'The Ten Articles of William I' with an introduction pp225–6.
22. TAM Bishop and P Chaplais *Facsimiles* 15, plate XIV.
23. O'Brien *God's Peace* p14. For details of the Church's peace, *Leges Edwardi Confessoris* 1 and 2, O'Brien pp159, 160.

The old customary laws of England survived.[24] No king in England had ever thought they showed weakness in the central administration and the Norman kings were content to keep them as the foundation of their legal system. Of course, they were not appropriate for the great land disputes which arose from the dispossession of the English greater landowners. William I had to settle those himself. Those decisions, as political as they were legal, rarely have anything to do with arbitration, public or private, though the work of the king's commissioners recorded in Domesday Book in 1086 reveals much about the ways in which disputes were then managed. The royal courts have been the focus of attention of legal historians and the courts and judicial procedures which grew in part from them influenced the future Common Law; but they are outside the scope of this book.

The legal system for most disputes of most people remained as traditionally English as the language spoken in the assemblies of shires and hundreds where law was transacted.[25] That suited everybody, including William I, who saw no more advantage in imposing Norman law than Norman language, except to provide for new conditions. Indeed, for the first few years, he issued writs in Anglo-Saxon, **10.4**, and, when the written language changed, it was to Latin not Anglo-Norman.

The continuing diversity of customary law does not seem to have presented William I's new regime with problems. *Domesday Book* records many examples. The salt works of Cheshire had their own quite specific laws to deal with the exigencies of their trade.[26] On the border with Wales, in Hereford, the English burgesses kept their old customary laws and the French burgesses had their privileges.[27] And at Caerleon it was noted that there were three Welshmen who lived there under Welsh law, '*lege Walensi viventes*'.

The Norman kings did not need to lay down much new law to determine how disputes should be decided between the great landlords, the five hundred or so nobles to whom William I granted land rights. William I's law-making was not like modern legislation. It consisted of letters, which historians now call writs, primarily concerned to confirm the existing law, both customary and legislation, and to re-establish the legal system of Edward the Confessor, the *laga Edwardi*.

---

24. We have detailed accounts of their rich diversity in *Domesday Book*, discussed below. For recent general accounts of the events leading to the Norman Conquest and their political background, Huscroft *Ruling England 1042–1217*; NJ Higham *The Death of Anglo-Saxon England*.

25. There is perhaps a late example of this way of proving the applicable customary law in *Lanfranc v Odo* (1072) 106 *Selden Society* 5 p8, discussed below, **10.14**, **10.15**, and Baker *Introduction* p6. Compare Jane Martindale '*His Special Friend*' p45 on a Poitevin charter of cAD1032.

26. *Domesday Book* vol 1 folio 268r.

27. *Domesday Book* vol 1 folio 179r.

William Rufus left no trace of legislation. William's next son, Henry I, in his coronation charter of 5 August 1100, declared like his father that he intended to restore the good old customary law of Edward the Confessor and he sent copies to the bishops and chief magnates in every shire. He was not afraid to admit that he needed to get rid of 'bad customary laws', *malas consuetudines*, which his brother had allowed.[28]

10.8 1. ... I abolish all the bad customary laws by which the kingdom of England was unjustly oppressed...

10.9 12. I firmly establish the peace in all my kingdom and order that it be kept from now on.

10.10 13. I give you back, *reddo*, the law of King Edward, *lagam Eadwardi*, with those amendments by which my father amended it with the counsel of his barons.

Though Henry I did make one or two new laws, none of them related to dispute resolution. No legislation has survived,[29] but he made his intentions about the legal system clear in a letter of about 1110:[30]

10.11 Henry, King of the English, greets Bishop Samson, Urse d'Abitot and all his barons of Worcestershire, French and English. Let it be known that I grant and direct that henceforth my shire and hundred assemblies shall sit in the same places at the same times as they sat in the time of King Edward and not otherwise. And I forbid my sheriff to have them sit otherwise for his own convenience on his own business. For I will see to it, whenever I will, that they are sufficiently summoned for my own requirements as I wish. If henceforth any litigation shall arise about the division or seizure of lands between lords who hold land direct from me, then it shall be dealt with in my court. If it is between the men of any lord who holds land from me, then the litigation shall be dealt with in the court of their lord. If it is between the men of different lords, it shall be dealt with in the shire assembly. It shall be by trial by battle unless it shall be stood over for them. And I will and direct that everyone from the shire shall go to the shire and hundred as they did in the time of King Edward....

'Stood over' would include being interrupted so that the dispute could be submitted to arbitrators, as litigation sometimes was to avoid the judicial duel, even after the battle had commenced, **10.69**.

A charter has survived from AD1135, probably issued by Stephen at his coronation. It follows the formula:[31]

10.12 Be it known that I have granted and by this charter of mine I have confirmed to all my barons and men of England all the liberties and good laws which my

28. The Latin text is easiest to find in William Stubbs *Select Charters*, an English translation in DC Douglas and GW Greenaway *English Historical Documents 1042–1189* p400. The royal promise to observe Edward's laws remained in the coronation oath until 1688, JGA Pocock *The Ancient Constitution and the Feudal Law* pp229–30.

29. Pollock and Maitland *History of English Law* I p96.

30. Stubbs *Select Charters* p122.

31. Stubbs *Select Charters* p142; Douglas and Greenaway *English Historical Documents* p402.

uncle Henry, king of the English, gave and granted and I grant all the good laws and good customary laws which they had in the time of King Edward.

So, until the end of our period, kings thought it worthwhile to confirm by their writ the old legislation and customary laws, *leges et consuetudines*, of good old King Edward – for whatever they were worth and whatever they meant by then.

THE LITERARY SOURCES

There had been compilations of legal documents for the client's needs for many years, such as the documents proving title to land preserved in the Worcester Cartulary. There is some evidence, too, of St Aethelwold's interests in keeping records at the end of the tenth century.[32] Some documents may have been preserved not just as evidence of legal acts and the rights which flowed from them but for more general use, perhaps as precedents. But, after the Conquest, for the first time in English history, some of those who were beginning to make a profession of the law began to compile legal materials to be used in their daily practice:[33]

> The Conqueror had amended and confirmed the *laga Eadwardi*; Henry I had confirmed the *laga Eadwardi* and his father's amendments of it. Where then could the law of Edward, that is to say, the law of Edward's time, be found? No doubt a good deal of it was to be found in the code of Cnut and in the yet earlier dooms. But the language in which they were written was unintelligible to Frenchmen, and was fast becoming unintelligible even to Englishmen... Despite the large words of the Norman kings, the old dooms in their integrity could not fit the facts of the new age. Thus what was wanted was no mere translation of ancient texts, but a modernized statement of the old law, a practicable *laga Eadwardi*.

The first surviving attempt to publish a full description of English law was written at some time between 1116 and 1118, the so-called *Laws of Henry I*, in Latin *Leges Henrici Primi*.[34] Little is known of the author, who was probably a cleric performing middle-ranking administrative and legal services, probably for Archbishop Gerhard of York. He almost certainly also wrote the *Quadripartitus* a little earlier but he did not finish it because, having completed the first and second parts, he decided to write the *Leges* instead.[35] Otherwise there is no sign of any third or fourth parts, which were to have been on *causae*, actions, and on theft, except for some bits

32. Barbara Yorke ed *Bishop Aethelwold*, particularly the essays of Patrick Wormald and Michael Lapidge.
33. Pollock and Maitland *History of English Law* I p97; TFT Plucknett *Early English Legal Literature* pp19–41. Chibnall *Debate* is essential on the scholarly literature.
34. LJ Downer ed *Leges Henrici Primi*, with text, translation and notes, and an introduction on which this account relies heavily.
35. Felix Liebermann ed *Quadripartitus*; *Gesetze* pp529–47; TFT Plucknett *Early English Legal Literature* pp24ff.

incorporated into the *Leges*. The first part of the four of *Quadripartitus*, 'In Four Parts', as it has been called since the sixteenth century, is a translation into awful Latin[36] of all the Anglo-Saxon laws which the author could get his hands on, in this order: Cnut, Alfred, Ine, Aethelstan, Edward, I and II Edmund, Aethelred, Edgar and III Edmund, with odds and ends like *Judex* and *Dunsaete*. The only omissions of importance are the laws of Aethelberht, of Hlothhere and Eadric and of Wihtred. The second part is 'certain necessary writings of our own day', mainly concerned with what would now be called 'public law', including the coronation charter of Henry I, some papers relating to Archbishop Gerhart and, most important for our purposes, Henry I's decree on the courts of shire and hundred.

There is not much new to be learned about Anglo-Saxon England from the first part, because we have the Anglo-Saxon originals, but the *Leges* are a treasure house of information about the law in the author's own day, sixty years after the Conquest. 'The plan was to produce a treatise which would embrace quite widely the law of his day... he made a conscious effort to record law which was up to date and valid.'[37] The *Leges* are therefore a source of the greatest importance, not only for information about the background of the legal system of their time but, more particularly, for the small but crucial glimpses of dispute resolution.

A later compilation, the so-called *Laws of Edward the Confessor*,[38] from about 1136, claims to record the very laws of Edward the Confessor, the *laga Edwardi*, which his cousin William I and his successors made the foundation of their legal systems. It begins in the prologue with the story of William I in 1070 taking down the laws of Edward the Confessor from sworn Anglo-Saxon experts:[39]

10.13 After the fourth year of King William's acquisition[40] of this land, with the advice of his barons, he had summoned through every county in the land noble Englishmen, wise and learned in their own law, so that he could hear from them the customary laws (*consuetudines*). So, when twelve had been chosen from each county in all the land, they first swore a solemn oath before him that they would,

36. It would have been easier for him to write in French, his mother tongue. His grasp of Anglo-Saxon was not secure. Presumably he was writing for a 'literate' audience, which then meant 'able to read Latin'.
37. Downer *Leges* pp3, 5. Pollock and Maitland *History of English Law* I p101 fn1: 'He is not pretending to set forth the *laga Eadwardi* as it stood in Edward's day; he states it in what he thinks to be its modern and practicable shape.'
38. Felix Liebermann *Über die Leges Edwardi Confessoris*; *Gesetze* pp627–70; O'Brien *God's Peace and King's Peace* is a comprehensive edition, translation and commentary. He shows that the text cannot be earlier than 1096, pp45–8, and argues for a date in Stephen's reign. I have more confidence in his arguments than he allows himself.
39. O'Brien *God's Peace* p158 (prologue).
40. This word, carefully chosen to avoid any element of conquest rather than lawful inheritance, is also used in the *Leis Willelme* prologue and in the *Consuetudines et Justicie* of Normandy, CH Haskins p506.

as far as they were able, keep to the right track and declare the rules in force (*sancita*) of their laws and customs, leaving nothing out nor changing anything by straying from the path.

10.14 When King William himself heard it and other laws of the kingdom, he considered it of great worth, and wanted it to be observed throughout the kingdom because, he said, his ancestors and those of all the barons from Normandy had come from Norway, and their law, when it was honourable, they should follow well, since it was deeper and more honourable than all others, that is those of the Britons, English, Picts. But all the compatriots who had narrated the laws pleaded very strongly with him to let them have the laws and customs under which their ancestors had lived and they themselves were born, because it was hard for them to adopt laws and adjudicate according to ones which they did not know.[41]

Few scholars now believe that story of how the customary laws were collected and some have rejected it as worthless.[42] Their negative confidence is puzzling when the methods and results of Domesday Book are considered, as they are in a later section of this chapter, which shows how customs and customary laws were recorded there. Domesday Book was more than a register of title to land. Not only does it record the outcome of disputes, which needed to be settled before ownership could be established, it occasionally sets out the customary law. There, on its first page, it declares how customary law was established in Kent:[43]

10.15 The men of four *lathes*[44] (Borough *lathe*, Eastry *lathe*, Limen *lathe*, Wye *lathe*) agree that these are the customary laws of the king [details of various breaches of the peace and other offences]. In relation to adultery, the king has throughout Kent the fine from the man and the archbishop from the woman except from the land of Holy Trinity etc.

No one has ever cast doubt on the validity of that source. It rings so true. How is it that the method by which it was established, enquiry of local trustworthy men, should be accepted without question, but the story in *Laws of Edward the Confessor* be so easily and totally rejected?

Moreover, there is other evidence of expert witnesses being called on in William I's time to give evidence of the relevant customary law.[45]

---

41. O'Brien *God's Peace* p193 (chapter 34).
42. O'Brien's is the best assessment, pp31–6.
43. Vol 1 folio 1, now easily accessible in the Alecto Historical Editions *Domesday Book: A Complete Translation*. There are other statements of local customary law, e.g. vol 1 folio 154 for Oxford: 'If any outsider chooses to live in Oxford and have a house there and dies there with no kin, the king shall have whatever he leaves.' Also e.g. for Berkshire, Lincoln, Chester and the salt works in Cheshire. H Ellis *General Introduction to Domesday* 189. The definitive work on the legal aspects is now Robin Fleming *Domesday Book and the Law*.
44. A *lathe* was an administrative district in Kent, a division of the shire, comprising several hundreds.
45. RC Van Caenegem *English Lawsuits* pp7–16.

10.16 In 1072,[46] ... by the king's command and at the archbishop's insistence the whole shire was ordered to assemble without delay, to bring together all the *Francigeni* and especially the English who were expert in the old laws and customary laws, *consuetudines*, to determine the liberties and customary rights, *consuetudines*, which the Church of Christ has in its own lands and ought to have in the royal lands. They all assembled at Penenden and sat for three days, because there was much litigation about proving by evidence the ownership of lands and discussion of the customary laws... And all the wise men present there heard the evidence and gave judgment...

10.17 Aethelric, Bishop of Chichester, a very old man, *vir antiquissimus*, learned in the laws and customary laws, *leges et consuetudines*, of the English, was carried there in a carriage on the king's orders.

So there would have been nothing unusual in William I giving instructions for evidence to be taken of the Anglo-Saxon 'laws and customary laws'. Even if the *Laws of Edward the Confessor* is a complete fabrication, the very fact that someone at the end of our period thought it worthwhile to concoct it, indeed declared it to be the fount of the living law, is significant. The author, a contemporary of the author of *Leges Henrici Primi*, was an official, perhaps a reeve, of Anglo-Norman family from the northern Danelaw.[47] He would not have perpetuated a myth without some motive and his motive may be clear: the clergy, at least, wanted to emphasise that the laws of Edward were still in force in the middle of the twelfth century. It must always be borne in mind, of course, that there is no incontrovertible direct evidence that Edward the Confessor ever laid down any laws at all. No manuscript even pretends to contain a record from his time.

The *Leis Willelme* survive in three versions, two in Anglo-French and one in a Latin translation, the earliest original probably dating from 1150–70.[48] Again it is an attempt to state the contemporary law. There is one telling difference in the texts. The Latin of the introduction reads:[49]

10.18 These are the laws and customs which King William, after the acquisition, *post adquisitionem*, of England granted to be observed by the whole English people, that is, the same as those which his predecessor and cousin, King Edward, kept in the kingdom of the English.

The Anglo-French text reads:

10.19 These are the laws and customs which King William, after the conquest of the country, *apres le cunquest de la terre*, granted to the people of England. They are the same as those which his cousin, King Edward, kept before him.

---

46. DR Bates 'The Land Pleas of William I's Reign'.
47. O'Brien *God's Peace* pp93, 102.
48. JE Matzke *Lois de Guillaume le Conquérant*; Liebermann *Gesetze* pp492–520; Pollock and Maitland *History of English Law* I pp101–2.
49. Matzke *Lois* p1; Liebermann *Gesetze* pp492–3.

Conquest or acquisition? Perhaps there was no point in dissimulating the reality of conquest to French speakers but there was no need to be so blunt to those who read the Latin, which would have included the literate English.

These compilations were not forgeries or fakes. They uniformly proclaimed their purpose to be to establish what the law was at the time they were written. In the middle of the twelfth century, by order of the writs of successive Norman kings, William the Conqueror and his sons and then Stephen, the old law of the Anglo-Saxon Edward had been reconfirmed as the common law of the kingdom, subject to royal amendment.

What can be gleaned from these collections? If one can rely on what is unequivocally stated in the *Leges Henrici Primi*, then the old Anglo-Saxon customary laws, as amended, were in force well into the twelfth century:[50]

10.20 6. On the division of the kingdom of England into three parts, in the diversity of the laws of the shires and regions.

10.21 6.1 The kingdom of England is divided three ways,[51] into the regions of the Wessex people, Mercians and Danes.

10.22 6.1a It has two archbishoprics, many bishoprics (15) and 32 shires.

10.23 6.1b The shires are divided in turn into *centuriae* and *sipessocna*,[52] the *centuriae* or hundreds into *decaniae* or tithings, and the pledges of lords.

10.24 6.2 There is a threefold division of English law in the same way, one of Wessex, one of Mercia and one the Danelaw.

10.25 6.2a Above this is we place the awe-inspiring authority of the royal majesty, which we stress must be considered to prevail continually and beneficently over the laws.

10.26 6.3 They are different in many ways but in many ways the same.

10.27 6.3a The laws of the shires themselves differ in many ways from region to region, according of course to how the professionals' greed and malign and detestable practices have introduced more grievous categories of harm to the legal system.

That is quite a full description of the relations between the old law and the new. At the base was the customary law, varying from place to place. Lawyers manipulated it, sophisticating it to their own ends. Nevertheless the customary laws of the shires, and of areas both larger and considerably smaller, if proved satisfactorily, would prevail over the general customary law, itself divided into the old three major categories: West Saxons, Mercians and Danes.[53] The growing multiplicity of customary law areas was accompanied by frequent, almost commonplace, grants of multifarious jurisdictions

---

50. *Leges Henrici Primi* 6.1, 6.1a, 6.1b, 6.2, 6.2a, 6.3, 6.3a.

51. The author's Latin can be so bad as to be comic, as here. The word he uses for 'three ways', *triphariam*, seems to exist only as the name of a diuretic herb.

52. *Sipessocna* is an odd word, made up of the words for ship and jurisdiction. The author sensibly keeps the Anglo-Saxon word when he can find no Latin equivalent.

53. Paul Brand 'Local Custom' has shown that this was still so in the thirteenth century.

to lords, ecclesiastical and lay. There was a need for a more uniform system, organised and developed by the central government. That became the Common Law, but not quite yet; its early development is just outside our period.

All the law now was law because it had been expressly confirmed by the king:[54]

> **10.28** What is to come will provide a fuller account of all these things, just as we have discovered by evidence and reliable oral accounts they were in the time of the most blessed King Edward.

Of course the king could make any law he liked overriding the customary law, as he could repeal and amend the laws of his predecessors, though whether or not he could enforce it was a different matter. Stephen certainly could not. Moreover, no king and none of the authors pretended that the whole of the law was comprehended in any document. It was still possible to prove the customary law from group memory in the customary oral ways in the customary assemblies.

ASSEMBLIES

From the Conquest, everyone in the kingdom was made subject to the king's jurisdiction, or, as it was put, had the benefit of the king's peace. That was a statement of centralisation of power, in an enlarged state, one realm. The feud remained but under the king's control. Cnut's laws show the beginnings of the shift. William I, another foreign conqueror, reinforced it by putting one of his own people in each assembly of hundred, shire or borough. William's *comites* were the successors in office of the Anglo-Saxon ealdormen, the earls of Cnut and Edward, who represented the king in the shires. They came to take a share in the profits of the shire assemblies. Not they but the thegns, the lesser landowners, still gave judgment there. One local thegn, the sheriff, was the earl's deputy but the king's representative, and a sheriff presided at both shire and hundred.

William I also granted away jurisdiction over some breaches of the peace, those for which a money payment to the grantee could suffice; but he kept to himself the more serious offences. The king might grant the jurisdiction of a hundred to an individual or institution. William Rufus granted the hundred of Normancross to the abbey of Thorney and Stephen granted the hundred of Stowe to St Edmund's church.[55]

Though those at the highest level of power in Anglo-Saxon England lost their lands and their positions at the Conquest, the same classes as before provided the members of the assemblies of shire and hundred and borough until the fifteenth century. To run his legal system William I had, as well as

54. *Leges Henrici Primi* 8.6, 8.7.
55. Stubbs *Select Charters* p122.

his own Normans, the same kinds of wealthy English landowners, not of the top rank, but those who had always done that kind of work for the king. Whenever he wished, William I ensured his control by appointing earls and bishops to preside at shire assemblies.

Most of the king's higher officials were Normans. But those who heard claims, oaths and testimony from English-speakers were still predominantly English. They had to declare, understand and apply English law. Compilations like the *Laws of Edward the Confessor*, the *Laws of Henry the First* and the *Laws of William* no doubt had their uses for both English and French speakers, though there is no record of any of them or any other laws being cited.[56]

The *Leges Henrici Primi* state that all shires should hold assemblies twice a year at fixed places and appointed times,[57] as established by ancient decree and recently restated by the king, and should be attended by a long list of office-holders, making up a quite different body from the old Anglo-Saxon, which had been composed of thegns, with the bishop and earl attending:

> **10.29** 7.2 Bishops, earls, sheriffs, deputies (*vicarii*), hundredsmen (*centenarii*), ealdormen (*aldermanni*), stewards (*prefecti*), reeves (*prepositi*), barons, vavasours, village reeves (*tungrevii*) and the other lords of lands.

This swollen committee had first to deal with church matters, then those in which the king had an interest, and then the causes of individuals. These were best settled:[58]

> **10.30** 7.3a Those whom the shire moot finds in dispute it shall bring together in love or dispose of by decision.

So far as possible, reconciliation in Christian charity was sought. Adjudication, though often necessary, was second best.

The hundred was subject to the same rules, though it must meet twelve times a year, at a week's notice. The lord must attend and his steward (*dapifer*) or priest and reeve and the better sort (*meliores homines*).

Some of these officers were still no doubt Anglo-Saxon, the hundredsmen and ealdormen and reeves. The Norman bishops and barons and the vavasours who held land from them were not required to attend the hundred. One of the better sort is to preside over the hundred and be called the ealdorman or alderman in Latin, now quite distinct from the Norman earl.[59] Presumably the hearing was conducted in Anglo-Saxon for the most part, the taking of evidence certainly. Every male from his twelfth year must be in a tithing and therefore in a hundred, except for *conducticii*, *solidarii* and

---

56. O'Brien *God's Peace* p16.
57. *Leges Henrici Primi* 7, 7.1, 7.2.
58. DM Stenton *English Justice* p7: 'It was a habit of mind prepared to take every opportunity of ending civil suits by compromise between the parties.'
59. *Leges Henrici Primi* 8.1a.

stipendarii, different members of a lord's household, for whom their lord took separate responsibility.[60]

The writ from the end of Edward the Confessor's reign, **9.41**, shows that disputes over land were normally heard in the assembly of one or sometimes more shires:[61]

> The writ once sealed was handed over to the beneficiary and produced by him at a meeting of the shire court. There it was 'published', that is, read aloud, which explains why the writ… was couched in the vernacular; after publication the writ was returned to the grantee for safe keeping.

Royal interference in the shire assemblies did not start with the Conquest. There is plenty of evidence of royal officials attending in Cnut's time, **9.35**: 'Tofig the Proud came there on the king's errand', as if the presence of the sheriff and ealdorman and the bishop were not enough. Edward the Confessor's widow Edith is known to have written to the hundred of Wedmore to inform them of her grant of land there:[62]

> **10.31** Lady Edith, widow of King Edward, sends friendly greetings to all the hundred of Wedmore. Take note that I have granted to Bishop Giso the land at Mark… And I tell you to deem me a just doom about Wudemann to whom I entrusted my horses and who has kept back my rent for six years, both in honey and money.

The use of royal letters to set the assembly's business had become regular by 1084. According to the *Leges Henrici Primi*, all legal causes could be divided first into two categories, those which might be bought off and those which could not. But there were also those which belonged to the king. The reality was that the king could intervene in any case he liked. He could also delegate or sell or grant away jurisdiction and often did. In the most troubled times, as in Stephen's reign, only a judgment of the king was final and not always permanent even then. Whenever there were alternative jurisdictions, there was forum shopping. Just like today, parties would go wherever they thought they would have the greatest chances of success and reliable enforcement.[63]

Still the underlying legal system was Anglo-Saxon and the laws which it applied still purported to be those of good old king Edward. But it is clear that by the end of William I's reign there were the makings of a centralised royal system of justice, which the king imposed as he thought fit. How it

---

60. *Leges Henrici Primi* 8.2a, 8.3.
61. Bishop and Chaplais *Facsimiles* ppx–xi.
62. Robertson *Anglo-Saxon Writs* p72.
63. It is not unknown today in former British colonies in West Africa for parties to choose between revived indigenous tribunals and the successors of the colonial courts, according to the advice of sophisticated lawyers trained in the Common Law. It has often helped me to think of Norman courts as colonial.

worked can be seen from two of William's writs to Lanfranc, Archbishop of Canterbury, who was a central figure in his administration. Both are preserved in the *Liber Eliensis*, written c1170. The first probably dates from 1082:[64]

> **10.32** William King of the English greets Lanfranc Archbishop of Canterbury... Stay the litigation about the lands which William de Eu, Ralph FitzWaleran and Robert Gernon are claiming; and, if they refuse to deal, *placitare*, with this matter in the same way that they would have dealt with it in the time of King Edward and in just the same way as the abbey was then observing the customary laws, *consuetudines*, I will that you make sure they do observe them in every respect, in accordance with how the abbot can establish them through his charters and his witnesses.

Placitare presents problems to the translator. Its meanings range from the earlier 'negotiate a settlement' to the later standard technical usage 'plead in a lawsuit'.[65] I have therefore used the inert phrase 'deal with this matter'. The king here is instructing Lanfranc to suspend litigation in which William, Ralph and Robert are claiming land from the abbot of Ely. It is usual to translate *placitare* as 'plead' but that is not justified here. The king is not telling the parties to plead at all, just the contrary. He is instructing them to stop the litigation and come to an agreement with the abbot according to the evidence of ownership, to be found in the abbot's documents and according to his witnesses, the men of the relevant hundred.

In another writ from about the same time or a little later, William I reiterates his policy on customary law:[66]

> **10.33** William, king of the English, greets Lanfranc Archbishop of Canterbury, Geoffrey Bishop of Coutances and Count Robert. I order you without delay to make sure that the Abbot of Ely has his benediction[67] and his lands and all his customary rights, *consuetudines*, as I have often told you in my writs. And whatever he has obtained by litigation as his own property, *de dominio*, let nothing be awarded to anyone without my permission; and do right to him at the place of litigation, *sede placitorum*, making sure that nobody cuts down his woods.

Here he also shows not only his readiness to insist on the application of the customary law to uphold customary rights but his willingness to intervene with his own solution, whatever customary law might require.

There are charters from this period recording transfers of land which do not disclose the disputes behind them. They did not need to. Better not to

---

64. *Liber Eliensis* II 124.
65. Alan Harding *Medieval Law* explains, in relation to Merovingian France: 'The first pleas (*placita*) of which we have record are a series of land-cases which came before a *palatium* for arbitration... A *placitum* was originally no more than a meeting consented to by the parties to a dispute and designed to reach a conclusion which "pleased" them'; and Paul Fouracre '*Placita* and the Settlement of Disputes'.
66. *Liber Eliensis* II 126.
67. *Benedictio* was a supernumerary offering.

get into arguments about the rights and wrongs of the dispute. Better just to set down the result. And it was the party which wanted the result recorded who kept the record. We do not hear the other side:[68]

> Any document recording a transaction involving laymen may well stem from an abnormal situation, generally one of conflict. Simpler transactions would be oral. The situation is made still more difficult by the fact that the written documents try to hide the very abnormality... as they aim to restore workable social relations.

The disputes which came before the king's own courts are outside our scope but they too followed the procedures with which all were familiar, the customary law of the shire courts, with the parties telling their versions of what they thought was relevant and would show they had the merits on their side.[69] What else could the new king's courts do but follow the ways they knew? Invent new ones? Not until after our period ends.

By far the richest source for how the assemblies of hundred and shire worked is Domesday Book.[70]

DOMESDAY BOOK

The *Anglo-Saxon Chronicles* record that at Christmas 1085 William I held court with the archbishops and bishops. The Archbishop of Canterbury presided, Lanfranc, who had been educated in Italy, where everyday business was carried on by professional lawyers.[71] William took the best counsel he could and thought carefully about the task he confronted: to record who owned what land throughout his kingdom. He had redistributed among his supporters land he took by conquest from those who opposed him. It amounted to more than half of England. It was a gigantic and unprecedented undertaking. He appointed commissioners from among his most trusted men. Their task was to make an inquiry, the Domesday Inquest as it is known, seeking the best evidence of ownership and recording it in one enormous record, which became Domesday Book. They went out on seven circuits to seek the testimony of those who could be expected to know best, the assemblies of hundred and shire. Those local government bodies could be depended on to provide the required information: 'the Normans inherited from the Anglo-Saxons an administration at shire level that was literate,

---

68. John Hudson *Land, Law, and Lordship* p4.
69. Paul Hyams 'Norms and Legal Argument Before 1150' is both imaginative and convincing, particularly on the significance of the *perambulatio* or 'view' p45, though he can hardly believe it: 'It almost looks like a custom designed for the purpose of raising and clarifying issues.' That is because it was!
70. There is a vast literature and much controversy, e.g. David Roffe *Domesday: The Inquest and the Book*.
71. 'it was precisely this everyday business we have in mind when we think of *Domesday Book*'; and mss of Justinian's *Codex* and parts of the *Digest* had recently been rediscovered, HR Loyn 'The Beyond of Domesday Book' p8.

active and continuous'.[72] Sometimes a document, a writ from William I, granted land to the present owner or a predecessor. The king's writ, of course, would settle the question – unless there were two.

Sometimes the testimony was conflicting or inconclusive and *Domesday Book* then merely records what evidence it had, leaving the matter unresolved. Some disputes were left to be determined by the king. But usually the assembly of the hundred decided. Only the king could settle disputes among those who held land directly from him; they were not within the jurisdiction of the shire assemblies unless the king asked them for help, the barons of course attending.

Domesday does provide some evidence of *conventiones*, even of parties (one a Norman lord, the other an English reeve) producing conflicting ones,[73] and of mediation, even after a *conventio* recording a concord. Wulfstan, bishop of Worcester, and Walter, abbot of Evesham, had a long-running dispute over land in Oswaldslow, Worcestershire. William I, towards the end of his reign, wrote from Normandy to Archbishop Lanfranc and Geoffrey, bishop of Coutances:[74]

> **10.34** You, Bishop Geoffrey, take my place to settle this matter, *istud deplacitandum*, so that Bishop Wulfstan shall have his right in full and see that he justly has the houses which he claims against the abbot.

A report of the proceedings gives further details:[75]

> **10.35** There was a great dispute about this matter between the bishop and the abbot. The abbot resisted for a long time, putting up an unjust defence... There was a meeting to hear the case. A great assembly was held in Worcester of the neighbouring shires and the barons before Bishop Geoffrey. The matter was discussed. The aforesaid claim of Bishop W was made against the abbot. The abbot defended it. The bishop called lawful witnesses who had seen these things in the time of King Edward and vouched for the said services for the benefit of the bishop. Eventually, on the orders of the king's justice and by decree of the barons, a decision was arrived at. Since the abbot said he had no witnesses against the bishop, the magnates, *optimatibus*, decided that the bishop should nominate his witnesses and produce them on the appointed day so that they could prove on oath the bishop's statement, and the abbot could produce whatever relics he liked. Both parties agreed. The appointed day arrived. Bishop W came and Abbot Walter and, by command of Bishop Geoffrey, the barons attended who had been at the previous hearing and decision. The abbot brought the relics, i.e. the corpse of St Ecgwin.

The bishop's witnesses were impressive both in number and quality, one of them the helmsman of King Edward's own ship, another Siward, 'a rich

---

72. Loyn 'The Beyond' p2.
73. Vol 2 folio 287b F2767; King 'Dispute Settlement' p117.
74. RC Van Caenegem *Lawsuits* I no15 pp37–41.
75. Dugdale *Monasticon* I no38 p602. The author writes from the bishop's side.

man from Shropshire'. They all swore that they owed their services to the bishop, not the abbot. The abbot gave in.

> **10.36** He accepted the advice of his friends and surrendered the oath to the bishop and recognised the whole of the complaint, and everything just as the bishop had claimed and so he agreed that he would make a concord with the bishop.

There were plenty of witnesses there to make sure there was no denial. Then followed a writ from William I to his sheriff of Worcestershire to enforce the agreed decision, 'as it was established and sworn, with the shire as witness'.

But it was not as simple as that. A document of 1086 shows that the parties continued to negotiate.[76]

> **10.37** This is confirmation of the agreement made between Bishop Wulfstan and Abbot Walter... The bishop claimed more there... so, because the abbot himself humbly accepted this, the bishop himself, at the request of those who were there, allowed the abbot himself and the brethren to have the land subject to an agreement that the abbot would make an honourable recognition and do service, in whatever way and for as long as the bishop should require it.

So the result was what might well have been achieved at the start, if the abbot had been less aggressive or, perhaps, the bishop less intransigent (or indeed the mediators more effective): the bishop's ownership was recognised by the assembly, the abbot had the use of the land subject to his submitting to the bishop and undertaking unspecified services.

When the Domesday commissioners were investigating ownership of Oswaldslow, Bishop Geoffrey wrote to them explaining what had happened:[77]

> **10.38** This was established and sworn before me and before Urse de Abetot, Osbern son of Escrop, and the other barons of the king, the whole shire making the decision and bearing witness, *judicante et testificante*.

The details of the services owed to the bishop are set out fully in another contemporary document:[78]

> **10.39** The whole shire of Worcester confirmed this evidence, the sacrament of the oath having been taken, before [the Domesday Commissioners by name] who had been sent out by the king to inquire into and describe the ownership and customary rights, *possessiones et consuetudines*, of the king and his magnates in this province and in many others at that time when the king ordered the whole of England to be described.

Having heard the testimony on oath of the whole shire, the commissioners made sure that ownership was recorded by being copied into the *autentica*

76. RC Van Caenegem *Lawsuits* I no15E p40.
77. RC Van Caenegem *Lawsuits* I no15D p39.
78. RC Van Caenegem *Lawsuits* I no15F p41.

regis cartula, Domesday Book, 'which is preserved in the royal treasury with descriptions of the whole of England'.

In the first two unsettled decades after the Conquest, many of those granted the land of the dispossessed English died and others forfeited their land for opposing the king.[79] What if they had themselves granted estates to others? There were endless opportunities for competing claims. Though there were no professional judges or lawyers yet, there were some who provided expert services to claimants. Disputes were already set to last for generations.

Within Domesday Book lies the best evidence of legal practice in Anglo-Norman England. Its legal aspects have been exhaustively examined by Robin Fleming:[80]

> Domesday Book read as a legal text also tells us much about the mechanics of justice; about the ways men of the Conqueror's generation protected what they had been given and what they had taken on their own. We can see, as well, how much they depended on old, familiar legal customs to defend property and how they developed new ways of protecting land at law. Domesday's legal information hammers home the oral and public nature of law in the period and the importance of communal memory in legal custom... the Domesday inquest was the crucible in which a new, hybrid Anglo-Norman law was forged.

In the preparation of Domesday Book, the assembly of the hundred or the shire or a joint meeting of more than one was called on to bear witness to ownership of land. Some entries say 'the hundred testifies'.[81] Sometimes the dispute went before both hundred and shire, 'the hundred and the shire bear witness to this'.[82] The hundred could not always come to a clear conclusion:[83]

> **10.40** TRW Ralph de Mortimer holds 1 hide in Swampton. TRE Cypping held it of the bishop and monks and it always belonged to the monastery but it was granted to him to hold for his life only, on his death to revert to the church. That is what the monks say but the hundred knows nothing of an agreement. But they do know this, that it belonged to the monastery and that it did not nor does it now pay geld, and they do not know why he still holds it.

They might deny all knowledge of who had the right to the land:[84]

> **10.41** Two of those who held were killed at the Battle of Hastings... The men of the hundred say they have never seen anything with the king's seal on it, nor a royal

---

79. 'Domesday Book recorded only two English lay tenants in chief of any significance', Hudson *Land, Law, and Lordship* p3.
80. Robin Fleming *Domesday Book and the Law* p6; she gives each of her selected entries a number, prefaced by F, and that is how they are cited here.
81. Vol 1 folio 38r F582.
82. Vol 1 folio 46v, in Neatham Hundred; folio 49v: 'Edwin holds Oakhanger and says that he bought it from King William but the shire does not know this.' Fleming *Domesday Book and the Law* p13 on joint assemblies.
83. Vol 1 folio 47r F632. TRW = *Tempus Regis Willelmi*, in King William's time; TRE = in King Edward's time.
84. Vol 1 folio 50 F658.

official giving seisin of this manor to Alwine Ret, who held the land before him who holds it now, and he has nothing there unless the king bear witness to it.

It was common for a Norman to claim ownership from a dispossessed Anglo-Saxon, called in Latin the *antecessor*, here Alwine Ret. Anyone 'killed at the battle of Hastings' was a traitor who had taken up arms against the lawful king, William, and therefore forfeiture was automatic. When the king granted that land, it went free from any lease, mortgage or other encumbrance that the antecessor might have created. Religious foundations were not happy with that; and one of the arguments they devised was that those who had granted them leases – loans of land as they were known then – had died before the Norman invasion and could not therefore have been traitors, so that the lease survived the transfer of ownership to the new Norman. Sometimes a lord was found to have granted the same land twice by mistake, **10.36**. Who had the better right, the first grantee because after that there was nothing for the lord to grant (as would be the case with a modern conveyance) or the second because that was presumably the grantor's more considered intention (as with a modern will)?

Usually the assembly gave clear advice and no doubt in most cases the king's commissioners, as they covered the country on seven circuits, registered ownership according to the uncontested sworn testimony – the 'communal memory' – of hundred or shire, or by command of the king's writ. If the title was disputed, the hundred might make its own decision. After relating that 'the men of Strafford Wapentake testify' to this ownership and 'say that Nigel ought to have' that, they show that the hundred (or wapentake in Yorkshire) could decide:[85]

> **10.42** The king has half the alms of the three feasts of St Mary, of St Mary's church, which belongs to Wakefield, and, by the decision (or judgment, *iudicio*) of the men of the Morley Wapentake, Ilbert and the priest in charge of the church have the rest.

Similarly in Essex:[86]

> **10.43** Godwine Woodhen appropriated three virgates of land at Hordon-on-the-Hill against the king, from the land of a free man, which still belongs to the king by the decision, *per iudicium*, of the hundred.

None of these entries states conclusively that the hundred's decision was part of the Domesday Inquest, though that can be inferred perhaps from an entry from Little Domesday Book for Suffolk, which deals with a dispute between two men both claiming to hold by different royal grants:[87]

85. Vol 1 folio 373v F1776; also vol 1 folio 165v F545; vol 1 folio 376r F1096.
86. Vol 2 folio 99a F2057.
87. Vol 2 folios 423b–424a F3105; similarly in vol 2 folios 338a–b F2890 and vol 2 377a F2962.

10.44 [Falkenham] was granted to Ralph, so he says. He offers the testimony of the hundred that he was seised first. But they do not know whether he was seised on the part of the king. They say that Ranulf claimed this land against Ralph and that Roger the sheriff fixed a date for them both to appear. Ranulf appeared but Ralph did not. Therefore the men of the hundred decided that Ranulf was seised. Ranulf now holds it but Ralph denies that he ever received a summons.

If the assembly did not consider itself able to resolve the dispute, it might record the differences and leave the conflicting claims to be decided by the king or one of his justices:[88]

10.45 They did not declare a decision but sent it for the king to decide.

10.46 They leave them for the king to decide.

10.47 William de Chernet claims this land... by inheritance from the antecessor, and he has adduced his evidence of this from old men of the better sort, *de melioribus et antiquis hominibus*, of the whole shire and hundred, and Picot has brought against it the evidence of villeins and low people and officials, prepared to maintain by oath, or the judgment of God, that the land was held by a free man... but William's witnesses will accept no law but that of King Edward until it is decided by the king.

A decision might be made by the king's barons:[89]

10.48 Thereafter both churches had the customary dues on their lands by the judgment of the king's barons who had heard the case.

Or by a bishop and barons and four shires together:[90]

10.49 Abbot Walter proved his right to these five hides at Ildeberga before [an assembly of] four shires and the Bishop of Bayeux and the king's barons. There are two ploughs and five villains and two bordars with two ploughs. It was worth 60 shillings in King Edward's time, later 50 shillings and 60 shillings now.

An entry for Alveston in Warwickshire shows that a powerful ecclesiastical lord might choose to overwhelm a competitor by heaping up his proofs and that William I's Queen Matilda (not to be confused with Stephen's rival for the crown) presided over a joint assembly of four shires:[91]

10.50 Bishop Wulfstan says that he won a dispute over this land before Queen Matilda in the presence of four shire assemblies; and that he has King William's writs for it; and the testimony of the shire of Warwick.

A meeting of four shires would be very large but no more numerous than the decision-making assemblies of Homer or classical Athens, or indeed the English Parliament, sitting as a court.

88. Vol 1 folio 58v F103; vol 1 folio 377 F1174; vol 1 folio 44v F622; JC Holt 'Some Agents and Agencies' p216.
89. Vol 1 folio 2r F900 '*iudicio baronum regis placitum tenuerunt*'.
90. Vol 1 folio 175v F1674.
91. Vol 1 folio 238v F1567.

Domesday Book also provides evidence of the survival of British people and even communities among the Anglo-Saxons, not only on the borders with Wales.[92] There were peasants, called *Walenses*, in English hundreds. One, called Mersete in Shropshire, 'had an English superstructure of lords, manors and place-names, overlying a largely Welsh substructure of peasants and farms'.[93] On the borders were Britons, of course, like the Dunsaete, **8.2–9**.

Thanks to the work on Domesday Book of generations of selfless scholars in different disciplines, most recently and in particular for our purposes Robin Fleming:[94] 'We can hear most clearly the voices of eleventh-century men speaking about the laws and customs of their world.' Whether intentionally or not, the Domesday Inquest and the permanent record of its findings in Domesday Book were a 'prerequisite for the eventual elaboration of the centralizing procedures of royal justice'.[95]

OATH, SURETIES, ORDEAL AND EVIDENCE

The decision-makers of Norman England followed the procedures of the Anglo-Saxon assemblies, adding trial by battle to the range of evidentiary techniques, not just for Normans. Oaths were regularly sworn and accepted as proof, though the Domesday commissioners seem to have preferred oral testimony supported by written evidence where that was available. Pledges were commonplace. The ordeal flourished. It played a part in twenty-one entries in the Domesday Book.[96] It was offered against the other side's oath by all kinds of parties, including women[97] and priests.[98] In one case a party's witnesses insisted on the judgment of the king, preferring the law of King Edward to the judgment of God, *judicium dei*.[99]

A party might combine the elements, giving a pledge to prove his title either by ordeal or battle.[100] There is such an air of routine about the records that it is hard to believe that those who offered to bear the ordeal, supposing that is the regular meaning of *ferre judicium* or *judicum*, expected to suffer the terrible injuries that ordeal is usually assumed to threaten. Domesday Book provides no evidence of it ever being applied. There it has all the appearance, at least to me, of a technical legal plea with its regular place in the proceedings before the king's commissioners and therefore presumably in the assemblies generally.

92. CP Lewis 'Welsh Territories'.
93. CP Lewis 'Welsh Territories' p136. Moreover 'all the Welsh manors in *Mersete* were taxed more leniently than ones inhabited by English or mixed populations'.
94. Fleming *Domesday Book* p11.
95. Fleming *Domesday Book* p34.
96. Fleming *Domesday Book* p524, index.
97. Vol 2 folio 137a F2230; vol 2 folio 277b F2723.
98. Vol 1 folio 336r F966.
99. Vol 1 folio 44v F622.
100. Vol 1 folio 377v F1190.

William Rufus is said to have thought little of *iudicium dei*. Fifty Englishmen were accused of taking and eating the king's deer. They were required to support their 'not guilty' plea by suffering the ordeal of the hot iron:[101]

> **10.51** Almighty God displayed their innocence to everybody by mercifully preserving all their hands from burning. By his just judgment he declared how unjust was the ill-will of those who wickedly wanted to destroy them. When the king was told of this, that the condemned men had all appeared together on the third day after the ordeal with their hands unburnt, he is said to have replied in a fury: 'What's this? God's the just judge? To Hell with anyone who believes that from now on! By this and by that,[102] in future they'll answer to my judgment not God's, which bends this way and that according to each man's prayer.'

There must have been some deterrence in the ordeal, though, because it could lead to a forced compromise:[103]

> **10.52** The Bishop of Bayeaux said that they must prove this very matter by the ordeal of the iron. And they promised to do so but were not able to do it. By the judgment of the other men of their shire they made a payment of three hundred pounds to the king.

This was at some time between 1177 and 1187, but it shows the survival of the ordeal until after our period ends. It has been suggested that: 'resolution of civil cases by the ordeals of fire and water was always rare: with the exception of a few post-Conquest instances, the ordeal was a criminal proof only'.[104] The Domesday records do not bear that out – twenty-one is more than a few – and Van Caenegem provides evidence of many other instances.[105] And Glanvill says that the ordeal was still standard practice when he wrote, c1188, but only in criminal prosecutions.[106]

LAWYERS AND JUDGES

The Norman kings still insisted that all ordinary legal business be transacted in the traditional courts of shire, hundred and borough, according to customary law, **10.3–10**. But this century saw the early buds of the professional practice and study of law which were to flower under Henry II.[107]

It was not that other laws were unknown or that nobody in England was educated in them. The king's own courts had the advantage of men who

101. Eadmer *Historia Novorum* 102, in Van Caenegem *Lawsuits* I, 150.
102. Presumably a euphemism for Rufus's actual words, which were too much for the scribe.
103. Rochester *Registrum Roffense* 31–2 in Van Caenegem *Lawsuits* 19.
104. Robert Bartlett *Trial by Fire* p27; also Paul Hyams 'Trial by Ordeal' pp107–34.
105. Including one reference to ordeal by water, 234.
106. GDG Hall ed *Glanvill* XIV 1: hot iron for a free man, water for a villein.
107. Paul Brand *The Origins of the English Legal Profession* prefers a later start. DM Stenton *English Justice*, Lecture 3 'Courts of Justice and the Beginning of the Legal Profession' tells a different story.

were not only learned in the law of the Church but had some experience of the Civil Law as practised on the Continent. Maitland believed that Lanfranc of Pavia, William I's right-hand man, was 'a lawyer of world-wide fame, the most famous of pleaders' who not only knew some Roman law but had been educated in a tradition that tried to harmonise the Lombard laws with Justinian's.[108] Lanfranc had been taught by Herlwin, abbot of Bec, whose biographer called him 'most learned in the laws of his native land' and 'practised in resolving disputes in lay matters'.[109] Doubt has been cast on the reliability of those sources and the conclusions drawn from them and perhaps 'the legal cast of Lanfranc's mature thinking should not be exaggerated'.[110]

Thomas Becket, who was busy by the end of our period, had studied law at Bologna and Auxerre. From William Rufus's time, some men with legal training were appointed as local judges, to judge in the king's place to the exclusion of the sheriff.[111]

There were other professionals of different kinds, both arguing and deciding, in all sorts of courts with conflicting jurisdictions. They were given many different names.[112] There were men in the hundred and the shire assemblies called justiciar, *iusticiarius*,[113] or *iudicator*, or *iudex*, or *iudicia*.[114] There were itinerant judges, the forerunners of the justices in eyre, who went on circuit and judged in the king's name. 'Local justiciars finally disappeared when Henry II felt free to make his first grand gesture towards a more centralised and efficient judicial administration.'[115] The itinerant judges were to become an integral part of it.

There were also members of the assemblies of shire or hundred who were recognised as having some quality which set them apart as fitted for decision-making. Sometimes they were called law-men, *lagemanni*, 'found operating in eleventh-century Chester, Lincoln, Stamford and York',[116] and in Cambridge, who may have been those called in Latin elsewhere *legales homines*, 'legal men', **10.67**.

108. Pollock and Maitland *History of English Law* p77.
109. JA Giles *Lanfranci Opera* I p270.
110. HEJ Cowdrey *Lanfranc* p8.
111. Stenton *English Justice* p65.
112. John Hudson *English Common Law* p31 sums up: 'First there were resident justices having a certain jurisdiction throughout one or more shires. Secondly, there were minor local officials responsible for attending to the king's pleas. Thirdly, individuals were appointed to hear particular cases as royal justices. And fourthly, there were "itinerant justices" sent on a circuit of counties to hear a wide variety of cases.'
113. E.g. Van Caenegem *English Lawsuits* 137 p107.
114. John Hudson *Historia Ecclesia* II 170 p172; Stenton *English Justice* pp57-58 referring to *Pipe Roll 31 Henry I*. Fleming *Domesday Book* F1688 on the four *iudices* of York; F269 the twelve *iudices* of Chester.
115. Stenton *English Justice* p68.
116. Fleming *Domesday Book* p12; and Ely, AG Kennedy 'Disputes About *Bocland*' pp184 and 195.

There were professional lawyers of some sort who helped the Abbot of Abingdon in his tussles with royal officials in William I's time, reading out charters in the Berkshire shire assembly, including two monks, blood brothers, Sacol and Godric:[117]

> **10.53** ... their eloquence, *facundia*, in secular affairs and their memory of past events were so great that people on all sides would readily approve a decision which they said was correct. Many other pleaders of the English, *de Anglis causidici*, were kept in the abbey at that time whose advice no wise man opposed.

Who were these *causidici*?[118] They were advocates retained to plead ecclesiastical causes, not quite professional lawyers yet, perhaps, but getting close. The author of the history of the church of Abingdon was writing at the end of our period about events nearly a century earlier. He was sometimes guilty of anachronism. But, even if he anticipated the activities of these *causidici*, what he wrote is evidence of their existence by his day. He mentions them again acting about 1050:[119]

> **10.54** Brihtwine... was talking big, all the more because he had with him a landbook, that is a document relating to the described land, because anyone who had a writing of that kind in his hand could argue about any land with greater confidence... It was proclaimed that an assembly, *consistorio*, of older men would consider the arguments of both sides and would decide who would have the better right to the ownership of the land in future. So, on the appointed day, it was considered and the *causidici*, who had been delegated there to fix who had the fair right, worked out which of the two claims was true and decided the abbot's case was the more just.

That would seem evidence of *causidici* working not as advocates but arbitrators in land disputes at some time in the eleventh or twelfth centuries.

The author of the *Leges Henrici Primi* practised as a lawyer of sorts and made an effort to understand law as a discipline. He may have had some education in Roman law and, as a cleric, in canon law.[120] His language suggests that he may have been educated in rhetoric. Like all his contemporaries who wrote in Latin, he calls *iudex* all those who made decisions in legal matters, even when using an Anglo-Saxon source from a time when there were no judges. What other word could he have used? He could not then have felt the same need as I do to avoid the anachronism or to discriminate between judge and arbitrator. Throughout the eleventh century the assemblies of shire and hundred and borough decided disputes as they had always done, by judgment of non-professionals.

---

117. Hudson *Historia Ecclesie* II p5 II 4. Could the writer have been remembering Catullus, **3.17**? How else can the juxtaposing of *facundia* and *causidici* be explained?
118. Kennedy 'Disputes About *Bocland*' p189.
119. Hudson *Historie Ecclesiae* I pp209–10.
120. MT Clanchy *From Memory* 2nd edn p18; Brand *Origins* pp9–12.

Moreover, the *Leges Henrici Primi* suggest that the respondent had the right to object to an outsider hearing the case. The decision-makers had to come from the locality and therefore be known to the parties:[121]

> **10.55** 5.2 No judgments shall be pronounced by a stranger, or by a *iudex* or in a place or at a time which is not his own.
>
> **10.56** 5.3a He shall affirm or object whether the witnesses and *iudices* and parties are acceptable to him and whether he agrees to the *iudices*.

The author eventually tries to put the matter beyond doubt:

> **10.57** 5.5 The *iudices* should definitely not be anyone other than those the respondent has chosen.
>
> **10.58** 5.5a Nor should he be heard nor should a decision be made before they have been chosen.
>
> **10.59** 5.5b If anyone puts off agreeing to the chosen ones, nobody shall talk to him [or perhaps share the sacrament with him, *communicare*] until he obeys.
>
> **10.60** 5.13 Anyone charged before his own *iudex* may plead his cause if he wishes, and if he is charged before a *iudex* who is not his own, he may keep silent, if he wishes.
>
> **10.61** 5.6 If any dissent arises among the peers in making their decision on the matters in dispute, the opinion of the majority shall prevail.

These rules show how hard it is to define away public arbitration, as if it should not be included in a study of arbitration for lack of some element of consensual choice. When everyone felt more strongly than we do about belonging to their groups, of family and larger, consent did not usually come into it. When, as here, it was brought to their attention, they made provision for disagreement.

By the time of the *Laws of Edward the Confessor*, the office of royal judge was established but he was not called in Latin *iudex*, the general name for a decision-maker. A new name had to be created to denote this embryonic professional:

> **10.62** 3. Wherever a royal justice, *iusticia*, or any other justice, *iusticia*, whoever he is, holds the pleas of a justice, *iusticia*, if the bishop's minister is there and institutes a claim of Holy Church, that claim shall be finished first, as reasonably as possible on that day.

That is clear evidence of the establishment of a royal judicial officer.[122] Ordeals had to be administered by a priest but from this time a royal justice must also attend:

> **10.63** 9. On the day when there is to be an ordeal, the bishop's minister shall attend the ordeal with his clergy and the royal justice, *iusticia regis*, and the legal men of the district.

---

121. *Leges Henrici Primi* 5.2.
122. Francis West *The Justiciarship in England* p7.

These royal justices, who had the Latin name *iusticia*, must not be confused with the justiciar, *iusticiarius*, who acted as the king's deputy throughout this period. It is true that some justiciars did judicial work. William I's Geoffrey de Coustances, for example, was not yet called justiciar but acquired a reputation for legal skills before he became a leading member of the Domesday Inquest team. Any judging they did until after the death of Stephen was in land disputes between the Norman lords, lay and ecclesiastical, and too political to fall within the scope of this book.[123]

Though something of a lawyer himself,[124] the author of the *Leges Henrici Primi* thought little of the contributions of his colleagues to the development of the law, **10.27**: 'the professionals' greed and malign and detestable practices have introduced more grievous categories of harm to the legal system', in that case by creating artificial differences between the customary laws of different shires. And that is not all:

> **10.64** 6.4 Indeed, there is so much wrongheadedness in affairs and such a quantity of evils that the definite truth of the law or the fixed provision of a remedy is rarely able to be found; but to everybody's greater confusion a new method of bringing claims is worked out, a new trick to hurt is found, as if what there was before did not do enough harm, and the one who does most harm to most people is judged most highly.
>
> **10.65** 6.6 Finally, the misfortunes of this world are so many and full of such great worries and obfuscated by so many tricks that it seems better to totally avoid claims and the uncertain chances of litigation.

There is no doubt about the author's concern that the old, simpler processes of the assemblies were being corrupted by the activities of the *professores*. But who were they? The author of *Leges Henrici Primi* speaks of '*professio nostra*'.[125] He later uses *professio* to mean any distinct expert body,[126] but here he is talking about a body to which he himself belongs. What does it do? Something for which the *Leges Henrici Primi* were written. And that was to instruct in law:

> **10.66** 8.7 If indeed the earlier or later chapters may teach anything relevant to our profession, whether they rejoice in the natural law or legal or moral decree, and it may be I do not fully accomplish this from the great variety of circumstances, at least I am offering good will in all directions.

Though it is more usual for legal historians to date the genesis of the English legal profession from the time of Henry II, when our period has ended,

---

123. David Bates 'The Origin of the Justiciarship'.
124. His training in rhetoric may be evidenced by the little irrelevant insertions he makes in the belief that they ornament his text, e.g. 6.5: 'Only to those we cannot do without do we proffer respect and love – with hellish (*stigia*, Stygian?) hypocrisy'. And a few Latin legal tags, e.g. 5.28b: '*Reum non facit nisi mens rea*: guilt is not established without a guilty mind'.
125. *Leges Henrici Primi* 8.7.
126. *Leges Henrici Primi* 9.8.

earlier chapters have shown that there were lawyers in England long before that, in Roman times and thereafter. It should not surprise us, therefore, if the first evidence of their activities, not only in the royal courts but in the customary assemblies, appears at the end of the eleventh century.[127] They were not, of course, a self-conscious body like a modern profession, nor are they likely to have been employed full-time in litigation. They were not graduates of any uniform training. *Professio* in Latin is not an exact synonym for profession in English. But the *Leges Henrici Primi* was written for an express purpose: to set out for somebody's use the relevant, applicable law, to be applied in litigation.

There is no evidence of regular legal education, intended to prepare lawyers for practice before 1154. Though the famous Italian scholar Vacarius was teaching in England, perhaps in Oxford, in the reign of Stephen, and wrote a book for English students of the Roman law,[128] the evidence for his teaching career is later.[129]

THE CHURCH

Perhaps in April 1072, William I wrote a letter to all his sheriffs with instructions for the future administration of justice in ecclesiastical matters. The Anglo-Saxons had dealt with such disputes in their ordinary assemblies of hundred and shire, where clergy attended and no doubt took the leading roles as appropriate. William I was happy for that to continue in the shires, where the greater disputes were heard and a bishop co-presided, but no longer in the hundreds. Two copies of the letter survive, one to all in the diocese of Lincoln; this is a translation of part of the other:[130]

> **10.67** William by the grace of God king of the English to Ralph Bainard, Geoffrey de Manneville, Peter de Valognes and to my other faithful men of Essex, of Hertfordshire and of Middlesex, greetings. Know you all, and my other faithful men who are in England, that I have decided, with the common council and on the advice of the archbishops and bishops and abbots and all the leading men of my kingdom, that the episcopal laws, which up to my times in the kingdom of the English have not been kept well or according to the instructions of the holy canons, should be amended.
>
> Therefore I order and by royal authority instruct that no bishop or archdeacon shall any further deal with disputes in the hundred, nor bring for the decision

---

127. The best monograph is Paul Brand *The Origins of the English Legal Profession* (1992), who does not deal with this evidence. In 'The Origins of the English Legal Profession' (1987) he disagrees with RC Palmer 'The Origins of the Legal Profession in England' (1976).
128. Francis de Zulueta *The Liber Pauperum of Vacarius*.
129. Francis de Zulueta and Peter Stein *The Teaching of Roman Law in England Around 1200* xxii–xxvii. Zulueta, the Oxford Regius Professor of Civil Law, had claimed Vacarius for Oxford; Stein, his Cambridge counterpart, shows that claim to be questionable.
130. Liebermann *Gesetze* I 485; Stubbs *Select Charters* pp99–100.

of laymen a cause which relates to the control of souls. But anyone who shall have been called to appear about any cause or accusation shall come to the place which the bishop shall have chosen and nominated. There shall he reply to the cause or accusation, and not according to the hundred but according to the canons and episcopal laws shall he do right to God and his bishop.

Respondents who fail to turn up may be excommunicated and the king promises his terrestrial help if the bishop needs it. The king expressly forbids any official of his or anyone else to interfere with the bishop's jurisdiction.

From this it is clear that William I had no doubts about his authority and responsibility for ecclesiastical disputes, and that he preferred the more straightforward ones to be dealt with in courts – not assemblies – set up and run by the bishops and later the archdeacons. Appeals might lie to the Pope. The jurisdiction of the shire assemblies was not affected.

There is little evidence of the ecclesiastical courts making use of mediation and arbitration in Norman times, though more of the clergy themselves as peacemakers. Like Maitland, I wish that the myths told of fewer miracles and more mortgages, or in my case mediations, but they sometimes allow a glimpse of saintly techniques.

William of Malmesbury wrote a life of Wulfstan, bishop of Worcester, who died in 1095.[131] He tells the story of a dispute which was probably resolved well before that date. Wulfstan went to Gloucester to consecrate a church. There was a big crowd, despite Wulfstan's sermon going on for most of a day. His subject was peace:[132]

> **10.68** Very many who had previously been irreconcilable were on that day brought to peaceful resolutions. People encouraged one another and, if anyone should think he ought to refuse, the bishop was consulted.

But one dispute was intractable. William the Bald had killed a man by accident; his five brothers would accept no reconciliation payment. The abbot of Gloucester had tried and failed many times to reconcile the parties. When brought before Wulfstan they rejected his entreaties out of hand. They would rather be excommunicated. So Wulfstan, though wearing his bishop's best, threw himself in the dirt at their feet, promising them masses in both Worcester and Gloucester. They scorned him. The crowd shouted curses on them. The most violent brother went mad, foaming at the mouth and chewing the earth. The other brothers begged for mercy.[133]

> **10.69** Fear of him had wrenched respect from them. Concern for their brother brought humility. They feared that their wicked act would be punished as his had

---

131. RR Darlington *Vita Wulfstani* pp38–9; Van Caenegem *Lawsuits* no139.
132. Van Caenegem *Lawsuits* no139.
133. PR Hyams 'Feud in Medieval England' pp2–4 sets this in context.

been, all being equally involved. The sight of these things moved him to mercy and straight after mass he restored health to the sufferer, safety to the others and peace to all.

Many a modern mediator has begged the Almighty for similar powers.

MEDIATION AND ARBITRATION

The sources provide plenty of evidence for a continuing preference for compromise and settlement, mediated if necessary, before, during, or after the formal proceedings:[134]

> **10.70** 3. On the handling and determination (and classification) of causes.
> 3.1 All causes are to be tried by the *iudices* with true reason of deliberation and decided with equality and with no regard to person, or, if the practice will allow, to be settled by peace.

Leges Henrici Primi says that this was incorporated into legislation:[135]

> **10.71** 49.5a for an agreement prevails over the law and love over a judgment.

And shows a similar preference for love rather than adjudication in directing the shire assembly to bring the parties together 'in love', **10.30**.[136]

Even the Norman landholding class's preference for trial by battle, the judicial duel, to decide ownership and accusations of theft, usually gave way to compromise:[137]

> They were never – as some legal historians have supposed – the sole method used to reach a decision or to secure a settlement in litigation over property. Indeed many disputes over land during the years of Anglo-Norman rule were not in practice settled by formal adjudication, but by amicable agreement or arbitration often reached through collective action or pressure.

This continued in Normandy, where William I acted as arbitrator to avoid a dispute ending in trial by battle and bloodshed, where a clerical party was claimant.

A writ of Henry I directed that a dispute between the cathedral church of Canterbury and St Augustine's monastery there be determined with the assistance of arbitrators, all laymen, who were to decide what we would now call questions of both law and fact between archbishop and abbot.[138]

---

134. *Leges Henrici Primi* 3 and 3.1. John Hudson discusses the use of mediation at this time in 'Interpretación de Disputas' pp898–903.
135. *Leges Henrici Primi* 49.5a '*pactum enim legem vincit et amor iudicium*'.
136. The chirograph incorporating the agreement might then terminate with the words: 'This is the settlement of love', '*hec est composicio amoris*', King 'Dispute Settlement' p121.
137. Jane Martindale 'Between Law and Politics' p124.
138. DM Stenton *English Justice* pp115–23 provides text and translation.

The archbishop had the right to dues paid for use of the harbour at Sandwich. The abbot had land on the other side of the river and some vessels preferred to dock there, the abbot taking harbour dues. In 1127, Henry I sent a letter saying how their disputes should be dealt with:[139]

> **10.72** He ordered that a gathering of wise men who lived by the sea should meet at Sandwich where they were to consider what rights each church should have and confirm their findings by oath, so that thereafter they would be kept firm and intact.

Archbishop William, who was of course a party, presided. He told the meeting that they must tell the truth without fear or favour. Nearly all were ready to say that they had never known any harbour dues to be payable to anyone other than the archbishop. But they wanted to know what the king had written. The letter was read out:

> **10.73** Henry, King of the English, greets the Archbishop of Canterbury, the Abbot of St Augustine's and the Sheriff of Kent. By the oath of twelve legal men of Dover and twelve legal men of the region of Sandwich, who are not men of the archbishop or abbot, establish the truth in the claim between them about the customary rights, *consuetudinum*, as they were in the time of my father and Archbishop Lanfranc and Archbishop Anselm. Let the archbishop and the abbot have such customary rights as it shall be established their antecessors had at that time. In this way let each church have its right in full.

So the whole assembly chose 24 wise old men, who knew what they were talking about, *bonum testimonium habentes*. At least 21 of them had English names. They found for the archbishop and each swore an oath in the same formula. Then 'the great assembly bore witness to these things'.[140] It was still important that the whole assembly approved the award.

In a dispute between the Bath cathedral priory and a layman, Modbert, heard on 30 June 1121 in the bishop's own court, where all those attending might be expected to favour the church's claim, Modbert produced a letter from William, the son of Henry I, which said, in common form: 'I order you to give justly to Modbert seisin of the land which Grenta of Stoke held, as during his lifetime he left it to him.' That was a clear enough royal command, it would seem. But what did 'justly' mean? What if the evidence showed that Grenta on his deathbed had acknowledged that he only rented the land from the church?

---

139. DM Stenton *English Justice* pp119–21 and p21: 'There are no records revealing more plainly the extent to which the Anglo-Norman judicial administration depended for its efficiency on the cooperation of English free men of repute, capable of giving good testimony.'

140. This is about as regular and solemn a formula of Roman law as one can imagine. Gaius *Institutes* 2.104, on making a will in the old-fashioned way, requires the testator to say: 'These things, just as they have been written on these wax tablets, thus I give, thus I leave, thus I attest, and so you, Roman citizens, bear witness for me, *testimonium mihi perhibetote!*'

Moreover, the church had a charter from Cynewold, no less, king of Wessex in the ninth century, granting the land to the church. The arguments on both sides went on too long for the bishop:[141]

10.74 Because the different contradictory arguments spun out the case too long, the bishop said: 'As the day is coming to an end and we have other business to deal with, it is preferable that those of you whom we know are not advocates or supporters of the parties should consider the matter carefully and decide by what resolution the matter should be laid to rest.' So those who appeared senior in years or more learned in the law withdrew from the assembly. They thought carefully and responsibly about every single thing they had heard. When they came back, one spokesman said on behalf of all: 'Considering all the circumstances of this matter, we have resolved to fix it that the one who claims to be the heir at law shall conclusively prove what he has asserted a little while ago in support of his claim, by at least two free and lawful witnesses from the family of the church, appointed today and produced within a week, or by a chirograph with credible signatures. But if he cannot produce either, he shall never be heard again.'

We are not told how many arbitrators were thus appointed but their award was acclaimed by the assembly, everyone declaring it 'worthy and just'. Modbert had been put upon his proof; that is, if he could produce witnesses or a deed, he would win the dispute and the land. If he could not, he could hardly complain, at least formally, though the royal letter had done no more than get the matter heard and the witnesses had to be from the 'family of the church'.

Mediation played its part in managing the disputes of the time.[142] How it worked then in Oxford is shown in splendid detail in the records of the Abbey of Abingdon. At some time between AD1111 and 1117, a dairy farmer called Ermenold failed to pay the rent he owed to Abbot Faritius of Abingdon for land near Oxford Bridge. The abbot took the land back and seized his livestock. Ermenold got Walter, archdeacon of Oxford, and Richard of Standlake to persuade the abbot to give back the livestock by standing surety for him and agreeing a date for a hearing. They all failed to appear, so the abbot brought a complaint against the sureties:[143]

10.75 Because they were his manorial dependants and friends, they intervened and mediated between him and Ermenold and arranged for him to ask the abbot for mercy. He would grant to the abbot and church of Abingdon whatever land he had for his own procurement, within or without the borough, whether his own or held on mortgage[144] (except from the king, or a lord or bishop). But those who

141. Van Caenegem *Lawsuits* no226.
142. Lawrence of Durham (c1114–1158) shows in his exercises in rhetoric how a mediator might have worked then; his euphuism would get him nowhere now, Mia Münster-Swendsen 'Setting Things Straight'.
143. Hudson *Historia Ecclesiae* 204 pp204–7; Van Caenegem *English Lawsuits* I 209 pp178–9.
144. 'Mortgage' is an anachronism. I have used it because it is more familiar than and near enough to the technically correct term 'gage'. No doubt the land was charged in some way as surety.

were creditors of the land, if they could release the land from the abbot's mortgage, would get it back. If not, the abbot and monks would keep it.

The abbot further granted to that man that, if he wanted to become a monk, he would make him a monk in Abingdon. But, if he preferred to live as a layman in the town of Abingdon, he would be found a suitable place to live and be given provisions for one monk and one servant.

This was done in the said Ermenold's house, with the consent of his wife and son William, in the presence of the said Walter and Richard of Standlake and many others. And afterwards it was published and granted in the same manner with the same agreement in the portmoot.

This detailed settlement, mediated by friends of both parties, shows every sign of careful negotiation, and was made enforceable by its 'registration' in the traditional assembly, the portmoot, the town of Oxford's equivalent to a shire assembly. It is easy to imagine the circumstances. The work of a dairy farmer was no easier then than it is today. Perhaps Ermenold was getting old and found it hard to keep up with the labour it took to produce enough surplus to pay the abbot's rent. His business dealings were getting too much for him, too. It was not unusual for older men to become monks. His wife and grownup son were brought into the settlement. There is no sign that there was anything at all unusual about this mediation. How lucky we are to have such a record!

The parties might be brought to a settlement and then agree that their compromise be made binding by the decision, *iudicium*, of the archbishop:[145]

10.76 This agreement was made at Canterbury in the presence of the Lord Archbishop Lanfranc and written by his command between Bishop Gundulf and Gilbert of Tonbridge. By the Lord Archbishop's decision, *iudicium*, Gilbert must pay every year one *solidum* to the Lord Bishop Gundulf for the land of St Andrew's which Gilbert holds, until he gives him other land of his worth one solidum a year, or its equivalent.

Another form of mediation was by the use of go-betweens. In a quarrel between two lords, negotiations would be carried on by their men on their behalf, even after the date for the trial by battle had been set.[146]

At the very end of our period, a chirograph records the resolution of a dispute between the prior of Southwick and Herbert de Boarhunt about some exchanges of land they had made. Herbert fell ill and conceded for the good of his soul but, while he was still well, the parties had withstood efforts to mediate:[147]

10.77 A dispute and conflict had arisen, to settle and pacify which the justice, *justicia*, of Lord Porchester and neighbours and friends of the church met many

145. Van Caenegem *Lawsuits* I no136 p107.
146. Martindale 'Between Law and Politics' 139; King 'Dispute Settlement' p124.
147. Van Caenegem *Lawsuits* I no343 pp298–301.

times but could not put an end to the business in a way that would satisfy the demands of each party.

Presumably Lord Porchester's *justicia* had some legal background and was called in to help with the mediation because of it.[148] Then, after Herbert's death, arbitrators were chosen by the parties in a clever but unusual way: the prior chose four of the friends of Alexander, Herbert's son who had taken over; Alexander chose four of the prior's men; and together the prior and Alexander chose another two.[149] Their names are recorded. They swore to tell the truth. They sorted out the details of the lands and their boundaries and their award was 'recognised by lawful neighbours and sworn men'.

A compromise might be worked out even during the brutal Norman process of trial by battle. At some time about 1147, so the story goes,[150] Edward refused to acknowledge the overlordship of the prior and canons of St Frideswide, Oxford, over his land in Headington. The judicial duel began:

10.76 Eventually, after many exchanges between the fighters, although Edward's champion had lost his vision in the contest, which had escaped the notice of the prior and his side, they both sat down, since neither of them dared attack the other. Peace was established like this: the said Edward did homage to the prior and for that would hold it as his hereditary right, paying for it 19 shillings per annum, and having to make suit for it in the court of the prior of St Frideswide, Oxford, just like the other free men of that landholding.

We are not told who brought about the settlement. The writer is more concerned to disclose the shocking consequences: Edward was succeeded by his nephew Robert, then came his son Roger, then Roger's daughter, the present owner, who is given no name. The prior sold her wardship to Gocelin the marshal for six marks. Gocelin left her and her unnamed mother with Simon de Wancy, who raped her while she was still a little girl, *puella parvula*, and then married her off to his under-age son.

CONCLUSIONS

By the end of this period, the Norman kings had fathered a new legal system, whose mother was the old Anglo-Saxon law. The Common Law was still in gestation but its birth was imminent. It had its father's energy and its mother's indigenous native acceptability. Together they produced an extraordinarily healthy, practical and inventive creature, well able to manage disputes, offering a wide range of possibilities in litigation and

---

148. There was a connection because the Southwick priory had earlier been at Porchester. Or could it be that *justicia* here means not a person but the jurisdiction, or the body of local law, of the lord of Porchester? That would fit better the most common use of the word at that time, though the *Leges Henrici Primi* uses it in the sense of a judicial officer.
149. Van Caenegem *Writs* p74.
150. Van Caenegem *Lawsuits* no316.

through alternatives in arbitration and mediation. But that was just a little while into the future. Soon there would be a system of returnable writs, royal letters in standard form, sent to the sheriff with instructions to bring the parties before a royal court. Professional lawyers with some relevant training would argue the law before full-time judges. But that was not yet and even then the old assemblies continued for a while, doing most of the jobs they always had done.

11 CONCLUSIONS

> One can too easily assume that the development of the Anglo-Saxons and of
> other peoples in northern Europe was from the chaotic to the orderly, from the
> *ad hoc* to the schematized, and from weaker rule to stronger ... Much of the
> nature and power of Dark Age states may have derived from institutions and
> habits of mind whose origins were prehistoric.
>
> James Campbell in Campbell, John and Wormald *The Anglo-Saxons* p241

> Some local usages, it is quite possible, may be relics of a prehistoric society
> and of an antiquity now immeasurable, saved by their obscurity through the
> days of Celt, Saxon and Norman alike. There is no better protection against the
> stronger hand; bracken and lichens are untouched by the storm that uproots oak
> and beech.
>
> Frederick Pollock and FW Maitland *The History of English Law* I pxcix

INTRODUCTION

In Chapter 1 the scope was set, of area, time and emphasis. Those limits
have proved to be appropriate. In particular, hard as it has been, this has
remained a history of the practice of dispute resolution, though laws and
legal records, so far as they could be discovered, have provided most of
the evidence. No attempt has been made to write a history of legal doctrine
or even of the legal systems, and there is still a need for a comprehensive
description of English law's Anglo-Saxon foundations.

Rarely in this period would those who had to mediate or arbitrate have
referred to rules. If they did, it would be as tools to help to mend the broken
peace, which was the preponderant object of their work:[1]

> The historian should beware of assuming that in the absence of expressed inter-
> pretations of the law and given the silence of doctrine, there were no disputes:
> for many disputed points could be settled by compromise without the case
> ending in a judicial determination.

Of course, there were rules then but they had different sources, just as
there were languages and concepts whose use fluctuated. Reading history
backwards carries the risks inherent in using the familiar to think about

---

1. Michael Lobban 'Introduction' to Andrew Lewis and Michael Lobban *Law and History*
    p7. There is much of relevance in the other contributions, particularly Paul Hyams
    'Norms and Legal Argument Before 1150' and in John Hudson 'Court Cases and Legal
    Arguments'.

and describe the unfamiliar. We have only an educated imagination to protect us from anachronism. If it has done nothing else, this study of dispute resolution has provided some evidence that the functions of the practice were often the same then as now. While there is plenty of evidence that technologies have developed, there is little to show that people have become more efficient, more subtle, more honest, let alone wiser in managing their disputes.

DEFINITION

Enforcement is all. There is no point in submitting a dispute to any form of management unless the outcome produces some step towards a resolution which the parties can rely on. Today the parties can take awards of arbitrators and mediated agreements to state courts for enforcement. That was not possible in the period which this study covers. Then, at all times except perhaps in parts of Roman Britannia, the parties had to rely on pressures to conform which flowed from belonging to a community. They were usually enough. The parties knew that. What can be accurately described as public arbitration was the normal way of resolving any dispute which either a party or the community considered important enough.

Indeed, it is only possible to think about arbitration as an alternative to litigation when public arbitration in customary assemblies gives place – at first slowly and in part – to litigation within a state apparatus of government, as happened under the Norman kings. That is why this study cannot satisfy two essential elements of some modern definitions of arbitration. First, the definition by distinction from litigation is irrelevant when there is no litigation, properly defined, with which to contrast it. Secondly, the requirement that arbitration be consensual, demanding a free choice by the parties both of the process and of the arbitrators, is anachronistic when applied to societies where such emphasis on individuality was unknown. But, by Norman times at least, the arbitrators must be known to the parties. They could not be strangers, **10.55**. Respondents could object to anyone they had not themselves chosen, **10.57**.

Everything was public knowledge. The simple 'all or nothing' conclusion of modern litigation was not subtle enough for such a world. The result depended on many factors not thought appropriate for consideration today. Everyone understood that fighting and self-help resulted not just from the victim's anger but from community pressure, from the victim's need to respond to a wrong in a way which satisfied the community's sense of honour. A family could not easily live with shame. But there was another countervailing pressure from the community to resolve the problem peacefully, that is without damage to the community, by methods which the community provided. If you followed the procedures set down by the community, what we call customary law, no shame could result. And how cleverly the assembly manipulated this element in the Inkberrow case, **8.57**! Make the winner say that he would have been satisfied with the result if he had been in the loser's position!

> Then Leofric's friends and Wulfstan's friends said that it would be better if they were to come to an agreement... Leofric and two thegns were to swear an oath that Leofric would have been satisfied with that amount if the decision had gone against him as it had for Wulfstan.

It was the whole community, as represented by the hundred or shire or borough which approved the outcome of these proceedings. Whoever adjudicated, whatever settlement was agreed, it was essential throughout our period, as it had been at the time of Homer, that the whole assembly approved the award, 'the whole shire making the decision', **10.38**.

There is no evidence of professional arbitration in England as there is in contemporary Ireland, where the *brithem* was a legal expert who regularly heard disputes.[2] Nor is there any sign of the *bonus homo*, the single private arbitrator of Roman law, even in Roman Britannia. Any mention of *boni homines* or *legales* or *meliores* or *seniores*, men old or wise or otherwise distinguished for their qualities, is in the process of public arbitration. There those men of distinction – or wealthy enough in land – were a necessary part of the process.[3] The determination, whoever produced it and however it was brought about, would only stick if those with authority in the group were satisfied with it. When the Anglo-Saxon for *boni homines*, *god man*, is found, they are acting as 'witnesses', a role which there included representing the whole assembly.[4]

No problems were perceived in theory or arose in practice if witnesses took part in mediating a settlement or even in adjudicating as arbitrators. The more knowledge of facts and law relevant to the dispute were diffused and shared, the easier it would be to get consensus and the more likely the settlement would stick. The important difference from modern procedures is that those who were helping to bring about a settlement were considered (however far that might be from reality) to be the friends of both sides.[5]

Why does no evidence survive of private arbitration? The simple answer might be that awards would be performed forthwith and that nothing would be written and kept to record them and, if it did, it would not survive. But that does not explain why there is no mention of ad hoc private arbitration anywhere at any time. It is more likely that there was no place for private

---

2. Richard Sharpe 'Dispute Settlement in Medieval Ireland' pp183–8: 'there survive a considerable number of arbitral awards', citing Mac Niocaill (1967) 2 *Irish Jurist* (NS) 299–307.
3. Susan Reynolds *Kingdoms* pp12–66; Chris Wickham in Davies and Fouracre *The Settlement of Disputes* p232.
4. E.g. **8.61**; it must be remembered both *man* and *homo* do not specify gender and, in this case, it is clear the *menig god man* included women.
5. Susan Reynolds 'Medieval Law' p489.

arbitration when the public system was so comprehensive. There would be no way to enforce a private award. The response to a theoretically possible seeker of private arbitration would be similar to that to someone who wanted a contract enforced that had been entered into privately: 'there is no such thing'.[6]

PROCEDURE

Many have made the mistake of assuming that procedure in the assemblies was less rational, more ritualistic, the further back you go. The evidence is all to the contrary in this period. All decent people believed in the power of the oath. That belief long predates Christianity but was confirmed by the Church. If you believed in the Church's basic teachings, and there was rarely any opportunity for discussing alternatives and few are likely to have allowed themselves the luxury of free thought, to break a solemn oath had unpleasant and eternal repercussions. Usually there was evidence available. The lawmakers tried to insist that there should be as far as possible, for example by requiring witnesses for a valid sale of cattle. When those who knew the facts gave their testimony, it ought to be reliable. It looks as though that sort of evidence was always given due weight. And both those who gave the evidence and those who weighed it swore oaths to do right.

The decision of the assembly often relied on documents, usually royal grants, which knocked the bottom out of one party's case and regularly led to a settlement: 'disputes where the parties do appear to accept the worth of documentary evidence impress with a sense of genuine conciliation';[7] and 'One does not fabricate superfluous written evidence if one expects to win by out-swearing or out-remembering one's opponents'.[8] But still, at the end of our period, even the most important legal transactions, transfers of land, might well be perfected without documents of any kind:[9]

> In the eleventh and twelfth centuries... unless possession was challenged and a case came into the court of lord or king, land for the most part changed hands in an unrecorded ceremony, leaving no trace.

No documentary trace for us now, but we may be sure there were plenty of witnesses, to add seriousness at the time and survive to give evidence for the foreseeable future.

Sometimes the assembly could be misled. Some parties or their witnesses were forsworn. Documents could be forged. But the system worked. There were few complaints or calls for change. Even those which survive, like

---

6. Indeed, private contracts were discouraged in England, though not on the continent, PJ Geary 'Extra-Judicial Means'.
7. Kennedy 'Law and Litigation' p172.
8. Wormald 'Charters' in *Legal Culture* p298.
9. Marjorie Chibnall 'Clio's Legal Cosmetics' p31.

Gildas's tirade against the tyrants who wilfully failed to apply the right law, **4.8**, do not call for reforms in procedure.

Nor did procedures change with governments. When newcomers take power, why should they want to interfere with the way in which private disputes are managed? They rarely do, in any time or place, unless their authority is threatened. The Romans left well alone, as did the Chinese emperors and as the Chinese rulers of Hong Kong do today. The Germanic invaders, from the earliest Anglo-Saxons to William the Conqueror, left existing systems to do the work of dispute management. William and his Norman successors were at pains to emphasise their confirmation of the good old laws, customary mainly but with the addition of legislation for which they took credit.

And so the procedure at the end of our period had not changed significantly:[10]

> There was no 'marvellous suddenness' about the emergence of the Common Law. For, to judge from recorded proceedings, pre-Conquest dispute settlement was not 'archaic' but, in most senses of the word, 'medieval'.

SUBJECT MATTER

Because all arbitration and mediation were handled by the group, if the group was comprehensive enough there was no reason to limit the scope of its jurisdiction. No need was seen for the limitations of the Roman law, which excluded from arbitration by *compromissum* such matters as personal status, succession and legitimacy, public order offences and some matters reserved to the praetor. Rome had alternative official venues: in England there was nowhere else to go.

When disputes arose in ecclesiastical affairs, if they were clearly confined to God's work, they could be handled within the ecclesiastical hierarchy and, if necessary, an appeal might go to the Pope. Ordinary disputes where the clergy were one or both parties – and the surviving records are disproportionately about them – would go to the ordinary assemblies, where the clergy would take the lead in managing them. It was not until after the Conquest that church courts were created with exclusive jurisdiction.

Even the killing of a prince might be the subject of mediation, though there 'seemed to be potential for more bitter fighting between these fierce kings and peoples', the seventh-century Northumbrians and Mercians, **6.16**.

THE LAW AND LEGAL SYSTEM

The community knew the law, at least most of its general substance. If an assembly did not know the details, it knew where to find them, in the

10. Wormald 'Charters' p168.

memories of the old and wise. Throughout this period that was the customary law, *consuetudo*, which the ideology of all such communities assumes is unchanging, but which changes constantly and imperceptibly and may be expressly altered by royal command. After the Conquest, the Norman kings reiterated that the customary law of the time of Edward the Confessor was the underlying law of the land, and they were careful to imply that it was now the law because they said so. They made known their will on this point, even if they published no other laws. When kings considered intervention necessary, as they did from the time of Aethelberht's legislation to deal with conflicting customary laws, they published their law, at first only to those who had to apply it but later to those they ruled. But:[11]

> It was no more than marginally adjustable to a demonstrably changing world. Nobody saw this more clearly than Charlemagne and Alfred, the most competent as well as inspired of early medieval kings. For all the former's hundred-plus capitularies or the latter's ideologically gravid Mosaic preface, they barely altered the fundamental law of their realms.

This book ends as the Common Law begins. There is no clean break but it is a good place to stop because so much changes from the beginning of the reign of Henry II. The distinctions between Norman and English people were dissolving into unimportance. The old forms of Anglo-Saxon were no longer spoken or written and the monks stopped adding to the *Anglo-Saxon Chronicle*. Literature was starting to be written in many dialects of what we now call Middle English.[12]

The Constitutions of Clarendon, restating the old law on Church and State, the Assizes of Clarendon, laying down the criminal law, and the Assize of Novel Disseisin, transforming the civil law, are just a decade away. The assemblies lose their primacy. Royal governments forbid the feud. Royal courts and royal law become more important and pervasive. There are trained lawyers and judges and books about law. They create their own privileges, even their own language. When the history of dispute management under the Common Law is written, it will have a more modern look, with arbitration and mediation more recognisably separate and private.[13]

FINALE

We all have our preconceptions, prejudices and slants. It is so much easier to take in new notions from whatever media we prefer than it is to recognise

11. Wormald, preface to *Legal Culture* pxiv.
12. Marjorie Chibnall *Debate* pp128–9.
13. The recent work of Dorothy Reynolds has shed much light particularly on the last years of our period and the century which followed, 'The Emergence of the Professional Law in the Long Twelfth Century' and the discussion of that paper: Paul Brand 'The English Difference: The Application of Bureaucratic Norms within a Legal System', Piotr Górecki 'A View from a Distance', CM Radding 'Legal Theory and Practice in Eleventh-Century Italy' and Susan Reynolds' reply 'Variations in Professionalism', with many comparative insights.

old unjustified assumptions, which clutter up our view. Sometimes it needs a shock to show us how dirty our reading glasses have become. As I write these final sentences, I have just read yet again in the newspaper that physicists are realising that the very foundations of their science need to be rethought. Just in time, as I was preparing this manuscript for publication, my wife heard a radio programme and bought me Stephen Oppenheimer's new book, *The Origins of the British*. As it says on the back cover: 'British prehistory will never look the same again', and even the most recent accounts of Anglo-Saxon invasions must be questioned. I read today in her copy of *BBC History* about cocaine and tobacco in Ancient Egyptian mummies, which, if substantiated, puts all ideas of early trade in a new perspective – or at least tells us something of the habits of those who handled them in modern times.

It would be an odd scholar for whom greater knowledge did not increase humility. It is so obvious that uncertainty is better than confidence in assumptions, however longstanding or highly favoured. So much scholarship depends on serendipity as well as thorough literature searches. Aldhelm's letter apologising for not accepting an invitation to spend Christmas with the bishop provides the only bit of hard evidence for the study of law in England then, all the more convincing because neither the writer nor those who preserved the letter meant to tell us anything about it. How many millions of similar trivia have been lost, with all the flashing insights they could have given us – and all the corrections of simple and repeated slips? When all the searching, sifting and sorting are done, there are still just a few scraps; nearly all the bits are missing. And still they do not fit, nor do we know their relative importance.

But, if historians could ask for evidence to help them to describe with confidence how disputes were resolved in this period, they would surely ask, first, for legislation laying down the legal system. That we have, law after law reiterated throughout Anglo-Saxon times and even after the Conquest, providing that disputes shall be settled if possible, adjudicated if not, by the traditional assemblies according to customary law as amended by royal dooms, which provided both legislation to be followed and authoritative decisions to extrapolate from. Secondly, if we were really greedy, we might ask for a description, preferably by an arbitrator, not in a form in which he might wish to make something of it for historians, but ideally describing what actually happened, in an attempt to persuade the appropriate authority to enforce the award. We have it in the Fonthill letter! Old Ordlaf, in his own words, in his own hand even, putting down (with no thought of future readers) all he could muster to persuade the king that he had done everything necessary to secure enforcement of the award. And all from the time of Alfred! What more can we ask for? We have all we need to show that the age-old system for the management of disputes for the health of the community was, as it had been for the ancient Greeks, a form of public arbitration, which had mediation as its first object and in default adjudication by a popular assembly.

And yet, if we could know all there was to know about the past, what good would it do? Would it help to solve present problems? Not directly, perhaps, but it would be enough if it clarified our minds and saved us from avoidable and repeated error. This has special relevance in the ever-changing world of legal concepts:[14]

> It need not matter that current frameworks of legal explanation do not correctly explain what the past cases were really about: but if past cases turn out not to be capable of sustaining the analytical explanation imposed on them, we may be forced to rethink the present, in order to be more sceptical about modern models. Equally, if we look to history to test our contemporary analytical categories, we might find seams of doctrine that have been buried away which might be fruitfully explored in a modern context.

No one has a right to rely on bad history, even from ignorance. Perhaps even the most modest and embryonic contribution may at least disturb too comfortable a reliance on common assumptions. It would be nice to think so but all conclusions must be tentative. It is too much to dream, with that would-be mediator the Duke of Exeter, 'And I, I hope, shall reconcile them all.'[15]

---

14. Michael Lobban 'Introduction' p15.
15. William Shakespeare *King Henry VI Part III* Act 1 Scene 1, last line.

Appendix A

LANGUAGES OF DISPUTE IN ENGLAND BEFORE THE COMMON LAW

INTRODUCTION

There may doubtless be some little British and Roman blood in us, just as some Welsh and Latin words crept into the English tongue from the very beginning. But we may be sure that we have not much of their blood in us, because we have so few of their words in our language... It has turned out much better in the end that our forefathers did thus kill or drive out nearly all the people whom they found in the land... I cannot think that we should ever have been so great and free a people as we have been....

Sir Edward Freeman *Old English History for Children* pp27–9[1]

To understand how disputes are managed, at any time and place, it is important to know what languages are used and how. Do all the people in a jurisdiction speak the same language? Is there a social difference between the languages? Can parties to a dispute use their own language? Do they choose arbitrators or mediators who speak their language? What happens if the parties speak different languages? All these questions arise in England, from prehistoric times until AD1154, the terminus of our period. Until writing started and some of what was written was preserved, we have to rely on other disciplines: especially anthropology, archaeology and genetics. From Roman colonial times, there is relevant literature, in Latin, Anglo-Saxon and Anglo-Norman, but not all the answers can be found even then. In any case, is what is written ever a true reflection of what is spoken?[2]

1. I have to thank Markku Filppula, Juhani Klemola and Heli Pitkänen 'Early Contacts Between English and the Celtic Languages' p4 for this quotation and the collection of essays they edited, *The Celtic Roots of English*, for many insights. Not only has Freeman's *Old English History for Children* been popular for nearly 140 years, for much of that time in Dent's Everyman's Library, it is still in print. This is just one of the worst examples of scholarship perverted by racism; not only Gildas and Bede but Gibbon, Macaulay and Stubbs fell into the trap: Nicholas Higham 'The Anglo-Saxon/British Interface' p29.
2. It would be futile to attempt to provide a comprehensive bibliography of the linguistic literature, even the most relevant; the items cited in the footnotes, though, should provide sufficient leads. Most recently, help has come from Nick Higham ed *Britons in Anglo-Saxon England*.

Most historians have assumed, and some have argued, that all the people of Iron Age England spoke the languages which became Welsh, Cornish, or Irish, what we now call Celtic. None, including the historical linguists, have satisfactorily explained (at least to me) how Anglo-Saxon dialects took hold and developed so quickly between the end of the Roman colonial rule (cAD425) and the time of Bede (born AD672 or 673), when Anglo-Saxon provided a literary language to compete with Latin. Though I cannot answer my own questions to my own satisfaction, at least I can dispose of Freeman's assumptions, offer a synthetic and tentative solution and place dispute resolution in a clearer background, even if it is still patchy and often only in outline.

PREHISTORY

Each to his own job and the cows will be well looked after.[3]

Nobody knows what languages were used in prehistoric England. The *kind* of languages may be guessed. In particular, it may be possible to know something about the languages used by those who repopulated England after the last Ice Age, as described in Chapter 2. Help comes from two disciplines, genetics and linguistics.

If, as is now generally agreed, the new immigrants came from a 'Basque homeland', they no doubt spoke the languages of their places of origin. We cannot assume that those languages were the forerunners of modern Basque. There is some evidence, archaeological and genetic, that later incomers brought new languages of which traces remain. Though it is neither easy nor safe to link genetic evidence to language change, it must be taken into account. Oppenheimer's research shows:[4]

> Given the distribution of Celtic languages in southwest Europe, it is most likely that they were spread by a wave of agriculturalists who dispersed 7,000 years ago from Anatolia, travelling along the north coast of the Mediterranean to Italy, France, Spain and then up the Atlantic coast to the British Isles. There is a dated archaeological trail for this. My genetic analysis shows exact counterparts for this trail... right up to Cornwall, Wales, Ireland and the English south coast.
>
> Celtic languages and the people who brought them probably first arrived during the Neolithic period. The regions we now regard as Celtic heartlands actually had less immigration from the Continent during this time than England... Wales and Cornwall have received about 20 per cent, Scotland and its associated islands 30 per cent, while eastern and southern England, being nearer the continent, has received one third of its population from outside over the past 6,500 years.

3. The dangers of trespassing into disciplines where one is not at home are fearful and I have tried to keep in mind the French proverb: '*Chacun son métier, les vaches seront bien gardées.*'
4. Stephen Oppenheimer 'Myths'; Barry Cunliffe *Facing the Ocean*.

If the Celtic parts spoke early forms of Welsh (sometimes called Brittonic or Brythonic), Cornish, Irish and other dialects, what was spoken in the rest of England? The generally accepted conclusion is that all spoke some kind of Celtic language:[5] 'As a general model, it is probably reasonable to infer that the peoples of mainland Britain spoke a range of P-Celtic dialects, with the closest linguistic similarities between adjacent groupings.' But could there have been a significant number of people in England whose language was a different branch of Indo-European, one more akin to the Germanic rather than the Brittonic/Celtic? The question may be raised here in the words of Oppenheimer:[6]

> The possible relationships of language to archaeology and genetics are all specu-
> lative and can be misleading. But the genetics tells us the Welsh/English genetic
> border is perhaps of Neolithic or earlier antiquity, and the archaeology tells us
> that there were always two separate sources of cultural flow into the British
> Isles, with Ireland and the British Atlantic coast relating southwards, and the
> east coast of England relating across the North Sea. If the prehistoric language
> split followed the same Neolithic geographical divide, the cultural and linguistic
> divisions between the English and the rest could be just as old too.

This is the first hint of what will become a useful tool: the rough and ready division of England into highland and lowland zones, Map 1.

I argue in Chapter 3, on the disinterested authority of Julius Caesar, **3.4**, and Tacitus, **3.5**, that those in Kent, and perhaps others between the south coast and the Thames, were speaking a language not much different from that of the Belgae across the Channel. This is the conclusion of Oppenheimer:[7] 'One possibility is that the Belgae spoke Germanic languages, perhaps ancestral to Dutch or Frisian, which they carried to England even before the Roman invasion.' The great weight of opinion among linguists, on the other hand, is that the Belgae spoke Celtic dialects of some sort.[8] Yet I believe that the rapid acceptance in England of variants of Germanic languages, in the fifth, sixth and seventh centuries, is partly explained by the existence in parts, perhaps only pockets, of the lowland zone of communities speaking languages sufficiently similar to be mutually comprehensible. As Whatmough concluded:[9] 'Not only fundamental agreements, but borrowings, back and

5. David Mattingly *Imperial Possession* p52.
6. Oppenheimer *Origins* p260.
7. Oppenheimer *Origins* p271. I have been persuaded by the arguments of his Chapter 7: 'What Languages were Spoken in England before the "Anglo-Saxon Invasions"?', which deals with all the evidence, including that of place-names, coins and inscriptions.
8. Joshua Whatmough *The Dialects of Ancient Gaul* p3: 'it is certain that a Western Germanic dialect was spoken in Belgica in regions adjoining the river Rhine (the later Germania inferior) from which it tended to spread westwards'; P-H Billy *Thesaurus Linguae Gallicae* ppi, ii; EM Wightman *Gallia Belgica* pp11–12: 'the aristocracy probably spoke one language (Celtic), the poorer folk another'.
9. Whatmough *Dialects of Ancient Gaul* p36.

forth, made for some superficial points of agreement between Germanic and Keltic especially in frontier regions.'

Another factor has not been explored as thoroughly as it deserves: pidgins. Where individuals from different language groups need to communicate, they always find the means. Linguists have learned much about the processes by which pidgins are created, drawing widely on the vocabularies of the different groups but usually settling on a preferred though modified syntax quite quickly. We know nothing of the pidgins used in prehistoric times but it would be surprising if some of the languages we know from later evidence did not start in that way.[10]

Another technique is to adopt one language as the *lingua franca*. That language will be affected by the native languages of all those who adopt it. Celtic became the *lingua franca* of the Atlantic seaboard from Portugal to Scotland.[11]

BRITANNIA

> When I last saw Londinium it was a field of ash... Now it was a new
> administrative capital. I caught smells both familiar and exotic, and
> heard six languages in the first ten minutes.
> Marcus Didius Falco, according to Lindsey Davis *The Silver Pigs* p89

What then were the languages of England under the Romans?

Latin   Latin was the language of colonial administration, and all regular soldiers had the opportunity and plenty of incentive to learn it. Civil servants had to know it. There is evidence to show that it was used not only by the English upper classes but by many whose trade or other activities brought them into conversation with Latin speakers,[12] including some of the women with whom they lived and the children they had by them. Writing about AD98, Tacitus described the spread of Latin in Britannia under the influence of his father-in-law, governor Agricola:[13]

> **A.1** He educated the sons of the leading men in the liberal arts and thought more
> highly of the natural abilities of the Britons than the educated accomplishments
> of the Gauls, so that those who had until recently been contemptuous of the
> Latin language became keen to acquire fluency in it.

10. JA Holm *Pidgins and Creoles*. Theo Vennemann suggests that there were Semitic
    influences on Celtic, 'Semitic → Celtic → English'. I have observed that ordinary people
    – not scholars – are able to pick up enough of the language of others more easily where
    they have no access to formal language teaching. Enough but minimal. Their aspirations
    are different and they are less self-conscious.
11. Cunliffe *Facing the Ocean* pp558–60, 565.
12. A good range of sources for the use of Latin in London from cAD84 onwards is in Morris
    Londinium pp222–3, including a joke written by a brickmaker on a tile, presumably for
    other workers to read.
13. Tacitus *Agricola* 21.

Until an edict of Septimius Severus in AD197, soldiers below the rank of centurion were not allowed to marry during their service in the legion.[14] The civil servants were also part of the military administration and subject to the same restrictions. But there is no doubt that they had relations, temporary or more permanent, with British women. There was nothing to stop other Roman colonials from marrying women who spoke British languages. From the beginning of the third century there were no bars of any kind to intermarriage. Is it more likely that spouses communicated in some British language rather than in Latin? Did they speak a Romance pidgin? Would their children speak their mothers' language? And the next generation? Would it usually depend on their social status? There are a number of rough Latin graffiti which suggest that Latin was commonly used in the towns.[15]

We know that commanding officers had their wives with them from their letters which have survived from a Northumbrian fort, Vindolanda.[16] More than a thousand documents written on wood have been preserved there on Hadrian's Wall because they were submerged in water. About AD100 Claudia Severa, wife of Commander Aelius Brocchus, wrote to her friend, possibly her sister, Sulpicia Lepidina, wife of Flavius Cerialis, Commander of Vindolanda, inviting her to her birthday party:[17]

> A.2 Claudia Severa to her Lepidina, greetings! I send you a warm invitation, sister, to come on 10 September to celebrate my birthday. See that you come to us to make the day happier for me by your company if you come. Give my regards to your Cerialis. My Aelius and my little son send their regards too.
> *I look forward to seeing you, sister. Fare you well sister, my dearest soul, as I hope to fare well. Ciao!*
> [address]   To Sulpicia Lepidina of Flavius Cerialis, from Severa

What is of special interest is that, though the letter was as usual dictated to and written by a secretary, the sentence printed in italics is a P.S. in Claudia's own hand, showing that she was not only at home in Latin, but able both to read and write it.

Other letters show that a distinctive business Latin was commonly used in trade. Though none so far is evidence of a dispute, this shows the background (300 denarii was a soldier's annual salary):[18]

14. Lindsay Allason-Jones *Women in Roman Britain* pp58–9.
15. Higham *Rome, Britain and the Anglo-Saxons* p32; Peter Schrijver 'The Rise and Fall of British Latin'.
16. AK Bowman *The Roman Writing Tablets from Vindolanda*.
17. It is the earliest surviving writing in Latin by a woman anywhere, AK Bowman and JD Thomas 'New Texts from Vindolanda' pp137–40. The tablet is on display in the Roman Britain room at the British Museum, London and pictured in Potter and Johns *Roman Britain* p58.
18. AK Bowman, JD Thomas and JN Adams 'Two Letters from Vindolanda' pp43–52 plus two plates, which show that the letter was written left-handed in a hurry.

A.3 That hundred pounds of sinew from Marinus, I'll settle that. Since you wrote to me about this he has not mentioned it. I have written to you several times that I've bought about 1,000 pecks (*modii*) of grain, so I must have cash. If you don't send me some, at least 500 *denarii*, I am going to lose what I've given as deposit, around 300 *denarii*, and that will be an embarrassment.

Those who were comfortable in their command of Latin were no doubt more likely to make use of the Roman legal system and arbitration in the Roman style; there would be other factors, including cost and accessibility, to inhibit their use by others.

Latin was spoken widely in many parts of Britannia and still in England long after the Romans had left but by a minority, it has been assumed.[19] Recently, that assumption has been challenged:[20]

> The success of linguistic Romanization within the Empire is clearly demonstrated by the disappearance of all other languages that were being spoken when the legions marched in, apart from... Albanian, Basque and British Celtic... Yet... In the later days of the Empire the man in the street spoke Latin and possibly nothing but Latin.

So presumably the women would have no choice but to speak it too.

That British Latin at first showed strong influences from existing mother tongues, which were no doubt in turn affected by the Latin being learned. This produced:[21]

1. types of Brittonic and English with a Latin substratum as a result of language shift from Latin to Brittonic and English;
2. types of Latin with heavy borrowing from Brittonic and/or English, ultimately leading to language death.

It must be a rich transfusion which produces in the target language a replacement of such basic terms as 'arm' and 'leg', which British took from Latin at this time: *braich* from *bracchium* and *coes* from *coxa*. Such interchange must have importance for our later quest to understand how Anglo-Saxon took hold so quickly and completely, if it did.

British Languages Both the indigenous people and many of the occupying forces must have spoken the British languages which prevailed before the Romans came.[22] Though there was no other language than Latin

---

19. Thomas Charles-Edwards 'Language and Society among the Insular Celts AD400–1000' pp703–36; Glanville Price *The Languages of Britain* pp158–69.
20. Schrijver 'The Rise and Fall of British Latin' p87. His approach is heart-warming: 'this is exactly the kind of recovery operation that a historical linguist is supposed to be capable of performing'.
21. Schrijver 'The Rise and Fall of British Latin' p88.
22. KH Jackson *Language and History in Early Britain* pp76ff is the standard reference, though his methods have been shown to be faulty by AS Gratwick '*Latinitas Britannica*' in Nicholas Brooks *Latin and the Vernacular Languages in Early Modern Britain* pp1–79. MJ Harper *The History of Britain Revealed* especially pp62–73 argued in 2002 that the British spoke a form of English before the Anglo-Saxons came; and in the nineteenth century HC Coote *The Romans of Britain*.

in which Claudia could have *written* to Lepidina, and they must surely
have spoken Latin to one another, it is quite likely that their native tongues
came from Belgic Gaul:[23]

> Those who made up the garrison were not themselves Roman, or even Italian,
> by birth. In fact they had only been members of the Roman imperial club for
> a century or so. Most of the troops were Batavians or Tungrians from the Low
> Countries (modern Netherlands and Belgium) around the mouth of the Rhine,
> part of what Julius Caesar called Gallia Belgica.

The recent research in genetics suggests that a large part of south-eastern
Britannia, and some other parts as well, were then inhabited by people
whose stock came from more northern parts, across the Channel or the
North Sea. What languages did they bring with them? Are the Belgic Gauls
more likely to have spoken some other branch of the Indo-European family
of languages? Could it have been Germanic? Tacitus observed the similarity
of the way of life of the Gauls and Britons, 3.5: 'Their speech is not much
different at all.'[24] If those Britons were descended from incomers from
Belgic Gaul or further north, Britannia may have been partly populated
by Germanic speakers when the Romans first invaded. Neither they nor
the Romans have left us anything to tell us so directly. But we know that
Germanic immigrants had been settling in Britannia for centuries before
the Romans left.[25] Moreover, German soldiers came to make up most of
the Roman armies in the West and many served in Britannia and, when
their service was over, settled here.[26] Not only were soldiers given land
when they retired, fragments of tablets recording land sales show there was
a market in which Germans could have bought land.[27] But this is surmise,
prompted perhaps too strongly by an urge to explain how Anglo-Saxon
dialects could so quickly and completely have become the common speech
of England, if they did as is commonly assumed when the Romans left. This
unsolved problem must be left for further discussion in the next section.

AFTER THE ROMANS

> Another language spreads from coast to coast,
> Only perchance some melancholy Stream

23. David Miles *Tribes* p122.
24. Tacitus *Agricola* 12: *sermo haud multum diversus.* Saussure would have classified *sermo*
    as *parole* rather than *langue.*
25. There was a *civitas* called Belgae, which included Portsmouth and Winchester, *Venta
    Belgarum.* After the reorganisation of the provinces cAD396, Continental Belgae were
    divided into *Belgica Prima*, including Amiens and Reims, and *Belgica Secunda*, with
    Trier and Metz; Mattingly *Imperial Possession* pp228–9.
26. There is plenty of archaeological evidence but it is suggestive rather than decisive, e.g.
    from Dorchester, Mattingly *Imperial Possession* p346.
27. Tomlin 'A Five-Acre Wood' and Mattingly *Imperial Possession* p461. Coote *Romans
    of Britain* pp82–112 argues with his accustomed force, and a wealth of examples of
    boundary markers, that the whole of Britannia was centuriated by Roman surveyors.

> And some indignant Hills odd names preserve,
> When laws, and creeds, and people all are lost!
>
> William Wordsworth *Monastery of Old Bangor*[28]

It is useful to divide England crudely into two parts just for the purposes of discussing language. The highland zone is the more northerly and westerly part, the lowland zone the south and east. The dividing line runs from the mouth of the River Humber (some prefer the Tees) on the north-east coast down to the mouth of the Exe on the south-west. We can be fairly sure that most of the inhabitants of the highland zone when the Romans left spoke some dialect of what became Welsh and Cornish, though a few spoke an Irish version.[29] Many of those in the lowland zone may well have done so too but there were other competitors. What was left of Latin? Could there have been some who spoke a language from a Germanic branch of Indo-European? There is no direct evidence.

No literature has survived in any of those languages, just a few inscriptions. The oldest writing in prose or poetry is in Old English, or Anglo-Saxon as it is called here because that is its common name. Except for a few scraps, it all dates from after the beginning of the seventh century and starts with the dooms of Aethelberht, king of Kent. Does that mean that some form of Anglo-Saxon was the spoken language of those under Anglo-Saxon lordship then? In Kent or all the Anglo-Saxon lands? Were there differences between the languages of the highland and lowland zones? How and when did Anglo-Saxon spread? Was it the spoken language of all classes or just the higher? Had education anything to do with it? Was it ever more than the language of literature and how closely did the written language express the spoken? It is now accepted that:[30]

> English elites had already become well-established across great swathes of the east and south of the lowland zones of the old diocese of Roman Britain by the end of the fifth century and their hold strengthened during the sixth.

The speed of the advance of an incoming language must depend to some degree on the number of incomers, however socially advantageous the new language is. No literary evidence provides an answer. The earliest evidence is not of any kind of English but of Latin.

Latin Latin, of course, had been the language of the Roman administration and continued to be the only literary language in the fifth and sixth centuries.[31] Both Gildas and Patrick wrote it well, though Patrick's style was simple as befitted a missionary who regretted that his education had

---

28. From *Ecclesiastical Sonnets* XII, on the song of Taliesin.
29. M Gelling 'Why Aren't We Speaking Welsh?'
30. Nicholas Higham 'The Anglo-Saxon/British Interface' p36; he explains convincingly the interplay of religions.
31. Andy Orchard 'Latin and the Vernacular Languages'.

been terminated abruptly by enslavement. Its use continued even where it was no longer needed for administration; the best evidence comes from parts of England (and Wales) in epitaphs on standing stones of the fifth to seventh centuries, some in Latin in a cursive script, others in a Celtic language, written in a native script, Ogham:[32]

> The Latin language used in these inscriptions is literate and well-informed. It is not the product of ignorant backwoodsmen grappling with an unfamiliar tongue, but spoken Latin of a high order, employing all sorts of clever word-play which was fashionable in the late- and post-Roman world... They are quite common, and it seems reasonable to suppose that they could have been read by more than just the highest echelons of society.

Pryor provides no evidence to support the assertion of '*spoken* Latin of a high order'; the evidence for that will be mustered later. The 'word-play' was not just for the amusement of those who created the inscriptions. Whoever the audience were, they had to know more than the crude Latin of the graffiti and the informal language of the Vindolanda letters.

Not all the Latin would satisfy a classical scholar. At some time in the fifth or sixth century a gravestone was carved with the Latin inscription:

A.4 CANTIORI HIC IACIT VENEDOTIS CIVE FUIT [C]ONSOBRINO MA[G]LI MAGISTRAT....

'Here lies Cantiori. He was a citizen of Gwynedd. Cousin of Maglus the magistrate....' Why should anyone care who Maglus's cousin was? On a sixth-century stone from a churchyard near Carmarthen is an inscription in Latin and Irish (but not British). The Latin reads:

A.5 MEMORIA VOTEPORIGIS PROTICTORIS

'In memory of Protector Voteporix (or Votepor)'. 'Protector' was the title of an officer in the Roman army. Why should anyone want to pay for that to be permanently proclaimed in what is now Wales cAD600?[33] Epitaphs are not cheap. Someone thought the Roman status of the dead men was worth carving. Chapman Stacey's conclusion on the Votepor stone is illuminating though cautious:[34]

> Perhaps the only certain message communicated by this stone is the infinite complexity of personal and political identity in western Britain in the sixth century. Here we have a memorial inscribed in Latin and Irish to a ruler in Britain, yet British is the language that appears nowhere on the stone (other than in the name Votepor). It invokes in its inscription the Roman army title of *protector* in its characterization of the nature of the authority exercised by the

32. Pryor *Britain AD* p189.
33. Robin Chapman Stacey makes a dazzling success of answering that question in 'Texts and Society' in Charles-Edwards, *After Rome* pp243–47.
34. Chapman Stacey 'Texts and Society' p246.

deceased, and yet the man of whom that title is alleged lived in a Britain from which the last Roman troops had departed a century and a half earlier.

Where did such Latin users come from? Some in the British west were priests, like St Patrick, who travelled back and forth from the south-west coast of Britain to what is now Ireland. A scholar who has made the most microscopic study of the charters concludes:[35]

> But one can reasonably infer from the literary tradition of the fifth-century Romano-Britons Pelagius, Saint Patrick, and Faustus of Riez, the mid-sixth-century Britons Gildas and Vinniau, the late-sixth-century Irishmen Saint Columba of Iona and Mo-Sinu maccu Min and Saint Columban of Bangor, and a host of seventh-century Cambro-Latin, Hiberno-Latin, and Anglo-Latin authors, as from the epigraphic tradition illustrated by scores of inscribed stones from the fifth, sixth, and seventh centuries, that after withdrawal of Roman military and civilian administration in A.D. 410 the Church maintained in these islands schools that produced writers capable of thinking and writing in literary Latin of a high register.

Nor must we ignore the slight evidence of literature, for example Ausonius's Silvius Bonus Britannus, **4.4**. Written and read, the Latin kept alive by education was available for legal use and, possibly, for managing some disputes. But what of spoken Latin? The strength of Schrijver's arguments, relying on carefully presented linguistic evidence, persuades me to accept his conclusions:[36]

> The conclusion must be that Latin was the main language of the British Lowland Zone by the end of the Roman era. If Latin influence, first lexical and then also structural, was due to extensive borrowing in a situation of language shift in favour of Latin, Brittonic in the Highland Zone must have been on the brink of being superseded by Latin, which implies that Brittonic in the heavily Romanized Lowland Zone was not as fortunate and had already been superseded by Latin. If on the other hand Latin influence was due to initial lexical borrowing followed by Latin substratum influence, as I have attempted to argue, the influx of Latin speakers into the Brittonic language pool must have been considerable enough to restructure the whole language. Either way, we are looking at a scenario in which Latin was the main if not the only language of the British Lowlands.

Schrijver's more recent work makes broader claims, positing separate language families in the highland and lowland zones: Highland British Celtic, which became Welsh and Cornish in the highland zone; Lowland British Celtic which was heavily influenced by the syntax and sound system of the Latin spoken widely in the lowland zone,where there were no doubt many bilingual in Latin and Celtic.[37] Though it was in the lowland zone that

---

35. DR Howlett *Sealed From Within* p101.
36. Schrijver 'The Rise and Fall of British Latin' p102.
37. Peter Schrijver 'What Britons Spoke' p165. He draws parallels with developments in Gaul and even in Italy pp166–7.

Latin prevailed and Celtic died out, the highland zone was not unaffected. Highland British Celtic adopted hundreds of Latin words during the time of Roman colonial rule. That influence diminished there as Latin ceased to be the prestige language. Nevertheless, says Schrijver, even the Celtic speakers had a Latin accent, and:[38]

> Lowland British Celtic... was, as far as can be observed, identical with northern Gaulish. Spoken British Latin was to all intents and purposes identical with the type of Romance underlying Old French... The most important border of modern Britain over many centuries of its history has been not the English Channel but the one that runs right through it, from northeast to southwest.

Celtic and Germanic Languages The fact that Celtic/Brittonic languages eventually died out in most of England and became restricted to the future Cornwall and the Welsh borders is no evidence for what happened to those who spoke them. Many languages are dying today with no decrease in the people who are losing their ability to speak the old as they learn a new language more useful to them. For a generation or two they remain bilingual but soon the language of lower status becomes confined to people of lower status and, unless other influences prevail, the younger generations seek both cultural stimulus and economic advantage from acquiring the language of power. The various dialects of the different high-status groups become assimilated as happened in England in the last century, and many of those in the lower groups copy that new register of privilege.[39] Always the resulting spoken languages are a product both of the incoming language and that which was spoken before, which provides a substratum of the new.[40] Very few who acquire a second language speak without a trace of their mother tongue.[41]

If this assessment is true, the language which the first Anglo-Saxons heard in the southern zone was Latin, though there were no doubt pockets of Celtic and Celtic was what they would have heard in the highland zone. They have left no record of that. There must have been incentives for some of those Latin-speakers to learn an Anglo-Saxon dialect quickly – orally, of course, because few if any could have seen it written. The fact that all the written evidence is in Anglo-Saxon does not mean of itself that everyone could speak any of its variant written dialects, which it seems were not imported separately but developed here.[42] It may merely have taken over

38. Schrijver 'What Britons Spoke' p171.
39. There is a countervailing imperative, which is why I find it hard to understand the speech of some young poor people. Their quality of life depends upon them being at home in the language milieu of their peers and they see little use for more 'standard' English.
40. Richard Coates 'The Significances of Celtic Place-Names' p74: 'I know of no case where such an ascendancy has imposed its own language incorrupt.'
41. Kalevi Wiik 'On the Origins of the Celts' p286.
42. 'No region or group was essentially characterized by linguistic differences inherited from pre-invasion dialect geography', John Hines 'Philology' p31.

from Latin as the language of power. Writers and the scribes who copy their manuscripts are rarely likely to be interested at all in the language spoken by ordinary people. Moreover, the language of an eleventh-century manuscript is unlikely to represent accurately the text, let alone the speech, of its sixth-century original.

Language is what is spoken. Written documents are not photographs of speech. They tell us only so much, directly or uncontroversially, about how their scribes spoke. They need not speak the language they write. Writers follow the conventions of those they learn from. Rarely do they attempt to invent signs – there are just a few new ones in Anglo-Saxon – to make a good fit with the sounds they hear, as those sounds change. They would not have the first idea of how to start. All is learned convention, even graffiti. Just imagine how hard it would be for scholars a thousand years from now to discover how we speak English from how we write: 'know what I mean?' or 'nowadameen?' What has happened to the 'k' and 'w' in 'know', the 'h' in 'what' and the 'a' in 'mean'? We would find it hard to make sense of modern English written phonetically. We rely on our knowledge of the conventions of writing. Few writers today attempt to reproduce the sounds of speech.

Much has been made of the lack of British words in written Anglo-Saxon and 'we *must* provide an explanation for the paucity of lexical borrowing'.[43] Could it be that Anglo-Saxon writers would take care to avoid British vocabulary as 'low' or 'common' or 'vulgar', all adjectives we are familiar with from our own education? Historians and linguists until recently have concentrated on lexis but now it is clear that other British elements, including sound and syntax, crept in unnoticed. The very fact that written Anglo-Saxon did not change much over centuries shows that it did not represent the spoken dialects. When, after the Conquest, it was no longer the prestige language, contemporary spoken English came to be written. We call that form Middle English. There were different dialects. They had lost many of the inflexions of the antique written language, as one would expect of pidgins.[44]

The Germans who colonised Francia gave up their own languages and adopted the Latin of the peoples they conquered but whose culture they envied and whose administrative skills they needed. Five hundred years later, a second wave of Northmen moved into Normandy and on a much smaller scale did the same. Modern French is modern Latin, with only traces of the German of the Franks and little detectable from the Gauls. But in England the Germanic languages produced the power language. Anglo-Saxon dialects eventually replaced Latin, Celtic and any pre-existing Germanic languages wherever the Anglo-Saxon speakers became the powerful class. They had

---

43. Richard Coates 'Invisible Britons' p189.
44. There were changes of usage like the adoption of the auxiliary verb 'do', Hildegard Tristram 'Why Don't the English Speak Welsh' pp203-207 and her conclusions p214.

no Roman background and they needed and wanted none. They had no use for spoken Latin. They were pagan and their own culture mattered to them more as powerful immigrant minorities among more numerous indigenous peasants, whom as warriors they did not greatly respect, as is clear from their poems. We know little of the languages spoken by the great majority.

Even when the Normans conquered England and replaced the English-speaking aristocracy, they continued to speak their contemporary Latin, i.e. Anglo-Norman, for only a few generations.[45] Though few ever learned Anglo-Saxon, soon they too learned to speak what English was becoming, perhaps partly to accommodate them, what we now call Middle English.

What does all this say for the acquisition of Anglo-Saxon dialects in England in the fifth and sixth centuries? Scholars do not like mysteries. They would rather provide an unsatisfactory answer than no answer at all (and struggle mightily to establish it) and readers expect them to do so. But Catherine Hills, having reviewed the evidence, concludes:[46]

> More inscriptions will be found, and they will provide further evidence about the early use and development of the Germanic languages, but it seems unlikely there will ever be sufficient material of this kind to answer questions about population and language change.

What can be said with confidence is that various dialects of Anglo-Saxon were spoken by the Anglo-Saxon ruling class and became the written language of royal edicts from the beginning of the seventh century. Bede says that the earliest poet to have written in Anglo-Saxon was Caedmon, a Celtic name if ever there was one. It is unlikely that Anglo-Saxons had adopted a fashion of giving Celtic names to their children, even if they had Celtic mothers. Anglo-Saxon was Caedmon's mother tongue and he spoke no Latin:[47]

> **A.6** Whatever he learned through interpreters from holy scripture, he himself would, in a flash, *post postillum*, express in the most attractive and moving verse composed in his own language, i.e. of the Angles.

He may, of course, have been bilingual in a Celtic and an Anglo-Saxon dialect. 'His own language' may have meant 'the language in which he naturally wrote' rather than his mother tongue.

45. Rolf Berndt 'The Linguistic Situation in England'.
46. Catherine Hills *Origins of the English* p52. But wonderful insights are already being found into voice production from scientific work on skeletal remains. A sufficiently untrammelled imagination may conceive of ways to produce evidence of how the dead once spoke.
47. Bede *Ecclesiastical History* 4.24; Caedmon = Cadfan, a king of Gwyneth. Wallace-Hadrill, *Bede's Ecclesiastical History* p165 does not agree: 'Too much is made of his name', believing it can be explained by 'some degree of bilingualism'. If *post postillum* means 'in a flash', it is contradicted only a page or so later: 'He turned into the sweetest poetry everything that could be learned by listening, rehearsing it to himself and ruminating on it like an animal chewing its cud.'

We have little evidence of how and when, or even if, the use of Anglo-Saxon dialects spread among the ordinary people of non-Anglo-Saxon origin.[48] It now seems most likely, at least to me, that Latin and perhaps some kinds of Germanic language had been spoken for centuries before the creation of the Anglo-Saxon kingdoms, at least in those parts where immigrants had settled from Gallia Belgica.[49] The Celtic languages were later restricted to the last remaining non-English parts of the island, which became Wales and Cornwall.[50] And the English Edward I did not finally conquer the Britons in Wales until 1282.

It seems likely that many parts of the highland zones were still administered in much the same way as they had been, even after they fell under Anglo-Saxon control.[51]

There are just one or two tantalising bits of physical evidence of the use of a Germanic language in England in the fifth century. A form of Anglo-Frisian is found on all kinds of objects, combs and coffins, brooches and bracteates (thin little medallions), sword fittings, pots and buckets. Most of

48. There is still something to learn from an older generation of scholars: 'When the English speakers settled down with their Celtic-speaking wives, the Britons must have adopted English, and there must have been a period, at least a generation, when they were bilingual... indicated by those instances where a name which is plural in British is plural in Anglo-Saxon, such as British *Dubrās*, which appears in Anglo-Saxon as the plural *Dofras*, Dover. The people who transferred this name into English understood what a British plural was and could speak Anglo-Saxon. Similarly those who translated Celtic *Lann Mihacgel* into Michaelchurch. Later hybrids are compounds of two words with the same meaning; Celtic *cēd* means 'wood', *wudu* in Anglo-Saxon, so whoever created English Cheetwood must have had a poor grasp of Celtic and thought that the sound 'Cheet' was a proper name for the wood referred to.' Kenneth Jackson 'The British Language during the Period of the English Settlements' p66. Higham expresses caveats, *Rome, Britain* p196, and considers the evidence of place-names, pp198–208, concluding: 'The study of place-names imposes no constraints on the numbers of Britons who became anglicised, simply because the numbers of the several language groups involved were not likely to have been the determining factor in the process of language transfer.' Matthew Townend *Language and History* pp47–57 'Norse Speakers and English Place-Names'.
49. EM Wightman *Gallia Belgica*.
50. The Isle of Man, which is still not part of England, has its own Manx language, derived not from British but Old Irish.
51. Campbell, John and Wormald *Anglo-Saxons* p41: 'The cow rendered annually by many villages in medieval county Durham was called *vacca de metreth*; *metreth* has as its main element the Welsh word *treth*, meaning tribute... what is recognizably the same system of local organization which stretches in a continuous belt from Wales, across northern England and far into Scotland... There is comparable evidence elsewhere, above all in the West Midlands, where, for example, the British term *cylch* was used in the Middle Ages as far east as Staffordshire to describe certain renders.' James Campbell uses 'Wales' and 'Welsh' as well as 'British' to describe the land, people and language of the Britons. I know from experience how long it can take for a dialect to die. Up to the end of the Second World War, when speaking to those of my grandparents' generation, I used the Anglo-Saxon *heo* for 'she'. We pronounced it 'oo', as we did not aspirate vowels at the start of words. That was at the southern extreme of what in Anglo-Saxon times was called 'between Ribble and Mersey'.

them cannot be dated before AD500, but there are a significant few which come from early in the fifth century. The inscriptions are in a Germanic language written in the runic alphabet, known as *futhorc* or *futhark*. Three clay pots from Norfolk bear the word *alu*, ale.[52] A gold bracteate from Suffolk bears a warrior's head, the she-wolf suckling Romulus and Remus and an inscription in runes.[53] But perhaps the earliest, carved as early as AD425 or even earlier,[54] is a bit of the anklebone of a roedeer, found in Caistor, near Norwich in an urn full of knucklebones, presumably to be used in a game. It bears the single word *raïhan*, roebuck.[55] The person who put this word on the bone to ensure it was not confused with the other three dozen sheep bones in the pot knew what it meant. Presumably it was there to communicate its meaning to anyone handling them. It was in a Germanic language, which scholars after intense linguistic inquiry call Anglo-Frisian. Whether it was made in England or abroad, the subject of much controversy, is not important to us. Its owner and those playing the game in Norfolk understood it, long before the Saxon invasions noted by Gildas and Bede.

Further interdisciplinary research will provide more evidence of Germanic languages in England before the coming of the Anglo-Saxons and progress is promising, particularly in Kent. It may even provide an answer to the question which remains: why is there no reference to language use in any surviving source? Could it be pure accident, or is it more likely that all those whose writings have survived took it for granted that their readers knew the obvious?

One thing is clear but not given sufficient emphasis. There were huge sound changes brought about by the interplay of Celtic and Anglo-Saxon dialects. To me they look like the effects of the mother tongue Celtic substratum on the newly learned Anglo-Saxon and give some support to my suggestion that many people in England could then communicate in different kinds of pidgin.[56] Moreover, it is now accepted that the interplay of Celtic and Anglo-Saxon produced in each a loss of word endings, the inflections of nouns and pronouns, verbs and adjectives, which have all but disappeared in modern Welsh and English.[57] That process is characteristic of pidgins.

52. J H Looijenga 'Runes Around the North Sea' p166.
53. Bengt Odenstedt 'The Runic Inscription on the Undley Bracteate'.
54. David Crystal *The Stories of English*, with a picture p22.
55. Odenstedt 'Runic Inscription' p118; Looijenga 'Runes' pp167–8. The inscriptions on many such objects state the obvious: 'comb', 'knucklebone', or even in one case 'deerhorn'. But I may be forgiven for pretending to prefer the interpretation of the great runic scholar who says it means 'this belongs to Raihan', or rather 'to Roebuck', Bammesberger pp389–408.
56. This is not the place and I am not the person to argue this out but there is evidence of all kinds, e.g. of place-names: Stephen Yeates 'River-Names: Celtic and Old English' shows that Welsh *gwyn* + neo-Brittonic *$*r\bar{e}sg$* = Windrush (rather than White Marsh).
57. HLC Tristram 'Attrition of Inflections in English and Welsh'.

For now we must avoid finding answers where there are none. The study of language has not yet answered the questions of how Anglo-Saxon spread, if it did, let alone the size of the influx of foreigners. There is some evidence and strong arguments that in Roman times Celtic was superseded by Latin, not only in lowland Britain but in what are now the Netherlands, Belgium and parts of northern France. People there spoke a similar Latin, Northwestern Romance, affected by a substratum of similar Celtic, North Sea Celtic.[58] The spoken languages of England had many bilingual speakers. There may have been adequate pidgins for others. Through the mediation of these different tongues, within a century or two, the written language was Anglo-Saxon and some no doubt spoke it. But there is no evidence that most did.

ANGLO-SAXON AFTER AETHELBERHT

> I am more an antique Roman than a Dane... .
>
> William Shakespeare *Hamlet* Act 5 Scene 2

The Anglo-Saxon kings were not at first Christian. The Christian clergy throughout the rest of Britain, of what is often called the Celtic church to distinguish it from the Roman church governed by the Pope, were literate of course, but in Latin. We do not know whether they could write in the British languages, whatever they were then. There is some evidence that there were some Anglo-Saxons who could write their own language in runes, a non-Roman script. But that evidence is limited to inscriptions and coins and just a few scraps of literature,[59] though it has been suggested that:[60] 'the overall stability and continuity of runic practice in England presupposes that runes were used regularly' and 'there is good evidence for a remarkable understanding of the runic system among the Anglo-Saxons'.

We are told that the Latin then spoken in England was 'better', that is closer to the written Latin of the classical Roman authors, than the 'Italianate' speech of those who in AD597 were sent from Rome with Augustine to the Anglo-Saxon court of Aethelberht of Kent.[61] Neither Augustine's team nor the British clergy were literate in Anglo-Saxon. Yet somehow statements of Kentish law were first written down in that language. By whom? Bede says:[62]

58. Schrijver 'The Rise and Fall of British Latin' p109.
59. 'There is a handful of slightly longer texts, the most significant being the inscriptions on the Auzon (Franks) Casket and lines from *The Dream of the Rood* which were engraved on the Ruthwell Cross', Susan Kelly 'Anglo-Saxon Lay Society' p37, a helpful introduction for both Anglo-Saxon and Latin charters.
60. René Derolez 'Runic Literacy among the Anglo-Saxons' in Alfred Bammesberger and Alfred Wollmann eds *Britain 400–600: Language and History* p400.
61. DR Howlett *The Celtic Latin Tradition of Biblical Style*; but also AS Gratwick '*Latinitas Britannica*'. 'Better' is an aesthetic judgment we retain from school, with no linguistic significance.
62. Bede *Ecclesiastical History* I 25. Tacitus had written 500 years before that there was little difference between the speech of the Gauls and the British, **3.5** and the discussion of British languages there.

A.7 So on this spot landed Augustine, servant of the Lord, and his companions, they say about forty of them. On the order of the blessed Pope Gregory, they had taken interpreters from the people of the Franks and they sent a message to Aethelberht announcing they had come from Rome.[63]

What language did 'the people of the Franks' speak then?[64] The interpreters must have spoken Frankish, the Germanic language of the Franks, which was mutually comprehensible with the Anglo-Saxon dialects of Kent. They would have also spoken the form of oral Latin that was to become French, which we call Gallo-Latin. They must surely have been literate in Latin and may have been able to write in Frankish, though by this time it was probably spoken less than Gallo-Latin. Their own laws were in Latin, though the manuscripts have some Frankish glosses. There is no direct evidence but it is likely that there were scholars among the Christian British, clergy and lay, who could write in Latin, and some even in pagan Kent to handle diplomatic correspondence at least. There is no evidence that any of them could write in Anglo-Saxon, even if that was the language they spoke.

Augustine's Frankish interpreters may have been the first to acquire the technical skills to make it possible to write down dooms in a Germanic tongue, though Bede does not say that.[65] Whoever first wrote the dooms down, and whenever, most of them surely must have existed orally in the Anglo-Saxon used in the Kent royal administration, so that was the language (and presumably the dialect) in which it would be natural to write them when the necessary skill could be called on. That writing was what those scribes decided best represented the sounds they heard.[66] We must not assume that they produced an accurate phonetic equivalent. Writing cannot hope to represent speech precisely. It works only because writer and reader share its conventions:[67]

> The phonetic transcription of an unwritten language by means of an alphabet is a very sophisticated operation which requires not only literary but also linguistic expertise including grammar and syntax... Christian missionaries had that expertise as early as the fourth century, whilst it is reasonable to believe that no one in Britain could have possessed this knowledge until at least a generation after the... mission.

63. This last sentence reads more naturally if it means that the message was sent in Anglo-Saxon, presumably to endear Augustine to Aethelberht. On early interpreters, Constance Bullock-Davies *Professional Interpreters*.
64. Kelly 'Anglo-Saxon Lay Society' p58: 'Much ink has been spent on the question of the mutual intelligibility of Frankish and English.'
65. Is it too wildly speculative to suggest that this may explain some of the *hapax legomena* (words found nowhere else) in the dooms of Aethelberht, e.g. *hion* in 36?
66. 'It is generally accepted that Old English spelling down to the eleventh century was roughly phonetic.' JD Pheifer *Old English Glosses* plvii.
67. Giorgio Ausenda in John Hines *The Anglo-Saxons* p232. Christian missionaries still create scripts for languages in Papua New Guinea.

It has been suggested that they wrote soon after they arrived. It is unlikely that they could have inserted the privileges of the clergy before Aethelberht was converted, probably not later than AD600. They would by then have had at most three years to develop their skills. There is, however, nothing in the laws themselves which suggests that date and other sources are few. And it must always be remembered that the only text we have of Aethelberht's dooms is in a manuscript written not less than five hundred years after his death.

The way in which the laws are presented gives a clue to how they were created. It is clear – at least to me – that there are strings of mnemonic formulas in different parts of Aethelberht's laws,[68] but fewer signs of them in the later laws of Hlothhere and Eadric (c685) and Wihtred (695), both from Kent, or in the laws of Ine of Wessex (c688–694).[69] Laws *created* in writing do not need the same mnemonics and follow different schemes from oral dooms written down later.

ALFRED AND AFTER

> Between wars and the frequent worries of this present life, the king… would read aloud from books in Anglo-Saxon and especially would learn Anglo-Saxon poems off by heart.
>
> Asser *Life of King Alfred* 76

When Alfred became king of the West Saxons in 871, most of the north was held by the Danes. Not only did Alfred restrict the advance of the Danes, he consciously set out to establish written English, setting a standard by his own published works. In that part of England called the Danelaw, a different language was spoken, at least by the upper class. But it was not entirely alien. It was roughly mutually comprehensible with the dialects of Alfred's kingdom, having the same Germanic base as them and closer still to the other forms of Old Norse which later Viking invaders spoke.

Alfred learned Latin in later life and translated from Latin to Anglo-Saxon, totally committed to a policy of spreading literacy in his mother tongue. So why did Asser choose to write his biography in Latin? Alfred said hardly anyone in his kingdom could read Latin at the start of his reign. Asser translated many place-names into British.[70] Did he assume his audience would recognise the towns and rivers better if he gave their

---

68. Most obviously in the list of injuries, which go roughly from head to toe, or rather from hair to toenail.
69. This was argued by Lorraine Miller, as related by John Hines in the discussion of Patrizia Lendinara's paper 'Kentish Laws' in Hines *Anglo-Saxons* p237.
70. Keynes and Lapidge always speak of 'Welsh' but there was no such place as Wales then. Asser calls the people who lived there *Britones* (once *mediterraneos Britones*, Britons in the midlands?) and 'in their language' is *sermone Britannico* or *Britannice*. Until just before the Norman Conquest, Grufydd ap Llewelyn was still styled *rex Britonum*, Chapter 9 above, fn3.

British names, sometimes in an obsolete form,[71] as well as Latin. If so, they must have spoken British languages first. Yet, when he writes of something in 'both languages', he says expressly that means Latin and Anglo-Saxon.[72] British was just not a written language then. Neither was the language spoken by Alfred's subjects. He expressly stated that none of them could follow the Divine Service even in Anglo-Saxon, by which he can only have meant the language he was translating into for their benefit.[73]

Certainly Alfred ruled a polyglot kingdom:[74]

A.7 Many Franks, Frisians, Gauls, Pagans (i.e. Vikings), Britons, Scots and Bretons of their own accord subjected themselves to his dominion, nobles of course as well as commoners.

Few of those 'foreigners and incomers', whom Alfred was careful to foster, would be literate at all but, if they were, it would be in Latin. Perhaps it was just that Asser wanted to preserve his account of Alfred in the eternal language, as he must have regarded Latin, and for all truly literate readers everywhere. Or, more simply, it was the only language in which he could write.

In 878 Alfred spent twelve nights with Guthrum, the Viking king, not only concluding a treaty but persuading him to become a Christian. There is no hint of interpreters. The Vikings were illiterate, being heathen and uninstructed by the Church, and the treaty was written and survives in Anglo-Saxon.[75]

Orosius's *Seven Books of Histories Against the Pagans*, a history of Rome written about AD410, was translated into Anglo-Saxon with a supplement which tells the stories of Ohthere, a Norwegian traveller, and of Wulfstan, an English traveller to Scandinavia, relating their adventures to Alfred the Great.[76] Ohthere spoke to Alfred in Old Norse. The Anglo-Saxon text includes many Old Norse words, which the Anglo-Saxon hearers and the writer of the account appear to comprehend.

A century later, sometime between 978 and 988, Aethelward, ealdorman of Wessex, wrote a Latin chronicle. He was interested in language questions and understood Old Norse, incorporating and commenting on Norse place-names.[77]

---

71. E.g. *Frauu* for the River Frome in Asser *Life of King Alfred* 49, Keynes and Lapidge *Alfred* p82.
72. Asser *Life of King Alfred* 75.
73. Henry Sweet ed *King Alfred's West-Saxon Version of Gregory's Pastoral Care.*
74. Asser *Life of King Alfred* 76.
75. Liebermann *Gesetze* pp126–8; Attenborough *Laws* pp98–101, which expressly deals with trade between Danes and Anglo-Saxons.
76. JM Bately *The Old English Orosius*; Townend *Language and History* pp90–109.
77. A Campbell *The Chronicle of Aethelweard*; Matthew Townend *Language and History* pp110–28.

There were many dialects of English in Anglo-Saxon England.[78] Traces of some of their differentiating characteristics can still be detected in present-day regional differences, for example short and long 'a' in 'path' or aspirated initial vowels. Northumbrian, Mercian, West Saxon and Kentish are just rough categories into which many kinds of speech have since been sorted, depending on their written survivals.

MORE NORTHMEN: DANES AND VIKINGS

> Sweetly sang the monks in Ely
> As King Cnut rowed near.
> Row, lads, row, nearer to the shore
> And the monks' song let us hear!
>
> Cnut's Song, _Liber Eliensis_ 2.85

Not bad for a foreign king, whose mother tongue was not Anglo-Saxon![79]

Care must be taken not to fall into the habit of thinking of languages as disembodied entities that can exist apart from those who speak and write them. Incomers bring their own languages with them. Somehow, some of them must converse with those they have invaded. From the end of the eighth century, there were frequent incursions, not only but mainly into the north-east of England by invaders from Scandinavia we now call Vikings. They spoke Old Norse. As well as diplomatic relations, there was easy trade between the parts. The Vikings and the Danes understood one another and there is ample evidence that Anglo-Saxon speakers could communicate with them too.[80] A community of Danes lived in Oxford, where in 1018 Danes and English held a meeting and agreed to abide by the law of Edgar, presumably each understanding what the other was saying well enough. All the literary evidence of language use is in Anglo-Saxon, apart from a few scraps of Old Norse preserved in runic writing.

Anglo-Saxon and Old Norse were the offspring of the same North-West Germanic language spoken where the first Germanic invaders came from

---

78. The only scientific distinction between 'language' and 'dialect' that I know is political; compare the mutually incomprehensible 'dialects' of China, say of Canton and Shanghai, with the more mutually comprehensible 'languages' of Norway, Sweden and Denmark, at least in their higher registers: 'a language is a dialect with an army'; Einar Haugen _The Scandinavian Languages_.

79. _Merie sungen the muneches binnen Ely_
    Tha Cnut ching reu ther by.
    Roweth cnites noer the lant
    And here we thes muneches saeng.

    The chronicler goes on to write that this and following verses became a hit: 'They are still sung in public today (cAD1200, nearly two centuries later) by choirs and remembered in proverbs'; so they must have been originally sung in some dialect of Anglo-Saxon, not translated by the scribe or others.

80. Townend _Language and History_ argues convincingly for mutual comprehensibility of Anglo-Saxon and the incomers' Scandinavian.

in the fifth century. Though they had grown apart:[81] 'the phonological systems of the two languages had remained remarkably similar'. Many of the sound-changes were regular and, therefore, speakers of the other language could comprehend more easily by mentally making the necessary switch. Cultural affinities would help, as would the context of the conversation. And the speakers would make allowances. Hearers might recognise a noun easily, if it was the word for pig and they were in a market. But they might not be able to detect the meaning of suffixes which denoted its number or sex, or the case endings which showed whether it was the subject or object of the verb. As a result, inflections became indistinct and unnecessary, word order taking their place.

These processes affected the language of dispute resolution. Naturally, where legal concepts were specifically Danish or Viking, with no Anglo-Saxon equivalent, the Old Norse word was retained, for example *lahslit*, a penalty which applied only to Danes in II Cnut 27, **9.11**. A doom of Aethelred, from about 994, makes it clear that Anglo-Saxon and Old Norse speakers took part in the same legal processes, for example:[82]

> **A.8** If a claim is made that our fellow-countryman has stolen cattle or killed someone, and one of the claimants is a Viking, *sceithman*, and one a fellow-countryman, the defendant may not make a formal denial.

Sceithman is one who comes off a raiding ship; not, one would have thought, a great compliment or appropriate for use in legislation. But by that time perhaps it had lost its piratical connotations.

Aelfric wrote in Anglo-Saxon in Aethelred's reign at the end of the tenth century in the south-west of England. He starts off using the Anglo-Saxon word for law, *ae*, consistently, then brings in the Old Norse word, *lagu*, until *ae* is completely replaced.[83]

In 1016 Cnut divided England up with Edmund Ironside. The *Anglo-Saxon Chronicle* records:[84]

> **A.9** Both kings came together at Alney near Deerhurst and became partners, *feolagan*, and oath-brothers, *wedbrothra*.

Feolagan is an Old Norse, not an Anglo-Saxon word. Did the kings use both words themselves, to strengthen their pact? These two words have quite different meanings to start with. Others, which originally were synonyms, could be given different shades of meaning: 'shirt' and 'skirt'.

We know little or nothing of how the Norse-speakers felt about language because few were literate at first and when they learned to read and write

81. Townend *Language and History* p41; 'the recorded instances of lexical substitution reveal an ability to make every important phonemic substitution' p63. Townend provides the 'empirical evidence for pragmatic intelligibility' p64.
82. II *Aethelred* 7.
83. Townend *Language and History* pp128–43.
84. Townend *Language and History* p7.

it was in Latin or Anglo-Saxon and they tell us nothing. By the time of the Norman Conquest, monolingual speakers of Old Norse were few and in remoter parts. The argument in favour of mutual intelligibility is powerful and probably explains what happened most of the time. There is no evidence that the mixed marriages resulted in many offspring who were bilingual, though it usually does. If it produced any pidgins, there is no evidence. Equally, there is nothing to show that Anglo-Saxons and Old Norse-speakers did not modify the way they spoke to one another, producing a simplified speech, which would never, of course, have been written down.[85]

If personal experience is allowable as evidence, with argument built on it, then it may be of interest, if only to explain some of my biases. I grew up speaking two dialects, one quite restricted to a small area around Stalybridge on the border of north-east Cheshire and south-east Lancashire, the other a variety of Northern Standard English (NSE). Most of the local dialect speakers, but not quite all, could understand (though not speak) NSE. Many speakers of NSE could understand the local dialect well enough, if they came into daily contact with it. I doubt if any (unless it was their mother dialect) could speak it, except for comic effect, and none would, for social reasons. I spoke the local dialect to my grandparents and others of their generation, and also to the rougher boys at primary school. I spoke NSE (or as near as I had got to it) to my parents, teachers, girls at school and the world at large. I find it easy to understand how Anglo-Saxon and Norse speakers communicated, how they adapted their speech as they needed, and how the dialect that was less useful gave way, even before mass media. There was nothing like a pidgin. There were no interpreters. Within a generation or two, other forces were creating new language barriers, for example for immigrants, and the same skills were being used to overcome them and with similar results for the surviving dialects of English, including the loss of some of the last remaining inflections and the adverbial form, no longer in daily use but withering on a daily basis.

LANGUAGES IN ENGLAND FROM 1066 TO 1154

> Yet are there good grounds for supposing that any such language or dialect as Anglo-Norman ever existed? Is it not a mere cobweb of the philologist's brain?
> HG Richardson, review of *Year Books of Edward II XXIII and XXIV*

Bottom	I cry your worship's mercy, heartily:
	I beseech your worship's name.
Cobweb	Cobweb.
Bottom	I shall desire you of more acquaintance, good master Cobweb... .

William Shakespeare *A Midsummer Night's Dream* Act 3 Scene 1

85. This is a subject too large and controversial to be further addressed here, Townend *Language and History* pp200–10, and the sources he cites.

Introduction[86]   The languages used in the management of disputes in England between 1066 and 1154 included Latin, French and English, written and spoken; but it is not obvious what languages were spoken and written when, by whom, in what contexts and for what purposes.[87] The questions can only be addressed by applying to the primary sources the techniques not only of the historian but also of scholars of literature and language.

Latin was the formal language of record. French and English were competing vernaculars. English was at first Anglo-Saxon in its various forms, including a Danish dialect, spoken mainly in the Danelaw. By the end of our period it had started to transmute into regional dialects of Middle English. Written Anglo-Saxon was preserved artificially until the twelfth century but was not spoken. The last Anglo-Saxon Chronicle for 1132–54 shows a shift towards spoken English.[88] But what was French? Some have asserted that it was the tongue imported by the Normans and that they imposed it on the English. Some, like HG Richardson in the quotation above, could see no difference from the forms of French spoken on the Continent. It is hard to compare the written forms, because the great bulk of the surviving literature was created in England, very little in France.[89]

I shall try to set out the known references to the use of French, more familiarly known as Anglo-Norman, in England in this period, in chronological order as always to try to avoid the dangers of reading back later developments.[90] I shall call 'French' any of the vernacular languages which came to England with the Conqueror and keep 'Anglo-Norman' for the kind of French which developed here.

---

86. Much of this part is based on my 1990 working paper 'Chronology of a Cobweb'. More recent scholarship and stimulating discussions with my PhD student Gordon Fisher have made me think again. There is still no more delightful introduction than MD Legge 'Anglo-Norman as a Spoken Language'. Wales, which was not yet ruled by the kings of England, and Cornwall, which was, had their own languages at this time but my lack of knowledge arbitrarily excludes them.

87. DR Howlett *English Origins of Old French Literature* and the earlier but still important: MK Pope *From Latin to Modern French*; Johan Vising *Anglo-Norman Language and Literature*; MD Legge *Anglo-Norman Literature and Its Background* and 'La Précocité'; RM Wilson 'English and French in England (1100–1300)'; Ian Short 'Bilingualism in Anglo-Norman England'; DA Kibbee *For to Speke Frenche Trewely*.

88. HLC Tristram 'Attrition of Inflections in English and Welsh' pp119 and 125.

89. DR Howlett *English Origins of Old French Literature* p165: 'For the first century of its existence, most French literature was English.'

90. There is no agreement on the best names for the language or languages which developed in England from languages imported from what is now France. Anglo-Norman is perhaps the most familiar but 'insular French' is more accurate. I have used Anglo-Saxon inaccurately as the name for Old English and offer that as a weak excuse for using Anglo-Norman for convenience here. It has its own modern dictionary: William Rothwell *Anglo-Norman Dictionary*. Law French is different and comes later, outside our period: JH Baker *Manual of Law French*.

The Background   William I spoke a French dialect from Normandy. His ancestors were Danes – his paternal line, that is – the word 'bastard' (it is said) having been introduced into English as his epithet. Little is known about his mother, said to have been a tanner's daughter. About AD911 Charles the Simple, king of France, had granted William's ancestor Rollo 'certain districts bordering the coast, along with the city of Rouen'.[91] By then Rollo's Viking forebears had been there already for a century or so and may have been speaking some kind of French. The story goes that Rollo's successor had to send his son away to school to learn his ancestral language.[92]

The Norman dialect was already well known in the English royal household by the time of the Conquest. In 1002 Ethelred the Unready married Emma, daughter of the Duke of Normandy and great-aunt of William I. Their son, Edward the Confessor, spoke his mother's language. His court included Normans and seemed quite French to the English. William's companions must have spoken different dialects; the beginnings of a standard French come only when Francien became dominant in the fourteenth century.[93]

At his coronation, William I asked his French-speaking and English-speaking subjects in their own languages to accept him as their king and, in their own languages, they shouted that they would.[94] It was said that he tried in vain to learn Anglo-Saxon.[95] But the only surviving copy of his letter to the mayor and bishop of London, confirming their customary rights, is in Anglo-Saxon, **10.6, 10.7**.

At the time of the Conquest and for a while afterwards, the great majority of those who had come to England then, and the women who followed later, could speak no English. Not all were native speakers of the language of the Normans but they must have been able to communicate with one another in some sort of 'French', perhaps a Latin pidgin of some kind.[96] French religious orders quickly established themselves in England, with more than a hundred houses by 1135.[97] They could not have taught in English straight away.

The Records   In the process first of colonial conquest and then of military pacification and the establishment of a civilian administration, what happened

---

91. According to Flodoard *Historia Remensis Ecclesiae* in *Monumenta Germaniae Historica, Scriptores* xiii (1881) p577, cited by David Bates *Normandy Before 1066* p2, now accessible and translated in Steven Fanning and BS Bachrach *The Annals of Flodoard of Rheims*.

92. Jules Lair ed *Dudo: De Moribus et Actis Primorum Normanniae Ducum* pp168-169; Bates *Normandy Before 1066* thinks it an unlikely story, p21, and Dudo 'a thoroughly unworthy source', pxii. But the Scandinavian language 'had ceased to be spoken in Normandy by the early eleventh century', Peter Rickard *History of the French Language* p35.

93. HJ Chaytor *From Script to Print* p36. 'Francien' is a nineteenth-century coinage.

94. MJ Chibnall ed and tr *Ecclesiastical History of Orderic Vitalis* II 157.

95. Chibnall *Orderic Vitalis* II 215.

96. Pope *From Latin* pp425–6.

97. Johan Vising, *Anglo-Norman Language and Literature* p12.

to the language of the Normans? Anglo-Norman did not immediately become a literary language.[98] There is less evidence for the eleventh than for later centuries but one thing is clear: almost at once the language of official record changed from English to Latin. An examination of 487 writs and charters surviving from the reigns of William I and William II, the 34 years from 1066 to 1100, put the score at:[99]

Anglo-Saxon	19
Both Anglo-Saxon and Latin	9
Latin	459
Any kind of French	nil

William I kept on at least some of Edward the Confessor's secretariat but very few documents have survived from it in Anglo-Saxon and none in French. No other vernacular derived from Latin took a hold in England. Latin was read by all scholars, indeed *literatus* meant 'able to read Latin', but by this time it was not spoken much in England except by the clergy in ritual, and sometimes in ceremonial and diplomatic work. English had become the working spoken language of the civil service by the time of the Domesday Inquest, **A.16**.

The Literary Evidence There is almost no contemporary written evidence of the use of any kind of French in England before 1100 but twelfth-century authorities can sometimes be trusted. Orderic Vitalis was born near Shrewsbury in 1075 of a French father and English mother. He wrote in 1141 of his father, a Norman priest called Odelirius, sending him to Normandy to become a monk:[100]

A.10 So, as a boy of ten, I crossed the Channel and arrived in Normandy as an exile, knowing no one, unknown to all. Like Joseph in Egypt I heard a language which I could not understand.

Orderic had learned Latin before he went abroad. So the unknown language he heard in Normandy must have been some kind of French. It also follows that he had not learned his Latin in French, as later authorities say it was always taught in England. Therefore Orderic, first generation son of a Norman colonist, whose mother tongue was presumably Anglo-Saxon, and who already had a primary education, could not understand the French spoken in Normandy in 1085, less than twenty years after the Conquest.

98. But Maitland's marvelous *bon mot* cannot be true: 'French would become Latin if you tried to write it at its best', Pollock and Maitland *History of English Law* I p82, because he was speaking of the twelfth century, by which time there were written forms of French and of laboured attempts to put vernacular French into Latin. I owe this insight to Gordon Fisher.
99. David Mellinkoff *The Language of the Law* p66; Van Caenegem *Royal Writs*. For the reign of William I, David Bates *Regesta Regum Anglo-Normannorum*.
100. Chibnall *Orderic Vitalis* IV 176 and V 134–5.

The writings of the time show the relative socio-economic positions of Anglo-Saxon and Anglo-Norman. A recurring theme in medieval literature is that of the dumb given the power of speech by a miracle. The first of these stories in Anglo-Norman tells us something about speech in England no later than the first decade of the twelfth century. It comes from the *Life of St John of Beverley*:[101]

> **A.11** Soon the dumb man uttered words and, though he had never before been able to speak at all, he now began to speak French as well as English, and all those who were standing around were flabbergasted.

The report of an inquest held in the shire assembly of York in 1106 tells how royal justices took evidence of the customary law:[102]

> **A.12** from the wisest Englishmen of that city... And Asketinus de Bolomer, who was then sheriff of the North Riding, was interpreter.

The 'wisest' spoke English, the justices did not – or not that of York.

At some time in the first half of the twelfth century, foreign clergy visited the monastery of St Alban's. They were almost certainly French. They were not able to speak English. They had to tell their tale in Latin. That must mean that the monks of St Alban's could not understand their visitors' French.[103]

Perhaps the most famous story about French in England at the end of our period is of St Wulfric and his friend Brihtric, a parish priest. The saint's biographer, John of Ford, considerately provides us with the saint's own words:[104]

> **A.13** There was a dumb man brought to me and I prayed to my Lord for him and placed my hand on him and behold, the man speaks properly and without impediment, not only in English but in French as well! That priest [Brihtric] was most upset when he saw it and he was so indignant he did not understand, and he came up to me in such a temper and said:

> 'Look, I've been your servant for years and years but up till now I've done it all in vain, and I've proved that clearly today. This fellow is a stranger and it would have been quite enough if you had freed his tongue so that he could speak but you've fondly furnished him with the double power of speech. Yet you haven't given *me* ability to speak French, and you know that, when I go before the bishop or archdeacon, I am forced to be as silent as a mute.'

Wulfric knew no more French than Brihtric. But Wulfric did not need it. His business was miracles and healing. But poor old Brihtric was a parish

---

101.   J Raine ed *William Ketell's Life* I 1 pplii–lvi, 299.
102.   AF Leach *Visitations* pxlviii.
103.   HT Riley *Gesta Abbatum Monasterii S. Albani* IV 1 88.
104.   M Bell ed *Wulfric of Haselbury* 29.

priest; his bishop and archdeacon, who used French, expected him to acquire a bit of learning.[105]

By that time a writer could be self-conscious about the differences between the French she had learned and that of mother-tongue speakers. An anonymous nun wrote:[106]

> **A.14** I know an artificial French from England
> Which you won't find anywhere else.
> And those of you who learned French elsewhere
> Can put it right as you know best.

The Linguistic Evidence   Anglo-Norman literature begins with a translation of the *Voyage of Saint Brendan*, which the monk Benedeit l'Apostile made c1120 for Adeliza, Henry I's second queen.[107] Its language already shows dialectal variations from what can be reconstructed as the French spoken on the Continent. Differences of pronunciation can be detected.[108] Moreover, careful reading of that text provides evidence of Anglo-Norman's lexical assimilation from English.[109] Benedeit's vocabulary also includes French words not found elsewhere.

The objection can at once be raised that these distinctions reveal no insular dialectal pronunciations at all but are 'rather the poetic licences of a literary language'; but 'non-Insular literary allusions from the following century allow us to opt with relative confidence' for distinct Anglo-Norman pronunciation.[110] These allusions come from the later (1180) *Roman de Renart*,[111] where the fox passes himself off as an Englishman by speaking a comic French and in the even later *Deux Anglois et l'Anel*,[112] where fun is made of the distinction between the nasalised and unnasalised *n*, or rather of the lack of that distinction in Anglo-Norman. The joke depends on the Englishmen's confusion of *asnel*, donkey, with *agnel*, lamb. But these later writers cannot tell us anything directly about language use before 1154. Much more telling is the evidence from the text of Benedeit's *Voyage* itself:[113]

---

105. Bishop Odo of Canterbury is recorded as preaching in French about the end of our period; JS Brewer *Chronica Monasterii de Bello* 163; Wilson 'English and French' p48.
106. Ö Södergård *La Vie d'Edouard* verses 7–10; no doubt a forebear of Chaucer's Prioress.
107. Or possibly Maud, his first queen, MD Legge 'Rise and Fall' p2.
108. Ian Short and Brian Merrilees *The Anglo-Norman 'Voyage of St Brendan'* pp12–13 list the 'few divergencies from the hypothetical Continental standard, though there are a small number sufficiently attested to make them significant' e.g. Benedeit rhymes [u] 14 times with what in continental French would be [y]; 'in another 21 rhymes to identify [n] and [l] with their palatal counterparts'.
109. Short and Merrilees, *St Brendan* p15 e.g. *haspe* and *rap*.
110. Ian Short 'On Bilingualism' p469.
111. Ian Short 'On Bilingualism' p472.
112. Ian Short 'On Bilingualism' p469.
113. Ian Short 'On Bilingualism' p470.

When... Benedeit incorporates into his narrative the two Anglo-Saxon words *raps* 'ropes' and *haspes* 'clasps', it is the presence of other English words in poems such as Gaimar's *Estoire des Engleis*, the *Horn*, and the Anglo-Norman *Alexander* which permits us to conjecture that this sort of lexical assimilation perhaps characterised the spoken as well as the literary French of the time.

It does more. It tells us that the writer was thinking in English. It would surprise those who today work in a bilingual milieu if it were seriously suggested that in Norman England lexical assimilation was not common-place to some degree. There was certainly plenty of assimilation from French into English. No such assimilation from English would be likely in Normandy. Therefore Anglo-Norman would have tended to diverge from continental French, only the frequent and ready intercourse between the two dialects providing a countervailing force. Of course, there may be a great difference between what was written and spoken.

The Latin texts written in England in this period often incorporated French and English where there was no classical or later Latin word available to the author, or where it was essential to retain the specificity of the English or French word that was in the author's mind. Professor Van Caenegem has collected and edited reports of cases and writs of this period.[114] These are rich sources of examples, not only the technical legal formulas, '*sac et soc et tol et theam et infangenetheof*', but in the language of common speech of farmers: *bladum*, *wicam*, *weram*, *lada*, *crofta*, *cuherd*, *pleiseiz*, and even whole phrases: '*1 hafdracram inter suos duos marliz in suis garstunis*' and '*mensurari debet ad mayne flod ut sit plena de banke en banke*'.[115] Nigel, bishop of Ely, used the English word *harred*, unchanged and undeclined, because there is no Latin equivalent for 'hounds on a leash'.[116]

A controversy between German and French editors of Anglo-Norman verse does not need to be resolved to be illuminating. They have disagreed about scansion. Some editors have fallen into the temptation to meddle with the Anglo-Norman texts so that they fit the rhythms of French verse coming from the Continent at the same time or later.[117] Continental French verse, like much of its more modern counterparts, is based on the number of syllables in the line. Some editors have attributed variations from these perceived norms to the ineptitude of the poets in Norman England: they had no ear or they could not count. No such tinkering is needed if the editor accepts the obvious: they sang to different music. Not only did they have French as a second language, so that they took words from English when they needed them. They also, much more fundamentally, had the rhythms of English deepest within them and wrote their words to fit its music. English

114. Van Caenegem *Lawsuits* and *Writs*.
115. Van Caenegem *Lawsuits* I nos 255 and 343.
116. Johnson *Richard Fitz Nigel* p135.
117. RC Johnston 'On Scanning Anglo-Norman Verse'.

verse depends not on syllables but on stress; so does Anglo-Norman. AE Housman, poet and editor, put it best:[118]

> I suppose we could all write verses if we were allowed to have our own way with the language. For instance: I propose to make English poetry on French principles. What do I require of my readers?... I only ask them to weaken the English accent till it is no stronger than the French, and to count accurately up to twelve. Here are four alexandrines:
>
> > Why does not the lobster ever climb trees or fly?
> > Can he not? Or does he think it looks silly?
> > I have made these verses as well as I am able:
> > You must be to blame if they sound disagreeable.
>
> Observe the *rime riche*!

Not only verse, the linguistic evidence shows that everything written in Anglo-Norman was different from contemporary continental French. 'Anglo-Norman literature possessed a distinctly local character, and was, in fact, often thoroughly English in everything except the medium'.[119]

Conclusions on the Twelfth Century The best evidence of language use in England in the later years of our period comes from just after its end. Richard Fitz Nigel became the royal Treasurer about 1158. He acquired judicial experience as an itinerant justice. About 1176–79 he wrote in Latin a manual of practice for the Treasury, in the form of a dialogue between Master and Student.[120] Student asks Master whether the secret killing of an Englishman gives rise to the murder-fine, *murdrum*,[121] in the same way as the death of a Norman. Master replies:[122]

> **A.15** At the beginning it should not have done, as I told you, but now that English and Norman live among one another and Englishmen marry Norman women and vice versa, the nations are so mixed up that you can scarcely tell them apart these days – freemen I mean – which are of English and which of Norman origin.

Fitz Nigel, who had both Norman and English ancestors, could hardly have made it clearer. With no thought of the linguistic importance of what he was writing, he plainly said he could not tell the difference between them. Among other useless tests must have been any attempt to distinguish them by their speech. They all spoke the same language with similar accents.[123]

---

118. AE Housman, book review in (1899) 13 *Classical Review*.

119. HE Allen 'Mystical Lyrics' p470.

120. Johnson *Richard Fitz Nigel*.

121. No one could risk translating this Anglo-Saxon technical legal word because an accused's life could depend on it.

122. Johnson *Richard Fitz Nigel* p43.

123. Or, possibly, languages; they could in theory have all been equally bilingual, and that has been seriously suggested, MD Legge, *Anglo-Norman and the Historian* p166. But we know that Orderic and the nun had to learn their French.

Fitz Nigel's freemen were all speaking English by not long after our period ends and possibly well before.

Moreover, Student asks Master not to try to coin new Latin words for English things:[124]

> **A.16** But I'm asking you, if you don't mind, not to be ashamed to use ordinary words, *communibus verbis*, for the things themselves, whatever you like, but don't create further difficulties by making up words we're not used to.

And later, when Master's false modesty begins to irritate Student, he reminds him: [125]

> **A.17** I got you to agree to use ordinary and usual words, *communibus et usitatis verbis*, for ordinary things.

This is a clever literary device to overcome the objections of the purists who would look askance at neologisms. Such critics existed then as they still do today in England, France, Germany, or China. But needs prevail over niceties. Fitz Nigel found it more efficient to write words in actual use in the daily speech of his government office. He therefore adopted (and declined) *hida* as a Latin word for the measure of land which the stylist Bede had centuries before rendered as *familia*.[126] But he left proper names in Anglo-Saxon: *Merchenlage, Danelage, Westsexenlage*.[127]

When Fitz Nigel talks about common, usual, well known or ordinary words, he means English. When he wants a Latin word for 'common' in the sense of homely or 'non-U', he uses *agrestis*. This evidence is enough to show that the working spoken language not only of the assemblies of shire and hundred but even of the civil service was then English. And Fitz Nigel tells me, at least, that English was the language in which the Doomsday commissioner's scribes took their notes:[128]

> **A.18** Finally, lest anything should seem to be lacking from the highest level of supreme forethought, he took counsel and then sent out the most able men he had by him, on circuit throughout the realm. Thus they made a careful description of all the land – woods, pastures and meadows and cultivated land too – and, having taken notes in the common language, *verbis communibus annotata*, edited it into a book, *in librum redacta est*.

He may even have had access to those notes in his office, or what was left of them a century after they were made.

---

124. Johnson *Richard Fitz Nigel* p6; *communibus verbis* could mean 'in words common to both languages', as 'common law' might sometimes at first have meant common to both French and English. But that makes poor sense here. There would be no shame in accomplishing such a feat.
125. Johnson *Richard Fitz Nigel* p45.
126. Johnson *Richard Fitz Nigel* p63.
127. Fitz Nigel's contemporary Glanvill has *bladis, toftis, esterlingorum, fruisseto, faldas, stikis*, but he must be kept outside our period.
128. Johnson *Richard Fitz Nigel* p63.

The evidence collected in this appendix, linguistic, literary and historical, shows at least that in Anglo-Norman England:

1. English was spoken generally.
2. Some French was written and spoken.
3. French had to be learned by those who were not French.
4. The French – written and spoken – in England was noticeably different from that in Normandy.
5. Anglo-Norman vocabulary included words taken from English.
6. English writers of Anglo-Norman verse used English not French rhythms.
7. Latin was used for records and charters and formal documents.

GENERAL CONCLUSIONS

It is essential to respect the limits of the contributions that language studies can make to historical enquiry in general and dispute resolution in particular and to keep in mind some truisms:

1. Until the invention of the gramophone, the only contemporary evidence of the speech of earlier centuries was written.
2. A distinction must be kept between the language of the author and that of the scribe.[129]
3. Copyists may not have written what they read.
4. Scribes can copy what they cannot understand and even, at a pinch, if they cannot read at all.[130]
5. Much of the surviving evidence is in later copies made centuries after it was first written down.
6. Conventions of orthography are a mask; the letters of the conventional alphabet were the only tools scribes had to capture speech.
7. The best evidence is provided unconsciously by a writer who is unaware of the significance of the writing for later scholars.

Some claims can be substantiated and some conclusions drawn which can be taken back into the discussion of the development of dispute management in this period. At least we can be confident that, by the end of it, English was the language spoken throughout the whole of England (though not Wales and Cornwall) by the vast majority of people of both English and Norman ancestry. There were many different dialects, traces of which survive today. Though French had disappeared from ordinary use, many people had been bilingual and Anglo-Norman had had profound and massive influence. Many French words were adopted, enriching

---

129. LE Menger *The Anglo-Norman Dialect* p.7: 'In only one Anglo-Norman text are we sure that the author and scribe were one and the same person'; MK Pope 'Etude sur la Langue'. Compare for Latin Claudia Severa's birthday invitation and for Anglo-Saxon Ordlaf's Fonthill Letter.
130. Clanchy *From Memory to Written Record* pp97, 100; Wormald *Uses of Literacy* p95: 'Charlemagne could speak Latin and enjoy *The City of God* but he never learned to write.' Higher education taught students how to dictate but not usually how to write.

Middle English with synonyms. Moderated no doubt through pidgins, the influence of French had accelerated the structural changes that contact with Celtic had begun, such as the loss of inflections.[131] English, though the language in which notes were taken, was not yet a literary language. Literature was in Anglo-Norman. Records were in Latin. The king's own courts used Anglo-Norman and the shire and hundred courts used English, with interpreters if needed. Centuries would pass before French left the courts and Latin the records, and by then all disputes were managed in Modern English.

131. A process which still continues, e.g. under the influence of Caribbean usage imported into the major cities and through popular culture.

Appendix B

A NOTE ON THE TEXT OF THE LAWS OF HLOTHHERE AND EADRIC 8[1]

> How crucial for the solution of some of the problems in legal growth may be the
> solution of questions of dialect!
>
> HD Hazeltine 'The Laws of the Anglo-Saxons' p397

There is only one text of the eighth century Laws of Hlothhere and Eadric.
It is contained in a manuscript, the *Textus Roffensis*, compiled in the
twelfth century.[2] We have nothing more than that one source to rely on. We
know that punctuation and even word division were not uniform or regular
when it was first written and we need not accept that which survives in our
present manuscript. Most important, we should assume neither that the
original author intended nonsense, nor that later copyists would necessarily have noticed it if introduced later. We have no idea how many times
it was copied or of the quality of the intermediate scribes. They did not
have to be able to understand the content to be given the job of copyist.
When, therefore, we find that what is now commonly understood to be the
meaning could not be the intention of any half-competent legislator, we
must look at the text again.[3]

Our suspicions will be strengthened if there is a flaw in the writing. They
will be all but confirmed if the common reading requires the acceptance
of at least three words that are found nowhere else. But acceptance of any
suggested alternative will depend on the method by which it is arrived at,
as well as the sense it makes.

1. Copied probably in 1130. For the purposes of this note Hlothhere and Eadric are assumed
   to have issued this legislation together, though that is unlikely.
2. Now in the Kent County Archives in Maidstone. A facsimile has been produced by
   Peter Sawyer in two parts, Pt 1 containing the legislation, *Early English Manuscripts in
   Facsimile VII: Textus Roffensis I*. Oliver *Beginnings* has text, translation and commentary,
   with a diplomatic transcription, pp183–94.
3. 'That conjecture will entice its adversaries to do what they have never done before, to
   read the passage with attention. If they can attempt a defence… let them attempt it by all
   means: if it succeeds, I shall claim half the credit.' AE Housman *D Ivnii Ivvenalis Satvrae*
   pxxx. They may do so with all the greater relish because it is suggested not by a Housman
   but a tremulous amateur whose knowledge of Anglo-Saxon is rudimentary.

The part which I believe requires emendation is Liebermann 8, section 6 in Oliver's edition, lines 18 to 22 in her transcription:[4]

mannan
B.1 *Gif man oÞerne sace tihte. 7he Þane, mote anmedle oÞÞe an Þin ge.symble seman Þam oðrum byrigean .gesel le 7 Þam riht awyrce Þeto hiom cantwara de man gescrifen.*

Oliver's translation,[5] agreeing with the German of Liebermann and based on his text, reads:

> If a person brings a charge against another in a matter, and he should meet that person in the assembly or public meeting, the person [charged] is always to give surety to the other and carry out that right [= judgment] which the judges of the Kentish people may appoint for them.

The major problem is with the first line, which Liebermann[6] edits as:

B.2 *Gif man oÞerne sace tihte. 7he Þane mannan mote an medle oÞÞe an Þinge....*

Attenborough[7] and Oliver accept that reading, merely bringing the super-script into the gap below it. But in this context the chance meeting – 'if... he should meet that person in the assembly' makes no sense. Men attended their own assemblies. Attendance was compulsory. They did not attend the assemblies of other groups. They would not have been welcome unless invited. Legal process cannot depend on a defendant happening to be at some public gathering and the claimant bumping into him by chance. No one then or now would make a law to provide for it. It does not read like a general statement arising from a particular decision. What has 'chance' got to do with it? Some other meaning must have been intended. I believe the text allows us to read exactly what we would expect the doom at that time to do.

There is no difficulty with the first conditional clause: *tihte*, third person singular present subjunctive of *tihtan*, is also found in this sense of 'make a claim' in the Laws of Wihtred 23. 'Bring a charge' is too technical. 'Charge' can only be criminal. This is long before the modern distinction between crime and tort/delict. *Sacu* is any dispute and *sace* is the dative. So the clause reads: 'If a person makes a claim against another in a dispute.'

It is the next few words that raise the problem. The gap in the manuscript after *Þane* and the *mannan* written in a smaller superscript partly above the gap and partly over *mote* leave room for speculation; indeed they demand it.

Wilkins,[8] followed by Thorpe,[9] reads the first line as:

4. Oliver *Beginnings* p189 lines18–22.
5. Oliver *Beginnings* p131; there is a full description of the earlier editions at pp251–6.
6. Liebermann *Gesetze* I p10: *Hlothaere und Eadric* 8.
7. Attenborough *Laws* p18.
8. David Wilkins *Leges Anglo-Saxonicae Ecclesiasticae et Civiles* 1721 p8.
9. Benjamin Thorpe *Ancient Laws and Institutions of England*.

B.4 *Gif man oÞerne sace tihte. 7 he Þane mannan mote anmedle oÞÞe anÞinge*

and translates it into Latin: '*Si quis alterum criminis postulet, & tunc eum ad conventum vocet vel citet*' – 'if someone charges another with a crime and then summons or cites him to a meeting.' Presumably he is translating *Þane* as '*tunc*, then'. The word for 'then', though, is *Þanne* or *Þonne* and is not found as *Þane*, which must be the masculine singular accusative demonstrative pronoun, an alternative form to *Þone*. Wilkins had to translate *Þane* as 'then', though, because he wanted the object of his verbs to be *mannan*, a man. But the normal accusative is *mann* not *mannan*. It is easy to get rid of the unwanted *-an*, though; it goes well with *mote*, which is dative, so that *an mote* gives 'to a meeting'.

The first phrase, *Þane mann*, then makes sense 'the man', though *mann* is superfluous. It means 'man', though, not 'one' or 'a person'; it is not the same word as *man*, so there is a problem with the sense.

Then we are left with just the verbs *anmedle* and *anÞinge*, presumably synonyms meaning '*vocet vel citet*', 'summons or cites'. The problem is that neither *anmedle*[10] nor *anÞinge* are found anywhere else. So Wilkins gets good sense out of it but his readings cannot stand.

What is to be done? To look at what is there, to make no assumptions and to accept no *hapax legomena* unless we cannot manage without them. We can start by running the letters together to produce what may have been nearer to the original script, four hundred or more years before it took its present form in the *Textus Roffensis*.

B.5 *7heÞanemannanmoteanmedleoÞÞeanÞinge*

We can be sure that 7 = 'and'; *he* = 'he'; *Þane* = 'him'. Leave aside the insertion *mannan* for a moment: *mote* is a known word, the dative singular of the noun *mot*, a meeting. Nowhere is it found as a verb in the sense 'meet', but only in the sense 'may' or 'might' or 'should' or 'must'. Then let it mean here 'in a meeting'; *anmedle* is unknown as a verb but it can be a phrase *an medle*, meaning 'in a meeting', if *medel* can be admitted as an alternative to *meðel*; *oÞÞe an Þinge* causes no problems: 'or in an assembly', *Þing* elsewhere in the literature having an element in it of a meeting dealing with a dispute.

So we are left with a clause: 'If a person makes a claim against another in a dispute, and he... in a meeting, a meeting, or a meeting'. We may leave aside for the moment the problem of differentiating the synonyms, which must be there for a purpose, which could be merely stylistic but can be shown to be much more than that. Our first task is to make sense of the superscript *mannan*. Why, first of all, is there a superscript there at

---

10. There is a noun *anmedla* but it means 'pomp'.

all? Because the scribe of the *Textus Roffensis* first wrote something in the line and later, looking back on it, saw it was wrong, rubbed it out, but did not have enough space in the erasure to fit what he wanted to put in. The original problem could have been that what he was copying did not make sense. We have no idea through how many hands the text had passed or what was its state when our scribe got it. Whatever that was, that is of little interest now. What we want to know is what was first written by the legislator in the time of Hlothhere and Eadric. That made good legal sense, we can be sure. Can we make a guess what that sense was? To fill the gap we want something like: 'makes a claim'.

What we have is *mannan*. If we take two letters off the end, *an* fits nicely before *mote* and produces the sort of triple noun phrase so loved by writers and rhetoricians since evidence began: *an mote, an medle oÞÞe an thinge*. But what do we do with *mann*? We could leave it as it is, intruding itself into the sense, but *Þane* does the job better on its own.

First we must remember that we do not know how big the space was which the original mistaken letters took up. So we should not be put off if our conjecture exceeds four letters. We know that what we lack is a verb. It would be pleasing if one could be found that made sense. What about the verb *manian*? It is used often in the sense we want: to make a claim against someone. The third person present indicative is *manaÞ*. It fits for sense and almost for size, making the clause read:

B.6 *Gif man oÞerne sace tihte 7 he Þane manaÞ an mote, an medle oÞÞe an Þinge*
If a person makes a claim against another in a dispute, and he lays a claim against him in a moot, a medley or a gathering.

Now we are left with the task of differentiating the meanings of the three kinds of meeting, which we can only do, not by finding elegant synonyms from *Roget* but discovering what they meant to Hlothhere and Eadric. First we must be sure what the rest of the paragraph means. Though there are two erasures and insertions, they are of no importance but there is just one further textual difficulty.

Using the same method of running all the letters together, we get:

B.7 *SymblesemanÞamoðrumbyrigeangeselle*
   7ÞamrihtawyrcePetohiomcantwarademangescrifen

The 7 makes a convenient uncontroversial break so that we have two parts we can deal with separately. *Symble* means 'always'. The next five letters can be taken together, *seman*, or split into *se man*. The next eight are clearly *Þam* and *oÞrum*. Then *byrigeangeselle* is clearly *byrigean geselle*.

We cannot allow ourselves to be influenced by the fact that the manuscript now has *seman* as one word, even less by the pleasure it would give that *seman* means 'arbitration'. *Seman* does not make sense and *se man* does: *symble se man Þam oÞrum byrigean geselle* means word for word 'always the one to the other surety gives up' or 'the one always gives surety to the other'. So the whole so far reads: 'If a person makes a claim against another in a dispute, and he lays a claim against him in a moot, a medley or a gathering, the one always gives surety to the other'.

7ÞamrihtawyrceÞetohiomcantwarademangescrifen can be broken down into *7 Þam riht awyrce Þe to hiom cantwara deman gescrifen* with the meaning: 'and to him does right that to him of-the-Kentish-people decision-makers awarded'. *Dema* is usually translated 'judge' but there were no judges in the time of Hlothhere and Eadric. The word 'judge' carries too many false meanings to the modern eye.[11] Nor would it be justified to translate it 'arbitrator', though there were mediators and arbitrators then.[12] It is important not to find answers to problems by making distinctions that the source did not. Clumsy as it may seem, unless we keep the word in the original as 'dema', we have no alternative but to find a phrase which does not make the distinction, such as 'decision-maker'. The full clause then would read: 'and does the right to him which the decision-makers of the Kentish people award.'

Why mention the Kentish people? To make it clear that they were the ones to make the decision, not anyone else. Who else could it have been? All the different peoples, clans if you will, that Hlothhere and Eadric were addressing. What about the three kinds of meetings? The etymology of the three words is not within my powers. The dictionaries do not say enough to support the suggestion that they can be distinguished linguistically to represent the meeting-words of different clans, different groups of incomers who had settled within the realm of Hlothhere and Eadric. Yet it seems likely that the distinction arises from different traditions or dialects. The *Oxford English Dictionary* says that *mōt* is not found on its own but only in compounds like *gemot* until the twelfth century. My conjectural text would be the first occasion. Tentatively I suggest that it has the general meaning of 'meeting', without more. Perhaps *medle* has a different Kentish source.[13] *Þing* is of Scandinavian origin, meaning 'a formal meeting to resolve a dispute', the dictionaries suggest.

We could then fill up the gaps and render the whole passage, without forcing our own meaning on to any words:

> If a person makes a claim against another in a dispute and lays a claim against him in a moot, a medley, or a meeting, the one always gives surety to the

---

11. The argument is fully set out in *Roman Arbitration* p15.
12. The *sæmend* who *gesemed* in **6.3** and Bishop Cyneheard in **6.17**.
13. *Medle* is the *mæðl* of the first part of Aethelberht's laws 1.7, **5.9**: 'Assembly's peace, 2 payment'.

other and does the right to him which the decision-makers of the Kentish
people award.

Having laboriously established the meaning of this part, we can fit it into
the whole. Fortunately there are few difficulties with the rest of the text and
they do not need treatment in an appendix of this kind.[14]

14. Aliki Pantos '*In Medle odde an Ðinge*: the Old English Vocabulary of Assembly' is
    affected by the misreading of the text but full of helpful linguistic insights, e.g. p184: 'the
    evidence therefore suggests that a shift took place in the vocabulary of assembly in the
    course of the Anglo-Saxon period', with more at p188.

CHRONOLOGY

The purpose of this simple list of dates is to help the reader to see more easily, though not quite at a glance, the sequence of and relations between the more important events in the period this book covers, from the beginnings of human occupation of Britain to AD1154, when Henry II became king. There are those who insist that a crude and unqualified chronology is worse than none at all but they may be of that wondrous company who can keep dates in their heads. I hope it is not presumptuous of me to assume, to be on the safe side, that there are enough readers who, like me, need even an undependable set of hooks upon which to hang bits of knowledge. Almost all the dates are approximate,[1] unless there was some natural phenomenon then, like an eclipse, but I hope the sequences are about right. I have made no attempt to resolve any controversies. The abbreviation c, for about, means the date is approximate; a ? denotes a guess. The x sign between dates means that the date falls somewhere in between them. Kings and emperors have their names in bold. King is shown by k, death by d, birth by b, marriage by m.

BC	PREHISTORY (all dates approximate and most contentious)
500,000–130,000	Lower Palaeolithic
170,000	First humans in England
130,000–40,000	Middle Palaeolithic; Neanderthals
70,000	Modern humans emigrate from Africa
40,000–13,000	Early Upper Palaeolithic; Crô-Magnons
30,000	First modern humans in Britain
22,000	Last Glacial Maximum begins; humans leave England
15,000	Last Glacial Maximum ends; humans come back
13,000–10,000	Late Upper Palaeolithic
10,000–5,000	Mesolithic
9,000 (or later)	English Channel separates Britain from the Continent
6,000	Farming in England
5,000	Early Neolithic; first pottery
4,000	Bronze Age starts in England
3,500	Traditional date of Middle Neolithic; causewayed enclosures, barrows
3,000–2,150	Traditional date of Late Neolithic; Stonehenge
1,300	First use of wheel
750	First use of iron
750–450	Early Iron Age
450–150	Middle Iron Age
c320	?Voyage of Pytheas to Britain
150–AD43	Late Iron Age; formation of larger tribal groups

---

1. EJ Bickerman *Chronology of the Ancient World* revd edn 1980.

BC	ROMAN BRITAIN
55–54	Caesar invades Britain; **Cassivelaunus** of South Britain agrees to pay tribute
51	Caesar's *De Bello Gallico*
27	Augustus inaugurates the Roman Empire
4	Traditionally birth of Christ

AD	
4	Rome recognises **Cunobelinus** (Cymbeline) of the Catuvellauni k of Britain
40	Arminius, son of **Cunobelinus**, takes refuge with **Caligula**, who, deluded, declares he has conquered Britain.
43	Rome invades Britain; defeat of **Caratacus** k of South-East
61	Revolt and d of **Boudicca**
79–84	Agricola's conquest of North Britain
122	Invasion of **Hadrian**, starts Wall
180	Romans fail in North and withdraw behind **Hadrian's** Wall
208	**Septimus Severus** divides Britannia into two provinces
211	**Septimus Severus** d at York; **Caracalla's** *Constitutio Antoniniana* gives citizenship to all free inhabitants of Empire
285	**Carausius**, commander of British fleet, claims to be emperor *of* (not in) Britannia **Diocletian** divides Empire East/West
293	**Alectus** kills **Carausius**; claims to be emperor *in* Britannia
296	**Constantius** crushes revolt
305	**Constantius** succeeds **Diocletian** in West
306	**Constantius** d at York; his son **Constantine** emperor
312	**Constantine** reunites East and West
313	Christianity tolerated
314	British bishops attend Arles synod
343	**Constans** in Britain
360	Scots break treaty with Rome; Picts and Scots cross Hadrian's Wall
c360	Pelagius b
367	Picts and Scots attack with Saxon allies
369	**Theodosius** drives them back; ?new Northern province of Valentia
383	**Magnus Maximus** claims to be emperor, conquers Spain and Gaul, kills **Gratian**
388	**Theodosius** kills **Magnus Maximus** at Aquilea
395	**Theodosius** d; empire divided East/West
406	Vandals, Suevi and Alans cross the Rhine and invade Gaul
407	**Honorius** recognises **Constantine III** as ruler in Britain
409	**Constantine III** in Spain; British *civitates* expel **Constantine III's** officials
410	Visigoths sack Rome; **Honorius** 'tells Britons to defend themselves'
418	Franks settle in Gaul
420	Pelagius d
429	Germanus of Auxerre and ?Lupus of Troyes in Britain to combat Pelagianism
432	Patrick taken to Ireland

435	Germanus's second visit
436	Roman troops leave
438	Theodosian Code
441–442	*Anglo-Saxon Chronicle* for 452: 'The British provinces were brought under the authority of the Anglo-Saxons'
446x452	Britons appeal to Aetius, leading Roman general
449	?Jutes into Kent; Angles and Saxons into West Britain
457	?Hengest in Kent
461	?Mansuetus, bishop of the Britons, attends Council of Tours
469	?**Riothamus**, k of Britons, fights for Roman Empire against Visigoths
476	End of Western Roman Empire; Goth **Odoacer** in Rome
c482	**Clovis** k of Francia; Merovingians 486-751
486	**Clovis** defeats Roman governor in Gaul
491	Saxons in Sussex
496	**Clovis** defeats Alemanni
500	Lex Romana Visigothorum/Burgundiorum
	?British defeat Angles at battle of Mount Badon
	Clovis Christian; Saxon kingdom of Wessex
508–511	Lex Salica
511	**Clovis** d; four sons divide his kingdom
527	Saxon kingdoms of Essex and Middlesex
	Justinian
528–534	**Justinian's** legislation
533	**Justinian's** Digest
534	**Justinian's** Code 2nd edition
?540	**Theudebert I** of Franks claims authority over some Britons
c540	Gildas b (author of *De Excidio Britanniae*)
c550	Anglian kingdoms of East Anglia, Mercia and Northumbria founded
	Dionysius Exiguus *Decretals*
c560	**Aethelberht** m Bertha, great-great-granddaughter of **Clovis**
563	Columba founds Iona
570	Mohammed b
577	West Saxons defeat Britons at battle of Deorham
586–592	**Hussa**, k of Bernicians, fought four other British kings
592	Northumbria (Bernicia plus Deira) supreme
597	Augustine arrives in Kent
597x600	**Aethelberht** Christian
c600	Augustine opens school in Canterbury, teaching in Latin
602	Augustine founds see of Canterbury
613x615	Aethelfrith of Bernicia defeats Britons at battle of Chester
614x616	**Aethelberht's** dooms
614	**Chlothar II** invites bishop of Rochester and abbot of St Peter's to Council of Paris
616	**Aethelberht** d; kingdom of Kent under Wessex
616–633	**Edwin**, k of Northumbria; Christian 625
632	Mohammed d
c660	Aldhelm studying law in Canterbury
672	Bede b
c686	Dooms of **Hlothhere** and **Eadric**

686	**Eadric** d
688x694	Dooms of **Ine**
695	Dooms of **Wihtred**
716–757	**Aethelbald** k of Mercia
725	**Wihtred** d; Kent under Mercia
731	Bede's *Historia Ecclesiastica Gentis Anglorum*
734	Bede's letter to Ecberht, bishop of York
735	See of York created
	Offa's silver penny
736	Bede d
751	**Pepin** k of French, end of Merovingians, start of Carolingians
757	**Offa** k of Mercians
771	**Charlemagne** k of French
779	**Offa** k of English
782–783	Danish attacks
793	**Offa** annexes East Anglia
796	**Offa** treaty with **Charlemagne**; **Offa** d; **Coenwulf** k
800	**Charlemagne** emperor
802	**Egbert** k of Wessex; **Charlemagne's** Laws
c810	Nennius *Historia Britonum*
814	**Charlemagne** d
821	**Coenwulf** d
825	**Ecgberht** takes Mercia
828	**Ecgberht** recognised as over-king
835	**Ecgberht** defeats Danes, and Britons in Cornwall
842	Danes attack London; ransom paid
843	**Louis the Pious** d
849	**Alfred** b
851	Danes sack Canterbury
855	**Aethelwulf** of Essex and his son **Alfred** pilgrims to Rome
865	'Great Army' lands
866	Danes take York
870	Danes take East Anglia
871	**Alfred** k of Wessex; *Anglo-Saxon Chronicle* begins
876	Danes in Northumbria
877	Mercia partitioned between English and Danes
878	Danes attack Wessex; **Alfred** defeats Guthrum; Danelaw treaty
886	**Alfred** takes London
893	Danish attacks; **Alfred** defeats Danes
895	**Alfred** defeats Danish fleet
899	**Alfred** d; **Edward the Elder** k
910	**Edward the Elder** takes Oxford and London
913	**Edward the Elder** takes Essex from Danes
917	**Edward the Elder** takes English Mercia
925	**Edward the Elder's** Laws I and II; **Edward the Elder** and Guthrum
	Edward the Elder d; **Athelstan** k
926	**Athelstan** takes Northumbria; **Athelstan** I and II
937	**Athelstan** defeats Danes, Scots and Britons
939	**Athelstan** d; **Edmund** k; **Edmund** I, II and III
947	**Eadred**

955	**Edwy** k of Wessex
959	**Edmund** d; **Edgar** k; **Edgar** I, II, III, IV
960	Dunstan archbishop of Canterbury
970	*Exeter Book*
973	Eight kings submit to **Edgar**
975	**Edgar** d; **Edward the Martyr** k
979	**Edward the Martyr** d; **Aethelred** k; **Aethelred** I and II
979–1016	**Aethelred**
987	**Hugh Capet** k of France, end of Carolingians
c995	Battle of Maldon
1002	**Aethelred** m Emma daughter of Duke Richard I of Normandy
1013	**Aethelred** and family flee to Normandy
1013–1014	**Swein**
1014	Return of **Aethelred**
1016	**Edmund Ironside**, son of **Aethelred**, rules with **Cnut**
1016–1035	**Cnut**
1017	**Cnut** m Emma, widow of **Aethelred**, mother of **Edward the Confessor**
1019–1035	**Cnut** king of Denmark
1020–1023	Laws of **Cnut**
1035–1040	**Harold Harefoot**, son of Cnut
1035–1087	William duke of Normandy
1040–1042	**Harthacnut**, son of Cnut
1042–1066	**Edward the Confessor**, son of **Aethelred,** stepson of **Cnut**
1045	**Edward** marries Edith, daughter of Godwin
1053–1066	Harold Godwin's son earl of Wessex
1055	**Gruffydd ap Llewellyn** 'k of the Britons' ruler of all Wales
1062–1095	Wulfstan bishop of Worcester
1063	**Gruffydd ap Llewellyn** d. Wales falls apart
1066	**Harold Godwinson**
1066	**Harold Hardrada**
1066	**Edgar Aetheling**
1066	Battle of Hastings 14 October
1066–1087	**William I** (consecrated Christmas Day)
1070–1089	Lanfranc archbishop of Canterbury
1085	**William I** orders Domesday survey
1087–1100	**William II Rufus**
1087–1088	Domesday Book
1100–1135	**Henry I**
1106–1135	**Henry I** duke of Normandy
1114	*Quadripartitus*
1116x1118	*Leges Henrici Primi*
1130	First surviving Pipe Roll
1135–1154	**Stephen**
c1136	*Laws of Edward the Confessor*
1139	**Matilda** invades
1141	**Matilda** captures Stephen, but then defeated
1148	**Matilda** leaves England
1150x1170	*Leis Willelme*
1153	Henry of Anjou, Matilda's son, invades, acknowledged as heir
1154–1189	**Henry II**
c1170	*Liber Eliensis*

BIBLIOGRAPHY

Any bibliography, however expansive, cannot help but be select. It necessarily depends on its creator's choices. The aims of this one are first to help the reader follow the trails and secondly to give proper acknowledgment to those whose work this book depends on.

Anon *The History of Count Zosimus, Sometime Advocate and Chancellor of the Roman Empire* London, J Davis 1814

A

Richard Abels 'King Alfred's Peace-Making Strategies with the Vikings' (1991) 3 *Haskins Society Journal* 23–34

Henry Adams and others *Anglo-Saxon Law* Boston, Little Brown 1905 reprinted Rothman 1972

JW Adamson *The Illiterate Anglo-Saxon and Other Essays on Education, Medieval and Modern* Folcroft PA, Folcroft P 1946, repr 1969

RA Adkins and MR Petchey 'Secklow Hundred Mound and Other Meeting Place Mounds in England' (1984) 141 *Archaeological J* 243–51

Aldhelm see Rudolphus Ehwald

Michael Alexander *The Earliest English Poems* Harmondsworth, Penguin 1966

Lindsay Allason-Jones *Women in Roman Britain* London, British Museum 1989

HE Allen 'The Mystical Lyrics of the Manuel des Pechiez' (1918) 9 *Romanic Review* 154–93

Ammianus Marcellinus see JC Rolfe

Appian *Roman History* see Horace White

MS Arnold and others eds *On the Laws and Customs of England: Essays in Honor of Samuel Thorne* Chapel Hill NC, U of North Carolina P 1981

FL Attenborough *The Laws of the Earliest English Kings* New York, Russell 1963

Giorgio Ausenda 'Current Issues and Future Directions in the Study of the Early Anglo-Saxon Period' in Hines *The Anglo-Saxons* 411–50

B

JH Baker *An Introduction to English Legal History* London, Butterworths 4th edn 2002

— *Manual of Law French* Aldershot, Scolar P 2nd edn 1990

JN Bakhuizen van den Brink 'Episcopalis Audientia' (1956) 19:8 new series *Mededelingen der Koninklijke Nederlandse Akademie van Wetenschappen, afd Letterkunde* 245–301, reprinted Amsterdam, Noord–Hollandsche Uitgevers 1956

Alfred Bammesberger and Alfred Wollmann eds *Britain 400–600: Language and History* Heidelberg, Heidelberg UP 1994

MW Barley and RPC Hanson eds *Christianity in Britain, 300–700* Leicester, Leicester UP 1968

Frank Barlow *Edward the Confessor* London, Eyre Methuen 2nd edn 1978

— *William Rufus* London, Methuen 1983

JT with JP Barrett *A History of Alternative Dispute Resolution: The Story of a Political, Cultural, and Social Movement* San Francisco, Jossey-Bass 2004

Robert Bartlett *Trial by Fire and Water: The Medieval Judicial Ordeal* Oxford, Clarendon P 1986

Steven Bassett ed *The Origins of the Anglo-Saxon Kingdoms* London, Leicester UP 1989

— 'In Search of the Origins of Anglo-Saxon Kingdoms' in Bassett *Origins* 3–27

Janet Bately *John Joscelyn and the Laws of the Anglo-Saxon Kings* in Korhammer 435–66

JM Bately *The Old English Orosius* London, Early English Text Society 1980

David [= DR] Bates 'Charters and Historians of Britain and Ireland: Problems and Possibilities' in MT Flanagan and JA Green *Charters and Charter Scholarship* Basingstoke, Palgrave Macmillan 2005 1–14

— 'The Land Pleas of William I's Reign: Penenden Heath Revisited' (1978) 51 *Bulletin of Historical Research* 1–19

— *Normandy Before 1066* London, Longman 1982

— 'The Origin of the Justiciarship' (1981) 4 *Anglo-Norman Studies* 1–12

— *Regesta Regum Anglo-Normannorum: The Acta of William I (1066–1087)* Oxford, Clarendon P 1998

Mary Bateson *Borough Customs* 2 vols (1904) 18 Selden Society; (1906) 21 Selden Society

Guy de la Bédoyère *The Golden Age of Roman Britain* Stroud, Tempus 1999

— 'How Roman was Britain' *BBC History* June 2006 40–2

— *Roman Britain: A New History* London, Thames and Hudson 2006

M Bell ed *Wulfric of Haselbury by John of Ford* (1932) 47 Somerset Record Society

P Bellwood *First Farmers: The Origins of Agricultural Societies* Oxford, Blackwell 2004

— and C Renfrew eds *Examining the Language/Farming Dispersal Hypothesis* Cambridge, McDonald Institute for Archaeological Research 2005

Rolf Berndt 'The Linguistic Situation in England from the Norman Conquest to the Loss of Normandy (1066–1204)' in Roger Lass ed *Approaches to Historical Linguistics: An Anthology* New York, Holt, Rinehart and Winston 1969

Dorothy Bethurum 'Stylistic Features of the Old English Laws' (1932) 27 *Modern Language Review* 263–79

EJ Bickerman *Chronology of the Ancient World* Ithaca NY, Cornell UP revd edn 1980

Pierre-Henri Billy *Thesaurus Linguae Gallicae* Hildesheim, Olms-Weidmann 1993

DA Binchy *Celtic and Anglo-Saxon Kingship* Oxford, Clarendon P 1970

WdeG Birch *Cartularium Saxonicum* London, Whiting 3 vols 1885–93, reprint New York, Johnson 1964

AR Birley tr *Tacitus: Agricola and Germany* Oxford, Oxford UP 1999

— *The Roman Government of Britain* Oxford, Oxford UP 2005

E Birley *Roman Britain and the Roman Army* Kendal, Titus Wilson 1976

TAM Bishop and P Chaplais eds *Facsimiles of English Royal Writs to AD 1100* London, Oxford UP 1957

278 Early English Arbitration

EO Blake *Liber Eliensis* London, Royal Historical Society, Camden 3rd series 1962

JE Bogaers 'King Cogidubnus in Chichester: Another Reading of *RIB 91*' (1979) 10 *Britannia* 243–54

John Bossy ed *Disputes and Settlements: Law and Human Relations in the West* Cambridge, Cambridge UP 1983

AK Bowman *The Roman Writing Tablets from Vindolanda* London, British Museum 1983

— and JD Thomas 'Vindolanda 1985: The New Writing Tablets' (1986) 76 *Journal of Roman Studies* 120–3

— and JD Thomas 'New Texts from Vindolanda' (1987) 18 *Britannia* 125–42

— JD Thomas and JN Adams 'Two Letters from Vindolanda' (1990) 21 *Britannia* 33–52

Mark Boynton and Susan Reynolds 'The Author of the Fonthill Letter' (1996) 25 *Anglo-Saxon England* 91–5

William Boys *Collections for an History of Sandwich in Kent* Canterbury, printed for the author 1792

Richard Bradley *The Prehistory of Britain and Ireland* Cambridge, Cambridge UP 2007

— *The Social Foundations of Prehistoric Britain: Themes and Variations in the Archaeology of Power* London, Longmans 1984

Paul Brand 'The English Difference: The Application of Bureaucratic Norms within a Legal System' (2003) 21 *Law and History Review* 383–7

— 'Local Custom in the Early Common Law' in Stafford, Nelson and Martindale 150–9

— *The Origins of the English Legal Profession* Oxford, Blackwell 1992

Keith Branigan *Roman Britain: Life in an Imperial Province* London, Reader's Digest 1980

Rolf Brendt 'The Linguistic Situation in England from the Norman Conquest to the Loss of Normandy (1066–1204)' in Roger Lass ed *Approaches to Historical Linguistics: An Anthology* New York, Holt 1969 369–81

JS Brewer ed *Chronicon Monasterii de Bello* London, Anglia Christiana Society 1846

AR Bridbury ed *The English Economy from Bede to the Reformation* Woodbridge, Boydell 1992

— 'The Dark Ages' in Bridbury *The English Economy* 43–55

— 'Seventh Century England in Bede and the Early Laws' in Bridbury *The English Economy* 56–85

RH Britnell *The Commercialisation of English Society 1000–1500* Manchester, Manchester UP 2nd edn 1996

Johannes Brøndsted *The Vikings* Harmondsworth, Penguin 1965

Nicholas Brooks 'The Creation and Early Structure of the Kingdom of Kent' in Bassett 55–74

— ed *Latin and the Vernacular Languages in Early Modern Britain* Leicester, Leicester UP 1982

Marie-Bernadette Bruguière *Littérature et Droit dans la Gaule du Ve Siècle* (Toulouse doctoral thesis 1968) Toulouse, Espic 1974

CG Bruns ed *Fontes Iuris Romani Antiqui* 7th ed by Otto Gradewitz, Tübingen Mohr 1909

JJ Buchanan and HT Davis *Zosimus Historia Nova: The Decline of Rome* San Antonio, Trinity UP 1967

Constance Bullock-Davies *Professional Interpreters and the Matter of Britain* Cardiff, U of Wales P 1966

D Bullough and R Collins eds *Ideal and Reality in Frankish and Anglo-Saxon Society: Studies Presented to JM Wallace-Hadrill* Oxford, Blackwell 1983

Colin Burgess *The Age of Stonehenge* London, Dent reprinted 2002

John Burke *An Illustrated History of England* London, Book Club Associates new edn 1985

Vratislav Busek 'Episcopalis Audientia, eine Friedens- und Schiedsgerichtsbarkeit' (1939) 28 *Zeitschrift der Savigny-Stiftung für Rechtsgeschichte: Kanonistische Abteilung* 453ff

Arthur Bryant *Set in a Silver Sea* London, Collins 1984

C

Caesar *Gallic War* see HJ Edwards

Helen Cam 'An East Anglian Shire-Moot of Stephen's Reign' (1924) 39 *English Historical Review* 568–71

— *Law-Finders and Law-Makers in Medieval England* London, Merlin P 1962

— *Liberties and Communities in Medieval England* London, Merlin P 1963

A Campbell *The Chronicle of Aethelweard* London, Nelson 1962

Brian Campbell *The Writings of the Roman Land Surveyors: Introduction, Text, Translation and Commentary* London, Society for the Promotion of Roman Studies 2000

James Campbell 'Anglo-Saxon Courts' in C Cubitt ed *Court Culture in the Early Middle Ages* Leiden, David Brown 2003 155–69

— *The Anglo-Saxon State* London, Hambledon 2000

— *Essays in Anglo-Saxon History* London, Hambledon 1986

— Eric John and Patrick Wormald *The Anglo-Saxons* Oxford, Phaidon 1982

C Capelli and 14 others 'A Y Chromosome Census of the British Isles' (2003) 13 *Current Biology* 979–84

Paul Caspers *Der Gute- und Schiedsgedanke im Kirchlichen Zivilgerichtsverfahren: ein Kirchenrechtliche Untersuchung über das Wesen der Episcopalis Audientia* Düsseldorf, Triltsch 1954

SM Caza *Maces* http://otlichnik.tripod.com/medmace1.html

HM Chadwick 'The End of Roman Britain' in Chadwick *Studies in Early British History* 9–20

— and others *Studies in Early British History* Cambridge, Cambridge UP 1959

Nora Chadwick *The Celts* Harmondsworth, Penguin 1971

Pierre Chaplais 'The Royal Anglo-Saxon "Chancery" of the Tenth Century Revisited' in Mayr-Harting and Moore 41–51

Robin Chapman Stacey 'Texts and Society' in Charles-Edwards *After Rome* 220–57

Thomas Charles-Edwards ed *After Rome* Oxford, Oxford UP 2003

— 'Anglo-Saxon Kinship Revisited' in Hines *The Anglo-Saxons* 171–210

— 'Early Medieval Kingships in the British Isles' in Bassett *Origins* 28–39

— 'Introduction' in Charles-Edwards *After Rome* 1–20

— 'Language and Society among the Insular Celts AD400–1000' in MJ Green ed *The Celtic World* 703–36

— 'Law in the Western Kingdoms Between the Fifth and the Seventh Century' in Averil Cameron, Bryan Ward-Perkins and Michael Whitby eds *The Cambridge Ancient History: Late Antiquity: Empire and Successors AD 425–600* XIV Cambridge, Cambridge UP 2000 260–88

— 'Nations and Kingdoms: a View from Above' in Charles-Edwards *After Rome* 23–58

MP Charlesworth *The Lost Province or the Worth of Britain* Cardiff, U of Wales P 1949

HJ Chaytor *From Script to Print* London, Sidgwick and Jackson 1966

FL Cheyette '*Suum Cuique Tribuere*' (1970) 6 *French Historical Studies* 287–99

Marjorie Chibnall 'Clio's Legal Cosmetics: Law and Custom in the Work of Medieval Historians' (1997) 20 *Anglo-Norman Studies* 31–43

— *The Debate on the Norman Conquest* Manchester, Manchester UP 1999

— ed and tr *Ecclesiastical History of Ordericus Vitalis* II Oxford, Clarendon P 1990

HD Chickering Jr tr *Beowulf* New York, Anchor Books 1977

VG Childe *Prehistoric Communities of the British Isles* London, Chambers 1940

MT [= Michael] Clanchy *From Memory to Written Record* Oxford, Blackwell 2nd edn 1993

— 'Law and Love in the Middle Ages' in *Law and Human Relations* London, Past and Present 1980 1–14 (separately paged) and in Bossy 47–67 'Medieval Mentalities and Primitive Legal Practice' in Stafford, Nelson and Martindale 83–94.

— 'Remembering the Past and the Good Old Law' (1970) 55 *History* 165–76

GN Clark *Historical Scholarship and Historical Thought* Inaugural Lecture Cambridge, Cambridge UP 1944

John Clarke 'Roman and Native, AD80–122' in IA Richmond *Roman and Native* 28–59

Richard Coates 'Invisible Britons: the View from Linguistics' in Higham ed *Britons in Anglo-Saxon England* 172–191

— 'The Significances of Celtic Place-Names in England' in Filppula, Klemola and Pitkänen 47–85

Bertram Colgrave and RAB Mynors eds *Bede's Ecclesiastical History of the English People* Oxford, Oxford UP 1969

JP Collas ed *Year Books of Edward II Volume XXV* (1964) 81 *Selden Society* particularly 'Problems of Language and Interpretation' xiv–cxxviii

RG Collingwood and RP Wright *The Roman Inscriptions of Britain* Oxford, Oxford UP 1965

Rob Collins and James Gerrard *Debating Late Antiquity in Britain AD300–700* Oxford, Archaeopress BAR British Series 365 2004

Roger Collins 'The Role of Writing in the Resolution and Recording of Disputes' in Davies and Fouracre 207–14

— 'Visigothic Law and Regional Custom in Disputes in Early Medieval Spain' in Davies and Fouracre 85–104

John Collis *The Celts: Origins, Myths, Inventions* Stroud, Tempus 2003

RV Colman 'Domestic Peace and Public Order in Anglo-Saxon Law' in JD Woods and DAE Pelteret eds *The Anglo-Saxons: Synthesis and Achievement* Waterloo Ontario, Wilfrid Laurier UP 49–61

— 'Reason and Unreason in Early Medieval Law' (1973) 4 *J of Interdisciplinary History* 571–91

Gabriel Cooney ed *Brú na Bóinne: Newgrange, Knowth, Dowth and the River Boyne* Dublin, Archaeology Ireland 2003

HC Coote *The Romans of Britain* London, Norgate 1878

Daniel de Coppet 'Gardens of Life, Gardens of Death in Melanesia' (1981) 8–9 *Kabar Seberang* 22–32

HEJ Cowdrey *Lanfranc: Scholar, Monk, and Archbishop* Oxford, Oxford UP 2003

MH Crawford ed *Roman Statutes* London, Institute of Classical Studies U of London 2 vols 1996

John Creighton *Britannia: The Creation of a Roman Province* London, Routledge 2006

Julia Crick review of David Howlett *Sealed from Within* (2001) 116 *English Historical Review* 925–6

HA Cronne 'The Office of Local Justiciar under the Norman Kings' (1937) 6 *U of Birmingham Historical Journal* 18–38

David Crouch 'A Norman *Conventio* and Bonds of Lordship in the Middle Ages' in Garnett and Hudson 299–324

David Crystal *The Stories of English* London, Allen Lane 2004

Barry Cunliffe *The Ancient Celts* Oxford, Oxford UP 1997

— *The Extraordinary Voyage of Pytheas the Greek* Harmondsworth, Penguin 2001

— *Facing the Ocean: the Atlantic and its Peoples 8000BC–AD1500* Oxford, Oxford UP 2001

— *Iron Age Communities of Britain* London, Routledge 3rd edn 1991

D

Richard Dammery 'Editing the Anglo-Saxon Laws: Felix Liebermann and Beyond' in DG Scragg and P Szarmach eds *The Editing of Old English* Woodbridge, Boydell 1994 251–61

RJE [= Richard] Dammery 'The Law-Code of King Alfred the Great: a Study, Edition and Translation' Trinity College Cambridge fellowship dissertation 3 vols 1990

— 'The Law-Code of King Alfred the Great: a Study, Edition and Translation' Cambridge U PhD thesis 2 vols 1991

JE Damon 'Advisors for Peace in the Reign of Aethelred Unraed' in Diane Wolfthal ed *Peace and Negotiation: Strategies for Co-Existence in the Middle Ages and the Renaissance* Brepols, Turnhout 2000 57–78

Ken Dark *Britain and the End of the Roman Empire* Stroud, Tempus 2000

— *Civitas to Kingdom: British Political Continuity 300–800* Leicester, Leicester UP 1994

— and Petra Dark *The Landscape of Roman Britain* Stroud, Sutton 1997

Petra Dark *The Environment of Britain in the First Millennium AD* London, Duckworth 2000

RR Darlington *The Vita Wulfstani of William of Malmesbury* (1938) 40 Camden Society 3rd series

David Daube *Forms of Roman Legislation* Oxford, Clarendon P 1956

M Daunt 'Old English Verse and English Speech Rhythm' (1946) 44 *Transactions of the Philological Society* 57

Wendy Davies *The Llandaff Charters* Aberystwyth, National Library of Wales 1979

— 'Local Participation and Legal Ritual in Early Medieval Law Courts' in Peter Coss ed *The Moral World of Law* Cambridge, Cambridge UP 2000 48–61

— 'People and Places in Dispute in Ninth-Century Brittany' in Davies and Fouracre 65–84

— and Paul Fouracre eds *The Settlement of Disputes in Early Medieval Europe* Cambridge, Cambridge UP 1986

HWC Davis 'The Anglo-Saxon Laws' (1913) 28 *English Historical Review* 417–30
— *England under the Normans and Angevins 1066–1272* London, Putnam 11th edn 1937
— Charles Johnson and HA Cronne eds *Regesta Regum Anglo-Normannorum* Oxford, Clarendon P 4 vols 1913–69
Lindsey Davis *The Silver Pigs* London, Sidgwick and Jackson 1989, Arrow Books paperback 2000
René Derolez 'Cross-Channel Language Ties' (1974) 3 *Anglo-Saxon England* 1–14
— 'Runic Literacy among the Anglo-Saxons' in Bammesberger and Wollmann 397–436
AS Diamond *Primitive Law Past and Present* London, Methuen 1971
CL Dier 'The Proper Relationship Between Lord and Vassal: Toward a Rationale for Anglo-Norman Litigation' (1994) 6 *Haskins Society Journal* 1–12
Myles Dillon 'Germanic and Celtic' (1943) 42 *Journal of English and Germanic Studies* 492–8
Domesday Book: A Complete Translation London, Penguin (Alecto Historical Editions) 2002
Philip Dixon 'Crickley Hill' (1981) 76 *Current Archaeology* 145–7
Guido Donini and B Ford Jr tr *Isidore of Seville's History of the Kings of the Goths, Vandals and Suevi* Leiden, Brill 1966
DC Douglas *William the Conqueror: The Norman Impact upon England* London, Eyre and Spottiswoode 1964
LJ Downer *Leges Henrici Primi* Oxford, Oxford UP 1972
William Dugdale *Monasticon Anglicanum* London, Longman 1817–30
DN Dumville 'Gildas and Maegwin: Problems of Dating' in Lapidge and Dumville 51–84
— 'The Terminology of Overkingship in Early Anglo-Saxon England' in Hines *The Anglo-Saxons* 345–73
AJ Dunkin *Corpus Juris Cantici: The Dooms, or the Saxon Laws of Kent* privately printed, np nd [173?]

E

Eadmer see M Rule
John Earle *A Handbook to the Land-Charters and Other Saxonic Documents* Oxford, Clarendon P 1888
KA Eckhardt *Gesetze der Angelsachsen 601–925* Göttingen, Musterschmidt 1958
— *Pactus Legis Salicae* and *Lex Salica* in *Monumenta Germaniae Historica, Legum Sectio I: Leges Nationum Germanicarum* IV 1 and 2 Hanover 1962, 1969
HJ Edwards *Caesar Gallic War* London, Heinemann and Boston, Harvard UP Loeb Classical Library 1917
Rudolphus Ehwald ed *Aldhelmi Opera* in *Monumenta Germaniae Historica: Scriptores* Berlin 4 vols 1913–19
Alvar Ellegård and Gunilla Åkerström-Hougen *Rome and the North* Jonsered, Paul Åströms 1996
Henry Ellis *A General Introduction to Domesday Book* London, British Museum 2 vols 1833, repr London, Frederick Muller 1971
G Eogan *Knowth and the Passage Tombs of Ireland* London, Thames and Hudson 1986

Jeremy Evans 'From the End of Roman Britain to the "Celtic West"' (1990) 9 *Oxford Journal of Archaeology* 91–103

MP Evison 'All in the Genes? Evaluating the Biological Evidence' in Hadley and Richards 277–94

F

Janet Fairweather tr *Liber Eliensis: A History of the Isle of Ely from the Seventh to the Twelfth Century, Compiled by a Monk of Ely in the Twelfth Century* Woodbridge, Boydell 2004

Rosamund Faith *The English Peasantry and the Growth of Lordship* London, Leicester UP 1997

Sally Falk Moore *Law as Process: An Anthropological Approach* London, Routledge and Kegan Paul 1978

Steven Fanning and BS Bachrach ed and tr *The Annals of Flodoard of Rheims, 919–966* Plymouth, Broadview P 2004

Neil Faulkner *The Decline and Fall of Roman Britain* Stroud, Tempus 2004
— 'The Case for the Dark Ages' in Collins and Gerrard

Markku Filppula, Juhani Klemola and Heli Pitkänen eds *The Celtic Roots of English* Joensuu, U of Joensuu Faculty of Humanities 2002
— 'Early Contacts Between English and the Celtic Languages' in Filppula, Klemola and Pitkänen 1–26

RO Fink *Roman Military Records on Papyrus* Cleveland, Ohio, Case Western Reserve UP for American Philological Association 1971

Katherine Fischer Drew *The Laws of the Salian Franks* Philadelphia, U of Pennsylvania P 1991

Richard FitzNigel see Charles Johnson; and Arthur Hughes

Magnús Fjalldal *Anglo-Saxon England in Icelandic Medieval Texts* London, U of Toronto P 2005

Robin Fleming *Domesday Book and the Law: Society and Legal Custom in Early Medieval England* Cambridge, Cambridge UP 1998

MT Flanagan and JA Green *Charters and Charter Scholarship in Britain and Ireland* Basingstoke, Palgrave Macmillan 2005

Richard Fletcher *Bloodfeud: Murder and Revenge in Anglo-Saxon England* Oxford, Oxford UP 2003
— *Who's Who in British History: Roman Britain and Anglo-Saxon England 55BC–AD1066* London, Shepheard-Walwyn 1989

Deanna Forsman 'An Appeal to Rome: Anglo-Saxon Dispute Settlement, 800–810' (2003) 6 *The Heroic Age* at www.heroicage.org/issues/6/forsman.html

Paul Fouracre ed *The New Cambridge Medieval History* I Cambridge, Cambridge UP 2004
— '*Placita* and the Settlement of Disputes in Later Merovingian Francia' in Davies and Fouracre 23–43
— 'Procedure and Practice in the Settlement of Disputes' in Davies and Fouracre 214–28

EA Freeman *The History of the Norman Conquest of England, its Causes and its Results* Oxford, Clarendon P 6 vols 1870
— *Old English History for Children* London, Macmillan 1869, reprint Whitefish, MT, Kessinger 2007
— *The Reign of William Rufus and the Accession of Henry the First* Oxford, Clarendon P 2 vols 1882

Sheppard Frere *Britannia: A History of Roman Britain* London, Pimlico 3rd edn 1991

G

Emmanuel Gaillard and John Savage eds *Fouchard Gaillard Goldman on International Commercial Arbitration* Amsterdam, Wolters Kluwer 1999

VH Galbraith *Domesday Book: Its Place in Administrative History* Oxford, Oxford UP 1974

Clive Gamble *The Palaeololithic Societies of Europe* Cambridge, Cambridge UP 1999

GN Garmonsway *The Anglo-Saxon Chronicle* London, Dent 1953

George Garnett '*Franci et Angli*: The Legal Distinctions Between Peoples After the Conquest' (1985) 7 *Anglo-Norman Studies* 109–37

— and John Hudson eds *Law and Government in Medieval England: Essays in Honour of Sir James Holt* Cambridge, Cambridge UP 1994

PJ Geary 'Extra-Judicial Means of Conflict Resolution' in *La Giustizia Nell'Alto Medioevo (Secoli V–VIII)* Spoleto, CISAM 1994 569–601, discussion 603–5

— *Phantoms of Remembrance: Memory and Oblivion at the End of the Millennium* Princeton, Princeton UP 1994

M Gelling 'Why Aren't We Speaking Welsh' (1993) 6 *Anglo-Saxon Studies in Archaeology and History* 51–6

JA Giles *Beati Lanfranci Archiepiscopi Cantuariensis Opera Quae Supersunt Omnia Nunc Primum in Anglia e Codicibus Manuscriptis Auctius et Emendatius Edidit*, Oxford, Parker 2 vols 1844

JP Gillam 'Roman and Native: AD122–197' in Richmond *Roman and Native* 60–90

Pierre-Roland Giot, Philippe Guigon and Bernard Merdrignac *The British Settlement of Brittany: The First Bretons in Armorica* Stroud, Tempus 2003

Julius Goebel Jr *Felony and Misdemeanour: A Study in the History of Criminal Law* Philadelphia, U of Pennsylvania P 1937, reprint 1976

Walter Goffart 'The *Historia Ecclesiastica*: Bede's Agenda and Ours' (1990) 2 *Haskins Society Journal* 29–45

CW Goodwin *The Anglo-Saxon Version of the Life of Saint Guthlac, Hermit of Crowland* London, Russell Smith 1848

Piotr Górecki 'A View from a Distance' (2003) 21 *Law and History Review* 367–76

Antonia Gramsden *Historical Writing in England c500 to c1307* London, Routledge and Kegan Paul 1974

RJS Grant *Laurence Nowell, William Lambarde, and the Laws of the Anglo-Saxons* Amsterdam, Rodopi 1996

AS Gratwick '*Latinitas Brittanica*: Was British Latin Archaic?' in Brooks ed *Latin and the Vernacular* 1–79

MJ Green ed *The Celtic World* London, Routledge 1995

D Greene 'Some Linguistic Evidence relating to the British Church' in MW Barley and RPC Hanson *Christianity in Britain 300–700* Leicester, Leicester UP 1968 75–86

Mechthild Gretsch 'The Language of the Fonthill Letter' (1994) 23 *Anglo-Saxon England* 57–102

Bill Griffiths *An Introduction to Early English Law* Hockwold-cum-Wilton, Anglo-Saxon Books 1995

Martin Grimmer 'Britons in Early Wessex: the Evidence of the Law Code of Ine' in Higham ed *Britons in Anglo-Saxon England* 102–14

OR Gurney *The Middle Babylonian Legal and Economic Texts from Ur* Oxford, British School of Archaeology in Iraq 1993

SL Guterman *From Personal to Territorial Law: Aspects of the History and Structure of the Western Legal-Constitutional Tradition* New Jersey, Scarecrow 1972

H

DM Hadley *The Northern Danelaw: Its Social Structure, 800–1100* Leicester, Leicester UP 2000
— and JD Richards eds *Cultures in Contact: Scandinavian Settlement in England in the Ninth and Tenth Centuries* Turnhout, Brepols 2002
Heinrich Härke 'Early Anglo-Saxon Social Structure' in Hines *The Anglo-Saxons* 125–70
— 'Invisible Britons, Gallo-Romans and Russians: Perspectives on Culture Change' in Higham ed *Britons in Anglo-Saxon England* 57–67
FE Halliday *A Concise History of England from Stonehenge to the Atomic Age* London, Thames and Hudson 1964
Alan Harding *Medieval Law and the Foundations of the State* Oxford, Oxford UP 2002
FE Harmer ed *Anglo-Saxon Writs* Stamford, Paul Watkins 2nd edn 1989
— *Select English Historical Documents of the Ninth and Tenth Centuries* Cambridge, Cambridge UP 1914
MJ Harper *The History of Britain Revealed* London, Nathan Carmody 2002
Jill Harries and Ian Wood *The Theodosian Code* Ithaca NY, Cornell UP 1993
PDA Harvey 'La Coutume dans la Vie Rurale Anglaise au Moyen Age' in Mireille Mousnier and Jacques Poumarède *La Coutume au Village dans l'Europe Médiéval et Moderne* Toulouse, Presses Universitaires de Mirail 2001 61–72
CH Haskins 'The Norman "Consuetudines et Justicie" of William the Conqueror' (1908) 23 *English Historical Review* 502–8
Einar Haugen *The Scandinavian Languages* London, Faber 1976
Christine Haughton and Dominic Powlesland *West Heslerton: The Anglian Cemetery* Yedingham, Landscape Research Centre 1999
F [= Francis] Haverfield (revd George Macdonald) *The Romanization of Britain* Oxford, Clarendon P 1922
— *The Roman Occupation of Britain* (revd George Macdonald) Oxford, Clarendon P 1924
Jacquetta Hawkes *Dawn of the Gods* New York, Random House 1968
Hiroshi Hayashi *Essays in Anglo-Saxon Law* Tokyo, privately printed, 2 vols 1990, 1992
HD Hazeltine 'The Laws of the Anglo-Saxons' (1913) 29 *Law Quarterly Review* 387–98
Hans Hecht ed *Ubersetzung der Dialoge Gregors des Grossen* Leipzig, Wigand's Verlag 1900
RH Helmholz *The Ius Commune in England: Four Studies* Oxford, Oxford UP 2001
— *The Oxford History of the Laws of England I: The Canon Law and Ecclesiastical Jurisdiction from 597 to the 1640s* Oxford, Oxford UP 2004
Martin Henig *The Heirs of King Verica: Culture and Politics in Roman Britain* Stroud, Tempus 2002
— 'Remaining Roman in Britain AD300–700: the Evidence of Portable Art' in Collins and Gerrard 2004
— and Paul Booth *Roman Oxfordshire* Stroud, Sutton 2000
Don Henson *The Origins of the Anglo-Saxons* Hockwold-cum-Wilton, Anglo-Saxon Books 2006

Hesiod *Works and Days* see ML West

Nicholas [= NJ =Nick] Higham 'The Anglo-Saxon/British Interface: History and Ideology' in Filppula, Klemola and Pitkänen 29–46

— ed *Britons in Anglo-Saxon England* Woodbridge, Boydell 2007

— 'Britons in Anglo-Saxon England: an Introduction' in Higham ed *Britons in Anglo-Saxon England* 1–15

— *The Death of Anglo-Saxon England* Stroud, Sutton 1997

— 'Historical Narrative as Cultural Politics: Rome, "British-ness" and "English-ness"' in Higham ed *Britons in Anglo-Saxon England* 68–79

— *Rome, Britain and the Anglo-Saxons* London, Seaby 1992

Catherine Hills 'Anglo-Saxon Attitudes' in Higham ed *Britons in Anglo-Saxon England* 16–26

— *The Origins of the English* London, Duckworth 2003

John Hines ed *The Anglo-Saxons from the Migration Period to the Eighth Century: an Ethnographic Perspective* Woodbridge, Boydell 1997

— 'Philology, Archaeology and the *Adventus Saxonum vel Anglorum*' in Bammesberger and Wollman 17–36

— 'Society, Community and Identity' in Charles-Edwards *After Rome* 61–101

FR Hoare *Constantius: The Life of St Germanus* in FR Hoare ed *The Western Fathers* London, Sheed and Ward 1954

LT Hobhouse, GC Wheeler and Morris Ginsburg *The Material Culture and Social Institutions of the Simpler Peoples* London, Routledge and Kegan Paul reprint with new introduction 1965

RH Hodgkin *A History of the Anglo-Saxons* London, Oxford UP 3rd edn 1952

A Hofmeister ed *Vita Sancti Lebvini Antiqua* in *Monumenta Germaniae Historica: Scriptores* XXX 2 Hanover 1934

WS Holdsworth *A History of English Law* London, Methuen 17 vols 1903–72

Leofranc Holford-Strevens *Aulus Gellius: An Antonine Scholar and his Achievement* Oxford, Oxford UP 2003

JA Holm *Pidgins and Creoles: Theory and Structure* Cambridge, Cambridge UP 1988

JC Holt ed *Domesday Studies* Woodbridge, Boydell and Brewer 1987

— '1086' in Holt *Domesday Studies* 41–64

Homer *Iliad* see AT Murray

Homer *Odyssey* see AT Murray

Tony Honoré 'Roman Law AD200–400: From Cosmopolis to Rechstaat?' in Simon Swain and Mark Edwards *Approaching Late Antiquity: The Transformation from Early to Late Empire* Oxford, Oxford UP 2003 109–32

ABE Hood ed *St Patrick: His Writings and Muirchu's Life* London, Phillimore 1978

Della Hooke 'The Anglo-Saxons in England in the Seventh and Eighth Centuries: Location in Space' in Hines *The Anglo-Saxons* 65–99

Brian Hope-Taylor *Yeavering: An Anglo-British Centre of Early Northumbria* London, HMSO 1977

DR [= David] Howlett *The Celtic Latin Tradition of Biblical Style* Dublin, Four Courts P 1995

— *The English Origins of Old French Literature* Dublin, Four Courts P 1996

— *Sealed from Within: Self-Authenticating Insular Charters* Dublin, Four Courts P 1999

John Hudson *The Formation of the English Common Law: Law and Society in England from the Norman Conquest to Magna Carta* London, Longman 1996

— ed and tr *Historie Ecclesie Abbendonensis: The History of the Church of Abingdon* Oxford, Clarendon P vol I 2007, vol II 2002
— ed *The History of English Law: Centenary Essays on 'Pollock and Maitland'* Oxford, Oxford UP Proceedings of the British Academy 89 1996
— 'La Interpretación de Disputas y Resoluciones: el Caso Inglés, 1066–1135' (1997) 17 *Hispania* 885–916
— *Land, Law and Lordship in Anglo-Norman England* Oxford, Clarendon P 1994
— 'Maitland and the Anglo-Norman Law' in Hudson *History of English Law* 21–46
Arthur Hughes, CG Crump and C [= Charles] Johnson *De Necessariis Observantiis Scaccarii Dialogus Commonly called Dialogus de Scaccario* Oxford, Clarendon P 1902
Gwilym Hughes ed *The Lockington Gold Hoard: An Early Bronze Age Barrow Cemetery at Lockington, Leicestershire* Oxford, Oxbow Books 2000
Peter Hunter Blair *Anglo-Saxon England* Cambridge. Cambridge UP 1977 reprinted London, Folio Society 1996
— *Roman Britain and Early England 55BC–AD871* London, Sphere 3rd impn 1974
PR [= Paul] Hyams 'The Common Law and the French Connection' 1981 *Proceedings of the Battle Conference* 77–92 and notes 196–202
— 'Feud in Medieval England' (1991) 3 *Haskins Society Journal* 1–21
— 'Norms and Legal Argument Before 1150' in Lewis and Lobban 41–61
— *Rancor and Reconciliation in Medieval England* New York, Cornell UP 2003
— 'Trial by Ordeal: the Key to Proof in the Early Common Law' in MS Arnold *On the Laws* 90–126

I

Isidore *Historia Gothorum* in *Monumenta Germaniae Historica (Auctores Antiquissimi)* IX 281 Berlin, 1877–1919 and see Donini

J

John Jackson *Tacitus Annals 13–16* London, Heinemann and Boston, Harvard UP Loeb Classical Library 1937
Kenneth Jackson 'The British Language during the Period of the English Settlements' in NK Chadwick ed *Studies in Early British History* Cambridge, Cambridge UP 1959 61–82
— *Language and History in Early Britain* Edinburgh, Edinburgh UP 1953
Edward James '*Beati Pacifici*: Bishops and the Law in Sixth-Century Gaul' in Bossy 25–46
— *Britain in the First Millennium* London, Arnold 2001
— 'The Origins of Barbarian Kingdoms: The Continental Evidence' in Bassett 40–52
MR James *Two Ancient English Scholars* Glasgow, Glasgow UP 1931 13–14
Charles Jarrosson *La Notion d'Arbitrage* Paris, LGDJ 1987
Edward Jenks 'The Development of Teutonic Law' in *Select Essays in Anglo-American Legal History* 3 vols London, Wildy reprint 1968 I 34–87
Sverker Johansson *Origins of Language – Constraints on Hypotheses* Amsterdam, Benjamins 2005
Eric John *Orbis Britanniae* London, Leicester UP 1966

Charles Johnson ed and tr with corrections by FEL Carter and DE Greenway *Dialogus de Scaccario: The Course of the Exchequer by Richard, Fitz Nigel* Oxford, Clarendon P 1983

RC Johnston 'On Scanning Anglo-Norman Verse' (1982) 5 *Anglo-Norman Studies* 153–64

JEA Jolliffe *The Constitutional History of Medieval England* London, Black 1937
— 'The Era of the Folk in English History' in *Oxford Essays in Medieval History Presented to HE Salter* Oxford, Oxford UP 1934 1–32

HL Jones *Strabo: Geography* London, Heinemann and Boston, Harvard UP Loeb Classical Library 2 vols 1924, 1925

ME Jones *The End of Roman Britain* Ithaca NY, Cornell UP 1996
— 'The Legacy of Roman Law in Post-Roman Britain' in Mathison 52–67
— 'St Germanus and the *Adventus Saxonum*' (1990) 2 *Haskins Society Journal* 1–11

Juvenal *Satires* see GG Ramsay; JEB Mayor

K

Susan Kelly 'Anglo-Saxon Lay Society and the Written Word' in McKitterick *Uses of Literacy* 36–62

JM Kemble *Codex Diplomaticus Aevi Saxonici* London, English Historical Society 6 vols 1839–48
— *The Saxons in England* London, Quaritch 2 vols 2nd edn 1876

AG Kennedy 'Cnut's Law Code of 1018' (1982) 11 *Anglo-Saxon England* 57–81
— 'Disputes About *Bocland*: the Forum for their Adjudication' (1982) 14 *Anglo-Saxon England* 175–95
— 'Law and Litigation in the *Libellus Aethelwoldi Episcopi*' (1995) 24 *Anglo-Saxon England* 131–83

F Kern *Kingship and Law in the Middle Ages* Oxford, Blackwell 1948

Soazick Kerneis 'L'Ancienne Loi des Bretons d'Armorique: Contribution à l'Étude du Droit Vulgare' (1995) 2 *Revue Historique du Droit Français et Étranger* 175–99

Simon [=SD] Keynes *Anglo-Saxon History: A Select Bibliography* www.wmich. edu/medieval/rawl
— 'Cnut's Earls' in AR Rumble ed *The Defence of Wessex: The Burghal Hidage and Anglo-Saxon Fortifications* Manchester, Manchester UP 1996 43–88
— 'Crime and Punishment in the Reign of King Aethelred the Unready' in Ian Wood and N Lund eds *People and Places in Northern Europe: Essays in Honour of Peter Hayes Sawyer* Woodbridge, Boydell 1991
— 'England 900–1016' in Reuter *The New Cambridge Medieval History* III 456–84
— 'The Fonthill Letter' in Korhammer 53–97
— 'Royal Government and the Written Word in Late Anglo-Saxon England' in McKitterick *Uses of Literacy* 226–57
— and Michael Lapidge tr *Alfred the Great: Asser's Life of King Alfred and Other Contemporary Sources* Harmondsworth, Penguin 1983

David Keys 'Erotic Ring Sheds Light on Slave Queen' *BBC History* July 2003 8

DA Kibbee *For to Speke Frenche Trewely: The French Language in England 1000–1600, its Status Description and Instruction* Amsterdam, Benjamins 1991

Edmund King 'Dispute Settlement in Anglo-Norman England' (1991) 14 *Anglo-Norman Studies* 115–30.

DP Kirby *The Earliest English Kings* London, Unwin Hyman 1991

Nikola Köpke and Jörg Baten 'The Biological Standard of Living in Europe During the Last Two Millennia' (2005) 9 *European Review of Economic History* 61–95

Michael Korhammer ed *Words, Texts and Manuscripts: Studies in Anglo-Saxon Culture Presented to Helmutt Gneuss on the Occasion of his 65th Birthday* Cambridge, Brewer 1992

GP Krapp and E van Kirk Dobbie eds *The Exeter Book* New York, Columbia UP 1936

Adam Kuper *The Reinvention of Primitive Society: Transformations of a Myth* London, Routledge 2005

Kurt von S Kynell *Saxon and Medieval Antecedents of the English Common Law* Lewiston NY, Studies in British History 2000

L

Jennifer Laing *Art and Society in Roman Britain* Stroud, Sutton 1997

Jules Lair ed *Dudo: De Moribus et Actis Primorum Normanniae Ducum* (Caen) Paris, Maisonneuve 1865

Peter Landau 'The Development of Law' in Luscombe and Riley-Smith *New Cambridge Medieval History* IV Pt1 113–47

Michael Lapidge 'Gildas's Education and the Latin Culture of Sub-Roman Britain' in Lapidge and Dumville 27–50

— and David Dumville *Gildas: New Approaches* London, Boydell 1984

— and Michael Herren tr *Aldhelm: The Prose Works* Cambridge, Brewer 1979

M [=Michael] Lapidge, J Blair, S Keynes and D Scragg *The Blackwell Encyclopedia of Anglo-Saxon England* Oxford, Blackwell 1999

LM Larson *The Earliest Norwegian Laws* New York, Columbia UP 1935

Roger Lass ed *Approaches to Historical Linguistics: An Anthology* New York, Holt, Rinehart and Winston 1969

RE Latham *Revised Medieval Latin Word-List from British and Irish Sources with Supplement* Oxford, Oxford UP 1965

Peter Lawrence *The Garia: An Ethnography of a Traditional Cosmic System in Papua New Guinea* Melbourne, Melbourne UP 1984

MK Lawson 'Archbishop Wulfstan and the Homiletic Element in the Laws of Ethelred and Cnut' (1992) 107 *English Historical Review* 565–86

— *Cnut: England's Viking King* Stroud, Tempus 2nd edn 2004

AF Leach *Visitations and Memorials of Southwell Minster* London, Camden Society 1891

Anne Lefebvre-Teillard 'L'Arbitrage en Droit Canonique' (2006) *Revue de l'Arbitrage* 5–34

Rodney Legg *Romans in Britain* London, Book Club Associates 1983

MD Legge 'Anglo-Norman as a Spoken Language' (1979) 2 *Anglo-Norman Studies* 108–17

— *Anglo-Norman Literature and its Background* Oxford, Clarendon P 1963

— 'La Précocité de la Littérature Anglo-Normande' (1965) 8 *Cahiers de Civilisation Mediévale* no.3–4 327–49

WW Lehman 'The First English Law' (1985) 6 *Journal of Legal History* 1–32

Patrizia Lendinara 'The Kentish Laws' in Hines *The Anglo-Saxons* 211–43

Andrew Lewis and Michael Lobban eds *Law and History* Oxford, Oxford UP (6 Current Legal Issues 2003) 2004

CP Lewis 'The French in England Before the Norman Conquest' (1994) 17 *Anglo-Norman Studies* 123–44

— 'Welsh Territories and Welsh Identities in Late Anglo-Saxon England' in Higham ed *Britons in Anglo-Saxon England* 130–43

Felix Liebermann *Die Gesetze der Angelsachsen* Halle, Niemeyer 3 vols 1903

— 'King Alfred and the Mosaic Law' (1908–10) 6 *Transactions of the Jewish Historical Society of England* 21–31

— *Quadripartitus: ein Englisches Rechtsbuch von 1114* Halle, Niemeyer 1892

— *Über die Leges Edwardi Confessoris* Halle, Niemeyer 1896

Detlef Liebs *Römischer Jurisprudenz in Africa* Berlin, Duncker and Humblot 2005

— *Römischer Jurisprudenz in Gallien (2 bis 8 Jahrhundert)* Berlin, Duncker and Humblot 2002

Jack Lindsay *The Normans and their World* London, Purnell 1974

Peter Linehan and JL Nelson *The Medieval World* London, Routledge 2002

Andrew Lintott *Imperium Romanum: Politics and Administration* London, Routledge 1993

Joan Liversidge *Britain in the Roman Empire* New York, Praeger 1968

Michael Lobban 'Introduction: the Tools and the Tasks of the Legal Historian' in Lewis and Lobban 1–32

FD Logan *The Vikings in History* London, Routledge 3rd edn 2005

JH Looijenga 'Runes Around the North Sea and on the Continent AD150–700: Texts and Contexts' Groningen http://dissertations.ub.rug.nl/FILES/faculties/arts/1997/j.h.looijenga/titelinh.pdf (doctoral thesis 1997)

Henry [= Henry] Loyn *Anglo-Saxon England and the Norman Conquest* London, Longmans 1962

— 'The Beyond of Domesday Book' in JC Holt *Domesday Studies* 1–13

— 'Kinship in Anglo-Saxon England' (1974) 3 *Anglo-Saxon England* 197–209

— *The Vikings in Britain* Oxford, Blackwells 1994

Sam Lucy *The Anglo-Saxon Way of Death: Burial Rites in Ancient England* London, Sutton 2000

David Luscombe and Jonathan Riley-Smith *New Cambridge Medieval History* IV Pts1 and 2 Cambridge, Cambridge UP 2004

M

Michael McCormick *Origins of the European Economy: Communications and Commerce AD300–900* Cambridge, Cambridge UP 2001

CH McIlwain *The High Court of Parliament and its Supremacy: An Historical Essay on the Boundaries between Legislation and Adjudication in England* New Haven CT, Yale UP 1910

Robin McKie *Face of Britain* London, Simon and Schuster 2006

Rosamond McKitterick ed *The New Cambridge Medieval History* II Cambridge, Cambridge UP 1995

— ed *The Uses of Literacy in Early Medieval Europe* Cambridge, Cambridge UP 1990

FW Maitland 'The Body Politic' in HAL Fisher ed *The Collected Papers of Frederic William Maitland* Cambridge, Cambridge UP 3vols 1911 reprinted Abingdon, Professional Books 1983

— *Bracton's Note Book* London, Clay 3 vols 1887

— *The Constitutional History of England* Cambridge, Cambridge UP 1919

— *Domesday Book and Beyond* Cambridge, Cambridge UP 1897

— 'The Laws of the Anglo-Saxons' (1904) 200 *Quarterly Review* 139–57, reprinted in HAL Fisher *Collected Papers* I 447–73

— 'A Prologue to the History of English Law' in *Select Essays in Anglo-American Legal History* 3vols London, Wildy reprint 1968 I 7–33

Bronislaw Malinowski, *Argonauts of the Western Pacific* London, Routledge and Kegan Paul 1922

JC Mann 'Spoken Latin in Britain as Evidenced in Inscriptions' (1971) 2 *Britannia* 218–24

Nanno Marinatos *Minoan Religion: Ritual, Image and Symbol* Columbia, U of South Carolina P 1944

Fabrizio Marrella and Andrea Mozzato *Alle Origini dell'Arbitrato Commerciale Internazionale: L'Arbitrato a Venezia tra Medioevo ed Età Moderna* Padua, CEDAM 2001

Jane Martindale 'Between Law and Politics: The Judicial Duel under the Angevin Kings (Mid-Twelfth Century to 1204)' in Stafford, Nelson and Martindale 116–49

— '"His Special Friend?" The Settlement of Disputes and Political Power in the Kingdom of the French (Tenth to Mid-Twelfth Century)' (1995) *Transactions of the Royal Historical Society* 6th series V

I Martinez and 9 others 'Auditory Capacities in Middle Pleistocene Humans from the Sierra de Atapuerca in Spain' (2004) 101 *Publications of the Academy of the Natural Sciences of the United States of America* 9976–81

Gino Masi *L'Udienza Vescovile nelle Cause Laiche da Costantino ai Franchi: Spunti ed Orientamenti* Modena, Società Tipografica Modenese 1939

J Maskell 'Who Were the Belgae?' *Notes and Queries* 7th Series 3 July 1886, 2–3

RW Mathison ed *Law, Society and Authority in Late Antiquity* Oxford, Oxford UP 2001

David Mattingly *An Imperial Possession: Britain in the Roman Empire* London, Allen Lane 2006

JE Matzke *Lois de Guillaume le Conquérant en Français et en Latin* Paris, Picard 1899

TF Mayer ed *Thomas Starkey: A Dialogue between Pole and Lupset* London, Royal Historical Society Camden Fourth Series 37 1989

JEB Mayor ed *Thirteen Satires of Juvenal* Cambridge, Macmillan 1853

Henry Mayr-Harting and RI Moore *Studies in Medieval History Presented to RHC Davis* London, Hambledon 1985

Rob Meens 'Sanctuary, Penance and Dispute Settlement under Charlemagne: the Conflict between Alcuin and Theodulf of Orléans over a Sinful Cleric' (2007) 82 *Speculum* 277–300

David Mellinkoff *The Language of the Law* New York, Little Brown 1963

LE Menger *The Anglo-Norman Dialect* New York, Columbia UP 1904

Fritz Mezger 'Self-Judgment in Old English Documents' (1952) 67 *Modern Language Notes* 106–9

David Miles *The Tribes of Britain* London, Orion revised paperback edn 2006

WI Miller 'Avoiding Legal Judgment: the Submission of Disputes to Arbitration in Medieval Iceland' (1984) 28 *American Journal of Legal History* 95–134

— *Bloodtaking and Peacemaking: Feud, Law, and Society in Saga Iceland* Chicago, U of Chicago P 1990

Martin Millett *Roman Britain* London, Batsford new edn 2005

— *The Romanization of Britain: An Essay in Archaeological Interpretation* Cambridge, Cambridge UP 1990

SFC Milsom *Historical Foundations of the Common Law* London, Butterworths 2nd edn 1981

JEG de Montmorency 'Danish Influence on English Law and Character' (1924) 40 *Law Quarterly Review* 324–43

KO Morgan ed *The Oxford History of Britain* Oxford, Oxford UP 1988

Colin Morris '*Judicium Dei*: the Social and Political Significance of the Ordeal in the Eleventh Century' (1975) 12 *Studies in Church History* 95–112

John Morris ed and tr *Nennius: British History and the Welsh Annals* London, Phillimore 1980

— (revd Sarah Macready) *Londinium: London in the Roman Empire* London, Phoenix 2005

MA Morse *How the Celts Came to Britain: Druids, Ancient Skulls and the Birth of Archaeology* Stroud, Tempus 2004

Mia Münster-Swendsen 'Setting Things Straight: Law, Justice and Ethics in the *Orationes* of Lawrence of Durham' (2004) 27 *Anglo-Norman Studies* 151–68

Peter Murphy 'The Anglo-Saxon Landscape and Rural Economy: Some Results from Sites in East Anglia and Essex' in J Rackham ed *Environment and Economy in Anglo-Saxon England* York, Council for British Archaeology Research Report 89 1994

AC Murray ed *After Rome's Fall: Essays Presented to Walter Goffart* Toronto, U of Toronto P 1998

— *Germanic Kinship Structure: Studies in Law and Society in Antiquity and the Early Middle Ages* Toronto, Pontifical Institute of Mediaeval Studies 1983

AT Murray tr *Homer Iliad* London, Heinemann and Boston, Harvard UP Loeb Classical Library 2 vols 1924, 1925

AT Murray tr *Homer Odyssey* London, Heinemann and Boston, Harvard UP Loeb Classical Library 2 vols 1919

DE Murray 'Arbitration in the Anglo-Saxon and Norman Periods' (1961) *Arbitration Journal* 193–208

N

Stuart Needham 'The Gold and Copper Metalwork' in Gwilym Hughes *The Lockington Gold Hoard* 23–47

Hermann Nehlsen 'Aktualität und Effektivität Germanischer Rechtsaufzeichnungen' in Peter Classen ed *Recht und Schrift im Mittelalter* (23 Vorträge und Forschungen) Sigmaringen, Thorbecke 1977 449–502

K Nehlsen-Von Stryk *Die Boni Homines des Frühen Mittelalters* Berlin, Freiburger Rechtsgeschichtliche Abhandlungen (new series) 2 1981

Janet Nelson 'Dispute Settlement in Carolingian West Francia' in Davies and Fouracre 45–64

— 'Our Forefathers? Tribes, Peoples and Nations in the Historiography of the Age of Migration' in Murray *After Rome's Fall* 17–36

KS Newman *Law and Economic Organization: A Comparative Study of Pre-Industrial Societies* Cambridge, Cambridge UP 1983

F Noble (Margaret Gelling ed) *Offa's Dyke Reviewed* London, British Archaeological Reports, British Series 114 1983

Fredrick Nzwili 'Stories of Transformation' in *North Rift, Kenya: Changing a Volatile Region* September 21, 2005, www.oikumene.org/en/news/news-management/all-news-english

O

TP Oakley *English Penitential Discipline and Anglo-Saxon Law in Their Joint Influence* New York, Columbia UP 1923

BR [=Bruce] O'Brien *God's Peace and King's Peace: The Laws of Edward the Confessor* Philadelphia, U of Pennsylvania P 1999

— 'The *Instituta Canuti* and the Translation of English Law' (2002) 25 *Anglo-Norman Studies* 177–97

Bengt Odenstedt 'The Runic Inscription on the Undley Bracteate' (2000) 72 *Studia Neophilologica* 113–20

RM Ogilvie and IA Richmond eds *Tacitus: Agricola* Oxford, Clarendon P 1967

TJ Oleson *The Witenagemot in the Reign of Edward the Confessor: A Study in the Constitutional History of Eleventh-Century England* London, Oxford UP 1955

Lisi Oliver *The Beginnings of English Law* Toronto, U of Toronto P 2002

— 'The Language of the Early English Laws' PhD thesis Harvard U 1995, Ann Arbor U Microfilms International 1995

Stephen Oppenheimer 'Myths of British Ancestry' (2006) 127 *Prospect Magazine* http://www.prospect-magazine.co.uk/printarticle.php?id=7817

Stephen Oppenheimer *The Origins of the British: a Genetic Detective Story* London, Constable 2006

Bruno Oppetit *Théorie de l'Arbitrage* Paris, PUF 1998

Andy Orchard 'Latin and the Vernacular Languages: the Creation of a Bilingual Textual Culture' in Charles-Edwards *After Rome* 191–219

Ordericus Vitalis *The Ecclesiastical History of England and Normandy, Translated with Notes and the Introduction of Guizot by Thomas Forester MA* London, Bohn 4 vols 1851–56

Oxford Dictionary of National Biography: www.oxforddnb.com.catalogue.ulrls.lon.ac.uk

P

OJ Padel 'Place-Names and the Saxon Conquest of Devon and Cornwall' in Higham ed *Britons in Anglo-Saxon England* 215–30

DM Palliser ed *The Cambridge Urban History of Britain* I Cambridge, Cambridge UP 2000

Aliki Pantos '*In Medle odde an Đinge*: the Old English Vocabulary of Assembly' in Pantos and Semple 181–201

— 'The Location and Form of Anglo-Saxon Assembly-Places: Some Moot Points' in Pantos and Semple 155–80

— and Sarah Semple *Assembly Places and Practices in Medieval Europe* Dublin, Four Courts P 2004

SA Parfitt and 17 others 'The Earliest Record of Human Activity in Northern Europe' (2005) 483 *Nature* 1008–12

François Paschoud *Zosime: Histoire Nouvelle* Paris, Société d'Edition Les Belles Lettres 6 parts 1971–89

St Patrick see ABE Hood

Colin Pendleton 'Firstly, Let's Get Rid of Ritual' in Joanna Brück ed *Bronze Age Landscapes: Tradition and Transformation* Oxford, Oxbow 170–8

JG Peristiany 'Law' in *The Institutions of Primitive Society: A Series of Broadcast Talks* Oxford, Blackwell 1967 39–49

Dominic Perring '"Gnosticism" in Fourth Century Britain: The Frampton Mosaics Reconsidered' (2003) 34 *Britannia* 97–128

Lord Peston 'The 1997 Bernstein Colloquium: Arbitration – An Economist's View' (1998) 64 *Arbitration* 19–27

Henry Petrie and John Sharpe *Monumenta Historica Britannica or Materials for the History of Britain from the Earliest Period* I London, HM George IV 1848

JD Pheifer *Old English Glosses in the Épinal-Erfurt Glossary* Oxford, Clarendon P 1974

Stuart Piggott 'Native Economies and the Occupation of North Britain' in IA Richmond *Roman and Native* 1–27

LO Pike *The Public Records and the Constitution: a Lecture...with Plan of Evolution of the Chief Courts and Departments of Government* London, Oxford UP 1907

Mike Pitts *Hengeworld* London, Arrow 2001

— and Mark Roberts *Fairweather Eden: Life in Britain Half a Million Years Ago as Revealed by the Excavations at Boxgrove* London, Century 1997

Plan UK 'A Slice of Life in Tanzania 2007: Togetherness' London, Plan UK 2007, www.plan-uk.org

Pliny *Letters* see Betty Radice

TFT Plucknett *A Concise History of the Common Law* Boston, Little Brown 5th edn 1956, repr Law Book Exchange 2001

— *Early English Legal Literature* Cambridge, Cambridge UP 1958

— *Edward I and Criminal Law* Cambridge, Cambridge UP 1960

JGA Pocock *The Ancient Constitution and the Feudal Law* Cambridge, Cambridge UP 2nd edn 1987

W Pohl 'Ethnic Names and Identities in the British Isles: A Comparative Perspective' in Hines *The Anglo-Saxons* 7–32

Frederick Pollock 'Anglo-Saxon Law' (1893) 8 *English Historical Review* 239–71

— 'English Law Before the Norman Conquest' (1898) 14 *Law Quarterly Review* 291–306 and in *Select Essays in Anglo-American Legal History* 3 vols London, Wildy reprint 1968 I 88–107

Frederick Pollock and Frederic Maitland *The History of English Law Before the Time of Edward I* Cambridge, Cambridge UP 2nd edn 2 vols 1968

MK Pope *Etude sur la Langue de Frère Angier Suivie d'un Glossaire de ses Poèmes* Paris, U of Paris doctoral thesis 1903

— *From Latin to Modern French With Special Consideration of Anglo-Norman: Phonology and Morphology* Manchester, Manchester UP 1934

TW Potter and Catherine Johns *Roman Britain* London, British Museum, new edn 2002

DJ Powlesland 'Early Anglo-Saxon Settlements, Structures, Form and Layout' in Hines *The Anglo-Saxons* 101–24

— 'West Heslerton' (1981) 76 *Current Archaeology* 142–44

David Pratt *The Political Thought of King Alfred the Great* Cambridge, Cambridge UP 2007

Glanville Price *The Languages of Britain* London, Edward Arnold 1984

OH Prior 'Remarques sur l'Anglo-Normand' (1923) 49 *Romania* 1–25

Duncan Probert 'Mapping Early Medieval Language Change in South-West England' in Higham ed *Britons in Anglo-Saxon England* 231–44

Francis Pryor *Britain AD: A Quest for Arthur, England and the Anglo-Saxons* London, Harper Collins 2004

— *Britain BC: Life in Britain and Ireland Before the Romans* London, Harper Perennial 2004

— *Britain in the Middle Ages: An Archaeological History* London, Harper Collins 2006

— 'Invasion, What Invasion?' (2004) 5:9 *BBC History Magazine* 46–8

R

Charles M Radding 'Legal Theory and Practice in Eleventh-Century Italy' (2003) 21 *Law and History Review* 377–82

Betty Radice tr *Pliny: Letters* London, Heinemann and Boston, Harvard UP Loeb Classical Library 2 vols 1969

J Raine ed 'William Ketell's Life of Saint John of Beverley (1170–1180)' in *The Historians of the Church of York and its Archbishops* I, London, Longman Rolls Series LXXI 3 vols 1879

Sarah Rainsford 'The Turkish Peacemaker' *From Our Own Correspondent* BBC Radio 4 11 November 2006, reprinted (2007) 73 *Arbitration* 117–18

GG Ramsay *Juvenal and Persius* London, Heinemann and Boston, Harvard UP Loeb Classical Library 1918

WF Rankine 'Stone Maceheads with Mesolithic Associations from South-Eastern England' (1949) 15 *Proceedings of the Prehistoric Society* 70–6

Hastings Rashdall *The Universities of Europe in the Middle Ages* revd FM Powicke and AB Emden Oxford, Oxford UP 3 vols 1936

Richard Reece *My Roman Britain* Cirencester, Cotswold Studies 1988

Colin Renfrew *Archaeology and Language: The Puzzle of Indo-European Origins* London, Penguin 1987

— 'At the Edge of Knowability: Towards a Prehistory of Language' (2000) 10 *Cambridge Archaeological Journal* 7–34

Timothy Reuter 'Assembly Politics in Western Europe from the Eighth Century to the Twelfth' in Linehan and Nelson 432–50

— ed *The New Cambridge Medieval History* III Cambridge, Cambridge UP 2000

Andrew Reynolds *Later Anglo-Saxon England: Life and Landscape* Stroud, Tempus 1999

JM Reynolds 'Legal and Constitutional Problems' in JS Wacher ed *The Civitas Capitals* 70–5

Susan Reynolds 'The Emergence of Professional Law in the Long Twelfth Century' (2003) 21 *Law and History Review* 347–66

— *Fiefs and Vassals: The Medieval Evidence Reinterpreted* Oxford, Oxford UP 1994

— 'Government and Community' in Luscombe and Riley-Smith *New Cambridge Medieval History* IV Pt 1 86–112

— *Kingdoms and Communities in Western Europe, 900–1300* Oxford, Oxford UP 2nd ed 1997

— 'Medieval Law' in Linehan and Nelson 485–502

— 'Rationality and Collective Judgment in the Law of Western Europe Before the Twelfth Century' (2000) 5 *Quaestiones Medii Aevi Novae* 3–19

— 'Variations in Professionalism' (2003) 21 *Law and History Review* 388–90

JD Richards *Viking Age England* Stroud, Tempus new edn 2004

M Richards, K Smalley, B Sykes and R Hedges 'Archaeology and Genetics: Analysing DNA from Skeletal Remains' (1993) 25 *World Archaeology* 18–28

MP Richards 'The Manuscript Contexts of the Old English Laws: Tradition and Innovation' in PE Szarmach *Studies in Earlier Old English Prose* Albany NY, State U of New York P 1986 171–92

HG Richardson, review of JP Collas and TFT Plucknett *Year Books of Edward II* vols XXIII and XXIV (1954) 70 *Law Quarterly Review* 423–6

— and GO Sayles *Law and Legislation from Aethelberht to Magna Carta* Edinburgh, Edinburgh UP 1966

IA Richmond *Roman Britain* Harmondsworth, Penguin 2nd edn 1963

— 'Roman and Native in the Fourth Century AD and After' in Richmond *Roman and Native* 112–30

— ed *Roman and Native in North Britain* Edinburgh, Nelson 1948

Peter Rickard *A History of the French Language* London, Unwin Hyman 3rd edn 1993

RT Ridley tr *Zosimus: New History*, Sydney, Australian Association for Byzantine Studies 1982

HT Riley ed *Gesta Abbatum Monasterii Sancti Albani a Thoma Walsingham* London, Longman Green 3 vols 1867

TJ Rivers *The Laws of the Alamans and Bavarians* Philadelphia, U of Pennsylvania P 1977

— *The Laws of the Salian and Ripuarian Franks* New York, AMS P 1987

ALF Rivet and Colin Smith *Place Names of Roman Britain* London, Batsford 1979

Simon Roberts 'Changing Modes of Dispute Settlement: an Anthropological Perspective' in *Law and Human Relations* London, Past and Present 1980 1–24 (separately paginated)

— *Order and Dispute: An Introduction to Legal Anthropology* Harmondsworth, Penguin 1979

— and Michael Palmer *Dispute Processes: ADR and the Primary Forms of Decision-Making* Cambridge, Cambridge UP 2nd edn 2005

AJ Robertson ed and tr *Anglo-Saxon Charters* Cambridge, Cambridge UP 1939

— *The Laws of the Kings of England from Edmund to Henry I* Cambridge, Cambridge UP 1925 repr 2 vols Felinfach, Lanerch 2000

Derek Roebuck *Ancient Greek Arbitration* Oxford, HOLO 2000

— *The Background of the Common Law* Hong Kong, Oxford UP 2nd edn 1990

— '"Best to Reconcile": Mediation and Arbitration in the Ancient Greek World' (2000) 66 *Arbitration* 275–87

— 'Bricks Without Straw: Arbitration in Roman Britain' (2007) 23 *Arbitration International* 143–56

— *The Charitable Arbitrator: How to Mediate and Arbitrate in Louis XIV's France* Oxford, HOLO 2002

— 'The Chronology of a Cobweb: Anglo-Norman from 1066–1250' in *City Polytechnic of Hong Kong Language Working Papers* No2, October 1990 1–43

— 'Customary Law before the Conquest' (2006) 68 *Amicus Curiae* November/December 23–32

— *A Miscellany of Disputes* Oxford, HOLO 2000

— 'The Prehistory of Dispute Resolution in England' (2006) 72 *Arbitration* 93–103

— 'Sources for the History of Arbitration' (1998) 14 *Arbitration International* 235–343

— and Bruno de Loynes de Fumichon *Roman Arbitration* Oxford, HOLO 2004

David Roffe *Domesday: the Inquest and the Book* Oxford, Oxford UP 2000

— 'The Making of Domesday Book Reconsidered' (1994) 6 *Haskins Society Journal* 152–66

JC Rolfe *Ammianus Marcellinus* London, Heinemann and Boston, Harvard UP Loeb Classical Library 3 vols 1935–40

William Rothwell general editor *Anglo-Norman Dictionary* A–Z (with Louise Strong) London, Modern Humanities Association 7 fascicles 1977–1992, 2 vols 2nd edn A–C and D–E 2005

M Rule ed *Eadmer: Historia Novorum in Anglia* London, HMSO Rolls Series 1884

AR Rumble ed *The Reign of Cnut* Leicester, Leicester UP 1999

S

Peter Sack 'The Cult of the Eight Foot Yam: Primitive Provocations on Law and Development' in FC Hutley, Eugene Kamenka and Alice Erh-Soon Tay *Law and the Future of Society* Wiesbaden, Steiner 1979 318–33

Peter Salway *The Frontier People of Northern Britain* Cambridge, Cambridge UP 1967

— *Roman Britain* Oxford, Clarendon P 1981

— 'Roman Britain (c55BC–cAD440)' in KO Morgan 1–59

VE Sanchez 'Towards a History of ADR: The Dispute Processing Continuum in Anglo-Saxon England and Today' (1996) 11 *Dispute Resolution* 1–39

Andrew Sargent 'The North-South Divide Revisited: Thoughts on the Character of Roman Britain' (2002) 33 *Britannia* 219–26

Anne Savage *The Anglo-Saxon Chronicles* London, BCA 1983

PH Sawyer *Anglo-Saxon Charters: An Annotated List and Bibliography* London, Royal Historical Society 1968

— 'The Bloodfeud in Fact and Fiction' (1987) 63:2 *Acta Jutlandica* 27–38

— *Textus Roffensis: Rochester Cathedral MS. A.3.5.* (Early English Manuscripts in Facsimile, 7 and 11) Copenhagen, Rosekilde and Bagger 2 vols 1957, 1962

PH Sawyer and IN Wood eds *Early Medieval Kingship* Leeds, Leeds UP 1977

Paul Schaffner 'Britain's *Iudices*' in Lapidge and Dumville 151–5

RJ Schoek 'Early Anglo-Saxon Studies and Legal Scholarship in the Renaissance' (1958) 5 *Studies in the Renaissance* 102–10

Peter Schrijver 'The Rise and Fall of British Latin: Evidence from English and Brittonic' in Filppula, Klemola and Pitkänen 87–110

— 'What Britons Spoke Around 400AD' in Higham ed *Britons in Anglo-Saxon England* 165–71

JR Schwyter *Old English Legal Language: The Lexical Field of Theft* Odense, Odense UP 1996

— 'Syntax and Style in the Anglo-Saxon Law Codes' in Christine Ehler and Ulrich Schaefer eds *Verschriftung und Verschriftlichung: Aspekte des Medienwechsels in Verschiedenen Kulturen und Epochen* Tübingen, Gunter Narr 1998 189–231

Elmar Seebold 'Was ist Jutisch? Was ist Kentish?' in Bammesberger and Wollmann 335–52

— 'Kentish and Old English Texts from Kent' in M Korhammer ed *Words, Texts and Manuscripts: Studies in Anglo-Saxon Culture Presented to Helmut Gneuss* Cambridge, Brewer 1992

Frederic Seebohm *The English Village Community* London, Longmans Green 4th edn 1915

— *Tribal Custom in Anglo-Saxon Law* London, Longmans Green 1902

Sarah Semple 'Locations of Assembly in Early Anglo-Saxon England' in Pantos and Semple 135–54

W Senior 'Romanic Legal Influences' (1924) 40 *Law Quarterly Review* 483–94

— 'Roman Law in England Before Vacarius' (1930) 46 *Law Quarterly Review* 191–206

Richard Sharpe 'Dispute Settlement in Medieval Ireland: A Preliminary Enquiry' in Davies and Fouracre 169–89

— 'The Use of Writs in the Eleventh Century' (2000) 32 *Anglo-Saxon England* 247–91

PVD Shelley *English and French in England 1066–1100* Philadelphia, University of Pennsylvania P 1921

KL Shirley *The Secular Jurisdiction of Monasteries in Anglo-Norman and Angevin England* Woodbridge, Boydell 2004

Ian Short 'Bilingualism in Anglo-Norman England' (1979) 33 *Romance Philology* 476–9

— '*Tam Angli Quam Franci*: Self-Definition in Anglo-Norman England' (1995) 18 *Anglo-Norman Studies* 153–75

— and Brian Merrilees eds *Benedeit: The Anglo-Norman 'Voyage of St Brendan'* Manchester, Manchester UP 1979

AWB Simpson 'The Laws of Ethelbert' in Arnold *On the Laws and Customs of England* 3–15 and in AWB Simpson *Legal Theory and Legal History: Essays on the Common Law* London, Hambledon P 1987 1–17

AJP Sirks *The Theodosian Code: A Study* Friedrichsdorf, Editions du Quatorze Septembre 2007

CA Snyder *An Age of Tyrants: Britain and the Britons AD400–600* London, Sutton 1998

Östen Södergård ed *La Vie d'Edouard le Confesseur: Poème Anglo-Normand du XIIe Siècle* Uppsala, dissertation 1948

R Sohm tr Marcel Thévenin *La Procédure de la Lex Salica* Paris, A Franck 1873

Pernille Sørensen 'A Reassessment of the Jutish Nature of Kent, Southern Hampshire and the Isle of Wight' Oxford U DPhil thesis 2 vols 1999

JW Spargo 'Chaucer's Love-Days' (1940) 15 *Speculum* 36–56

RC Stacey *The Road to Judgement: From Custom to Court in Medieval Ireland and Wales* Philadelphia, Pennsylvania UP 1994

Pauline Stafford 'The Laws of Cnut and the History of Anglo-Saxon Royal Promises' (1982) 10 *Anglo-Saxon England* 173–90

— 'Political Ideas in Late Tenth-Century England: Charters as Evidence' in Stafford, Nelson and Martindale 68–82

— Janet L Nelson and Jane Martindale eds *Law, Laity and Solidarities: Essays in Honour of Susan Reynolds* Manchester, Manchester UP 2001

EG Stanley 'The Administration of Law in Anglo-Saxon England: Ideas Formulated by the Bible, Einhard and Hincmar of Rheims – But No Formal Mirror of Princes' in KE Olsen, A Harbus and Tette Hofstra eds *Germanic Texts and Latin Models: Medieval Reconstructions (Germania Latina 4)* Gröningen, Peeters Bvba 2002 53–71

— 'On the Laws of King Alfred: The End of the Preface and the Beginning of the Laws' in Jane Roberts and JL Nelson with Malcolm Godden *Alfred the Wise: Studies in Honour of Janet Bately on the Occasion of her Sixty-Fifth Birthday* Cambridge, Brewer 1997 211–21

JM Stearns *The Germs and Developments of the Laws of England, Embracing the Anglo-Saxon Laws Extant from the Sixth Century to AD 1066, as Translated into English under the Royal Record Commission of William IV, with the Introduction of the Common Law by the Norman Judges after the Conquest, and its Earlier Proferts in Magna Charta* New York, Banks 1889, repr on demand London, Kessinger 2005

KA Steer 'Roman and Native in North Britain: The Severan Reorganisation' in Richmond *Roman and Native* 112–30

Peter Stein *Legal Institutions: the Development of Dispute Settlement* London, Butterworths 1984

DM Stenton *English Justice Between the Norman Conquest and the Great Charter 1066–1215* London, Allen and Unwin 1965

Frank [= FM] Stenton *Anglo-Saxon England* Oxford, Oxford UP 3rd edn 1971

— *The Latin Charters of the Anglo-Saxon Period* Oxford, Clarendon P 1955

WH Stephenson *Asser's Life of King Alfred together with the Annals of Saint Neots Erroneously Ascribed to Asser* Oxford, Clarendon P new impression 1959

CE Stevens 'A Possible Conflict of Laws in Roman Britain' (1947) 37 *Journal of Roman Studies* 132–4

Strabo see HL Jones

Chris Stringer *Homo Britannicus: The Incredible Story of Human Life in Britain* London, Allen Lane 2006

William Stubbs *The Constitutional History of England in its Origin and Development* Oxford, Clarendon Press 3 vols 1897

Simon Swain and Mark Edwards *Approaching Late Antiquity: The Transformation from Early to Late Empire* Oxford, Oxford UP 2003

Michael Swanton *The Anglo-Saxon Chronicles* London, Phoenix revd paperback edn 2000

Henry Sweet ed *King Alfred's West-Saxon Version of Gregory's Pastoral Care* London, Early English Text Society 2 vols 1871–72 (Original Series 45 and 50)

Brian Sykes *Saxons, Vikings and Celts: The Genetic Roots of Britain and Ireland* New York, Norton 2006; published in England as *Blood of the Isles: Exploring the Genetic Roots of Our Tribal History* London, Corgi 2007

T

Tacitus *Annals* see John Jackson

Tacitus *Agricola* see RM Ogilvie and IA Richmond

Isaac Taylor 'Who Were the Belgae?' *Notes and Queries* 7th Series 3 July 1886 1–2

MG Thomas, MPH Stumpf and Heinrich Härke 'Evidence for an Apartheid-Like Social Structure in Early Anglo-Saxon England' (2006) *Proceedings of the Royal Society B* 1–7

EA Thompson 'Britonia' in Barley and Hanson 201–6

— *The Early Germans* Oxford, Clarendon P 1965

— *St Germanus of Auxerre and the End of Roman Britain* Woodbridge, Boydell 1984

— *Who was Saint Patrick?* Woodbridge, Boydell 1999

— 'Zosimus on the End of Roman Britain' (1956) 30:119 *Antiquity* 163–7

DE Thornton 'Some Welshmen in Domesday Book and Beyond: Aspects of Anglo-Welsh Relations in the Eleventh Century' in Higham ed *Britons in Anglo-Saxon England* 144–64

Benjamin Thorpe *Ancient Laws and Institutes of England* London, Commissioners on the Public Records 1840, reprinted Clark NJ, Law Book Exchange 2003

— *Diplomatarium Anglicum Aevi Saxonici: A Collection of English Charters, from the Reign of King Aethelberht of Kent to that of William the Conqueror* London, Macmillan 1865

RSO Tomlin 'A Five-Acre Wood in Roman Kent' in Joanna Bird, Mark Hassall and Harvey Sheldon eds *Interpreting Roman London: Papers in Memory of Hugh Chapman* Oxford, Oxbow 1996 209–15

— '"The Girl in Question": a New Text from Roman London' (2003) 34 *Britannia* 41–51
— 'A Roman Will from North Wales' (2001) 150 *Archaeologia Cambrensis* 143–56
Roland Torkar *Eine Altenglische Übersetzung von Alcuins de Virtutibus et Vitiis Kap 20* (Texte und Untersuchungen zur Englischen Philologie 7) Munich, Fink 1981
Matthew Townend *Language and History in Viking Age England* Turnhout, Brepols 2002
— ed *Wulfstan, Archbishop of York* Proceedings of the Second Alcuin Conference Turnhout, Brepols 2004
HLC [= Hildegard] Tristram 'Attrition of Inflections in English and Welsh' in Filppula, Klemola and Pitkänen 111–49
— 'Diglossia in Anglo-Saxon England, or What was Spoken Old English Like?' (2004) 40 *Studia Anglica Posnaniensia* 87–110
— 'Why Don't the English Speak Welsh?' in Higham ed *Britons in Anglo-Saxon England* 192–214
MH Turk ed *The Legal Code of Aelfred the Great* Boston, Ginn 1893 repr New York AMS P 1973
EG Turner 'A Writing Tablet from Somerset' (1956) 46 *Journal of Roman Studies* 115–18
RV Turner *Judges, Administrators and the Common Law in Angevin England* London, Hambledon P 1994
Joseph Tynan 'The Growth of the Saxon Laws' (1890) 11 *Irish Ecclesiastical Record* 3rd series 19–29

V

RC Van Caenegem *English Lawsuits from William I to Richard I* 2 vols (1990) 106 Selden Society; (1991) 107 Selden Society
— *Royal Writs in England from the Conquest to Glanvill: Studies in the Early History of the Common Law* (1959) 77 Selden Society
RL Venezky and A di P Healey *Microfiche Concordance to Old English* Toronto, Toronto UP 1980
Theo Vennemann 'English as a "Celtic" Language: Atlantic Influences from Above and from Below' in LHC Tristram ed *The Celtic Englishes II* Heidelberg, Winter 399–406
Johan Vising *Anglo-Norman Language and Literature* London, Oxford UP 1923
Giulio Vismara *Episcopalis Audientia* Milan, U Cattolica del Sacro Cuore 2nd series Scienza Giuridiche vol 54 1937 50–3
— *La Giuridizione Civile dei Vescovi (Secoli I–IX)* Milan, Giuffrè 1995
Hanna Vollrath 'Gesetzgebung und Schriftlichkeit: das Beispiel der Angelsächsischen Gesetze' (1979) 99 *Historisches Jahrbuch* 28–54

W

John [= JS] Wacher *The Civitas Capitals of Roman Britain* Leicester, Leicester UP 1966
— ed *Roman Britain* London, Book Club Associates 1978
IW Walker *Mercia and the Making of England* Stroud, Sutton 2000
JM Wallace-Hadrill *Bede's Ecclesiastical History of the English People: A Historical Commentary* Oxford, Oxford UP 1988

— *The Long-Haired Kings* London, Methuen 1962, Toronto, U of Toronto P reprint 1982

— *Early Germanic Kingship in England and on the Continent* Oxford, Oxford UP 1971

Clifford Walsh ed *Jowitt's Dictionary of English Law* London, Sweet and Maxwell 2nd edn 1977

Bryan Ward-Perkins 'Why Did the Anglo-Saxons not Become More British?' (2000) 115 *English Historical Review* 513–33

MG Welch 'Rural Settlement Patterns in the Early and Middle Anglo-Saxon Periods' (1985) 7 *Landscape History* 13–25

H Wessel *Das Recht der Tablettes Albertini* Berlin, Duncker and Humblot 2003

Francis West *The Justiciarship in England 1066–1232* Cambridge, Cambridge UP 1966

ML West *Hesiod: Works and Days* Oxford, Clarendon P 1996

JJS Wharton and Ivan Horniman *Wharton's Law Lexicon* London, Stevens 13th edn 1925

Joshua Whatmough *The Dialects of Ancient Gaul: Prolegomena and Records of the Dialects* Cambridge, Mass, Harvard UP revd edn 1970

HG Evelyn White tr *Ausonius* London, Heinemann and Boston, Harvard UP Loeb Classical Library 2 vols 1919–21

Horace White tr *Appian* London, Heinemann and Boston, Harvard UP Loeb Classical Library 4 vols 1912–13

SD White '*Pactum... Legem Vincit et Amor Judicium*: The Settlement of Disputes by Compromise in Eleventh-Century Western France' (178) 22 *American Journal of Legal History* 281–308

— *Re-Thinking Kingship and Feudalism in Early Medieval Europe* Aldershot, Ashgate 2005

F Whitehead 'Norman-French: the Linguistic Consequences of the Conquest' (1966–67) 109 *Memorials and Proceedings of the Manchester Literary and Philosophical Society* 78–83

Dorothy Whitelock *The Beginnings of English Society* Harmondsworth, Penguin 1952

— *English Historical Documents* I London, Eyre and Spottiswoode 1955

— 'Recent Work on Asser's Life of Alfred' in WH Stephenson *Asser's Life* cxxxii–clii

— *Sweet's Anglo-Saxon Reader in Prose and Verse* Oxford, Clarendon P 1967

— 'Wulfstan *Cantor* and Anglo-Saxon Law' in AH Orrick *Nordica et Anglica: Studies in Honour of Stefán Einarsson* The Hague, Mouton 1968 83–92

— 'Wulfstan and the Laws of Cnut' (1948) 63 *English Historical Review* 433–52

— ed *Wulfstan of York: Sermo Lupi ad Anglos* London, Methuen 3rd edn 1963

— 'Wulfstan's Authorship of Cnut's Laws' (1955) 70 *English Historical Review* 72–85

Chris Wickham 'Dispute Processes and Social Structures' in Davies and Fouracre 228–40

— 'Land Disputes and their Social Framework in Lombard-Carolingian Italy 700–900' in Davies and Fouracre 105–24

EM Wightman *Gallia Belgica* London, Batsford 1985

Kalevi Wijk 'On the Origins of the Celts' in Filppula, Klemola and Pitkänen 286–94

David Wilkins *Leges Anglo-Saxonicae Ecclesiasticae et Civiles* London, Gosling 1721

Ann Williams *Aethelred the Unready: The Ill-Counselled King* London, Hambledon 2003

Howard Williams 'Assembling the Dead' in Pantos and Semple 109–34

RM Wilson 'English and French in England (1100–1300)' (1943) 28 *History* 37–60

PH Winfield *The Chief Sources of English Legal History* Cambridge, Mass, Harvard UP 1925, reprint Hein 1983

Michael Winterbottom ed *Gildas: The Ruin of Britain and Other Works* London, Phillimore 1978

Ian Wood 'Administration, Law and Culture in Merovingian Gaul' in McKitterick *Uses of Literacy* 63–81

— 'Before and After the Migration to Britain' in Hines *The Anglo-Saxons* 41–54

— 'The Code in Merovingian Gaul' in Harries and Wood 161–9

— 'Disputes in Late Fifth- and Sixth-Century Gaul: Some Problems' in Davies and Fouracre 7–22

— 'The End of Roman Britain: Continental Evidence and Parallels' in Lapidge and Dumville 1–25

— 'Roman Law in the Barbarian Kingdoms' in Ellegård and Åkerström-Hougen 5–14

— and Niels Lund eds *People and Places in Northern Europe, 500–1600: Essays in Honour of Peter Hayes Sawyer* Woodbridge, Boydell and Brewer 1991

GE Woodbine 'The Language of English Law' (1943) 18 *Speculum* 395–436

Alex Woolf 'Apartheid and Economics in Anglo-Saxon England' in Higham ed *Britons in Anglo-Saxon England* 115–29

Greg Woolf *Becoming Roman: The Origins of Provincial Civilization in Gaul* Cambridge, Cambridge UP 1998

Patrick [= CP] Wormald 'Aethelred the Lawmaker' in David Hill ed *Ethelred the Unready: Papers from the Millennary Conference* British Archaeological Reports (British series 59) Oxford 1978

— *Bede and the Conversion of England: The Charter Evidence* Jarrow Lecture 1984

— 'Bede, the *Bretwaldas* and the Origins of the *Gens Anglorum*' in Wormald, Bullough and Collins 99–129

— 'Charters, Law and the Settlement of Disputes in Anglo-Saxon England' in Davies and Fouracre 149–186 and in Wormald *Legal Culture* 289–311

— '*Engla Lond*: the Making of an Allegiance' (1994) 7 *Journal of Historical Sociology* 1–24

— '*Exempla Romanorum* the Earliest English Legislation in Context' in Ellegård and Åkerström–Hoegen 15–28

— *The First Code of English Law* Canterbury, Canterbury Commemoration Society 2005

— 'Frederic William Maitland and the Earliest English Law' (1998) 16 *Law and History Review* 1–25 and in Wormald *Legal Culture* 45–69; also as 'Maitland and Anglo-Saxon Law: Beyond Domesday Book' in Hudson ed *History of English Law* 1–20

— 'Giving God and King their Due: Conflict and its Resolution in the Early English State' 2 *La Giustizia* 549–592 and in Wormald *Legal Culture* 333–57

— 'In Search of King Offa's "Law-Code"' in Wood and Lund *People and Places* pp25–45 and in Wormald *Legal Culture* 201–23

— '*Inter Cetera Bona... Genti Suae*: Law-Making and Peace-Keeping in the Earliest English Kingdoms' 1 *La Giustizia* 963–96 and in Wormald *Legal Culture* 71–80

— 'Introduction' in Davies and Fouracre 1–5
— 'Kings and Kingship' in Fouracre ed *New Cambridge Medieval History* I 571–604
— 'Law' in Lapidge et al *Blackwell Encyclopedia* 279–80
— *Legal Culture in the Early Medieval West: Law as Text, Image and Experience* London, Hambledon P 1999
— '*Lex Scripta* and *Verbum Regis*: Legislation and Germanic Kingship from Euric to Cnut' in Sawyer and Wood 105–38 and in Wormald *Legal Culture* 1–43
— *The Making of English Law* Oxford, Blackwell 1999
— 'Quadripartitus' in Garnett and Hudson 111–47
— 'The Uses of Literacy in Anglo-Saxon England and its Neighbours' (1977) *Transactions of the Royal Historical Society* 5th series 27, 95–114
— Donald Bullough and Roger Collins eds *Ideal and Reality in Frankish and Anglo-Saxon Reality. Studies Presented to JM Wallace-Hadrill* Oxford, Blackwell 1983

Y

DT Yates *Land, Power and Prestige: Bronze Age Field Systems in Southern England* Oxford, Oxbow 2006
Barbara Yorke ed *Bishop Aethelwold: His Career and Influence* Woodbridge, Boydell and Brewer 1997

Z

SP Zézas *Essai Historique de la Législation d'Angleterre depuis les Temps les Plus Réculés jusqu'au XII Siècle* Paris, Auguste Durand 1863
Frank Zinkeisen 'The Anglo-Saxon Courts of Law' (1895) 10 *Political Science Quarterly* 132–44
Zosimus *see* Anon; JJ Buchanan and HT Davis; François Paschoud; and RT Ridley
Francis de Zulueta *The Liber Pauperum of Vacarius* (1927) 44 Selden Society

INDEX

Compiled by Sue Carlton